CALIFORNIA'S
BEST TRIPS

33 AMAZING ROAD TRIPS

This edition written and researched by
Sara Benson

SYMBOLS IN THIS BOOK

✓ Top Tips	📖 History & Culture	📷 Essential Photo
🔗 Link Your Trips	👪 Family	🏃 Walking Tour
💬 Tips from Locals	🍷 Food & Drink	🍴 Eating
↪ Trip Detour	🌳 Outdoors	🛏 Sleeping

📞 Telephone Number	@ Internet Access	📋 English-Language Menu
🕐 Opening Hours	📶 Wi-Fi Access	👶 Family-Friendly
Ⓟ Parking	🥬 Vegetarian Selection	🐾 Pet-Friendly
🚭 Nonsmoking	🏊 Swimming Pool	
❄ Air-Conditioning		

MAP LEGEND

Routes
▬▬▬ Trip Route
▬▬▬ Trip Detour
▬▬▬ Linked Trip
▬▬▬ Walk Route
Tollway
Freeway
Primary
Secondary
Tertiary
Lane
Unsealed Road
Plaza/Mall
Steps
)= = Tunnel
Pedestrian Overpass
- - - Walk Track/Path

Boundaries
– – – International
- - - - State/Province
—ᴛ— Cliff

Hydrography
River/Creek
Intermittent River
Swamp/Mangrove
Canal
Water
Dry/Salt/ Intermittent Lake
Glacier

Route Markers
⑼⑺ US National Hwy
⑤ US Interstate Hwy
㊹ State Hwy

Trips
1 Trip Numbers
9 Trip Stop
🏃 Walking tour
↪ Trip Detour

Population
✪ Capital (National)
◉ Capital (State/Province)
● City/Large Town
○ Town/Village

Areas
▓ Beach
✝ Cemetery (Christian)
☓ Cemetery (Other)
▒ Park
Forest
Reservation
Urban Area
Sportsground

Transport
✈ Airport
Ⓑ BART station
Ⓣ Boston T station
⊕ Cable Car/ Funicular
Ⓜ Metro/Muni station
Ⓟ Parking
Ⓢ Subway station
⊕ Train/Railway
⊕ Tram
Ⓤ Underground station

2

Note: Not all symbols displayed above appear on the maps in this book

CONTENTS

Northern California
p73

Central California
p175

Southern California
p289

Contents cont.

Santa Barbara Bicycle touring in the wine country

Yosemite National Park Hikers on a quest for sublime views

WELCOME TO
CALIFORNIA

Starry-eyed newbies head to the Golden State to find fame and fortune, but you can do better. Come for the landscapes, stay for the sensational food, and glimpse the future in the making on America's creative coast. Live in California? Rest assured there's a gold mine of mom-and-pop restaurants, scenic routes and swimming holes yet to be discovered.

California's road trips will take you from the breezy, wildlife-rich Pacific Coast, to the towering redwoods of Big Sur and the north, to off-the-beaten-track deserts and Gold Rush towns, to big-name national parks such as Yosemite and Death Valley, and through the vine-strewn valleys of celebrated wine countries, starting with Sonoma and Napa.

From backcountry lanes to beachside highways, we've got something for you. And if you've only got time for one trip, make it one of our nine Classic Trips, which take you to the very best of California.

→

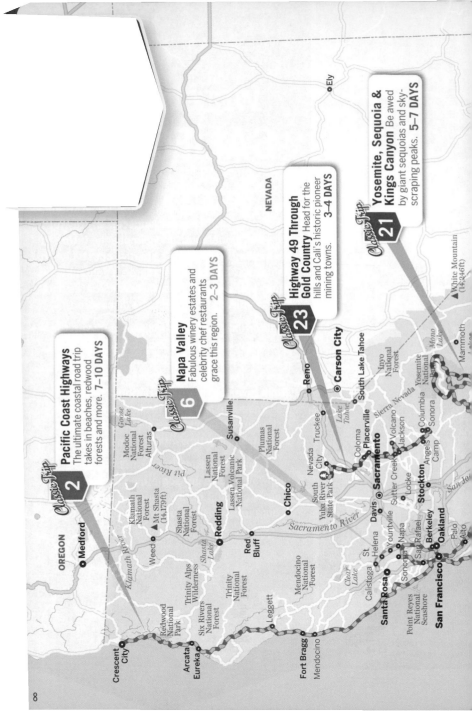

Classic Trip 2

Pacific Coast Highways The ultimate coastal road trip takes in beaches, redwood forests and more. **7–10 DAYS**

Classic Trip 6

Napa Valley Fabulous winery estates and celebrity chef restaurants grace this region. **2–3 DAYS**

Classic Trip 23

Highway 49 Through Gold Country Head for the hills and Cali's historic pioneer mining towns. **3–4 DAYS**

Classic Trip 21

Yosemite, Sequoia & Kings Canyon Be awed by giant sequoias and sky-scraping peaks. **5–7 DAYS**

OREGON

NEVADA

Medford

Ely

Crescent City

Arcata
Eureka

Redwood National Park

Klamath River

Six Rivers National Forest

Trinity Alps Wilderness

Weed

Klamath National Forest

Mt Shasta (14,179ft)

Shasta National Forest

Shasta Lake

Modoc National Forest

Alturas

Goose Lake

Pit River

Leggett

Trinity National Forest

Mendocino National Forest

Red Bluff

Redding

Lassen National Forest

Lassen Volcanic National Park

Plumas National Forest

Susanville

Fort Bragg
Mendocino

Clear Lake

Calistoga

St Helena

Chico

Yuba River State Park

Nevada City

Truckee

Reno

Carson City

South Lake Tahoe

Lake Tahoe

Santa Rosa

Sonoma

Napa

Yountville

Sacramento River

Davis

Sacramento

Coloma

Placerville

Sierra Nevada

Inyo National Forest

Yosemite National

Mono Lake

Point Reyes National Seashore

San Rafael

Berkeley
Oakland

San Francisco

Palo Alto

Sutter Creek

Locke

Stockton

Angels Camp

Jackson

Volcano

Columbia

Sonora

San Jo

White Mountain (14,246ft)

Mammoth

8

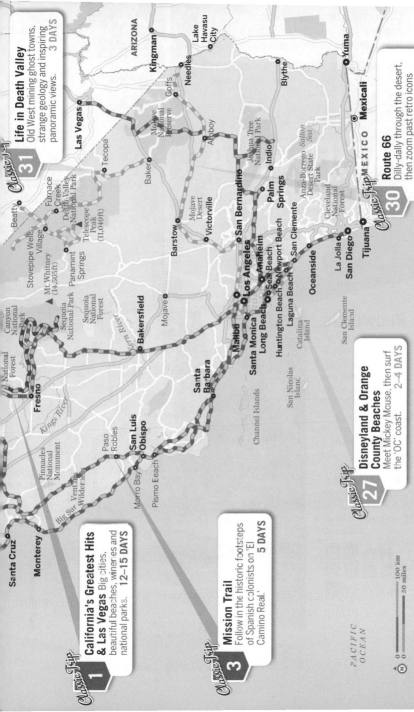

Classic Trip 31
Life in Death Valley
Old West mining ghost towns, strange geology and inspiring panoramic views. **3 DAYS**

Classic Trip 30
Route 66
Dilly-dally through the desert, then zoom past retro icons into LA. **3–4 DAYS**

Classic Trip 27
Disneyland & Orange County Beaches
Meet Mickey Mouse, then surf the 'OC' coast. **2–4 DAYS**

Classic Trip 1
California's Greatest Hits & Las Vegas Big cities, beautiful beaches, wineries and national parks. **12–15 DAYS**

Classic Trip 3
Mission Trail
Follow in the historic footsteps of Spanish colonists on 'El Camino Real.' **5 DAYS**

ARIZONA

Lake Havasu City
Kingman
Needles
Goffs
Mojave National Reserve
Amboy
Blythe
Joshua Tree National Park
Indio
Palm Springs
Anza-Borrego Desert State Park
Salton Sea
MEXICO
Mexicali
Yuma

Las Vegas
Beatty
Tecopa
Furnace Creek
Stovepipe Wells Village
Death Valley National Park
Telescope Peak (11,049ft)
Panamint Springs
Mt Whitney (14,505ft)
Baker
Mojave Desert
Barstow
Victorville
San Bernardino

Sequoia Canyon National Park
Sequoia National Park
Sequoia National Forest
Kern River
Bakersfield
Mojave
Los Angeles
Anaheim
Malibu
Santa Monica
Long Beach
Seal Beach
Huntington Beach
Newport Beach
Laguna Beach
San Clemente
Oceanside
La Jolla
San Diego
Tijuana
Cleveland National Forest

Kings River
Fresno
National Forest

Pinnacles National Monument
Paso Robles
San Luis Obispo
Morro Bay
Pismo Beach
Ventana Wilderness
Big Sur
Santa Barbara
Channel Islands
San Nicolas Island
Santa Cruz
Monterey
Catalina Island
San Clemente Island

PACIFIC OCEAN

100 km
50 miles

California's best sights and experiences, and the road trips that will take you there.

CALIFORNIA
HIGHLIGHTS

Redwoods

Ditch the cell phone and hug a tree, dude. California's towering giants grow along much of the coast, from Big Sur north to the Oregon border. It's possible to cruise past the trees – or even drive right through them at old-fashioned tourist traps – but nothing compares to the awe you'll feel while walking underneath these ancient ones. Explore Redwood National & State Parks on **Trip 12: Northern Redwood Coast**.

TRIPS 1 2
4 8 10 11 12
15

Redwoods Father and son enjoying the surrounding redwoods

Golden Gate Bridge View of San Francisco's iconic bridge and Fort Point

Golden Gate Bridge

Sashay out onto San Francisco's iconic bridge. Spy on cargo ships threading through the pylons and memorize 360-degree views of the rugged Marin Headlands, far-off downtown skyscrapers and the speck that is Alcatraz Island. Drive across this impressive 20th-century engineering feat on **Trip 2: Pacific Coast Highways**.

TRIPS 2 3 4 5

Palm Springs

A chic desert oasis ever since the early days of Hollywood and Frank Sinatra's Rat Pack. Do like A-list stars do here: lounge by your hotel's swimming pool, then drink cocktails from sunset till dawn. Break a sweat in hot-springs spas or on hiking trails that wind through desert canyons and mountain forests atop the head-spinning aerial tramway on **Trip 32: Palm Springs & Joshua Tree Oases**.

TRIPS 1 32

Disneyland

Where orange groves once grew, there Walt Disney built his fantasy Magic Kingdom in 1955. Beloved cartoon characters still waltz arm-in-arm down Main Street, USA, and fireworks explode over Sleeping Beauty's Castle. If you're a kid, or just hopelessly young at heart, this might really be 'the Happiest Place on Earth.' Make a date with Mickey on **Trip 27: Disneyland & Orange County Beaches**.

TRIPS 1 27

Yosemite National Park Hiker walking towards Yosemite Falls

BEST SCENIC ROUTES

- -

Pacific Coast Highway (PCH) Cruise oceanfront Hwy 1 in Orange County. **Trips** 2 27

- -

Avenue of the Giants Wind past the world's biggest redwood trees. **Trips** 2 11

- -

Kings Canyon Scenic Byway Descend into California's deepest river canyon. **Trips** 1 21

- -

Ebbetts Pass Scenic Byway Climb over the Sierra Nevada from Gold Country to Lake Tahoe. **Trip** 24

Yosemite National Park

In what conservationist John Muir called a temple, everything looks bigger, whether you're getting splashed by thunderous waterfalls, staring up at granite domes or walking in giant sequoia groves. For sublime views, perch at Glacier Point under a full moon or along high-elevation Tioga Rd on **Trip 21: Yosemite, Sequoia & Kings Canyon National Parks**.

TRIPS 1 21

Big Sur Bixby Creek Bridge over Big Sur's coastline

Big Sur

Hidden by redwood forests, the bohemian Big Sur coast keeps its secrets for those who will savor them: hidden hot springs, waterfalls and beaches where the sand is tinged purple or where gigantic chunks of jade have been found. Don't forget to look skyward to catch sight of endangered California condors soaring above craggy sea cliffs on **Trip 15: Big Sur**.

TRIPS `1` `2` `15`

BEST SMALL TOWNS

- - - - - - - - - - - - - - - - -

Bolinas A not-so-secret coastal hamlet in Marin County. **Trip** `4`

- - - - - - - - - - - - - - - - -

Calistoga For Napa Valley's blue-jeans-and-boots crowd and hot-springs lovers. **Trips** `1` `6`

- - - - - - - - - - - - - - - - -

Avila Beach Sunny beach boardwalk and a creaky fishing pier. **Trips** `2` `18`

- - - - - - - - - - - - - - - - -

Bodie California's most atmospheric Old West mining ghost town. **Trip** `22`

- - - - - - - - - - - - - - - - -

Arcata Bohemian counter-culture behind the Redwood Curtain. **Trips** `2` `12` `13`

Lake Tahoe Kayaking on the lake's clear blue waters

Santa Monica Pacific Park's Ferris wheel on Santa Monica Pier

Lake Tahoe

In summer, startlingly clear blue waters invite splashing around, kayaking and boating, while mountain bikers careen and hikers stride along trails threading through pine forests. In winter, after a thrilling day of skiing Olympic-worthy runs or snowshoe trekking, retreat to your cozy lakefront cottage to toast s'mores by the fire pit. **Trip 20: Lake Tahoe Loop** is ready to roll year-round.

TRIP

Monterey

Forget Hollywood visions of sun-soaked beaches. Instead imagine John Steinbeck and his novels of American realism set on this rugged peninsula. To meet local wildlife, hop aboard a whale-watching cruise in the bay or step inside Cannery Row's renowned aquarium. Then poke around the West Coast's oldest continuously operating lighthouse on **Trip 17: Around Monterey & Carmel**.

TRIPS

Santa Monica

Who needs LA traffic? Hit the beach instead. Learn to surf, ride a solar-powered Ferris wheel, catch jaw-dropping sunsets from an old-fashioned pier, amaze the kids at the aquarium's tidal touch pools or just dip your toes in the water and let your troubles float away. Experience it all on **Trip 1: California's Greatest Hits & Las Vegas**.

TRIPS

Joshua Tree National Park

Whimsical-looking Joshua trees define this park, where the Colorado and Mojave Deserts converge. This is one of California's top places to go rock climbing, but even kids can scramble around the larger-than-life boulders. Hikers seek out fan-palm oases fed by springs and streams. Come to see spring wildflower blooms on **Trip 32: Palm Springs & Joshua Tree Oases**.

TRIPS 1 32

Sonoma County

Amid the sun-dappled vineyards and pastoral ranchlands of 'Slow-noma,' the uniqueness of *terroir* is valued more than a winery's fine-art collection. In this down-to-earth wine region, which is also known for making fine artisanal food and craft beer and spirits, you might taste new vintages straight from the barrel. Who cares if it's not even noon yet? Relax. Conventions need not apply on **Trip 7: Sonoma Valley**.

TRIPS 5 7 8 9

(left) Sonoma County Vineyards and wine barrels on display;
(below) Joshua Tree National Park Boulders and Joshua trees

San Diego's Beaches

Cruise past impossibly white sands on Coronado's Silver Strand, then stop for cotton candy and a roller-coaster ride at Mission Beach. La Jolla sits pretty atop rocky bluffs, a whisper's breath from the sea, while beyond stretches an eclectic line-up of North County beach towns. Whatever you've been dreaming about for your SoCal beach vacation, find it on **Trip 28: Fun on the San Diego Coast**.

TRIPS

BEST ROADSIDE ODDITIES

Trees of Mystery Animatronic Paul Bunyan in the redwoods. **Trip** 12

Solvang Where windmills collide with Danish village kitsch. **Trips** 3 19

Elmer's Place Folk-art 'bottle trees' on Route 66. **Trip** 30

World's Biggest Dinosaurs Concrete behemoths outside Palm Springs. **Trip** 32

Mirage Volcano Erupting nightly on the Las Vegas Strip. **Trip**

19

Yosemite National Park Mule deer (Trip 21)

Beaches

California spoils you with over 1100 miles of Pacific coastline. Northern beaches are all about crashing waves, rocky tidepools and solitary strolls along the continent's edge. If you're dreaming of golden strands lapped by frothy surf and bronzed bods hanging out in lifeguard huts, head to SoCal.

27 Disneyland & Orange County Beaches Over 40 miles of surf, sand and sun in the OC.

28 Fun on the San Diego Coast Take your pick of ritzy or bohemian beach towns.

18 Around San Luis Obispo Steal away to the Central Coast's laidback beaches.

12 Northern Redwood Coast Walk rocky headlands past tidepools and barking sea lions.

History

Gold mining is the usual reason given for the madcap course of California's history. Yet Native American tribes, Spanish missionaries and conquistadors, Mexican ranchers, and later waves of immigration to the Golden State have all left traces to dig deeper for, too.

23 Highway 49 Through Gold Country Follow the footsteps of 19th-century gold seekers, bordello keepers and outlaws.

3 Mission Trail Trace the path of Spanish colonialists and Catholic priests through 'Alta California.'

31 Life in Death Valley Where the dreams of miners and pioneers are just ghosts today.

30 Route 66 Watch tumbleweeds roll along on America's 'Mother Road.'

Food & Wine

In California, star chefs' menus show off ingredients sourced from local farmers, fishers, ranchers and artisan food makers. And wine? Although Napa Valley is the most famous, California's other wine countries more than hold their own.

5 Bay Area Culinary Tour Sample farmers markets and the sources of California cuisine.

7 Sonoma Valley Napa's rustic-chic country cousin is a patchwork of pastoral farms and vineyards.

8 Healdsburg & Around Sip Zinfandel and pack a picnic basket full of locavarian treats.

19 Santa Barbara Wine Country Where the hit movie *Sideways* romped, find seriously sophisticated vintages.

San Juan Capistrano View of the beautiful mission complex (Trip 3)

Bringing Kids

The Golden State welcomes pint-sized travelers with open arms. Just keep them covered in sunblock and make sure they see something beyond Southern California's thrilling theme parks. Sunny beaches, cool mountains and lakes, and more outdoor fun awaits.

27 **Disneyland & Orange County Beaches** Families are all smiles at Disneyland. Afterwards cruise coastal Hwy 1.

21 **Yosemite, Sequoia & Kings Canyon National Parks** Amaze your kids with giant sequoia trees and huge waterfalls.

20 **Lake Tahoe Loop** No worries, no hurry: drive around the 'Big Blue' for swimming or skiing.

28 **Fun on the San Diego Coast** Tour the zoo's wild safari park, then treat tots to Legoland.

Parks & Wildlife

California's national and state parks protect an astonishing diversity of life zones, from misty redwood forests to snowy mountain peaks to marine sanctuaries where migratory whales breach.

21 **Yosemite, Sequoia & Kings Canyon National Parks** Don't miss the Sierra Nevada's prime-time parks, with wildflower meadows, vistas and wildlife galore.

12 **Northern Redwood Coast** See sandy beaches and calm lagoons where migratory birds flock, plus the tallest trees on earth.

14 **Volcanic Legacy Byway** Find alpine lakes, volcanic peaks, hot-springs 'hells' and more.

32 **Palm Springs & Joshua Tree Oases** Clamber through a wonderland of rocks and flowering desert gardens.

Backwoods Byways

Far from coastal California's bumper-to-bumper freeways, these scenic backroads and country highways let you finally lose the crowds – and maybe yourself – in cinematic landscapes of jagged peaks, rushing rivers and placid lakes.

13 **Trinity Scenic Byway** Watch for bald eagles (or Bigfoot!) as you dangle a fishing pole in lakes.

22 **Eastern Sierra Scenic Byway** Explore real Wild West landscapes, from Mt Whitney to the ghost town of Bodie.

24 **Ebbetts Pass Scenic Byway** Take this rugged route over the Sierra Nevada to Lake Tahoe.

25 **Feather River Scenic Byway** Wind through a peaceful river canyon up into the 'Lost Sierra.'

21

Climate

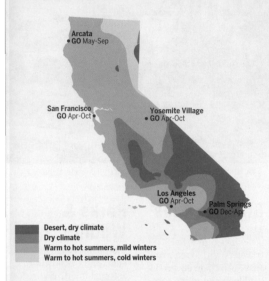

Arcata
GO May-Sep

San Francisco
GO Apr-Oct

Yosemite Village
GO Apr-Oct

Los Angeles
GO Apr-Oct

Palm Springs
GO Dec-Apr

Desert, dry climate
Dry climate
Warm to hot summers, mild winters
Warm to hot summers, cold winters

When to Go

High Season (Jun–Aug)

» Accommodations prices up 50% to 100% on average.

» Major holidays are even busier and more expensive.

» Summer is low season in the desert, where temperatures exceed 100°F (38°C).

Shoulder Season (Apr–May & Sep–Oct)

» Crowds and prices drop, especially on the coast and in the mountains.

» Mild temperatures and sunny, cloudless days.

» Typically wetter in spring, drier in autumn.

Low Season (Nov–Mar)

» Accommodations rates lowest along the coast.

» Chilly temperatures, frequent rainstorms and heavy snow in the mountains.

» Winter is peak season in SoCal's desert regions.

Your Daily Budget

Budget: Less than $75
» Hostel dorm beds: $25–55
» Take-out meal: $6-12

Midrange: $75–200
» Two-star motel or hotel double room: $75–150
» Rental car per day, excluding insurance and gas: $30–75

Top End: Over $200
» Three-star hotel or beach resort room: $150–300
» Three-course meal in top restaurant: $75–100

Eating

Roadside diners & cafes Cheap and simple.

Beach shacks Casual burgers, shakes and seafood.

National, state & theme parks Mostly so-so, overpriced cafeteria-style or deli picnic fare.

Eating price indicators represent the average cost of a main course at dinner:

$	less than $15
$$	$15–25
$$$	more than $25

Sleeping

Motels & hotels Ubiquitous along well-trafficked highways and in busy tourist areas.

Camping & cabins Ranges from rustic campsites to luxury 'glamping' resorts.

B&Bs Quaint, romantic inns in urban and rural areas.

Hostels Cheap and basic; almost exclusively in cities.

Sleeping price indicators represent the average cost of a double room with private bathroom during high season:

$	less than $150
$$	$150–250
$$$	more than $250

Arriving in California

Los Angeles International Airport (LAX) Taxis to most destinations in LA ($30 to $50) take 30 minutes to one hour. Door-to-door shuttles ($16 to $27) operate 24 hours. FlyAway bus runs to downtown LA ($9). Free airport shuttles to LAX City Bus Center & Metro Rail station.

San Francisco International Airport (SFO) Taxis into the city ($35 to $55) take 25 to 50 minutes. Door-to-door shuttles ($16 to $20) operate 24 hours. BART trains to downtown San Francisco ($8.95, 30 minutes) leave the airport between 5:30am and 11:45pm daily.

Cell Phones

The only foreign phones that will work in the USA are GSM multiband models. Network coverage is often spotty in remote and rural areas.

Internet Access

Wi-fi (free or fee-based) is available at most lodgings and coffee shops. Cybercafes ($6 to $12 per hour) are mostly in cities.

Money

ATMs are widely available. Credit cards are accepted almost universally and are usually required for reservations.

Tipping

Tipping is expected, not optional. Standard tipping is 18% to 20% in restaurants, 15% for taxi drivers, $1 minimum per drink in bars, and $2 per bag for porters.

Useful Websites

California Travel & Tourism Commission (www.visitcalifornia.com) Multilingual trip-planning guides.

Lonely Planet (www.lonelyplanet.com/usa/california) Destination info, hotel bookings, travelers forums and more.

Opening Hours

Businesses, restaurants and shops may close earlier and on additional days during the off-season (usually winter, and also summer in the deserts).

Bars ⏰5pm-2am daily

Business hours (general) ⏰9am-5pm Monday to Friday

Restaurants ⏰7:30am-10:30am, 11:30am-2:30pm & 5pm-9pm daily, some later Friday and Saturday

Shops ⏰10am-6pm Monday to Saturday, noon-5pm Sunday (malls open later)

CITY GUIDE

SAN FRANCISCO

Ride the clanging cable cars up unbelievably steep hills, snake down Lombard St's famous hairpin turns, cruise through Golden Gate Park and drive across the arching Golden Gate Bridge. Then go get lost in the creatively offbeat neighborhoods of California's capital of weird.

San Francisco Cable car on the city's street

Getting Around

Avoid driving downtown. Cable cars are slow and scenic (single-ride $7). MUNI streetcars and buses are faster but infrequent after 9pm (fares $2.25). BART (tickets from $1.95) runs high-speed Bay Area trains. Taxis cost $2.75 per mile; meters start at $3.50.

Parking

Street parking is scarce. Meters take coins, sometimes credit or debit cards; central pay stations accept coins or cards. Overnight hotel parking averages $35 to $55; downtown parking garages start at $2.50 per hour or $30 per day.

Where to Eat

The Ferry Building, Mission District and South of Market (SoMa) are foodie faves. Don't miss the city's outdoor farmers markets. Head to North Beach for Italian, Chinatown for dim sum and the Mission District for Mexican flavors.

Where to Stay

The Marina is near the family-friendly waterfront and Fisherman's Wharf. Union Square and SoMa are most expensive, but conveniently located for walking.

Useful Websites

San Francisco Travel (www.sanfrancisco. travel) Destination info, events calendar and accommodations bookings.

SF Station (www.sfstation.com) Nightlife, restaurants, shopping, events and the arts.

Lonely Planet (www.lonelyplanet.com/usa/ san-francisco) Travel tips, travelers' forums and hotel and hostel bookings.

Trips Through San Francisco:

`1` `2` `3` `4` `5`

TOP EXPERIENCES

➡ Golden Gate Bridge

Sunny days suit most cities just fine, but San Francisco saves its most dramatic Golden Gate Bridge views for when fog swirls around the towers, and romantics and photographers rejoice.

➡ Cruise to Alcatraz

No prisoner is known to have escaped alive from the USA's most notorious jail – but after you enter D-Block solitary, the swim through riptides might seem worth a shot.

➡ Ferry Building Feasts

Global food trends start in San Francisco. To see what's next on the menu, head to the Ferry Building, the city's monument to local, sustainable food.

➡ Golden Gate Park

Join San Franciscans doing what comes naturally: roller-discoing, drum-circling, sniffing orchids, petting sea stars and strolling toward the Pacific.

➡ Ride a Cable Car

Carnival rides can't compare to cable cars, San Francisco's vintage public transit. Regulars grip the leather hand-straps, lean back, and ride downhill slides like surfers.

➡ Mission District Murals

See garage doors, billboards and storefronts transformed into more than 400 visual portrayals of community pride, social commentary and political dissent. Balmy Alley has some of the oldest murals.

➡ Climb Coit Tower

Wild parrots might mock your progress up Telegraph Hill, but they can't expect to keep panoramic scenery like this to themselves.

LOS ANGELES

Loony LA is the land of starstruck dreams and Hollywood magic. You may think you know what to expect: celebrity worship, Botoxed blondes and endless traffic. But it's also California's most ethnically diverse city, with new immigrants arriving daily, infusing LA's ever-evolving arts, music and food scenes.

Getting Around

Freeway traffic jams are endless, but worst during extended morning and afternoon rush hours. LA's Metro operates slower buses and speedier subway and light-rail trains (fares $1.75), with limited night services. DASH minibuses (single-ride 50¢) zip around downtown. Santa Monica's Big Blue Bus (fare $1.25) connects West LA. Taxis cost $2.70 per mile; meters start at $2.85.

Parking

Street parking is limited. Meters take coins, sometimes credit or debit cards; central pay stations accept coins or cards. Valet parking is ubiquitous, typically $5 to $10 plus tip. Overnight hotel parking averages $30 to $50.

TOP EXPERIENCES

➡ Doing Downtown
Rub shoulders with fashionistas, sip cocktails in sleek lounges, sample global cuisine and get a dose of arts and culture in revitalized DTLA.

➡ Experience Venice
Get your freak on while milling with snake charmers, tarot readers, body builders and skaters along the boardwalk, not far south of Santa Monica's beautiful beach and pier.

➡ Seeing Stars in Hollywood
Traipse along the Hollywood Walk of Fame past historic theaters, then hit the bars and clubs for a night of tabloid-worthy debauchery.

➡ Getty Center at Sunset
Feel your spirits soar on a hilltop in West LA, surrounded by fantastic art, architecture, views and gardens.

Where to Eat
Food trucks and pop-up kitchens are a local obsession. Downtown LA cooks up a global mix, with Little Tokyo, Chinatown, Thai Town, Koreatown and Latin-flavored East LA nearby. Trend-setting eateries pop up in Hollywood, Santa Monica and Venice.

Where to Stay
For beach life, escape to Santa Monica or Venice. Long Beach is convenient to Disneyland and Orange County. Party people adore Hollywood and West Hollywood (WeHo). Culture vultures head to Downtown LA.

Useful Websites
LA Inc (www.discoverlosangeles.com) City's official tourism website for trip planning.

LA Weekly (www.laweekly.com) Arts, entertainment, dining and an events calendar.

Trips Through Los Angeles:

San Diego Balboa Park beyond the lily pond

SAN DIEGO

San Diego shamelessly promotes itself as 'America's Finest City.' Smug? Maybe, but it's easy to see why. The weather is idyllic, with coastal high temperatures hovering around 72°F (22°C) year-round. Wander Balboa Park's museums and gardens, laze on the beaches and then party in the Gaslamp Quarter after dark.

Getting Around

Driving is how most people get around. MTS operates a metro-area network of buses, trolleys and trains (one-way fare $2.25 or $2.50, day pass $5) with limited night and weekend services. Taxi meters start at $2.20, plus $2.30 per mile.

Parking

Street parking is crowded. Meters take mostly coins; central pay stations accept coins or cards. Valet parking, public lots and garages downtown cost from $10. Overnight hotel parking runs $25 to $45.

Where to Eat

Hit the Gaslamp Quarter for creative cuisine, Hillcrest for casual and international fusion eats, and beach towns for seafood and craft beer. Mexican food and the city's famous fish tacos are everywhere.

Where to Stay

Boutique and luxury hotels are in the Gaslamp Quarter and around downtown. Old Town has chain hotels and motels, as does Mission Valley inland. Beach towns nearby kid-friendly attractions have the biggest range of lodgings, from Coronado north to Carlsbad.

Useful Websites

San Diego.org (www.sandiego.org) City's official tourism site for trip planning and events.

San Diego Reader (www.sandiegoreader.com) Nightlife, arts, entertainment and an events calendar.

Trips Through San Diego: **2** **3** **28**

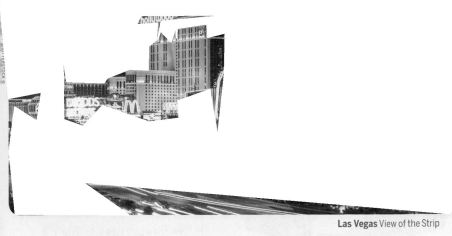

Las Vegas View of the Strip

LAS VEGAS

Rolling into Las Vegas, you'll feel like you're on a movie set. If you're behind the wheel and a Sin City first-timer, arrive after dark. As you approach the city, pull over and admire the neon glow from afar. Then cruise Las Vegas Blvd (aka the Strip).

Getting Around

Traffic jams on the Strip and the I-15 Fwy are common. Buses run 24/7 between the Strip and downtown (24-hour pass $8). Fast monorail trains (single-ride $5, 24-hour pass $12) make limited stops, mostly by the Strip. Taxi meters start at $3.45, plus $2.85 per mile.

Parking

Free self-parking and valet parking at casino hotels is rapidly disappearing downtown and on the Strip. Rates vary wildly. Street parking downtown is metered; bring coins since not all meters accept credit or debit cards.

Where to Eat

Casino hotels have the full gamut of dining options, from all-you-can-eat buffets to celebrity chefs' restaurants. Downtown, head to Fremont East and the Container Park to find local cateries. West of the Strip, Chinatown has scores of Asian kitchens.

Where to Stay

The Strip has the biggest range of casino hotels, from budget to luxury. Downtown has cheaper casino digs, sketchy motels and hostels. More casinos and chain motels and hotels are found just east and west of the Strip.

Useful Websites

Las Vegas Convention and Visitors Authority (www.lasvegas.com) Official tourist information site.

Las Vegas Weekly (www.lasvegasweekly.com) Nightlife, arts, dining, entertainment and an events calendar.

Trips Through Las Vegas: 1

For more, check out our city and country guides. www.lonelyplanet.com

The amazing thing about driving California's highways and byways is that things seem to get more dramatic with every winding mile – trees get bigger, mountain peaks higher and beaches more idyllic. It's enough for a lifetime of road trips.

Northern California (p73)

San Francisco is the launchpad for leisurely drives around coastal Marin County and NorCal's bucolic Wine Country, or more rugged adventures further north in the realm of ancient redwood groves, peaked volcanoes and sparkling mountain lakes.

Taste Napa Valley wine on Trip 6

See redwood trees on Trip

Central California
(p175)

Wind along the state's gorgeous Central Coast, stretched between San Francisco and Los Angeles, and bordered by beaches, lighthouses and vineyards. Or dart inland to the majestic Sierra Nevada, with its national parks, high-elevation passes, whitewater rivers and historical gold-mining country.

Get lost in Big Sur on Trip `15`

Discover Yosemite National Park on Trip `21`

Southern California (p289)

SoCal is a place of extremes, where you can motor from the lowest and hottest place on the continent to hot-springs oases in the desert outside LA. Or just kick back on the coast, where surfers, bronzed beach beauties and kids all cavort.

Hit the OC's beaches on Trip `27`

Drive into Death Valley on Trip `31`

CALIFORNIA

Classic Trips

RON THOMAS / GETTY IMAGES ©

3

What Is a Classic Trip?

All the trips in this book show you the best of California, but we've chosen nine as our all-time favorites. These are our Classic Trips – the ones that lead you to the best of the iconic sights, the top activities and the unique California experiences. Turn the page to see our cross-regional Classic Trips, and look out for more Classic Trips on the following pages:

Left: The Las Vegas Strip at night
Above: Spanish mission church in Santa Barbara

Classic Trip
California's Greatest Hits & Las Vegas

Like a top-10 playlist, this epic road trip hits the all-time greats of the Golden State (and some fascinating in-between spots), ultimately stopping in glitzy Las Vegas, Nevada.

TRIP HIGHLIGHTS

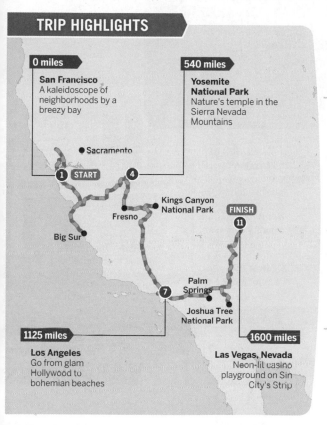

0 miles

San Francisco
A kaleidoscope of neighborhoods by a breezy bay

540 miles

Yosemite National Park
Nature's temple in the Sierra Nevada Mountains

● Sacramento

1 **START**

4

Kings Canyon National Park **FINISH**

Fresno

11

Big Sur

Palm Springs

7

Joshua Tree National Park

1125 miles

Los Angeles
Go from glam Hollywood to bohemian beaches

1600 miles

Las Vegas, Nevada
Neon-lit casino playground on Sin City's Strip

12–15 DAYS
1600 MILES /
2575KM

GREAT FOR...

BEST TIME TO GO

June to September for sunny days and snow-free mountain roads.

 ESSENTIAL PHOTO

Waterfalls and iconic peaks from Tunnel View in Yosemite Valley.

 BEST FOR FOOD & DRINK

Napa Valley wineries and star chefs' tables.

Santa Monica Colorful homes by the beach

Classic Trip

California's Greatest Hits & Las Vegas

1

California is a big place, so seeing its most famous places all in one trip could mean resigning yourself to driving dead-boring multi-lane freeways for hours on end. But you don't have to do that. Instead, this epic drive takes scenic state highways and local back roads to connect the dots, with a minimum of mind-numbing empty miles between San Francisco, Yosemite National Park, Los Angeles and Las Vegas.

Map labels:

Calistoga
Sacramento
Santa Rosa
2 Napa Valley
Sonoma
Yountville
Napa
San Rafael
START
Berkeley
San Francisco **1**
Oakland
p170
Palo Alto
San Jose
Santa Cruz
Monterey
Big Sur **3**
PACIFIC OCEAN

TRIP HIGHLIGHT

❶ San Francisco

In two action-packed days, explore **Golden Gate Park** (www.golden-gate-park.com; Stanyan St to Great Hwy; P 🚹; 🚌5, 7, 18, 21, 28, 29, 33, 44, MN), spy on sea lions lolling around **Pier 39** (www.pier39.com; Beach St & the Embarcadero, Pier 39; 🚹; 🚌15, 37, 49, F) at Fisherman's Wharf and saunter (p170) through the streets of busy **Chinatown** to the Italian sidewalk cafes of **North Beach**. Feast on an overstuffed burrito in the **Mission District** after wandering its mural-splashed alleys. Queue up at Powell and Market Sts for a ride on a bell-clanging cable car (fare $7) and then cruise to the infamous prison island of **Alcatraz** (📞Alcatraz Cruises 415-981-7625; www.nps.gov/alcatraz; day tours adult/child/family $33/21/100, night tours adult/child $40/24; 🕐call center 8am-7pm, ferries depart Pier 33 half-hourly 8:45am-3:50pm, night tours 5:55pm & 6:30pm; 🚹) out in the bay. Book Alcatraz tickets online at least two weeks ahead. At the foot of Market St, indulge your inner epicure at the **Ferry Building** (📞415-983-8030; www.ferrybuildingmarketplace.com; Market St & the Embarcadero; 🕐10am-6pm Mon-Fri, from 9am Sat, 11am-5pm Sun; 🚹; 🚌2, 6, 9, 14, 21, 31, MEmbarcadero, BEmbarcadero) food stalls, and stop by its **farmers**

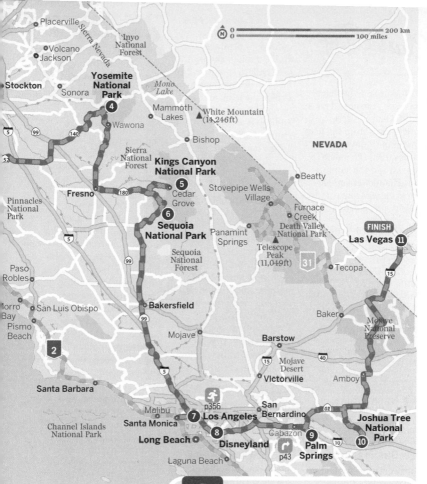

market ([☎]415-291-3276; www.cuesa.org; Market St & the Embarcadero; ⏰10am-2pm Tue & Thu, from 8am Sat; [♿][🚻]; [M]Embarcadero) year-round to wallow in the bounty of California-grown produce and gourmet prepared foods. Inside the historic **Castro Theatre** ([☎]415-621-6120; www.castrotheatre.com;

LINK YOUR TRIP

2 Pacific Coast Highways

California's most famous driving route hugs the Pacific Ocean from Mexico to Oregon. Join up in San Francisco, Big Sur or LA.

31 Life in Death Valley

California's biggest, wildest and most road trip-worthy national park is just over two hours' drive west of Las Vegas, Nevada.

Classic Trip

429 Castro St; ◷Tue-Sun; Ⓜ Castro), the crowd goes wild when the great organ rises from the floor and pumps out show tunes until the movie starts, and the sumptuous chandelier complements a repertory of silver-screen classics.

✖ 🛏 p46, p61, p71, p93

The Drive » Without traffic jams, it's an hour's drive from San Francisco to Napa, the nexus of Wine Country. Take Hwy 101 north over the soaring Golden Gate Bridge, stopping at the Vista Point on the far side of the bridge, and into Marin County. Zigzag northeast on Hwys 37, 121, 12 and 29 to reach downtown Napa.

- - - - - - - - - - -

❷ Napa Valley

The Napa Valley is famous for regal Cabernet Sauvignon, château-like wineries and fabulous food. The city of Napa anchors the valley, but the real work happens up-valley. Scenic towns along Hwy 29 include St Helena, Yountville and Calistoga – the latter more famous for its natural hot-springs water than its wine.

Start by the river in downtown Napa, where the **Oxbow Public Market** (✆707-226-6529; www. oxbowpublicmarket.com; 610 & 644 1st St; ◷9am-7pm

Wed-Mon, to 8pm Tue; Ⓟ♿) showcases all things culinary – produce stalls, kitchen shops, and everywhere something to taste – with emphasis on seasonal eating and sustainability. Come hungry, and top it all off with a scoop of organic Three Twins Ice Cream.

A dozen miles north of Napa, tour buses flock to the corporate-owned winery **Robert Mondavi** (✆707-226-1395, 888-766-6328; www.robertmondavi winery.com; 7801 Hwy 29, Oakville; tasting/tour from $5/20; ◷10am-5pm, store to 6pm; Ⓟ♿); if you know nothing about wine and can cope with crowds, the worthwhile tours provide excellent insight into winemaking. Driving back down-valley, follow bucolic Silverado Trail, which passes several other landmark, over-the-top wineries, including **Robert Sinskey** (✆707-944-9090; www.robertsinskey. com; 6320 Silverado Trail, Napa; tasting $25, incl tour $95; ◷10am-4:30pm; Ⓟ), where a dramatic hilltop tasting room resembles a small cathedral.

The Drive » From Napa, it's a four-hour drive of nearly 200 miles to the dramatic Big Sur coast. Head south over the Carquinez Bridge to Berkeley, then sail over the Bay Bridge into San Francisco, taking Hwy 101 south toward Silicon Valley. Detour on Hwy 17 over the mountains to Santa Cruz, then join Hwy 1 south past Monterey and Carmel-by-the-Sea.

- - - - - - - - - - -

❸ Big Sur

Highway 1 along Big Sur coast may be the most famous stretch of highway in the entire state. The road twists and turns a thousand feet above the vast blue Pacific, hugging the skirts of mile-high sea cliffs, above which California condors fly.

In the 1950s and '60s, Big Sur – so named by Spanish settlers who referred to the wilderness as *el país grande del sur* (the big country to the south) – became a bohemian retreat for artists and writers, including Henry Miller and the Beat Generation. Today it attracts new-age mystics, hippies and city slickers seeking to unplug on this emerald-green edge of the continent.

All along Hwy 1 in Big Sur's **state parks** (www. parks.ca.gov; parking fee $10, valid for same-day admission to all other parks), you'll find hiking trails through forests of redwoods (incidentally, the tallest trees on earth) and to magical waterfalls – don't miss McWay Falls, which tumbles onto an ocean beach.

✖ 🛏 p46

The Drive » It's about a five-hour, 220-mile trip from Big Sur to Yosemite Valley. Backtrack north on coastal Hwy 1 past Monterey, then veer inland through California's agricultural valleys, taking Hwy 152 east past San Luis Reservoir and crossing I-5, then continuing east toward Hwy 99. Outside Merced, join Hwy 140 – an all-weather highway normally open year-round – to Yosemite National Park.

TRIP HIGHLIGHT

❹ Yosemite National Park

With wild rock formations, astonishing waterfalls, vast swaths of granite and humbling Sierra Nevada peaks, **Yosemite National Park** (📞209-372-0200; www.nps.gov/yose; 7-day entry per car $30; 🅿 ♿) is no less than perfect. On your way in, stop at **Tunnel View** to drink in views of the Yosemite Valley, with iconic **Half Dome** and plunging **Bridalveil Fall** in the distance. Go deeper into the valley to see triple-decker **Yosemite Falls** up close, or to hike the **Mist Trail**, which climbs a rocky staircase beside mighty **Vernal and Nevada Falls**. Drive up to **Glacier Point** to catch a brilliant sunset.

The next day, detour along high-elevation Tioga Rd (closed in winter and spring) to wildflower-strewn **Tuolumne Meadows**, encircled by skyscraping peaks and granite domes. Picnic beside sparkling **Tenaya Lake** and pull over at roadside **Olmsted Point** for panoramic views over the rooftop of the Sierra Nevada. Then backtrack down to the valley and take Hwy 41 south, exiting the park

LOCAL KNOWLEDGE: HIKING HALF DOME

Just hold on, don't forget to breathe and – whatever you do – don't look down. A pinnacle so popular that hikers need a permit to scale it, Half Dome lives on as Yosemite Valley's must-reach-it obsession for millions. It's a day hike longer than an average work day, an elevation gain equivalent to almost 480 flights of stairs, and a final stretch of near-vertical steps that melts even the strongest legs and arms to masses of quivering jelly.

Reaching the top can only be done when the fixed cables are up, usually from late May until mid-October. To stem lengthy lines (and increasingly dangerous conditions) on the vertiginous cables, the park now requires that all day and overnight hikers obtain an advance permit. Half Dome permits go on sale by a preseason lottery in early spring, with a limited number available via another daily lottery two days in advance during the hiking season. Permit regulations and prices are subject to change; check the park website (www.nps.gov/yose/planyourvisit/hdpermits.htm) for current details.

near the **Mariposa Grove** of giant sequoia trees.

🍴 🛏 p46

The Drive » It's a straight shot south on Hwy 41 from Yosemite's south entrance to Fresno, then head east on Hwy 180, which eventually winds uphill and gains over 6000ft in elevation to enter Kings Canyon National Park. The 120-mile trip to Grant Grove Village takes about 2½ hours, without traffic.

❺ Kings Canyon National Park

From giant sequoia crowns down into one of the USA's deepest canyons, the twisting scenic drive in **Kings Canyon National Park** (📞559-565-3341; www.nps.gov/seki; 7-day entry per car $30; 🅿 ♿) is an eye-popping, jaw-dropping revelation.

At the northern end of the Generals Hwy, take a walk in **General Grant Grove**, encompassing the world's third-largest living tree, then wash off all that sweat with a dip down the road at **Hume Lake**. Get back on the **Kings Canyon Scenic Byway** (Hwy 180, closed in winter and spring), which makes a precipitous descent, and make sure you pull over to survey the canyon depths and lofty Sierra Nevada peaks from **Junction View**.

Classic Trip

WHY THIS IS A CLASSIC TRIP
SARA BENSON, WRITER

If you've only got one shot at seeing everything California is famous for – wine, beaches, mountains, deserts, big trees and even bigger cities – take this trip. It even includes a short hop across the Nevada state line to the casino capital of Las Vegas, a favorite weekend getaway for Californians year-round. The Sierra Nevada Mountains are best visited in summer; spring brings wildflower blooms to the deserts.

Top: Friends walking on Santa Monica beach
Left: Lupine wildflowers in the Sierra Nevada
Right: General Sherman Tree in Sequoia National Park

CHIARA SALVADORI / GETTY IMAGES ©

At the bottom of the canyon, cruise past Cedar Grove Village. Admire striking canyon views from verdant **Zumwalt Meadow**, a wildlife-watching hotspot with a boardwalk nature trail. At truthfully named **Road's End**, cool off by the sandy Kings River beach or make an 8-mile round-trip hike to **Mist Falls**, which roars in late spring and early summer.

🛏 p46, p237

The Drive ≫ It's only a 60-mile drive from Cedar Grove to the Giant Forest in Sequoia National Park, but it can take nearly two hours, thanks to hairpin turns and gawking drivers. Backtrack along the Kings Canyon Scenic Byway (Hwy 180) to Grant Grove, then wind south on the Generals Hwy through the sun-dappled forests of the Giant Sequoia National Monument.

- - - - - - - - - - - - - -

6 Sequoia National Park

Big trees, deep caves and high granite domes are all on the agenda for this day-long tour of Sequoia National Park. Arriving in the Giant Forest, let yourself be dwarfed by the majestic **General Sherman Tree**, the world's largest. Learn more about giant sequoias at the **Giant Forest Museum** (📞559-565-4480; www.nps.gov/seki; Generals Hwy, at Crescent Meadow Rd; ⏰9am-4:30pm; P 🚹). Snap a photo of your car driving through the **Tunnel Log**, or better

41

yet, leave your car behind and hop on the park shuttle for a wildflower walk around **Crescent Meadow** and to climb the puff-and-pant stairway up **Moro Rock**, granting bird's-eye canyon and peak views.

Picnic by the river at Lodgepole Village, then get back in the car and make your way to the chilly underground wonderland of **Crystal Cave** (www.explorecrystalcave.com; Crystal Cave Rd, off Generals Hwy; tours adult/youth/child from $16/8/5; May–Nov; P), where you can marvel at delicate marble formations while easing through eerie passageways. You must book tour tickets online in advance. Before sunset, take the dizzyingly steep drive down the Generals Hwy into the **Foothills** area, stopping at riverside swimming holes.

✖ 🛏 p47, p237

The Drive » After a few days in the wilderness, get ready to zoom down to California's biggest city. The fastest route to Los Angeles takes at least 3½ hours to cover 200 miles. Follow Hwy 198 west of Three Rivers to Hwy 65 south through the valley. In Bakersfield, join Hwy 99 south to the I-5 Fwy, which streams south toward LA.

- - - - - - - - - - -

TRIP HIGHLIGHT

❼ Los Angeles

Make a pilgrimage to **Hollywood**, with its pink-starred sidewalks, blingy nightclubs and restored movie palaces. In the San Fernando Valley, peek behind the scenes on a **Warner Bros Studio Tour** (☎818-972-8687, 877-492-8687; www.wbstudiotour.com; 3400 W Riverside Dr, Burbank; tours adult/child 8-12yr from $62/52; 9am-3:15pm Mon-Sat, extended hours Jun-Aug), or get a thrill along with screaming tweens at **Universal Studios Hollywood** (☎800-864-8377; www.universalstudioshollywood.com; 100 Universal City Plaza, Universal City; admission from $99, child under 3yr free; daily, hours vary; P) theme park.

Downtown LA is a historical, multi-layered and fascinating city within a city, known for its landmark architecture. Wander through the old town of **El Pueblo** (☎213-628-1274; www.elpueblo.lacity.org; Olvera St; tours 10am, 11am & noon; ; MUnion Station), then be awed by the **Broad** (☎213-232-6200; www.thebroad.org; 221 S Grand Ave; 11am-5pm Tue & Wed, to 8pm Thu-Sat, to 6pm Sun; P) museum of art (free, but reservations required) before partying at the **LA Live** (☎866-548-3452, 213-763-5483; www.lalive.com; 800 W Olympic Blvd; P) entertainment complex and worshiping at the star-spangled altar of the **Grammy Museum** (☎213-765-6800; www.grammymuseum.org; 800 W Olympic Blvd; adult/child $13/11; 11:30am-6:30pm Mon-Fri, from 10am Sat & Sun; P).

Don't leave town without hitting LA's sunny beaches. In laid-back **Santa Monica** and hipper **Venice**, you can mix with the surf rats, skate punks, muscled bodybuilders, yogis and street performers along a stretch of sublime coastline cradling the city.

✖ 🛏 p47, p70

The Drive » It's a tedious 25-mile trip south on the I-5 Fwy between Downtown LA and Anaheim. The drive can take well over an hour, especially in rush-hour traffic. As you approach Anaheim, follow the freeway signs and take exit 110b for Disneyland Dr.

**TOP TIP:
SAFE DRIVING IN
ALL WEATHER**

If you plan on driving this route in winter, be prepared for snow in the Sierra Nevada; carry tire chains in your car. During summer, the deserts can be dangerously hot; avoid overheating your car by not running the air-conditioning and by traveling in the cooler morning and late-afternoon hours.

🔟 Disneyland

When Walt Disney opened Disneyland on July 17, 1955, he declared it the 'Happiest Place on Earth.' More than 60 years later, it's hard to argue with the ear-to-ear grins on the faces of kiddos, grandparents, honeymooners and everyone else here in Anaheim.

If you've only got one day to spend at **Disneyland Park** (☎714-781-4565; https://disneyland.disney.go.com; 1313 Disneyland Dr, Anaheim; 1-day pass adult/child from $95/89, with Disney California Adventure $155/149; ☺open daily, seasonal hours vary; ⓟ ♿), buy tickets online in advance and arrive early. Stroll **Main Street, USA** toward Sleeping Beauty Castle. Enter **Tomorrowland** to ride Space Mountain. In **Fantasyland** don't miss the classic 'it's a small world' ride or racing downhill on the Matterhorn Bobsleds. Grab a FASTPASS for the Indiana Jones Adventure or the Pirates of the Caribbean before lunching in **New Orleans Square**. Plummet down Splash Mountain, then visit the Haunted Mansion before the **Fantasmic!** show and fireworks begin.

The Drive 》 A few different routes from Anaheim to Palm Springs all eventually funnel onto the I-10 Fwy eastbound from Los Angeles. It's almost a 100-mile trip, which should take less than three hours without traffic jams. Watch for the towering wind turbines on the hillsides as you shoot through San Gorgonio Pass. Take Hwy 111 south to downtown Palm Springs.

- - - - - - - - - - - -

🔟 Palm Springs

In the 1950s and '60s, Palm Springs was the swinging getaway of Sinatra, Elvis and dozens of other stars. Now a new generation has fallen in love with the city's mid-Century Modern charms: steel-and-glass bungalows designed by famous architects, boutique hotels with vintage decor and kidney-shaped pools, and hip bars serving perfect martinis.

North of downtown 'PS,' ride the revolving **Palm Springs Aerial Tramway** (☎760-325-1449, 888-515-8726; www.pstramway.com; 1 Tram Way; adult/child $25/17; ☺1st tram up 10am

DETOUR:
WORLD'S BIGGEST
DINOSAURS

Start: 🔟 Palm Springs

West of Palm Springs, you may do a double take when you see the **World's Biggest Dinosaurs** (☎951-922-8700; www.cabazondinosaurs.com; 50770 Seminole Dr, Cabazon; adult/child $10/9; ☺10am-6pm Mon-Fri, 9am-7pm Sat & Sun; ⓟ ♿). Claude K Bell, a sculptor for Knott's Berry Farm, spent over a decade crafting these concrete behemoths, now owned by Christian creationists who contend that God created the original dinosaurs in one day, along with the other animals, as part of his 'intelligent design.' In the gift shop, alongside the sort of dino-swag you might find at science museums, you can read about the alleged hoaxes and fallacies of evolution and Darwinism.

Mon-Fri, 8am Sat & Sun, last tram down 8pm daily; ⓟ ♿), which climbs 6000ft vertically in under 15 minutes. It's a little cooler as you step out into pine forest at the top, so bring warm clothing – the ride up from the desert floor is said to be the equivalent (in temperature) of driving from Mexico to Canada.

Down-valley in Rancho Mirage, **Sunnylands** (☎760-202-2222; www.sunnylands.org; 37977 Bob Hope Dr, Rancho Mirage; tours $20-40; ☺9am-4pm Thu-Sun, closed early Jun–mid-Sep; ⓟ) was the glamorous modern estate of the Annenberg family. Today it's nicknamed the 'West Coast Camp David' for summits that take place here between President Obama and world leaders. Explore the magnificent desert gardens or book

Classic Trip

ahead for tours of the stunning house with its art collection.

✗ 🛏 p47, p346

The Drive >> North of Palm Springs, take I-10 west to Hwy 62, which winds northeast to the high desert around Joshua Tree. The 35-mile trip goes by quickly; it should take you less than an hour to reach the park's west entrance. Resupply and fuel up first in the town of Joshua Tree – there's no gas, food or water inside the park.

- - - - - - - - - - - - -

⑩ Joshua Tree National Park

Taking a page from a Dr Seuss book, whimsical-looking Joshua trees (ac-tually tree-sized yuccas) symbolize this **national park** (✆760-367-5500; www. nps.gov/jotr; 7-day entry per car $20; ⏰24hr; P 🚻) at the convergence of the Colo-rado and Mojave Deserts. Allegedly, it was Mormon settlers who named the trees because the branch-es stretching up toward heaven reminded them of the biblical prophet pointing the way to the promised land.

Rock climbers know 'JTree' as the best place to climb in California, but kids and the young at heart also welcome the chance to scramble up, down and around the giant boulders. Hikers seek out hidden, shady,

desert-fan-palm oases fed by natural springs and small streams. Book ahead for fascinating guided tours of **Keys Ranch** (✆reservations 760-367-5522; www.nps.gov/jotr; tour adult/child $10/5; ⏰tour schedules vary, reservations required; P 🚻), built by a 20th-century desert homesteader.

Scenic drives worth taking inside the park include the side road to panoramic **Keys View** and the **Pinto Basin Rd**, which winds down to Cottonwood Spring, letting you watch nature transition from the high Mojave Desert to the low Colorado Desert.

✗ 🛏 p47, p347

The Drive >> It's a gloriously scenic back-road adventure to Las Vegas, three hours and nearly 200 miles away. From Twentynine Palms, Amboy Rd barrels east then north, opening up desert panoramas. At Amboy, jog east on Route 66 and north on Kelbaker Rd across I-40 into the Mojave National Preserve. North of the preserve, join the I-15 Fwy northbound to Las Vegas.

- - - - - - - - - - - -

`TRIP HIGHLIGHT`

⑪ Las Vegas, Nevada

Vegas is the ultimate escape. It's the only place in the world where you can spend the night partying in ancient Rome, wake up in Egypt and brunch under the Eiffel Tower, watch an erupting **volcano** (✆800-374-9000; www.mirage.com;

3400 Las Vegas Blvd S, Mirage; ⏰shows 8pm & 9pm daily, also 10pm Fri & Sat; 🚌Deuce) at sunset and get married in a pink Cadillac at midnight.

Double down with the high rollers, pick up some tacky souvenirs and sip a neon 3ft-high margarita as you stroll along the **Strip**. Traipse through mini versions of New York, Paris and Venice before riding the **High**

Las Vegas Fremont Street Experience

Roller (☎702-322-0591; www.caesars.com/linq; 3535 Las Vegas Blvd S; High Roller ride adult/child $23/17, after 5pm $37/27; ⊘11:30am-2am; [P] [♿]; Flamingo or Harrah's/Linq), the world's tallest Ferris wheel (for now). After dark, go glam at ultra-modern casino resorts like Cosmopolitan and Wynn.

So you like old-school casinos, vintage neon signs and dive bars more than celebrity chefs and clubbing? No problem. Head downtown to historic 'Glitter Gulch' along the **Fremont Street Experience** (www.vegas experience.com; Fremont St, btwn Main St & Las Vegas Blvd; ⊘shows hourly dusk-midnight or 1am; 🚌Deuce, SDX), a pedestrian-only zone with a **zipline** (www.vegas experience.com; rides $20-45;

⊘1pm-1am Sun-Thu, to 2am Fri & Sat; [♿]) canopy, nearby the **Mob Museum** (☎702-229-2734; www.themob museum.org; 300 Stewart Ave; adult/child 11-17yr $20/14; ⊘9am-9pm; [P]; 🚌Deuce). Afterward, mingle with locals at hip hangouts in the **Fremont East** entertainment district.

✕ 🛏 p47

Eating & Sleeping

San Francisco ❶

✖ La Taqueria — Mexican $

(📞415-285-7117; 2889 Mission St; items $3-11; 🕙11am-9pm Mon-Sat, to 8pm Sun; 🚹; 🚌12, 14, 48, 49, Ⓑ24th St Mission) SF's definitive burrito has no debatable saffron rice, spinach tortilla or mango salsa – just perfectly grilled meats, slow-cooked beans and classic tomatillo or mesquite salsa wrapped in a flour tortilla. They're purists at La Taqueria – you'll pay extra without beans, because they pack in more meat – but spicy pickles and *crema* (Mexican sour cream) bring complete burrito bliss.

🛏 Hotel Bohème — Boutique Hotel $$

(📞415-433-9111; www.hotelboheme.com; 444 Columbus Ave; r $225-295; 😊 @🛜; 🚌10, 12, 30, 41, 45) This boutique hotel is a love letter to the Beat era, with moody color schemes, Chinese umbrellas as light fixtures and photos from the Beat years on the walls. Rooms are smallish, some front on noisy Columbus Ave (quieter rooms are in the back) and bathrooms are teensy, but it's smack in North Beach's vibrant scene. No elevator or parking lot.

Big Sur ❸

✖ Big Sur Roadhouse — Californian $

(📞831-667-2370; www.bigsurroadhouse.com; 47080 Hwy 1; mains $6-13; 🕙8am-2:30pm; 🚹) This modern roadhouse glows with color-splashed artwork and an outdoor fire pit. At riverside tables, fork into upscale California-inspired pub grub like spicy wings, pork sliders and gourmet burgers, with craft beer on tap.

🛏 Ripplewood Resort — Cabin $$

(📞800-575-1735, 831-667-2242; www.ripplewoodresort.com; 47047 Hwy 1; cabins $110-250; Ⓟ 😊🛜) North of Pfeiffer Big Sur State Park, Ripplewood has struck a blow for fiscal equality by charging the same rates year-round. Throwback Americana cabins mostly have kitchens and sometimes even wood-burning fireplaces. Quiet riverside cabins are surrounded by redwoods, but roadside cabins can be noisy. Wi-fi in restaurant only.

Around Yosemite ❹

✖ Degnan's Loft — Pizza $

(www.travelyosemite.com; off Village Dr, Yosemite Village; mains $8-13; 🕙11am-9pm late May-Sep; 🖊🚹) Head upstairs to this convivial place with high-beamed ceilings and a many-sided fireplace, and kick back under the dangling lift chair for decent salads, lasagna and pizza.

🛏 Evergreen Lodge — Cabins, Campground $$$

(📞209-379-2606; www.evergreenlodge.com; 33160 Evergreen Rd, Groveland; tents $90-125, cabins $180-415; Ⓟ 😊 @🛜🏊) Outside Yosemite National Park near the entrance to Hetch Hetchy, this classic 95-year-old resort consists of a series of lovingly decorated and comfy cabins (each with its own cache of board games) spread out among the trees. Accommodations run from rustic to deluxe, and all cabins have private porches without distracting phone or TV. Roughing-it guests can cheat with comfy, prefurnished tents.

Kings Canyon National Park ❺

🛏 Cedar Grove Lodge — Lodge $$

(📞866-807-3598, 559-565-3096; www.visitsequoia.com; 86724 Hwy 180, Cedar Grove Village; r from $130; 🕙 mid-May–mid-Oct; Ⓟ 😊❄🛜) The only indoor sleeping option in the canyon, the riverside lodge offers 21 unexciting motel-style rooms. A recent remodel has dispelled some of the frumpy decor. Three ground-floor rooms with shady furnished patios have spiffy river views and kitchenettes.

Sequoia National Park ❻

✖ Ol' Buckaroo   American $
(📞559-799-3665; www.theolbuckaroo.com; 41695 Sierra Dr, Three Rivers; mains $8-16; ⏱8:30am-2:30pm & 5-9pm Sat & Sun, 5-9pm Thu, Fri & Mon) Line up outside this food truck early on weekends for cheddar waffles with fried chicken, or stop by for burgers, sliders and grilled cheese with crispy sweet-potato fries after dark, when strings of lights cast a glow over riverside picnic tables.

Los Angeles ❼

✖ Connie & Ted's   Seafood $$$
(📞323-848-2722; www.connieandteds. com; 8171 Santa Monica Blvd; mains $15-42; ⏱4-10pm Mon & Tue, 11:30am-10pm Wed & Thu, 11:30am-11pm Fri & Sat, 10am-10pm Sun) The design is an instant classic, and there are always up to a dozen oyster varieties at the stocked raw bar. Fresh fish is pan-fried or grilled to order. The lobster roll can be served cold with mayo or hot with drawn butter, and the shellfish marinara is a sacred thing.

🛏 Palihotel   Boutique Hotel $$
(📞323-272-4588; www.pali-hotel.com; 7950 Melrose Ave; r from $195; 🅿 @ 🛜) We love the rustic wood-paneled exterior, the polished-concrete floor in the lobby, the elemental Thai massage spa, and the 32 contemporary rooms with two-tone paint jobs, a wall-mounted, flat-screen TV, and enough room for a sofa. Some have terraces. Terrific all-around value.

Palm Springs ❾

✖ Tyler's Burgers   Burgers $
(📞760-325-2990; www.tylersburgers.com; 149 S Indian Canyon Dr; dishes $3-9; ⏱11am-4pm Mon-Sat; 🍴) This tiny shack in the center of downtown Palm Springs serves the best burgers in town, bar none. Waits are practically inevitable, which is presumably why there's an amazingly well-stocked magazine rack. Cash only.

🛏 Ace Hotel & Swim Club   Hotel $$
(📞760-325-9900; www.acehotel.com/ palmsprings; 701 E Palm Canyon Dr; r from $180; 🅿 😊 ❄ @ 🛜 🐾 🐕) Palm Springs goes Hollywood – with all the sass, but sans the attitude – at this former Howard Johnson motel turned hipster hangout. Rooms (many with patio) sport a glorified tent-cabin look and are crammed with lifestyle essentials (big flat-screen TVs, MP3 plugs).

Joshua Tree

✖ Crossroads Cafe   American $
(📞760-366-5414; 61715 Twentynine Palms Hwy, Joshua Tree; mains $6-12; ⏱7am-9pm Mon-Sat, to 8pm Sun; 🍴) The much-loved Crossroads is the go-to place for carbo-loaded breakfasts, dragged-through-the-garden salads and fresh sandwiches that make both omnivores (burgers, Reuben sandwich) and vegans (fake Philly with seitan) happy.

🛏 Harmony Motel   Motel $
(📞760-367-3351; www.harmonymotel.com; 71161 Twentynine Palms Hwy, Twentynine Palms; r $75-95; 🅿 😊 ❄ @ 🛜 🐾) This 1950s motel, where U2 stayed while working on the *Joshua Tree* album, has a small pool and large, cheerfully painted rooms; some have kitchenettes.

Las Vegas, Nevada ⓫

✖ Container Park   Fast Food $
(📞702-359-9982; www. downtowncontainerpark.com; 707 Fremont St; items $3-12; ⏱11am-11pm Mon-Thu, to 1am Fri & Sat, 10am-11pm Sun; 🚌Deuce) With food-truck-style menus, outdoor patio seating and late-night hours, food vendors inside the cutting-edge Container Park sell something to satisfy everyone's appetite.

🛏 Hard Rock   Casino Hotel $
(📞800-473-7625, 702-693-5000; www. hardrockhotel.com; 4455 Paradise Rd; weekday/ weekend r from $45/89; 🅿 ❄ @ 🛜 🐾) Sexy, oversized rooms and HRH suites at this shrine to rock 'n' roll pull in the SoCal party crowd. Free Strip shuttles for guests.

Classic Trip

Pacific Coast Highways

Our top pick for classic California dreamin' snakes along the Pacific coast for more than 1000 miles. Uncover beaches, seafood shacks and piers for catching sunsets over boundless ocean horizons.

TRIP HIGHLIGHTS

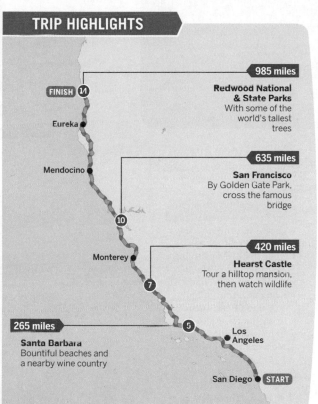

985 miles

Redwood National & State Parks
With some of the world's tallest trees

FINISH 14
Eureka

635 miles

San Francisco
By Golden Gate Park, cross the famous bridge

Mendocino

10

420 miles

Hearst Castle
Tour a hilltop mansion, then watch wildlife

Monterey

7

265 miles

Santa Barbara
Bountiful beaches and a nearby wine country

5

Los Angeles

San Diego START

**7–10 DAYS
985 MILES / 1585KM**

GREAT FOR...

BEST TIME TO GO
Year-round, but July to October for the sunniest skies.

 ESSENTIAL PHOTO
Golden Gate Bridge over San Francisco Bay.

 BEST TWO DAYS
Santa Barbara north to Monterey via Big Sur.

Big Sur A coastal stretch of Hwy 1

Classic Trip

2 Pacific Coast Highways

Make your escape from California's tangled, traffic-jammed freeways and cruise in the slow lane. Once you get rolling, it'll be almost painful to leave the ocean behind. Officially, only the short, sun-loving stretch of Hwy 1 through Orange and Los Angeles Counties can legally call itself Pacific Coast Highway (PCH). But never mind those technicalities, because equally bewitching ribbons of Hwy 1 and Hwy 101 await all along this route.

FINISH — Crescent City
Mt Shasta (14,179ft)
Redwood National & State Parks **14**
p172 — Arcata
13 Eureka
Fortuna
Redding
Red Bluff
Leggett
Mendocino & Fort Bragg
12
Willits
Around Point Arena **11**
Clearlake
Santa Rosa
Bodega Bay
Point Reyes National Seashore p57
Fairfield
Oakland
San Francisco **10**
p170
San Jose
Santa Cruz **9**
Monterey **8**
p284

PACIFIC OCEAN

0 — 100 km
0 — 50 miles

---

❶ San Diego

Begin at the bottom of the state map, where the pretty peninsular beach town of **Coronado** is connected to the San Diego mainland by the white-sand beaches of the **Silver Strand**. If you've seen Marilyn Monroe cavort in *Some Like It Hot*, you'll recognize the **Hotel del Coronado** (☏619-435-6611; www.hoteldel.com; 1500 Orange Ave, Coronado; **P** 🛝), which has hosted US presidents, celebrities and royalty, including the

Prince of Wales who gave up his throne to marry a Coronado divorcée. Wander the turreted palace's labyrinthine corridors, then quaff tropical cocktails at ocean-view Babcock & Story Bar.

Be thrilled by driving over the 2.1-mile-long **San Diego–Coronado Bridge**. Detour inland to **Balboa Park**. Head west, then south to Point Loma's **Cabrillo National Monument** (☏619-557-5450; www.nps.gov/cabr; 1800 Cabrillo Memorial Dr; per car $10; ☉9am-5pm; **P** 🛝) for captivating

bay panoramas from the 19th-century lighthouse and monument to the West Coast's first Spanish explorers. Roll north of **Mission Beach** and the old-fashioned amusement park at **Pacific Beach**, and suddenly you're in hoity-toity **La Jolla**, beyond which lie North County's beach towns.

 p60, p70

The Drive » It's a 50-mile trip from La Jolla north along coastal roads then the I-5 into Orange County (aka the 'OC'), passing Camp Pendleton Marine Corps Base and buxom-shaped San Onofre Nuclear Generating Station. Exit at San Clemente and follow Avenida del Mar downhill to the beach.

❷ San Clemente

Life behind the conservative 'Orange Curtain' is far different than in most other laid-back, liberal

---

LINK YOUR TRIP

15 Big Sur

Get lost on the rugged Big Sur coast, stretched between Hearst Castle and the painterly scenery of Carmel-by-the-Sea on the Monterey Peninsula.

28 Fun on the San Diego Coast

Start your California coastal road trip slowly with an extra couple of days in sunny San Diego.

California beach towns. Apart from glamorous beaches where famous TV shows and movies have been filmed, you can still uncover the California beach culture of yesteryear here in off-the-beaten-path spots like San Clemente. Home to living surfing legends, top-notch surfboard companies and *Surfer* magazine, this may be the last place in the OC where you can authentically live the surf lifestyle. Ride your own board or swim at the city's main beach beside San Clemente Pier. A fast detour inland, the community's **Surfing Heritage & Culture Center** (☎949-388-0313; www.surfingheritage.org; 101 Calle Iglesia, San Clemente; adult/student/child under 12yr $5/4/free; ☺11am-4pm Mon-Sat) exhibits surfboards ridden by the greats, from Duke Kahanamoku to Kelly Slater.

The Drive » Slingshot north on I-5, exiting onto Hwy 1 near Dana Point. Speed by the wealthy artists' colony of Laguna Beach, wild Crystal Cove State Park, Newport Beach's yacht harbor and 'Surf City USA' Huntington Beach. Turn west off Hwy 1 near Naples toward Long Beach, about 45 miles from San Clemente.

❸ Long Beach

In Long Beach, the biggest stars are the **Queen Mary** (☎877-342-0738; www.queenmary.com; 1126 Queens Hwy, Long Beach; tours adult/child from $29/20; ☺tours 10am-6pm or later; **P** **🚗**), a grand (and allegedly haunted) British ocean liner permanently moored here, and the giant **Aquarium of the Pacific** (☎tickets 562-590-3100; www.aquariumofpacific. org; 100 Aquarium Way, Long Beach; adult/senior/child $30/27/18; ☺9am-6pm; **P** **🚗**), a high-tech romp through an underwater world in which sharks dart and jellyfish float. Often overlooked, the **Long Beach Museum of Art** (☎562-439-2119; www. lbma.org; 2300 E Ocean Blvd, Long Beach; adult/seniors & students/child $7/6/free, Fri & 3-8pm Thu free; ☺11am-5pm Fri-Sun, to 8pm Thu; **P**) focuses on California modernism and contemporary mixed-media inside a 20th-century mansion by the ocean, while the urban **Museum of Latin American Art** (☎562-437-1689; www. molaa.org; 628 Alamitos Ave, Long Beach; adult/seniors & students/child $10/7/free, Sun free; ☺11am-5pm Wed, Thu, Sat & Sun, to 9pm Fri; **P**) shows off contemporary south-of-the-border art.

The Drive » Wind slowly around the ruggedly scenic Palos Verdes Peninsula. Follow Hwy 1 north past the South Bay's primetime beaches.

Curving around LAX airport and Marina del Rey, Hwy 1 continues north to Venice, Santa Monica and all the way to Malibu, almost 60 miles from Long Beach.

❹ Malibu

Leaving traffic-jammed LA behind, Hwy 1 breezes northwest of Santa Monica to Malibu. You'll feel like a movie star walking around on the public beaches, fronting gated compounds owned by Hollywood celebs. One mansion you can actually get a look inside is the **Getty Villa** (☎310-430-7300; www.getty. edu; 17985 Pacific Coast Hwy; ☺10am-5pm Wed-Mon, to 9pm Sat late May-late Aug; **P** **🚗**), a hilltop showcase of Greek, Roman and Etruscan antiquities and manicured gardens. Next to **Malibu Lagoon State Beach** (☎310-457-8143; www.parks. ca.gov; 3999 Cross Creek Rd; per car $12; ☺8am-sunset; **P**), west of the surfers by Malibu Pier, **Adamson House** (☎310-456-8432; www.adamsonhouse.org; 23200 Pacific Coast Hwy; adult/child $7/2; ☺11am-3pm Fri & Sat; **P**) is a Spanish-Moorish villa lavishly decorated with locally made hand-painted tiles. Motoring further west along the coast, where the Santa Monica Mountains plunge into the sea, take time out for a frolic on Malibu's mega-popular beaches like sandy Point Dume, Zuma or Leo Carrillo.

DETOUR: CHANNEL ISLANDS NATIONAL PARK

Start: ❹ Malibu

Imagine hiking, kayaking, scuba diving, camping and whale-watching, and doing it all amid a raw, end-of-the-world landscape. Rich in unique species of flora and fauna, tidepools and kelp forests, the islands of this **national park** (☎805-658-5730; www. nps.gov/chis) are home to nearly 150 plant and animal species found nowhere else in the world, earning them the nickname 'California's Galapagos.' Anacapa and Santa Cruz, the most popular islands, are within an hour's boat ride of Ventura Harbor, off Hwy 101 almost 50 miles northwest of Malibu on the way to Santa Barbara. Reservations are essential for weekends, holidays and summer trips. Before you shove off from the mainland, stop by the park's **visitor center** (☎805-658-5730, www.nps.gov/chis; 1901 Spinnaker Dr, Ventura; ⊙8:30am-5pm; 🅿) for educational natural history exhibits, a free 25-minute nature film and family-friendly activities.

✖ p60

The Drive » Hwy 1 crosses into Ventura County, winding alongside the ocean and windy Point Mugu. In Oxnard join Hwy 101 northbound. Motor past Ventura, a jumping-off point for boat trips to Channel Islands National Park, to Santa Barbara, just over 90 miles from Malibu Pier.

- - - - - - - - - - - - -

TRIP HIGHLIGHT

❺ Santa Barbara

Seaside Santa Barbara has almost perfect weather and a string of idyllic beaches, where surfers, kite flyers, dog walkers and surfers mingle. Get a close-up of the city's iconic Spanish Colonial Revival–style architecture along **State St** downtown or from the **county courthouse** (☎805 962-6464; http://sbcourthouse. org; 1100 Anacapa St; ⊙8am-4:45pm Mon-Fri, 10am-4:45pm Sat & Sun), its tower rising above the red-tiled rooftops. Gaze south toward the busy harborfront and **Stearns Wharf** (www.stearnswharf. org; ⊙open daily, hours vary; 🅿🏢) or north to the historic Spanish **mission church** (☎805-682-4713; www.santabarbaramission.org; 2201 Laguna St; adult/child 5-17yr $8/3; ⊙9am-5pm, last entry 4:15pm; 🅿🏢). Santa Barbara's balmy climate is also perfect for growing grapes. A 45-minute drive northwest along Hwy 154, visit Santa Barbara's **wine country**, made famous by the 2004 movie *Sideways*. Hit wine-tasting rooms in Los Olivos, then take Foxen Canyon Rd north past more wineries to rejoin Hwy 101.

✖ 🛏 p60, p70, p217, p319

The Drive » Keep following fast Hwy 101 northbound or detour west onto slow Hwy 1, which squiggles along the Pacific coastline past Guadalupe, gateway to North America's largest sand dunes. Both highways meet up again in Pismo Beach, 100 miles northwest of Santa Barbara.

- - - - - - - - - - - - -

❻ Pismo Beach

A classic California beach town, Pismo Beach has a long, lazy stretch of sand for swimming, surfing and strolling out onto the pier at sunset. After digging into bowls of clam chowder and baskets of fried seafood at surf-casual cafes, check out the retro family fun at the bowling alley, billiards halls and bars uphill from the beach, or dash 10 miles up Hwy 101 to San Luis Obispo's vintage **Sunset Drive-In** (☎805-544-4475; www.facebook.com/sunsetdrivein; 255 Elks Ln; adult/child 5-11yr $8/4; 🏢), where you can put your feet up on the dash and munch on bottomless bags of popcorn while watching Hollywood blockbuster double-features.

✖ 🛏 p60, p209

Classic Trip

WHY THIS IS A CLASSIC TRIP
SARA BENSON, WRITER

From the perfect sun-kissed beaches of Southern California to towering coast redwoods in foggy Northern California, this slice of Pacific Coast is a knockout. I've driven every mile of this route – in some spots, dozens of times – and never tired of the seascapes and surf. My favorite stretches are around Laguna Beach, Big Sur, north of Santa Cruz, and from Jenner to Mendocino and Westport.

Top: View to Pigeon Point Lighthouse, Pacific Coast
Left: Laguna Beach near San Clemente
Right: Neptune Pool at Hearst Castle

The Drive » Follow Hwy 101 north past San Luis Obispo, exiting onto Hwy 1 west to landmark Morro Rock in Morro Bay. North of Cayucos, Hwy 1 rolls through bucolic pasture lands, only swinging back to the coast at Cambria. Ten miles further north stands Hearst Castle, about 60 miles from Pismo Beach.

- - - - - - - - - -

TRIP HIGHLIGHT

❼ Hearst Castle

Hilltop **Hearst Castle** (info 805-927-2020, reservations 800-444-4445; www. hearstcastle.org; 750 Hearst Castle Rd, San Simeon; tours adult/child 5-12yr from $25/12; ⏱ from 9am; P 🚻) is California's most famous monument to wealth and ambition. William Randolph Hearst, the early-20th-century newspaper magnate, entertained Hollywood stars and royalty at this fantasy estate furnished with European antiques, accented by shimmering pools and surrounded by flowering gardens. Try to make tour reservations in advance, especially for living-history evening programs during the Christmas holiday season and in spring.

About 4.5 miles further north along Hwy 1, park at the signposted vista point and amble the boardwalk to view the enormous **elephant seal colony** that breeds, molts, sleeps, plays and fights on the beach. Seals haul out year-round, but the winter birthing and

55

mating season peaks on Valentine's Day. Nearby, **Piedras Blancas Light Station** (☎805-927-7361; www.piedrasblancas.gov; off Hwy 1; tours adult/child 6-17yr $10/5; ⏱tours 9:45am Tue, Thu & Sat Sep–mid-Jun, also 9:45am Mon & Fri mid-Jun–Aug) is an outstandingly scenic spot.

✗ p60

The Drive » Fill your car's gas tank before plunging north into the redwood forests of the remote Big Sur coast, where precipitous cliffs dominate the seascape, and tourist services are few and far between. Hwy 1 keeps curving north to the Monterey Peninsula, approximately a three-hour, 95-mile trip from Hearst Castle.

- - - - - - - - - - - - -

❽ Monterey

As Big Sur loosens its condor's talons on the coastal highway, Hwy 1 rolls gently downhill towards Monterey Bay. The fishing community of

Monterey is the heart of Nobel Prize–winning writer John Steinbeck's country, and although **Cannery Row** today is touristy claptrap, it's worth strolling down to step inside the mesmerizing **Monterey Bay Aquarium** (☎info 831-648-4800, tickets 866-963-9645; www.montereybayaquarium.org; 886 Cannery Row; adult/youth 13-17yr/child 3-12yr $40/30/25; ⏱9:30am-6pm Jun, to 6pm Mon-Fri, to 8pm Sat & Sun Jul-Aug, 10am-5pm or 6pm Sep-May; ♿), inhabiting a converted sardine cannery on the shores of a national marine sanctuary. All kinds of aquatic denizens swim in giant tanks here, from sea stars to pot-bellied seahorses and comical sea otters.

✗ 🛏 p61, p201

The Drive » It's a relatively quick 45-mile trip north to Santa Cruz. Hwy 1 traces the crescent shoreline of Monterey Bay, passing Elkhorn Slough wildlife refuge near Moss Landing boat harbor, Watsonville's strawberry and artichoke farms, and a string of tiny beach towns in Santa Cruz County.

- - - - - - - - - - - - -

❾ Santa Cruz

Here, the flower power of the 1960s lives on, and bumper stickers on surfboard-laden woodies shout, 'Keep Santa Cruz weird.' Next to the ocean, **Santa Cruz Beach Boardwalk** (☎831-423-5590; www.beachboardwalk.com; 400 Beach St; per ride $3-6, all-day pass $34-45; ⏱daily Apr-early Sep, seasonal hours vary; P ♿) has a glorious old-school Americana vibe and a 1911 Looff carousel. Its fun-for-all atmosphere is punctuated by squeals from nervous nellies on the stomach-turning Giant Dipper, a 1920s wooden roller coaster that's a national historic landmark, as seen in the vampire cult-classic movie *The Lost Boys*.

A kitschy, old-fashioned tourist trap, the **Mystery Spot** (☎831-423-8897; www.mysteryspot.com; 465 Mystery Spot Rd; admission $6; ⏱10am-4pm Mon-Fri, to 5pm Sat & Sun Sep-May, 10am-6pm Mon-Fri, 9am-7pm Sat & Sun Jun-Aug; P ♿) makes compasses point crazily, while mysterious forces push you around and buildings lean at odd angles; call for directions, opening hours and tour reservations.

✗ 🛏 p61, p193

The Drive » It's a blissful 75-mile coastal run from Santa Cruz up to San Francisco past Pescadero, Half Moon Bay and Pacifica, where Hwy 1 passes through the tunnels at Devil's

---

TROUBLE-FREE ROAD TRIPPING

In coastal areas, thick fog may impede driving – slow down, and if it's too soupy, get off the road. Along coastal cliffs, watch out for falling rocks and mudslides that could damage or disable your car if struck. For current highway conditions, including road closures (which aren't uncommon during the rainy winter season) and construction updates, call ☎800-427-7623 or visit www.dot.ca.gov.

Slide. Merge with heavy freeway traffic in Daly City, staying on Hwy 1 north through the city into Golden Gate Park.

- - - - - - - - - -

TRIP HIGHLIGHT

⑩ San Francisco

Gridlock may shock your system after hundreds of lazy miles of wide-open, rolling coast. But don't despair. Hwy 1 runs straight through the city's biggest, most breathable greenspace: **Golden Gate Park** (www.golden-gate-park.com; Stanyan St to Great Hwy; **P** 🚻; 🚌 5, 7, 18, 21, 28, 29, 33, 44, **M** N). You could easily spend all day in the conservatory of flowers, arboretum and botanical gardens, or perusing the **California Academy of Sciences** (📞 415-379-8000; www.calacademy.org; 55 Music Concourse Dr; adult/child $35/25; ☺ 9:30am-5pm Mon-Sat, from 11am Sun; **P** 🚻; 🚌 5, 6, 7, 21, 31, 33, 44, **M** N) and the **de Young Museum** (📞 415-750-3600; http://deyoung.famsf.org; 50 Hagiwara Tea Garden Dr; adult/child $10/7, 1st Tue of month free; ☺ 9:30am-5:15pm Tue-Sun, to 8:45pm Fri Apr-Nov; 🚌 5, 7, 44, **M** N) of fine arts. Then follow Hwy 1 north over the **Golden Gate Bridge**. Guarding the entry to San Francisco Bay, this iconic bridge is named after the straits it spans, not for its 'International Orange' paint job. Park in the lot on the bridge's south or north side, then traipse out onto the

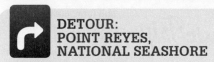

DETOUR: POINT REYES, NATIONAL SEASHORE

Start: ⑩ **San Francisco**

A rough-hewn beauty, **Point Reyes National Seashore** (📞 415-654-5100; www.nps.gov/pore; **P** 🚻) lures marine mammals and birds, as well as scores of shipwrecks. It was here that Sir Francis Drake repaired his ship the *Golden Hind* in 1579 and, while he was at it, claimed the indigenous land for England. Follow Sir Francis Drake Blvd west out to the point's edge-of-the-world **lighthouse** (📞 415-669-1534; www.nps.gov/pore; Sir Francis Drake Blvd; ☺ lighthouse 10am-4:30pm Fri-Mon, lens room 2:30-4pm Fri-Mon; **P**), whipped by ferocious winds, where you can observe migrating whales in winter. The lighthouse is about 20 miles west of Point Reyes Station off Hwy 1 along Marin County's coast.

pedestrian walkway for a photo.

🍴 🛏 p46, p61, p71, p93

The Drive » Past Sausalito, leave Hwy 101 in Marin City for slow-moving, wonderfully twisted Hwy 1 along the Marin County coast, passing nearby Point Reyes. Over the next 100 miles from Bodega Bay to Mendocino, revel in a remarkably uninterrupted stretch of coastal highway. More than halfway along, watch for the lighthouse road turnoff north of Point Arena town.

- - - - - - - - - -

⑪ Around Point Arena

The fishing fleets of Bodega Bay and Jenner's harbor-seal colony are the last things you'll see before PCH dives into California's great rural northlands. Hwy 1 twists and turns past the Sonoma Coast's

state parks packed with hiking trails, sand dunes and beaches, as well as underwater marine reserves, rhododendron groves and a 19th-century Russian fur-trading fort. At **Sea Ranch**, don't let exclusive-looking vacation homes prevent you from following public-access trailhead signs and staircases down to empty beaches and across ocean bluffs. Further north, guarding an unbelievably windy point since 1908, **Point Arena Lighthouse** (📞 877-725-4448, 707-882-2809; http://pointarenalighthouse.com; 45500 Lighthouse Rd; adult/child $7.50/1; ☺ 10am-3:30pm, to 4:30pm late May-early Sep; **P**) is the only lighthouse in California where you can actually climb to the top. Check in at the museum, then ascend the 115ft tower to inspect

JORDAN SIEMENS / GETTY IMAGES ©

Classic Trip

the Fresnel lens and panoramas of the sea and the jagged San Andreas Fault below.

📖 p61

The Drive >> It's an hour-long, 35-mile drive north along Hwy 1 from the Point Arena Lighthouse turnoff to Mendocino, crossing the Navarro, Little and Big Rivers. Feel free to stop and stretch at wind-tossed state beaches, parklands criss-crossed by hiking trails and tiny coastal towns along the way.

⑫ Mendocino & Fort Bragg

Looking more like Cape Cod than California, the quaint maritime town of **Mendocino** has white picket fences surrounding New England–style cottages with blooming gardens and redwood-built water towers. Its dramatic headlands jutting into the Pacific, this yesteryear timber town and shipping port was 'discovered' by artists and bohemians in the 1950s and has served as a scenic backdrop in over 50 movies. Once you've browsed the souvenir shops and art galleries selling everything from driftwood carvings to homemade fruit jams, escape north to worka-day **Fort Bragg**, with its simple fishing harbor

and brewpub, stopping first for a short hike on the ecological staircase and pygmy forest trail at oceanfront **Jug Handle State Natural Reserve** (📞707-937-5804; www. parks.ca.gov; Hwy 1, Caspar; 🕑sunrise-sunset; P 👪).

The Drive >> About 25 miles north of Mendocino, Westport is the last hamlet along this rugged stretch of Hwy 1. Rejoin Hwy 101 northbound at Leggett for another 90 miles to Eureka, detouring along the Avenue of the Giants and, if you have more time to spare, to the Lost Coast.

- - - - - - - - - - - - - -

⑬ Eureka

Hwy 101 trundles alongside **Humboldt Bay National Wildlife Refuge** (📞707-733-5406; www.fws. gov/refuge/humboldt_bay; 1020 Ranch Rd, Loleta; 🕑8am-5pm; P), a major stopover for migra-tory birds on the Pacific Flyway. Next comes the sleepy railroad town of Eureka. As you wander downtown, check out the ornate **Carson Mansion** (Ingomar Club; www.ingomar. org; 143 M St), built in the 1880s by a timber baron and adorned with dizzying Victorian tur-rets, towers, gables and gingerbread details. **Blue Ox Millworks & Historic Park** (📞707-444-3437; www. blueoxmill.com; 1 X St; adult/child 6-12yr \$10/5; 🕑9am-5pm Mon-Fri year-round, also 9am-4pm Sat Apr-Nov; P 👪) still creates Victorian detailing by hand using traditional carpentry and

19th-century equipment. Back by Eureka's harbor-front, climb aboard the blue-and-white 1910 **Madaket** (📞707-445-1910; www.humboldt-baymaritimemuseum.com; narrated cruise adult/child \$18/10; 🕑schedules vary; 👪), docked at the foot of C St. Sunset cocktail cruises serve from Cali-fornia's smallest licensed bar.

✕ 📖 p61, p153

The Drive >> Follow Hwy 101 north past the Rastafarian-hippie college town of Arcata and turnoffs for Trinidad State Beach and Patrick's Point State Park. Hwy 101 drops out of the trees beside marshy Humboldt

North Coast Hikers in a lush redwood forest

Lagoons State Park, rolling north towards Orick, just over 40 miles from Eureka.

TRIP HIGHLIGHT

⑭ Redwood National & State Parks

At last, you'll reach **Redwood National Park** (☎707-465-7335; www.nps. gov/redw; P ⛷). Get oriented to the tallest trees on earth at the coastal **Thomas H Kuchel Visitor Center** (☎707-465-7765; www.nps.gov/redw; Hwy 101, Orick; ☺9am-5pm Apr-Oct, to 4pm Nov-Mar; ⛷), just south of the tiny town of Orick. Then commune with the coastal giants on their own mossy turf inside **Lady Bird Johnson Grove** or the majestic **Tall Trees Grove** (free drive-and-hike permit required). For more untouched redwood forests, wind along the 8-mile **Newton B Drury Scenic Parkway** in **Prairie Creek Redwoods State Park** (☎707-488-2039; www.parks. ca.gov; Newton B Drury Scenic Pkwy; ☺9am-5pm May-Sep, to 4pm Wed-Sun Oct-Apr; ⛷), passing grassy meadows where Roosevelt elk roam, then follow Hwy 101 all the way north to **Crescent City**, the last pit-stop before the Oregon border.

Classic Trip

Eating & Sleeping

San Diego ❶

🛏 Pearl   Motel $$

([☑]877-732-7573, 619-226-6100; www.
thepearlsd.com; 1410 Rosecrans St; r $135-199;
[P][❄][📶][⛱]) The mid-century modern Pearl
feels more Palm Springs than San Diego. The
23 rooms in its 1959 shell have soothing blue
hues, trippy surf motifs and fishbowls. There's
a lively pool scene (including 'dive-in' movies on
Wednesday nights), or play Jenga or Parcheesi
in the groovy, shag-carpeted lobby. Light
sleepers: request a room away from busy street
traffic. On-site parking is limited and costs $10.

Malibu ❹

🍴 Neptune's Net   Seafood $$

([☑]310-457-3095; www.neptunesnet.com;
42505 Pacific Coast Hwy; mains $6-21;
⊙10:30am-8pm Mon-Thu, to 9pm Fri, 10am-8pm
Sat & Sun, closes 1hr earlier Oct-Apr; [👪][🐶]) Not
far past the Malibu line, Neptune's Net catches
Range Rovers, road bikes and rad choppers with
fried-shrimp-and-beer hospitality on inviting
wooden porches.

Santa Barbara ❺

🍴 Santa Barbara
Shellfish Company   Seafood $$

([☑]805-966-6676; www.sbfishhouse.com; 230
Stearns Wharf; dishes $4-19; ⊙11am-9pm;
[👪][🐶]) 'From sea to skillet to plate' sums up
this end-of-the-wharf seafood shack that's
more of a buzzing counter joint than a sit-down
restaurant. Chase away the seagulls as you
chow down on garlic-baked clams, crab cakes
and coconut-fried shrimp at wooden picnic
tables outside. Awesome lobster bisque, ocean
views and the same location for over 25 years.

🛏 El Capitan
Canyon   Cabin, Campground $$$

([☑]805-685-3887, 866-352-2729; www.
elcapitancanyon.com; 11560 Calle Real; safari
tent $155-170, yurt $205-225, cabins $225-425;
[P][⊙][📶][⛱]) Inland from El Capitán State
Beach, this 'glamping' resort is for those who
hate to wake up with dirt under their nails. No
cars are allowed up-canyon during peak season,
making this woodsy resort more peaceful.
Safari tents are rustic and share bathrooms,
while creekside cabins are more deluxe, some
with kitchenettes; all have their own outdoor
fire pit.

Pismo Beach ❻

🍴 Cracked Crab   Seafood $$$

([☑]805-773-2722; www.crackedcrab.com; 751
Price St; mains $12-39; ⊙11am-9pm Sun-Thu, to
10pm Fri & Sat; [👪]) Fresh seafood and regional
wines are the staples at this super-casual,
family-owned grill. When the famous bucket
o'seafood, full of flying bits of fish, Cajun
sausage, red potatoes and cob corn, gets
dumped on your butcher-paper-covered table,
make sure you're wearing one of those silly-
looking plastic bibs. No reservations, but the
wait is worth it.

Hearst Castle ❼

🍴 Sebastian's   American $

([☑]805-927-3307; 442 SLO-San Simeon Rd;
mains $8-12; ⊙11:30am-4:30pm Tue-Sun; [👪])
Down a side road across Hwy 1 from Hearst
Castle, this tiny historic market sells cold
drinks, Hearst Ranch beef burgers, giant deli
sandwiches and salads for beach picnics at San
Simeon Cove. Hearst Ranch Winery tastings are
available at the copper-top bar.

Monterey 8

✖ Monterey's Fish House   Seafood $$

(☎831-373-4647; 2114 Del Monte Ave; mains $10-25; ⏰11:30am-2:30pm & 5-9:30pm Mon-Fri, 5-9:30pm Sat & Sun; 🚼) Watched over by photos of Sicilian fishermen, dig into oak-grilled or blackened swordfish, barbecued oysters or, for those stout of heart, the Mexican squid steak. Reservations are essential (it's *so* crowded), but the vibe is island-casual: Hawaiian shirts seem to be de rigueur for men.

Santa Cruz 9

🛏 Pelican Point Inn   Inn $$

(☎831-475-3381; www.pelicanpointinn-santacruz.com; 21345 E Cliff Dr; ste $139-229; P ⊜ 🛜 🖥) Ideal for families, these roomy apartments near a kid-friendly beach come with everything you'll need for a lazy vacation, including kitchenettes. Weekly rates available. Pet fee $20.

San Francisco 10

✖ Greens   Vegetarian, Californian $$

(☎415-771-6222; www.greensrestaurant.com; Bldg A, Fort Mason Center, 2 Marina Blvd; lunch $16-19, dinner $20-27; ⏰11:45am-2:30pm & 5:30-9pm Tue-Fri, from 11am Sat, 10:30am-2pm & 5:30-9pm Sun, 5:30-9pm Mon; 🍴 🚼; 🚌28) Career carnivores won't realize there's zero meat in the hearty black-bean chili, or in the other flavor-packed vegetarian dishes, made using ingredients from a Zen farm in Marin. And oh!, what views – the Golden Gate rises just outside the window-lined dining room. The on-site cafe serves to-go lunches. For sit-down meals, including Sunday brunch, reservations are essential.

🛏 Argonaut Hotel   Boutique Hotel $$$

(☎800-790-1415, 415-563-0800; www.argonauthotel.com; 495 Jefferson St; r from $389; P ⊜ ❄ 🛜 🖥; 🚌19, 47, 49, 🚋Powell-Hyde) Fisherman's Wharf's top hotel was built as a cannery in 1908 and has century-old wooden beams and exposed brick walls. Rooms sport an over-the-top nautical theme, with porthole-shaped mirrors and plush, deep-blue carpets. Though all have the amenities of an upper-end hotel – ultra-comfy beds, iPod docks – some rooms are tiny with limited sunlight. Parking is $50.

Around Point Arena 11

🛏 Mar Vista Cottages   Cabin $$$

(☎707-884-3522, 877-855-3522; www.marvistamendocino.com; 35101 S Hwy 1, Gualala; cottages $185-305; P ⊜ 🛜 🖥) The elegantly renovated 1930s fishing cabins offer a simple, stylish seaside escape with a vanguard commitment to sustainability. The harmonious environment is the result of pitch-perfect details: linens are line-dried over lavender, guests browse the organic vegetable garden to harvest their own dinner and chickens cluck around the grounds laying the next morning's breakfast. It often requires two-night stays.

Eureka 13

🛏 Carter House Inns   B&B $$$

(☎707-444-8062, 800-404-1390; http://carterhouse.com; 301 L St; r $185-385; P ⊜ 🛜 🖥) Constructed in period style, this recently remodeled hotel is a Victorian lookalike, holding rooms with top-quality linens and modern amenities; suites have in-room whirlpools and marble fireplaces. The same owners operate four other sumptuously decorated lodgings: a single-level house, two honeymoon hideaway cottages and a replica of an 1880s San Francisco mansion, which the owner built himself, entirely by hand. Unlike elsewhere, you won't see the innkeeper unless you want to. Guests enjoy a complimentary hot breakfast in the understated, elegant **Restaurant 301** (dinner mains $24-40; ⏰5-8:30pm; 🍴).

Mission Trail

Follow the path of early Spanish colonists from San Diego to Sonoma, embracing the most intriguing of California's original missions, with atmospheric inns and eateries along the way.

TRIP HIGHLIGHTS

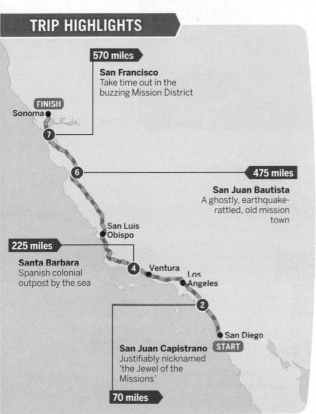

570 miles

San Francisco
Take time out in the buzzing Mission District

FINISH
Sonoma

7

6

475 miles

San Juan Bautista
A ghostly, earthquake-rattled, old mission town

San Luis Obispo

225 miles

Santa Barbara
Spanish colonial outpost by the sea

4 Ventura

Los Angeles

2

San Diego **START**

San Juan Capistrano
Justifiably nicknamed 'the Jewel of the Missions'

70 miles

5 DAYS
615 MILES / 990KM

GREAT FOR...

BEST TIME TO GO
April to October for sunny skies.

 ESSENTIAL PHOTO

Swallows returning to Mission San Juan Capistrano in March.

✓ **BEST FOR FOODIES**

San Francisco's Mission District.

Classic Trip

3 Mission Trail

It took over 50 years for a chain of 21 missions to be established along El Camino Real (the Royal Road), first forged by Spanish conquistador Gaspar de Portolá and Franciscan priest Junípero Serra in the late 18th century. Each mission was just a day's ride on horseback away from the next, but today you can drive the entire route in less than a week.

2   8   7
FINISH   Sonoma
San Francisco 7   p170
San Mateo
Redwood City
San Jose
Santa Cruz
Salinas
Monterey

PACIFIC
OCEAN

❶ San Diego

On July 1, 1769, a forlorn lot of about 100 Spanish soldiers and missionaries straggled ashore at San Diego Bay. After sailing for weeks up the coast from Baja California, many were sick and more than half had died. It was an inauspicious beginning for **Mission Basilica San Diego de Alcalá** (☏619-281-8449; www.missionsandiego.com; 10818 San Diego Mission Rd; adult/child $5/1; ☉9am-4:30pm; 🅿🚻), the oldest in California's chain of missions.

West atop Presidio Hill, the **Junípero Serra Museum** (☏619-232-6203; www.sandiegohistory.org; 2727 Presidio Dr; adult/child $6/3; ☉10am-4pm Fri-Sun early Jun-early Sep, 10am-5pm Sat & Sun early Sep-early Jun; 🅿🚻) recounts Native American struggles with mission life. Where the colonists' original military fort and church once stood, this 1920s Spanish Colonial Revival building echoes early mission architecture.

Nearby, **Old Town San Diego State Historic Park** (☏619-220-5422; www.parks.ca.gov; 4002 Wallace St; ☉visitor center & museums 10am-5pm daily May-Sep, to 4pm Mon-Thu Oct-Apr; 🅿🚻) preserves buildings from the Spanish, Mexican and early American periods, with an old-fashioned plaza surrounded by shops and cafes.

🍴 🛏 p60, p70

64

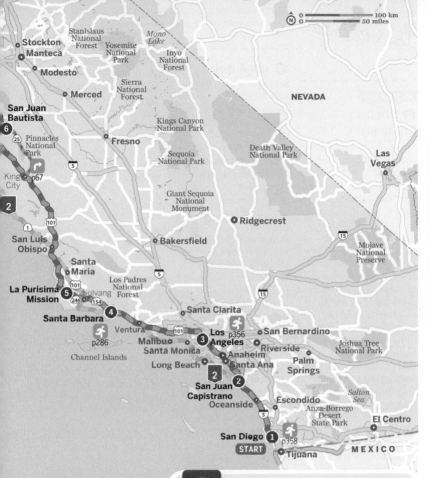

The Drive » El Camino Real, which is marked throughout California by free-standing bronze mission bells erected in the 1920s, follows I-5 north from San Diego. After more than 60 miles, exit onto Hwy 74 (Ortega Hwy), turn left and drive west to Mission San Juan Capistrano.

LINK YOUR TRIP

2 Pacific Coast Highways

California's mission trail intersects with the classic coastal route at San Diego, Los Angeles, Santa Barbara and San Francisco.

7 Sonoma Valley

Where this trip ends at Sonoma Plaza, you can start exploring Northern California's rustic-chic wine country.

❷ San Juan Capistrano

Archaeologists, engineers and restoration artists have done an exquisite job of keeping alive **Mission San Juan Capistrano** (☏949-234-1300; www. missionsjc.com; 26801 Ortega Hwy, San Juan Capistrano; adult/child $9/6; ⏰9am-5pm; ♿). Built around a series of 18th-century arcades, the mission complex encloses bubbling fountains and flowery gardens. The Serra Chapel, where the padre first celebrated mass in 1783, is considered California's oldest building, and even the mighty San Andreas Fault hasn't been able to topple it yet. Every year on March 19, the Festival of the Swallows celebrates the birds' return from their Argentine sojourn to make their nests in the mission's walls. One block west, by the train depot, the tree-shaded **Los Rios Historic District** collects quaint cottages and adobes housing cafes and gift shops.

✖ p70

The Drive » Get back on I-5 north for the often traffic-jammed 50-mile drive to downtown Los Angeles. Take the Alameda St/Union Station exit, turn right onto Main St and look for metered street parking or pay-parking lots.

❸ Los Angeles

Setting out from the valley's Mission San Gabriel Arcángel, just a few dozen Spanish colonists founded the 'City of Angels' in 1781, near the site of today's **El Pueblo de Los Angeles Historical Monument** (☏213-628-1274; www.elpueblo.lacity.org; Olvera St; ⏰tours 10am, 11am & noon; ♿; Ⓜ Union Station). Peek inside 19th-century historical buildings like the Avila Adobe and 'La Placita' plaza church and jostle down crowded block-long Olvera St, an open-air marketplace lined with Mexican food vendors and *folklorico* shops, then unwind in front of the wrought-iron bandstand, where mariachis often play on sunny weekend afternoons. Nearby, **La Plaza de Cultura y Artes** (☏213-542-6200; http://lapca.org; 501 N Main St; ⏰noon-5pm Mon, Wed & Thu, to 6pm Fri-Sun; ♿) vibrantly chronicles the Mexican American experience in LA.

✖ 🛏 p47, p70

The Drive » Follow Hwy 101 north of Downtown LA past Hollywood and west through the suburban San Fernando Valley all the way to the Pacific coast. Northwest of Ventura, another SoCal mission town with beautiful beaches, lies Santa Barbara, about 100 miles from LA.

❹ Santa Barbara

After a magnitude 6.3 earthquake hit Santa Barbara in 1925, downtown's **State St** was entirely rebuilt in Spanish Colonial Revival style, with whitewashed adobe walls and red-tile roofs. Head north to hillside **Mission Santa Barbara** (☏805-682-4713; www.santabarbaramission. org; 2201 Laguna St; adult/child 5-17yr $8/3; ⏰9am-5pm, last entry 4:15pm; Ⓟ ♿), another victim of historical quakes. From the front of its imposing Doric facade, itself a homage to an ancient Roman chapel, you can look up at the unique twin bell towers. Founded in 1786 on the feast day of Saint Barbara, the mission has been continuously occupied by Franciscan priests, having escaped Mexico's enforced policy of secularization that destroyed most of California's other missions. Artwork by Chumash tribespeople adorns the chapel. Look for a centuries-old cemetery out back.

✖ 🛏 p60, p70

The Drive » El Camino Real follows Hwy 101 north. For a more scenic route, take winding Hwy 154 up into the mountains and wine country. Turn left onto Hwy 246 (Mission Dr) toward the Danish village of Solvang, which has a pretty little mission, then keep driving west along Hwy 246 almost to Lompoc. It's a 50-mile trip from Mission Santa Barbara.

❺ La Purísima Mission

Drive through the hills outside Lompoc, past vineyards and commercial flower fields, to **La Purísima Mission State Historic Park** (☎805-733-3713; www.lapurisimamission.org; 2295 Purísima Rd, Lompoc; per car $6; ☺9am-5pm; [P] [♿]). Resurrected by the Civilian Conservation Corps (CCC) during the Depression era, almost a dozen buildings here have been restored to their original 1820s appearance. Amble past Spanish soldiers' living quarters, a weaving room and a blacksmith's shop, all beside grassy fields where cows, horses and goats graze.

The Drive 》 Follow scenic, rural Hwy 1 north to Pismo Beach, then rejoin Hwy 101 north to San Luis Obispo, a peaceful mission town that's a convenient place to break your journey. The next day, follow Hwy 101 north for 140 more miles past Salinas to Hwy 156, connecting east to San Juan Bautista.

TRIP HIGHLIGHT

❻ San Juan Bautista

Unknowingly built atop the San Andreas Fault, **Mission San Juan Bautista** (☎831-623-4528; www.oldmissionsjb.org; 406 2nd St; adult/child 5-17yr $4/2; ☺9:30am-4:30pm; [♿]) has the largest church among California's historical missions. The original chapel was toppled by

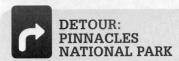

DETOUR: PINNACLES NATIONAL PARK

Start: ❺ La Purísima Mission

Named for the towering spires that rise abruptly out of the chaparral-covered hills, this **park** (☎831-389-4486; www.nps.gov/pinn; per car $15; [P] [♿]) is a study in geological drama, with its craggy monoliths, sheer-walled canyons and ancient volcanic remnants. Besides hiking and rock climbing, the park's biggest attractions are its endangered California condors and talus caves where bats live. It's best visited during spring or fall; summer's heat is too extreme. Camping is available near the east entrance off Hwy 25 between San Juan Bautista and King City, accessed via Hwy 101 north of San Luis Obispo.

the 1906 San Francisco earthquake. Scenes from Alfred Hitchcock's 1960s film *Vertigo* were shot here, although the climactic bell tower was just a special-effects prop. The old Spanish plaza opposite the mission anchors **San Juan Bautista State Historic Park** (☎831-623-4881; www.parks.ca.gov; 2nd St, btwn Mariposa & Washington Sts; museum adult/child $3/free; ☺10am-4:30pm). A short walk away, dusty downtown San Juan Bautista is crowded with Mexican restaurants and antiques shops.

The Drive 》 Backtrack west on Hwy 156 to Hwy 101, which speeds north past Gilroy's garlic farms to San Jose, then curves alongside San Francisco Bay and Silicon Valley. After almost 90 miles, you'll arrive in San Francisco: exit at Duboce Ave, turn left on Guerrero St, then right on 16th St to arrive at Mission San Francisco de Asís.

TRIP HIGHLIGHT

❼ San Francisco

Time seems to stand still at **Mission San Francisco de Asís** (Misión San Francisco de Asís; ☎415-621-8203; www.missiondolores.org; 3321 16th St; adult/child $5/3; ☺9am-4pm Nov-Apr, to 4:30pm May-Oct; [🚃]22, 33, [B]16th St Mission, [M]J), also known as Mission Dolores. With its gold-leafed altar and redwood beams decorated with Native American artwork, this is the only intact original mission chapel in California, its adobe walls having stood firm in the 1906 earthquake. Today, it's overshadowed by the ornate 1913 basilica, where stained-glass windows commemorate the 21 original California missions. The graveyard out back, where Kim Novak wandered in a daze in Hitchcock's *Vertigo*,

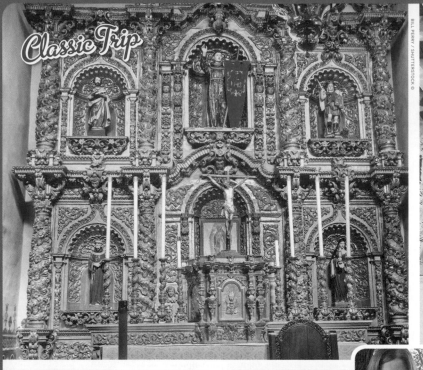

Classic Trip

WHY THIS IS A CLASSIC TRIP
SARA BENSON, WRITER

Driving up and down the state, I always wondered what those cast-iron mission bells placed beside Hwy 101 signified – that is, until I finally took an enlightening journey along El Camino Real. California's original road trip connects a string of Spanish colonial missions, beautified by sunny cloisters, adobe buildings and beautifully frescoed chapels. My favorite stop is at San Juan Capistrano.

Top: Golden altar at the Serra Chapel, San Juan Capistrano
Left: Statue of Saint Francis of Assisi at Mission Santa Barbara
Right: Interior of Mission San Francisco de Asís

is where 5000 Ohlone and Miwok who died in measles epidemics are memorialized, surrounded by the graves of early Mexican and European settlers. In the surrounding Mission District Mexican taquerías mix with California farm-to-table kitchens.

✗ 🛏 p46, p61, p71, p93

The Drive » Hwy 101 rolls up and down San Francisco's famous hills, from the Mission District to the Marina and the Presidio, finally exiting the city via the Golden Gate Bridge. North of the mission town of San Rafael, follow Hwy 37 east to Hwy 121 north, then take Hwy 12 north into downtown Sonoma, over a 40-mile drive from San Francisco.

— — — — — — — — — —

8 Sonoma

The wine country town of Sonoma is not only the site of the last Spanish mission established in California. It also happens to be the place where American settlers attempted to declare independence from Mexico in 1846. Mission San Francisco Solano is now part of **Sonoma State Historic Park** (📞707-938-9560; www.parks.ca.gov; adult/child $3/2; ⏱10am-5pm), which preserves military barracks and a mid-19th-century Mexican general's home. Its petite adobe chapel, dating from 1841, is also the finish line for El Camino Real.

✗ 🛏 p71, p113

Classic Trip

Eating & Sleeping

San Diego ❶

✕ El Agave — Mexican $$$

(📞619-220-0692; www.elagave.com; 2304 San Diego Ave; mains lunch $11-20, dinner $21-39; 🕙11am-10pm; P) Candlelight flickers in this romantic 2nd-floor, white-tablecloth, high-end place catering to cognoscenti. The mole is superb (there are 10 types to choose from), and there are a whopping 1500 different tequilas covering just about every bit of wall space and in racks overhead, enough that it calls itself a tequila museum.

🛏 Cosmopolitan Hotel — B&B $$

(📞619-297-1874; http://oldtowncosmopolitan. com; 2660 Calhoun St; r $139-195; 🕙front desk 9am-9pm; P ☺ 🛜) Right in Old Town State Park, this creaky, 10-room hotel restored to the 1870s has oodles of charm, antique furnishings, a possible haunting (!) and a restaurant downstairs for lunch and dinner. Don't go expecting modern conveniences like phones and TV, though there's free wi-fi. Breakfast is a simple affair centered on coffee and scones. Free parking.

San Juan Capistrano ❷

✕ Ramos House Café — Californian $$

(📞949-443-1342; www.ramoshouse.com; 31752 Los Rios St; weekday mains $16-20, weekend brunch $40; 🕙8:30am-3pm) The best spot for breakfast or lunch near the Mission, this Old West–flavored, wood-built house from 1881 is famous for organically raised comfort food flavored with herbs grown onsite. To find it, walk across the railroad tracks at the end of Verdugo St and turn right. Promptly reward yourself with apple-cinnamon beignets, basil-cured salmon lox or spicy crab-cake salad.

Los Angeles ❸

✕ Philippe the Original — Diner $

(📞213-628-3781; www.philippes.com; 1001 N Alameda St; mains $5-10; 🕙6am-10pm; 🚻) From LAPD hunks to stressed-out attorneys to smooching couples, everyone loves Philippe's, a French-dip sandwich institution. Order a crusty roll filled with meat (we go with the lamb 'double-dipped'), and hunker down at communal tables on the sawdust-covered floor. Cash only.

Santa Barbara ❹

✕ Bouchon — Californian $$$

(📞805-730-1160; www.bouchonsantabarbara. com; 9 W Victoria St; mains $26-36; 🕙5-9pm Sun-Thu, to 10pm Fri & Sat) The perfect, unhurried, follow-up to a day in the Wine Country is to feast on the bright, flavorful California cooking at pretty Bouchon (meaning 'wine cork'). A seasonally changing menu spotlights locally grown farm produce and ranched meats that marry beautifully with almost three dozen regional wines available by the glass. Lovebirds, book a table on the candlelit patio.

🛏 Inn of the Spanish Garden — Boutique Hotel $$$

(📞805-564-4700, 866-564-4700; www. spanishgardeninn.com; 915 Garden St; d from $309; P ☺ ❄ @ 🛜 ⛶) At this Spanish-colonial-style inn, casual elegance, top-notch service and an impossibly romantic central courtyard will have you lording about like the don of your own private villa. Beds have luxurious linens, bathrooms have oversized bathtubs, and concierge service is top-notch. Palms surround a small outdoor pool, or unwind with a massage in your room.

San Francisco ❼

✖ Pancho Villa   Mexican $

(☎415-864-8840; www.sfpanchovilla.com; 3071
16th St; burritos $5-10; ⊙10am-midnight; 🖉 🍴;
🖵14, 22, 33, 49, Ⓑ16th St Mission) The hero of
the downtrodden and burrito-deprived, Pancho
Villa supplies tinfoil-wrapped meals the girth
of your forearm and lets you add ammunition
at the fresh, heaping salsa bar. The line moves
fast going in, and as you leave, the door is held
open for you and your newly acquired Pancho's
paunch. Stick around for serenades by roving
mariachis.

🛏 Inn San Francisco   B&B $$

(☎415-641-0188, 800-359-0913; www.innsf.
com; 943 S Van Ness Ave; r $215-255, without
bathroom $165-225, cottage $385-475;
ℙ ⊜ @ 🛜🐾; 🖵14, 49) This stately Mission-
district inn occupies an elegant 1872 Italianate-
Victorian mansion, impeccably maintained,
packed with antiques. All rooms have fresh-cut
flowers and sumptuous mattresses with
featherbeds; some have a spa bath. There's
also a freestanding garden cottage that sleeps
up to six. Outside there's an English garden
and redwood hot tub open 24 hours (a rarity).
Limited parking: reserve ahead. No elevator.

Sonoma ❽

✖ Cafe La Haye   Californian $$$

(☎707-935-5994; www.cafelahaye.com; 140
E Napa St, Sonoma; mains $18-30; ⊙5:30-
9pm Tue-Sat) One of Sonoma's top tables for
earthy New American cooking, La Haye only
uses produce sourced from within 60 miles.
Its dining room gets packed cheek-by-jowl and
service can border on perfunctory, but the clean
simplicity and flavor-packed cooking make it
many foodies' first choice. Reserve well ahead.

🛏 El Dorado
Hotel   Boutique Hotel $$$

(☎707-996-3030; www.eldoradosonoma.com;
405 1st St W; r Sun-Thu $215-295, Fri & Sat $395-
495; ℙ ⊜ ❄ 🛜 🐾) Stylish touches, such as
high-end linens, justify rates and compensate
for the rooms' compact size, as do private
balconies, which overlook the plaza or rear
courtyard (we prefer the plaza view, despite
noise). No elevator.

Northern California Trips

San Francisco is the anchor of California's most diverse region, even if earthquakes have shown it isn't rock solid. From exploring the rugged beaches of the Lost Coast to floating down the tranquil Russian River, from poking around (and through) the redwoods to surmounting volcano summits, there's no shortage of natural places to explore and scenic roads to drive in Northern California.

Then there is the wine and food. The Napa Valley is world-famous for top-drawer Cabernet Sauvignon, Chardonnay and sparkling wines, but you can sip equally impressive vintages in Sonoma Valley, the nearby Russian River, Dry Creek and Alexander Valleys, as well as bucolic Anderson Valley near Mendocino. Then soak in some hot springs, where conversations start with, 'Hey, dude!' and end hours later.

Napa Valley Drinking wine among the vineyards
AE PICTURES INC / GETTY IMAGES ©

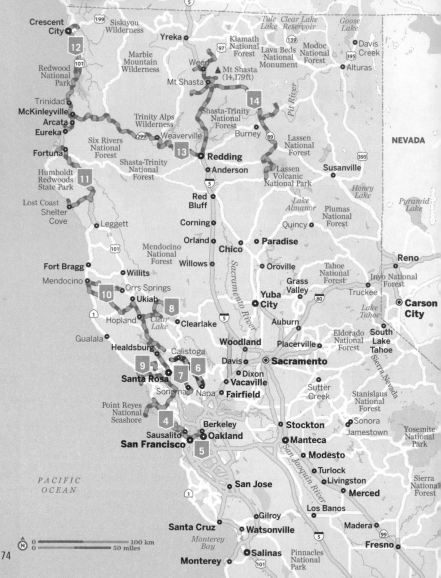

OREGON

Medford

Umpqua National Forest

Crater Lake National Park

Winema National Forest

Upper Klamath Lake

Summer Lake

Lake Albert

Crescent City

Siskiyou Wilderness

Yreka

Tule Lake

Clear Lake Reservoir

Goose Lake

Davis Creek

12

Redwood National Park

Marble Mountain Wilderness

Weed

Klamath National Forest

Mt Shasta

Mt Shasta (14,179ft)

Lava Beds National Monument

Modoc National Forest

Alturas

395

Trinidad

McKinleyville

Arcata

Eureka

Trinity Alps Wilderness

Shasta-Trinity National Forest

14

Pit River

NEVADA

Fortuna

Six Rivers National Forest

299

Weaverville

13

Burney

89

Lassen National Forest

Susanville

395

11

Humboldt Redwoods State Park

Shasta-Trinity National Forest

Redding

Anderson

Lassen Volcanic National Park

Honey Lake

Pyramid Lake

Lost Coast Shelter Cove

Leggett

Red Bluff

Lake Almanor

Plumas National Forest

Corning

101

Mendocino National Forest

Orland

Willows

Chico

Paradise

Quincy

Reno

Fort Bragg

Willits

Oroville

Grass Valley

Tahoe National Forest

Inyo National Forest

Mendocino

10

Orrs Springs

Ukiah

8

Sacramento River

Yuba City

Truckee

80

Carson City

Hopland

Clear Lake

Clearlake

Auburn

Lake Tahoe

South Lake Tahoe

Gualala

Healdsburg

9

Calistoga

7

6

Woodland

Davis

Placerville

Eldorado National Forest

Santa Rosa

Sonoma

Napa

Dixon

Vacaville

Fairfield

Sacramento

Sutter Creek

Sierra Nevada

Stanislaus National Forest

Point Reyes National Seashore

4

Berkeley

Stockton

Sonora

Jamestown

Yosemite National Park

Sausalito

Oakland

Manteca

San Francisco

5

Modesto

San Joaquin River

Turlock

Livingston

Merced

Sierra National Forest

PACIFIC OCEAN

San Jose

Gilroy

Los Banos

Madera

99

Santa Cruz

Watsonville

Monterey Bay

Salinas

Pinnacles National Park

Fresno

Monterey

101

0 — 100 km
0 — 50 miles

4 **Marin County 2–3 Days**
An eyeful of wildlife, wind-tossed beaches, Mt Tamalpais and bewitching Muir Woods. (p77)

5 **Bay Area Culinary Tour 2–3 Days**
Calling all foodies: taste the source of California's phenomenal farm-to-fork cuisine. (p87)

Classic Trip
6 **Napa Valley 2–3 Days**
Fabulous winery estates and celebrity chefs' restaurants grace this grand wine-producing region. (p95)

7 **Sonoma Valley 2 Days**
Tour a pastoral, down-to-earth part of Wine Country, starting from historic Sonoma. (p107)

8 **Healdsburg & Around 2–3 Days**
Go town-and-country style on a lazy wine-tasting trip, finishing at Clear Lake. (p115)

9 **Russian River & Bohemian Hwy 2 Days**
Meander ocean-view back roads, float in the river and taste fabulous vintages. (p123)

10 **Mendocino & Anderson Valley 3–4 Days**
Navigate byways lined with grapevines, redwoods and Pacific bluffs near dreamy Mendocino. (p131)

11 **Lost Coast & Southern Redwoods 3–4 Days**
Follow Avenue of the Giants, home to redwood trees and offbeat towns. (p139)

12 **Northern Redwood Coast 3–4 Days**
Stand agape at colossal forests in magnificent Redwood National & State Parks. (p147)

13 **Trinity Scenic Byway 3 Days**
From Mt Shasta to the sea, this backwoods route winds through Bigfoot country. (p155)

14 **Volcanic Legacy Byway 3 Days**
Volcanic peaks, hot springs and peaceful wilderness lakes dominate a naturalist's drive. (p163)

 DON'T MISS

Wine Tasting
Napa has the most famous names, but rustic-chic wineries in Sonoma County and beyond will charm you on Trips **6** **7** **8** **9** **10**

Conzelman Rd
Gawk at million-dollar views of San Francisco and the Pacific while exploring the hilly Marin Headlands on Trip **4**

Lost Coast
On this wild, windy stretch of shoreline that time forgot, lose yourself on black-sand beaches or hike to abandoned lighthouses on Trip **11**

Tall Trees Grove
Deep inside Redwood National Park, this ancient forest casts a spell over the lucky few who find it on Trip **12**

McArthur-Burney Falls
Between volcanic Mt Shasta and Mt Lassen, be mesmerized by an ethereal 129ft-high waterfall fed by natural springs on Trip **14**

Marin County

Follow twisted coastal highways and beckoning country backroads around Marin County as you drink in the stunning vistas from 19th-century lighthouses, dizzying ocean lookouts and the top of Mt Tamalpais.

TRIP HIGHLIGHTS

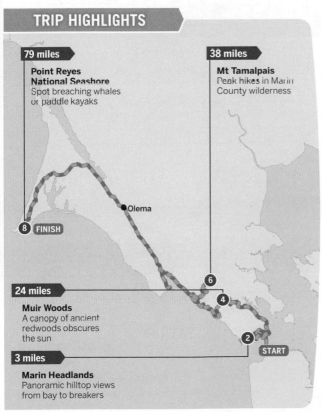

79 miles

Point Reyes National Seashore
Spot breaching whales or paddle kayaks

38 miles

Mt Tamalpais
Peak hikes in Marin County wilderness

● Olema

8 FINISH

24 miles

Muir Woods
A canopy of ancient redwoods obscures the sun

3 miles

Marin Headlands
Panoramic hilltop views from bay to breakers

6

4

2

START

**2–3 DAYS
100 MILES / 160KM**

GREAT FOR...

BEST TIME TO GO
April to October for dry, warmer days.

ESSENTIAL PHOTO

Views of Alcatraz, the Pacific Ocean and shimmering San Francisco from atop the Golden Gate Bridge.

BEST FOR FAMILIES

Take a walk under the rocketing redwood trees of Muir Woods.

Marin Headlands Point Bonita Lighthouse

4 Marin County

Leave behind the heady hills of cosmopolitan San Francisco by driving north across the wind-tunneling passageway of the Golden Gate Bridge. From there, the scenery turns untamed, and Marin County's undulating hills, redwood forest and crashing coastline prove a welcome respite from urban living. Finish up with exhilarating, end-of-the-world views at wild Point Reyes, jutting 10 miles out into the Pacific.

❶ Golden Gate Bridge

Other suspension bridges impress with engineering, but none can touch the **Golden Gate Bridge** (☎877-229-8655; www.goldengatebridge.org/visitors; Hwy 101; northbound free, southbound $6.25-7.25; ☒28, all Golden Gate Transit buses) for showmanship, with its soaring art-deco design. On sunny days it transfixes crowds with its radiant glow – thanks to 25 daredevil painters, who reapply 1000 gallons of 'International

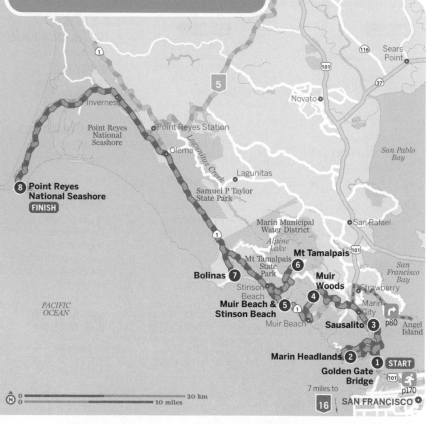

Orange' paint weekly. When afternoon fog rolls in, the bridge performs its disappearing act: now you see it, now you don't and, abracadabra, it's sawn in half.

There's no toll to pay when driving northbound over the turret-topped bridge, which first opened in 1937. On the Marin side of the span, pull into the parking lot and stroll around the **Vista Point** area. Sashay out onto the iconic bridge to spy on cargo ships threading through pylons painted 'International Orange.' Memorize the 360-degree views of the rugged Marin Headlands, downtown skyscrapers and the speck that is **Alcatraz**.

LINK YOUR TRIP

5 **Bay Area Culinary Tour**

From Point Reyes Station, drive meandering Point Reyes–Petaluma Rd northeast past green pastures for 19 miles to Petaluma.

16 **Along Highway 1 to Santa Cruz**

Wind south from San Francisco along Hwy 1 for more lighthouses, organic farms and your pick of sandy cove beaches.

The Drive » Immediately north of the bridge and the Vista Point turnoff, take the Alexander Ave exit and bear left before swinging back under the highway to ascend the bay-view ridgeline of Conzelman Rd. It's 2 miles to Hawk Hill, located just before the road becomes one-way.

- - - - - - - - - -

TRIP HIGHLIGHT

2 Marin Headlands

Near echoey WWII battery tunnels, bird watchers should stop to hike up **Hawk Hill**. Thousands of migrating birds of prey soar here from late summer to early fall, straddling a windy ridge with views of Rodeo Lagoon all the way to Alcatraz.

Stay west on Conzelman Rd until it ends in about 2 miles, then bear left towards the bay. The third lighthouse built on the West Coast, **Point Bonita Lighthouse** (☎415-331-1540; www.nps.gov/goga/pobo.htm; off Field Rd; ⊙12:30-3:30pm Sat-Mon; ⓟ) was completed in 1855, but after complaints about its ridgetop performance in fog, it was scooted down to the promontory in 1877. Three afternoons a week you can traverse a steep half-mile trail and cross through a dark rock tunnel – carved out with hand tools only – and over suspension bridges to inspect the beacon.

Continue north along the oceanview bluffs of Field Rd, joining westbound Bunker Rd after passing the **visitor center**

(☎415-331-1540; www.nps.gov/goga/marin-headlands.htm; Fort Barry; ⊙9:30am-4:30pm). At the end of the road, picnic-worthy **Rodeo Beach** awaits with breezy Pacific panoramas and hiking trails.

🛏 p84

The Drive » Turn around and take Bunker Rd eastbound (signed San Francisco). Pass through the timed one-way tunnel and continue straight ahead onto Murray Circle. Down by the waterfront, turn left onto Center Rd. The 5-mile drive takes 15 minutes or less.

- - - - - - - - - -

3 Sausalito

Just under the north tower of the Golden Gate Bridge, at East Fort Baker, families should stop by the **Bay Area Discovery Museum** (☎415-339-3900; www.baykidsmuseum.org; 557 McReynolds Rd; admission $14, 1st Wed of month free; ⊙9am-5pm Tue-Sun; ⓐ), an excellent hands-on activity museum specifically designed for children. Exhibits include a wave workshop, a small underwater tunnel and a large outdoor play area.

Follow East Rd as it curves alongside Richardson Bay, then take three quick rights onto Alexander Ave, 2nd St and Bridgeway Blvd. Perfectly arranged on a secure little harbor on the bay, Sausalito's pretty houses tumble neatly down a green hillside into a well-heeled downtown, and much of the town affords uninterrupted views of San Francisco and Angel Island.

Northwest of downtown, you can poke around Sausalito's picturesque houseboat docks off Bridgeway Blvd between Gate 5 and Gate 6½ Rds. Bohemian free spirits inhabit hundreds of these quirky homes that bobble in the waves amongst the seabirds

and seals. Structures range from psychedelic mural-splashed castles to dilapidated salt-sprayed shacks and three-story floating mansions.

✕ p84

The Drive ≫ Follow Bridgeway Blvd onto Hwy 101 north for less than a mile to the Hwy 1 exit. Ascend a mostly residential section of two-lane Hwy 1 and after 3 miles, follow signs to Muir Woods via the Panoramic Hwy.

❹ Muir Woods

Walking through an awesome stand of the world's tallest trees is an experience to be had only in Northern California and a small part of southern Oregon. The old-growth redwoods at **Muir Woods National Monument** (☎415-388-2595; www.nps.gov/muwo; 1 Muir Woods Rd, Mill Valley; adult/child $10/free;

DETOUR: ANGEL ISLAND

Start: ❸ Sausalito (p79)

Inland from Hwy 101, just over 8 miles northeast of Sausalito, is the well-to-do town of Tiburon (Spanish for 'shark'). There you can catch a **ferry** (☎415-435-2131; www.angelislandferry.com; 21 Main St; round-trip adult/child $15/13/1; 🚲) over to **Angel Island State Park** (☎415-435-5390; www.parks.ca.gov), which has historical sites, hiking and cycling trails, campgrounds and beaches in the middle of San Francisco Bay. Picnic in one of the island's protected coves while looking out at the geographically quite close but still distant-looking city.

Angel Island's varied history – it was a hunting and fishing ground for the Miwok people, served as a military base, an immigration station, a WWII Japanese internment camp and a Nike missile site – has left it with evocative old forts and bunkers to explore. You can get back to nature on 13 miles of hiking trails, including up Mt Livermore (788ft), granting panoramic views when it's not foggy, or by cycling the 6-mile perimeter loop road.

Nicknamed the 'Ellis Island of the West,' the **Angel Island Immigration Station** (☎415-435-5537; www.aiisf.org/visit; adult/child $5/3, incl tour $7/5; ⊙11am-3pm) operated from 1910 to 1940. It was primarily a screening and detention center for Chinese immigrants, who were at that time restricted from entering the US. Guided tours of the haunting historical site are given three times daily; arrive early to get tickets. It's a 1.5-mile walk, bicycle ride or shuttle trip (round-trip fare $6) from the ferry dock at Ayala Cove.

The best times to visit Angel Island are on summer weekends, when more of the historical buildings and sites are open, and when spring wildflowers bloom. Bring your own food, or grab sandwiches, salads, drinks and snacks from **Angel Island Café** (www.angelisland.com; Ayala Cove; mains $7-15; ⊙10am-3pm May-Oct, hours vary Nov-Apr; 🚲) near the ferry dock. For more information on bike rentals, shuttles and tram tours, visit www.angelisland.com.

Angel Island Enjoying stunning views from the island's summit

⊗8am-8pm mid-Mar–mid-Sep,
to 7pm mid-Sep–early Oct, to
6pm Feb–mid-Mar & early Oct–
early Nov, to 5pm early Nov–Jan;
P **🚻**) are the closest redwood stand to San Fran-
cisco. Logging plans were
halted when congressman
and naturalist William
Kent bought a section of
Redwood Creek, and in
1907 he donated 295 acres
to the federal govern-
ment. President Theodore
Roosevelt made the site
a national monument in
1908, the name honoring
John Muir, naturalist and
founder of the environ-
mental organization the
Sierra Club.

Muir Woods can
become quite crowded,
especially on weekends.
But even at busy times,
a short hike will get you
out of the densest crowds
and onto trails with huge
trees and stunning vistas.
Near the entrance, a
bustling cafe serves local
and organic sandwiches,
soups, baked goods and
hot drinks that hit the
spot on foggy days.

The Drive » Head southwest
on Muir Woods Rd (signed Muir
Beach/Stinson Beach) and
rejoin Hwy 1/Shoreline Hwy, a
spectacularly scenic and curvy
Pacific Ocean byway that winds
north. It's about 3 miles downhill
from Muir Woods to the turnoff
for Muir Beach.

- - - - - - - - - - -
**❺ Muir Beach &
Stinson Beach**
The turnoff from Hwy 1
for **Muir Beach** (www.nps.
gov/goga; off Pacific Way; **P**)
is marked by the north
coast's longest row of
mailboxes at mile marker
5.7, just before the Pelican
Inn. Another mile north-
west along Hwy 1, there
are superb coastal views
at **Muir Beach Overlook**,
where WWII scouts kept
watch from the surround-
ing concrete lookouts for
invading Japanese ships.

Over the next 5 miles,
Hwy 1 twists and makes
hairpin turns atop ocean
cliffs – both the road and

LOCAL KNOWLEDGE: WILDLIFE WATCHING

Want to see marine wildlife in Marin County? The following are a few choice spots: In the Marin Headlands, sea lions, seals and other injured, sick and orphaned marine creatures are rehabilitated at the **Marine Mammal Center** (☎415-289-7330; www.marinemammalcenter.org; 2000 Bunker Rd, Fort Cronkhite; ☺10am-5pm; Ⓟ♿), near Rodeo Beach, before being returned to the wild. Look for harbor seals hauled out on the rocks around Point Bonita Lighthouse.

In Bolinas, stroll along Wharf Rd to spot great blue herons, great egrets and snowy egrets, who build nests on the western shore of **Bolinas Lagoon** in springtime. At low tide, harbor seals often doze on sand bars in the lagoon itself. Outside town, drop by **Palomarin Field Station** (☎415-868-0655; www.pointblue.org; 999 Mesa Rd; ☺sunrise-sunset; Ⓟ♿), formerly the Point Reyes Bird Observatory, which is how it's still labeled on road signs, to watch bird-banding demonstrations most mornings.

At Point Reyes National Seashore, you can spot whales from **Point Reyes Lighthouse** (☎415-669-1534; www.nps.gov/pore; Sir Francis Drake Blvd; ☺lighthouse 10am-4:30pm Fri-Mon, lens room 2:30-4pm Fri-Mon; Ⓟ), where barking sea lions laze on the shore. At nearby **Chimney Rock**, a seasonal colony of elephant seals breed and give birth between December and March. Elsewhere in the park, hike out toward windy **Tomales Point** to observe free-ranging herds of tule elk.

the seascapes unfurling below will make you gasp. The highway eases as it rolls gently downhill to the town of **Stinson Beach**, a three-block strip of densely packed art galleries, shops, eateries and inns. A block west of Hwy 1, the three-mile-long beach itself is often blanketed with fog, but when the sun is shining, it's covered with surfers, families and picnickers. Swimming is advised only on calm summer days when the surf's not up.

✗ 🛏 p84

The Drive » In town, turn onto the Panoramic Hwy for Mt Tamalpais. It's a curvy 3.5-mile drive uphill to the state park's headquarters at Pantoll Station.

TRIP HIGHLIGHT

❻ Mt Tamalpais

Standing guard over Marin County, majestic 'Mt Tam' affords breathtaking 360-degree views of ocean, bay and hills rolling into the distance. The rich, natural beauty of the mountain and its surrounding area is inspiring – the 6300-acre **state park** (☎415-388-2070; www.parks.ca.gov/mttamalpais; per car $8; ☺7am-sunset; Ⓟ) is home to deer, foxes, bobcats and many miles of hiking and cycling trails.

Mt Tam was a sacred place to the coastal Miwok people for thousands of years before the arrival of European and American settlers. By the late 19th century, San Franciscans were escaping the bustle of the city with all-day outings on the mountain, and from 1896 to 1930, the 'world's crookedest railroad' (281 turns) connected Mill Valley to the summit (2571ft).

Turn left at Pantoll Station onto Pantoll Rd, then after almost 1.5 miles, turn right onto Ridgecrest Blvd, which climbs another 3 miles to a parking lot below **East Peak** summit. Follow the short, but steep hiking trail uphill to a fire lookout with commanding ocean-to-bay views.

The Drive » Backtrack downhill to Stinson Beach, turning right onto Hwy 1 northbound. Trace the eastern shore of Bolinas Lagoon, where waterfowl prowl during low tide and harbor seals often haul out. Take the first left after the lagoon and then go left on Olema–Bolinas Rd, continuing on Wharf Rd into central Bolinas. The 15-mile drive takes just over half an hour.

❼ Bolinas

Don't look for any signs directing you here. Residents from this famously private town tore the road sign down so many times that state highway officials finally gave in and stopped replacing it years ago. Known as 'Jugville' during the Gold Rush days, the sleepy beachside community is home to writers, musicians and fisherfolk. Stroll along the sand from access points along Wharf Rd or Brighton Ave.

Hikers veer off Olema–Bolinas Rd onto Mesa Rd and follow it northwest nearly 5 miles to road's end at Palomarin Trailhead, the tromping-off point for coastal day hikes into Point Reyes National Seashore. On a sunny day, pack some water and a towel and hightail it out to **Bass Lake**, a popular freshwater swimming spot reached by way of a 2.7-mile hike skirting the coast. Another 1.5 miles of walking brings you to the fantastic flume of **Alamere Falls**, which tumbles 50ft off a cliff to the beach below.

✗ p85

The Drive » Return to Hwy 1 and continue 9 miles northwest through Olema Valley. Just past the stop sign in Olema, turn left onto Bear Valley Rd and follow the brown Point Reyes National Seashore signs to the Bear Valley Visitor Center.

TRIP HIGHLIGHT

❽ Point Reyes National Seashore

A national park that covers much of the peninsula, wind-blown **Point Reyes National Seashore** (☎415-654-5100; www.nps.gov/pore; 🅿 ♿) shelters free-ranging elk, scores of marine mammals and all manner of raptors and wild cats. Beginning across the street from the **Bear Valley Visitor Center** (☎415-464-5100; www.nps.gov/pore; 1 Bear Valley Rd, Point Reyes Station; ⊙10am-5pm Mon-Fri, from 9am Sat & Sun; ♿), the short, paved **Earthquake Trail** reaches a 16ft gap between the two halves of a once-connected fence line, a lasting testimonial to the power of the magnitude 7.8 earthquake that rocked San Francisco in 1906.

Follow Bear Valley Rd north to Sir Francis Drake Blvd. Raptors perch on fence posts of historic cattle ranches, and the road bumps over rolling hills as it twists for almost 20 miles out to the lighthouse. Initially, the road parallels **Tomales Bay**, a thin channel that teems with harbor seals. In Inverness, **Blue Waters Kayaking** (☎415-669-2600; www.bluewaterskayaking.com; 12944 Sir Francis Drake Blvd; rentals/tours from $50/68; ♿) offers various bay tours or you can rent a kayak and paddle around the secluded beaches and rocky crevices on your own.

At the very end of Sir Francis Drake Blvd, Point Reyes Lighthouse (p82) endures ferocious winds as it sits below the headlands at the base of over 300 stairs. Not merely a beautiful beacon, it's also one of the best whale-watching spots along the coast, as gray whales pass by during their annual winter migration between Alaska and Baja. On weekends and holidays from late December through to mid-April, the road to the lighthouse is closed to private vehicles; visitors must take a shuttle bus ($7) from Drakes Beach.

🛏 p85

Eating & Sleeping

Marin Headlands ❷

🛏 Cavallo Point   Hotel $$$

(📞415-339-4700, 888-651-2003; www.
cavallopoint.com; 601 Murray Circle; r from
$365; P 😊 ❄ @ � 🐾 🐾) Spread over 45
acres of the Bay Area's most scenic parkland,
Cavallo Point is a buzz-worthy lodge that
flaunts a green focus, a full-service spa and
easy access to outdoor activities. Choose from
richly renovated rooms in the landmark Fort
Baker officers' quarters or more contemporary
solar-powered accommodations with exquisite
bay views (including a turret of the Golden Gate
Bridge).

🛏 HI Marin Headlands   Hostel $

(📞415-331-2777; www.norcalhostels.org/marin;
Fort Barry, bldg 941; r with shared bath $82-132,
dm $31-36; P 😊 @ �) Wake up to grazing
deer and dew on the ground at this spartan 1907
military compound snuggled in the woods. It
has comfortable beds and two well-stocked
kitchens, and guests can gather round a
fireplace in the common room, shoot pool or
play ping-pong. Hiking trails beckon outside.

Sausalito ❸

🍴 Avatar's   Indian $$

(📞415-332-8083; www.enjoyavatars.com; 2656
Bridgeway Blvd; mains $9-16; 🕚11am-3pm &
5-9:30pm Mon-Sat; 🥗 🍴) Boasting a cuisine
of 'ethnic confusions,' the Indian fusion dishes
here incorporate Mexican, Italian and Caribbean
ingredients and will bowl you over with their
flavor and creativity. Think Punjabi enchilada
with curried sweet potato or spinach and
mushroom ravioli with mango and rose-petal
alfredo sauce. All diets (vegan, gluten-free, etc)
are graciously accommodated.

🍴 Fish   Seafood $$

(📞415-331-3474; www.331fish.com; 350 Harbor
Dr; mains $13-36; 🕚11:30am-8:30pm; 🍴)

Chow down on seafood sandwiches, barbeque
oysters and a Dungeness crab roll with organic
local butter at redwood picnic tables facing
Richardson Bay. A local leader in promoting
fresh and sustainably caught fish, this place has
wonderful wild salmon in season, and refuses to
serve the farmed stuff. Cash only.

Muir Beach & Stinson Beach ❺

🍴 Parkside Café   American $$

(📞415-868-1272; www.parksidecafe.com; 43
Arenal Ave; dinner mains $11-28; 🕚7:30am-9pm,
coffee from 6am; 🥗 🍴) Famous for its hearty
breakfasts and lunches, this old-fashioned
eatery next to the beach serves wood-fired
pizzas and excellent coastal cuisine like
Tomales Bay oysters and king salmon at dinner,
when reservations are recommended.

🍴 Pelican Inn   Pub Food $$$

(📞415-383-6000; www.pelicaninn.com; 10
Pacific Way; dinner mains $14-34; 🍴) The
oh-so-English Pelican Inn is Muir Beach's only
commercial establishment. Hikers, cyclists
and families come for pub lunches inside its
timbered restaurant and cozy bar, perfect for
a pint, a game of darts and warming up beside
the open fire. The food is nothing mind-blowing
and the service is hit and miss, but the setting
is magical.

Upstairs are seven cozy rooms (from $215)
with half-canopy beds.

🛏 Sandpiper   Motel, Cabins $$

(📞415-868-1632; www.sandpiperstinsonbeach.
com; 1 Marine Way; r $145-200, cabin $225-240,
cottage $300-330; P 😊 �) Just off Hwy 1 and
a quick stroll to the beach, the 10 comfortable
rooms, cabins and cottage of the Sandpiper
have gas fireplaces and kitchenettes, and are
ensconced in a lush garden and picnic area.
Two-night minimum stay on weekends and
holidays between April and October.

Bolinas ❼

✕ Bolinas People's Store
Market $

(📞415-868-1433; 14 Wharf Rd; 🕐8:30am-6:30pm; 🖍) An awesome little co-op grocery store hidden behind the community center, the People's Store serves fair-trade coffee and sells organic produce, fresh soup and excellent tamales. Eat at the tables in the shady courtyard.

✕ Coast Cafe
American $$

(📞415-868-2298; www.coastcafebolinas.com; 46 Wharf Rd; mains $12-28; 🕐11:30am-3pm & 5-8pm Tue-Thu, to 9pm Fri, 8am-3pm & 5-9pm Sat, to 8pm Sun; 🖍🚺) The only 'real' restaurant in town, everyone jockeys for outdoor seats among the flowerboxes for fish and chips, barbecued oysters, or buttermilk pancakes with damn good coffee. Live music Thursday and Sunday nights.

Point Reyes Station

✕ Osteria Stellina
Italian $$

(📞415-663-9988; http://osteriastellina.com; 11285 Hwy 1; mains $15-24; 🕐11:30am-2:30pm & 5-9pm; 🖍) This place specializes in rustic Italian cuisine made from locally sourced produce, including pizza and pasta dishes and Niman Ranch meats. For dessert, the water-buffalo-milk gelato is the way to go.

Point Reyes National Seashore ❽

🛏 Cottages at Point Reyes Seashore
Cottage $$

(📞415-669-7250, 800-416-0405; www.cottagespointreyes.com; 13275 Sir Francis Drake Blvd; r $129-239; 🅿🚭🛜🗺🐾) Cottages at Point Reyes Seashore is a family-friendly place hidden away in the woods. It offers clean, modern kitchenette rooms in A-frame structures, and has a tennis court, hot tub, horseshoe pitches, barbecue pits and in-room DVD players. There's also a large garden and private nature trail. It's past the town, on the way down the Point Reyes peninsula.

🛏 HI Point Reyes
Hostel $

(📞415-663-8811; www.norcalhostels.org/reyes; 1390 Limantour Spit Rd; r with shared bath $105-130, dm $29-35; 🅿🚭@) Just off Limantour Rd, this rustic hostel has bunkhouses with warm and cozy front rooms, big-view windows and outdoor areas with hill vistas, and a newer LEED-certified building with four private rooms (two-night minimum stay on weekends) and a stunning modern kitchen. It's in a beautiful secluded valley 2 miles from the ocean and surrounded by lovely hiking trails.

Bay Area Culinary Tour

5

Combining country and city, this drive is a deeply satisfying taste of California's good earth, ending at revolutionary chef Alice Waters' touchstone restaurant Chez Panisse.

TRIP HIGHLIGHTS

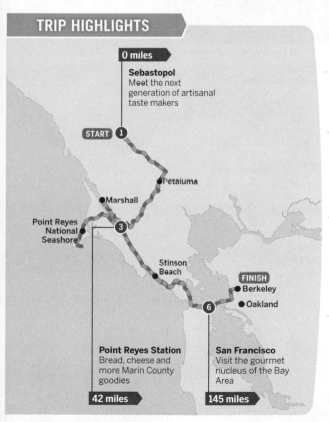

0 miles

Sebastopol
Meet the next generation of artisanal taste makers

START **1**

●Petaluma

●Marshall

3

Point Reyes
National
Seashore●

Stinson
Beach

FINISH
●Berkeley

●Oakland

6

Point Reyes Station
Bread, cheese and more Marin County goodies

42 miles

San Francisco
Visit the gourmet nucleus of the Bay Area

145 miles

2–3 DAYS
160 MILES / 255KM

GREAT FOR...

BEST TIME TO GO
Late summer or early fall, when farms deliver their tastiest bounty.

ESSENTIAL PHOTO
The lighthouse, bluffs and endless horizon at Point Reyes National Seashore.

BEST PICNIC
Briny oysters, local bread and cheeses, and Heidrun sparkling mead at Hog Island Oyster Company.

Bay Area Culinary Tour

Making a delicious loop around the Bay Area, you'll wander through the aisles of celebrated farmers markets and drop in on artisanal food and drink producers, from Hog Island oyster farm to Cowgirl Creamery and more. Thankfully, a hike at Point Reyes National Seashore will work up a healthy appetite. You'll need it on this straight-from-the-source trip to foodie heaven.

TRIP HIGHLIGHT

❶ Sebastopol

This western Sonoma farm town was founded in the 19th century, when apples were its main cash crop. Swing by in April for the **Apple Blossom Festival** (www.appleblossom fest.com) or in August for the **Gravenstein Apple Fair** (www.gravenstein applefair.com), both lively weekend celebrations of local food, wines and brews, accompanied by live music and more. In late summer and

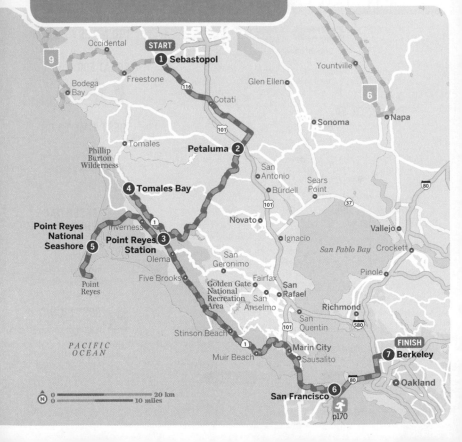

early autumn, you can pick your own apples at orchards on the outskirts of town along Sonoma County's **Farm Trails** (www.farmtrails.org).

But Sebastopol is about so much more than apples these days. Just look at the **Barlow** (☎707-824-5600; www.thebarlow.net; cnr Sebastopol & Morris Sts; ☺7am-9pm; P ♿), a former apple processing plant that has been re-purposed into a 12-acre village of food producers, artists, wine-makers, coffee roasters and spirits distillers who showcase West County's culinary and artistic diversity. Wander shed to shed, sample everything from microbrewed beer

LINK YOUR TRIP

6 Napa Valley

Cruise 26 miles east from Petaluma to Napa, the gateway to America's most famous wine region, home to several of California's best restaurants.

9 Russian River & Bohemian Highway

Starting in Sebastopol, revel in the country charms of 'Slow-noma,' stopping at orchards, vineyards and Freestone's famous bakery.

to nitrogen flash-frozen ice cream, and meet artisanal makers in their workshops.

✕ p129

The Drive ≫ Follow Hwy 116 south out of town for 8 miles to Cotati. Keep going across Hwy 101 (the speedier but more boring route to Petaluma) and turn right onto Old Redwood Hwy. After 3 miles, go left on pastoral Old Adobe Rd for 6 miles, turning left just past Petaluma Adobe State Historic Park.

- - - - - - - - - - -

❷ Petaluma

Near the elegantly slouching Victorians of Petaluma is **Green String Farm** (☎707-778-7500; www.greenstringfarm.com, 3571 Old Adobe Rd, Petaluma; ☺10am-5pm, to 6pm May-Sep; P). Bob Cannard has pioneered sustainable farming in the North Bay for 30 years, and you can taste the chemical-free fruits of his labors at the on-site farm store, which serves seasonal produce, local cheese and nuts. Instead of battling weeds with herbicides, Green String lets them coexist with cover vegetation and planted crops, creating a symbiotic ecosystem that yields a smaller crop but richer soil. The only weed eaters on hand are the fluffy sheep. Public tours are usually given on the first Saturday of the month, weather permitting.

Many farms around Petaluma are known

for raising chickens and selling fresh eggs and dairy products. Across Hwy 101 and west of downtown, the **Petaluma Creamery** (☎707-762-9038; www.petalumacreamery-cheeseshop.com; 711 Western Ave, Petaluma; items $3-7; ☺6am-7pm Mon-Fri, 8am-6pm Sat & Sun; ♿ ♿) has been in business for more than a century. Stop by to sample organic cheeses or for a scoop of lavender or Meyer lemon ice cream from the small specialty foods market and cafe.

The Drive ≫ From downtown Petaluma, take D St southwest to Red Hill Rd and follow Point Reyes–Petaluma Rd toward the coast, turning left onto Hwy 1 for Point Reyes Station. It's a relaxing 19-mile country drive; stop en route for Camembert or Brie at the **Marin French Cheese** factory store.

- - - - - - - - - - -

TRIP HIGHLIGHT

❸ Point Reyes Station

Surrounded by dairies and ranches, Point Reyes Station became a hub for artists in the 1960s. Today, it offers a collection of art galleries, boutique shops and excellent food. The tour of the town's edibles begins by fighting your way through the spandex-clad crowd of weekend cyclists to grab a crusty loaf of fire-baked Brick-maiden Bread at Bovine Bakery (p93). Next, step down the block to the restored barn that houses one of California's most sought-after cheese makers, the Cowgirl Creamery at Tomales Bay Foods (p93). Reserve a spot in advance for the Friday morning artisanal cheese-making demonstration and tasting ($5). In spring the must-buy is their St Pat's, a smooth, mellow round wrapped in wild nettle leaves. Otherwise, the Mt Tam (available year-round) is pretty damn good, and there's a gourmet deli for picking up picnic supplies. Heading north out of town, **Heidrun Meadery** (☏415-663-9122; www.heidrunmeadery.com; 11925 Hwy 1; tasting $15, incl tour $25; ⊙11am-4pm Mon & Wed-Fri, to 4:30 Sat & Sun) pours tasting sips of sparkling mead, made

from aromatic small-batch honey in the style of French champagne.

 p93

The Drive » Follow Hwy 1 north out of the tiny village of Point Reyes Station. Cruise for 9 miles along the east side of tranquil Tomales Bay, which flows many miles out into the Pacific. Just before the turnoff for rural Marshall–Petaluma Rd, look for the sign for bayfront Hog Island Oyster Company on your left.

----

❹ Tomales Bay

Only 10 minutes north of Point Reyes Station, you'll find the salty turnout for the **Hog Island Oyster Company** (☏415-663-9218; www.hogislandoysters.com; 20215 Hwy 1, Marshall; 12 oysters $13-$16, picnic fee per person

$5; ⊙shop 9am-5pm daily, picnic area from 10am, cafe 11am-5pm Fri-Mon). There's hardly much to see: just some picnic tables and BBQ grills, an outdoor cafe called Boat Oyster Bar and a small window vending the famously silky oysters and a few other picnic provisions. While you can buy oysters to go (by the pound), for a fee you can nab a picnic table, borrow shucking tools and take a lesson on how to crack open and grill the oysters yourself. Lunch at the waterfront farm is unforgettable – and very popular, so reserve ahead for a picnic table or for a seat at the Boat Oyster Bar's communal tables.

✖ 🛏 p93

CHEZ PANISSE PROTÉGÉS

Operating a restaurant for 45 years, lauded chef Alice Waters has seen a whole lot of people come through the kitchen. Of her alumni in San Francisco, try Michael Tusk, who offers elegant, seasonally inspired Californian cuisine at **Quince** (☏415-775-8700; www.quincerestaurant.com; 470 Pacific Ave; 4-/9-course tasting menu $165/220; ⊙5:30-9:30pm Mon-Thu, from 5pm Fri & Sat) and more rustic Italian fare at **Cotogna** (☏415-775-8508; www.cotognasf.com; 490 Pacific Ave; mains $17-38; ⊙11:30am-10:30pm Mon-Thu, to 11pm Fri & Sat, 5-9:30pm Sun; 🖗; 🚇10, 12), or Gayle Pirie, who operates **Foreign Cinema** (☏415-648-7600; www.foreigncinema.com; 2534 Mission St; mains $22-33; ⊙5:30-10pm Mon-Wed, to 11pm Thu-Sun, brunch 11am-2:30pm Sat & Sun; 🚇12, 14, 33, 48, 49, Ⓑ24th St Mission), a gourmet movie house in the Mission District.

More casual eateries by other Waters' protégés are found across the Bay in Oakland. Charlie Hallowell turns out immaculate wood-fired pizzas at a pair of neighborhood restaurants, **Pizzaiolo** and **Boot & Shoe Service** (☏510-763-2668; www.bootandshoeservice.com; 3308 Grand Ave; pizza from $10; ⊙5:30-10pm Tue-Thu, 5-10:30pm Fri & Sat, to 10pm Sun); you can tuck into earthy Californian dishes cooked over an open fire at Russell Moore's **Camino** (☏510-547 5035; www.caminorestaurant.com; 3917 Grand Ave; mains $20-25; ⊙dinner Wed-Mon, brunch Sat & Sun; 🚇12 AC Transit); and Alison Barakat serves what may be the Bay Area's best fried-chicken sandwich at **Bakesale Betty** (www.bakesalebetty.com; 5098 Telegraph Ave; sandwiches $8; ⊙11am-2pm Tue-Sat; 🖗).

Handmade California cheese

The Drive ❱❱ Backtrack 10 miles south on Hwy 1 through Point Reyes Station. Turn right onto Sir Francis Drake Blvd, following the signs for Point Reyes National Seashore, just on the other side of Tomales Bay.

- - - - - - - - - - - -

⑤ Point Reyes National Seashore

For another perfect picnic spot, look down the coast to **Point Reyes National Seashore** (☏415-654-5100; www.nps.gov/pore; Ⓟ Ⓗ). The windswept peninsula's rough-hewn beauty lures marine mammals and migratory birds. The 110 sq miles of pristine ocean beaches also offer excellent hiking and camping opportunities. For an awe-inspiring view, follow Sir Francis Drake Blvd beside Tomales Bay all the way out toward the **Point Reyes Lighthouse** (☏415-669-1534; www.nps.gov/pore; Sir Francis Drake Blvd; ☉lighthouse 10am-4.30pm Fri-Mon, lens room 2:30-4pm Fri-Mon; Ⓟ). Follow the signs and turn left before the lighthouse to find the trailhead for the 1.6-mile round-trip hike to **Chimney Rock**, where wildflowers bloom in spring.

🛏 p85

The Drive ❱❱ Leaving the park, trace the eucalyptus-lined curves of Hwy 1 south toward Stinson Beach and past one stunning Pacific view after the next. If you don't stop, you'll be back across the Golden Gate Bridge in about an hour and a half. From the bridge, follow Hwy 101 through the city to Broadway, then go east to the waterfront piers.

- - - - - - - - - - - -

TRIP HIGHLIGHT

⑥ San Francisco

From the center of the Golden Gate Bridge, it's possible to view the clock tower of the city's **Ferry Building** (☏415-983-8030; www.ferrybuildingmarket place.com; Market St & the

Embarcadero; 10am-6pm Mon-Fri, from 9am Sat, 11am-5pm Sun; [♿]; [🚌]2, 6, 9, 14, 21, 31, [M]Embarcadero, [B]Embarcadero), a transit hub turned gourmet emporium, where foodies happily miss their ferries slurping Hog Island oysters and bubbly. Star chefs are frequently spotted at the thrice-weekly Ferry Plaza Farmers Market (p93) that wraps around the building year-round. The largest market is on Saturday, when dozens of family farmers and artisanal food and flower vendors show up. From dry-farmed tomatoes to organic kimchi, the bounty may seem like an embarrassment of riches. If your trip doesn't coincide with a market day, never fear: dozens of local purveyors await indoors at the **Ferry Build-**ing Marketplace**. Take a taste of McEvoy Ranch and Stonehouse olive oils, Boccalone Salumeria sausages, fresh-baked loaves from Acme Bread Company and Humphry Slocombe ice cream.

✖️ 🛏️ p46, p61, p71, p93

The Drive » It is a straight shot over the San Francisco–Oakland Bay Bridge and into Berkeley via I-80 eastbound. Exit at University Ave and follow it east to Shattuck Ave, then go north of downtown Berkeley to the 'Gourmet Ghetto.'

- - - - - - - - - - - - -

❼ Berkeley

San Francisco might host a handful of banner dining rooms, but California's food revolution got started across the Bay, in Berkeley. You may spot the inventor of California cuisine, famed chef Alice Waters, in her element and in raptures at the **North Berkeley Farmers Market** (☎510-548-3333; www.ecologycenter.org; Shattuck Ave at Rose St; 3-7pm Thu; [♿] [♿]), run by the Ecology Center. It's in the so-called 'Gourmet Ghetto' – a neighbor-hood that marries the progressive 1960s ideals of Berkeley with haute-dining sensibility. The neighborhood's anchor, and an appropriate final stop, is Chez Panisse (p93), Alice Waters' influential restaurant. It's unpretentious, and every mind-altering, soul-sanctifying bite of the food is emblematic of the chef's revolutionary food principles. The kitchen is even open so diners can peek behind the scenes.

✖️ 🛏️ p93

NORTHERN CALIFORNIA 5 BAY AREA CULINARY TOUR

Eating & Sleeping

Point Reyes Station ❸

✖ Bovine Bakery
Bakery $

(☎415-663-9420; www.thebovinebakery.com; 11315 Hwy 1; most items $2-6; ⏰6:30am-5pm Mon-Fri, from 7am Sat & Sun; ⏏) **Don't leave town without sampling something buttery from one of the best bakeries in Marin County. A sweet bear-claw pastry and an organic coffee are a good way to kick off your morning.**

✖ Cowgirl Creamery at Tomales Bay Foods
Deli $

(☎415-663-9335; www.cowgirlcreamery.com; 80 4th St; deli items $3-9; ⏰10am-6pm Wed-Sun; ⏏) An indoor marketplace in an old barn sells picnic items, including gourmet cheeses and organic produce. Reserve a spot in advance for the artisanal cheesemaker's demonstration and tasting ($5); watch the curd-making and cutting, then sample a half dozen of the fresh and aged cheeses. All of the milk is local and organic, with vegetarian rennet in the soft cheeses.

Tomales Bay ❹

✖ Nick's Cove
Californian $$$

(☎415-663-1033; www.nickscove.com; 23240 Hwy 1, Marshall; dinner mains $26-35; ⏰11am-9pm; ⏏) At this vintage-1930s roadhouse perched over Tomales Bay, trophy heads are mounted on knotty pine walls and there's a roaring fireplace. Book a window table to birdwatch while you sup on impeccable seafood, wood-fired meats and local oysters – all sustainably farmed.

⛺ Dancing Coyote Beach Cottages
Bungalow $$$

(☎415-669-7200; www.dancingcoyotebeach. com; 12794 Sir Francis Drake Blvd; cottages $200-325; ⏏) Serene and comfortable, these four modern cottages back right onto Tomales Bay, with skylights and decks extending the views in all directions. Full kitchens contain locally sourced breakfast foods and fireplaces are stocked with firewood for foggy nights.

San Francisco ❻

✖ Ferry Plaza Farmers Market
Market $

(☎415-291-3276; www.cuesa.org; Market St & the Embarcadero; ⏰10am-2pm Tue & Thu, from 8am Sat; ⏏; ⓜEmbarcadero) The Ferry Building market showcases California-grown, organic produce, pasture-raised meats and gourmet prepared foods at moderate-to-premium prices – plus an excellent selection of food trucks on weekends.

⛺ Orchard Garden Hotel
Boutique Hotel $$

(☎888-717-2881, 415-399-9807; www. theorchardgardenhotel.com; 466 Bush St; r $190-390; ⏏2, 3, 30, 45, ⒷMontgomery) San Francisco's original all-green-practices hotel uses sustainably grown wood, chemical-free cleaning products and recycled fabrics in its soothingly quiet rooms.

Berkeley ❼

✖ Chez Panisse
Californian $$$

(☎cafe 510-548-5049, restaurant 510-548-5525; www.chezpanisse.com; 1517 Shattuck Ave; cafe dinner mains $20-32, restaurant prix-fixe dinner $75-125; ⏰ cafe 11:30am-2:45pm & 5-10:30pm Mon-Thu, 11:30am-3pm & 5-11:30pm Fri & Sat, restaurant seatings 5:30pm & 8pm Mon-Sat; ⏏) Foodies come to worship here at the church of Alice Waters, the inventor of California cuisine. It's in a lovely Arts and Crafts house in the Gourmet Ghetto.

⛺ Hotel Shattuck Plaza
Hotel $$

(☎510-845-7300; www.hotelshattuckplaza.com; 2086 Allston Way; r from $195; ⏏) Following a $15-million renovation and greening of this 100-year-old downtown jewel, a foyer of red Italian glass lighting, flocked Victorian-style wallpaper – and yes, a peace sign tiled into the floor – leads to comfortable rooms with down comforters, and an airy, columned restaurant serving all meals. Accommodations off Shattuck are quietest; cityscape rooms boast bay views.

Classic Trip

Napa Valley

6

The birthplace of modern-day Wine Country is famous for regal Cabernet Sauvignon, château-like wineries and fabulous food. Expect to be wined, dined and wowed by over-the-top architecture and art.

TRIP HIGHLIGHTS

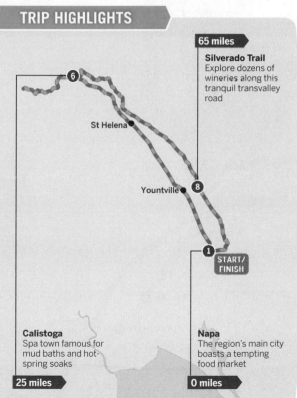

65 miles

Silverado Trail
Explore dozens of wineries along this tranquil transvalley road

St Helena

Yountville ● **8**

1

START/ FINISH

Calistoga
Spa town famous for mud baths and hot-spring soaks

25 miles

Napa
The region's main city boasts a tempting food market

0 miles

2–3 DAYS
90 MILES / 145KM

GREAT FOR...

BEST TIME TO GO

May for a presummer lull; September and October to experience 'the crush.'

 ESSENTIAL PHOTO

Three...two...one! Get ready for an eruption at Old Faithful Geyser.

 BEST FOR FOODIES

Book a star chef's restaurant table in tiny Yountville.

Napa Valley Hot-air balloon soaring over vineyards

95

Classic Trip

6 Napa Valley

California's premier viticultural region has earned its reputation among the world's best. Rolling hills, dotted with century-old oaks, turn the color of lion's fur under the summer sun. Swaths of vineyards carpet hillsides as far as the eye can see. Hundreds of wineries inhabit Napa Valley, but it's quality, not quantity, that sets the region apart – it competes with France and is an outpost of San Francisco's top-end culinary scene.

❶ Napa

The valley's workaday hub was once a nothing-special city of storefronts, Victorian cottages and riverfront warehouses, but booming real-estate values caused an influx of new money that has transformed Napa into a growing city of arts and food. Its number-one attraction, the Oxbow Public Market (p105) showcases all things culinary – from produce stalls to kitchen stores to fantastic edibles. It's foodie central, with an emphasis on seasonal and regional ingredients, grown sustainably. Graze your way through this gourmet market and plug into the Northern California food scene. Standouts include fresh oysters, Venezuelan cornbread sandwiches, excellent Cal-Mexican and certified-organic ice cream. Tuesday is locals night, with many discounts.

West of downtown, scrap-metal sheep graze Carneros vineyards at 217-acre **di Rosa Art + Nature Preserve** (☏707-226-5991; www.dirosaart.org; 5200 Hwy 121, Napa; admission $5, tours $12-15; ☉10am-4pm Wed-Sun; 🅿), a stunning collection of Northern California art displayed indoors in galleries and outdoors in sculpture gardens. Reservations are recommended for tours.

✕ 🛏 p105

The Drive » From Napa, Yountville is 9 miles north on Hwy 29, a divided four-lane road surrounded by vineyards and framed by low hills.

❷ Yountville

This one-time stagecoach stop is now a major foodie destination that once boasted of more Michelin stars per capita than any other American town. There are some good inns here, but it's deathly boring at night. You stay in Yountville to drink with dinner without having to drive afterward – but make reservations or you might not eat!

Ma(i)sonry (☏707-944-0889; www.maisonry. com; 6711 Washington St; ☉10:30am-4:30pm Sun-Thu, to 5:30pm Fri & Sat; 🅿) occupies a free-to-browse 1904 stone house and garden, transformed into a fussy winery collective and a gallery of overpriced rustic-modern *meubles* and art, some quite cool. Reservations recommended for wine tastings.

Yountville's modernist 40,000-sq-ft **Napa Valley Museum** (☏707-944-0500; www.napavalleymuseum.org; 55 Presidents Circle; adult/child $7/2.50; ☉11am-4pm Wed-Sun; 🅿), off California Dr, chronicles cultural history and showcases local paintings, and has good picnicking outside.

✕ 🛏 p105

The Drive » Go north to Oakville via 4 miles of vineyard vistas on Hwy 29, which slims to two lanes just outside of Yountville. Tracks for the Napa Valley Wine Train line the west side of the road.

❸ Oakville

But for its famous grocery (p105), you'd drive through the tiny settlement of Oakville (population 71) and never know you'd missed it. This is the middle of the grapes – vineyards sprawl in every direction.

The behemoth **Robert Mondavi** (☏707-226-1395, 888-766-6328; www.robert-mondaviwinery.com; 7801 Hwy 29, Oakville; tasting/tour from $5/20; ☉10am-5pm, store

LINK YOUR TRIP

7 Sonoma Valley
For lower-key wineries and early California historical sites, Hwy 12/121 is the main connector between Napa and Sonoma Valleys, just over a dozen miles apart.

8 Healdsburg & Around
From Calistoga, take Hwy 128 northwest less than 20 miles to more wineries in the Alexander and Dry Creek Valleys.

to 6pm; [P] [🚻]) winery is somewhat of a corporate-winery experience and you can expect a lot of company. That said, the grounds are gorgeous and it offers a good menu of tours and tastings for those who are new to wine. The winery also uses careful environ-mental practices in its farming, managing 1000 acres of naturally farmed vineyards.

✗ p105

The Drive » Rows of grapevines recede into the distance as you continue 2 miles north on Hwy 29 to Rutherford.

❹ Rutherford

Another blip of a town, Rutherford is more conspicuous, with its wineries putting it on the map. The valley views are spectacular at **Mumm Napa** (📞707-967-7700, 800-686-6272; www.mummnapa.com; 8445 Silverado Trail, Rutherford; tasting $18-40, tour $30; ☉10am-6pm; [P]), which makes respectable sparkling wines that you can sample while seated on a vineyard-view ter-race. No appointment necessary, or you can dodge crowds by paying extra to reserve a tasting on the oak terrace.

Meandering paths wind through the magical gardens and fruit-bearing orchards of **Frog's Leap** (📞707-963-4704; www.frogsleap.com; 8815 Conn Creek Rd, Rutherford; tasting $20-25, incl tour $25; ☉10am-4pm by appointment only; [P] [🚻] [🐾]) winery, surrounding an 1884 barn and farm-stead with cats and chickens. But more than anything, it's the vibe that's wonderful: casual and down-to-earth, with a major emphasis on *fun*. Sauvignon Blanc is its best-known wine, but the Merlot merits attention, and all are organic. There's also a dry, restrained Cabernet Sauvignon, atypical in Napa.

Round Pond (📞707-302-2575, 888-302-2575; www.roundpond.com; 875 Rutherford Rd, Rutherford; tasting $25-50, incl tour $75; ☉ by appoint-ment; [P]) estate tantalizes with fantastic food

NAPA VALLEY WINERIES

Cab is king in Napa. No varietal captures imaginations like the fruit of the Cabernet Sauvignon vine – Bordeaux is the French equivalent – and no wine fetches a higher price. Napa farmers can't afford *not* to grow Cabernet grapes. Other heat-loving varietals, such as Sangiovese and Merlot, also thrive here. Napa's wines merit their reputation among the world's finest – complex, with luxurious finishes.

A half century ago, this 30-mile strip of former stagecoach stops seemed forgotten by time, a quiet agricultural valley dense with orchards. Grapes had grown here since the Gold Rush, but grape-sucking phylloxera bugs, Prohibition and the Great Depression reduced 140 wineries in the 1890s, to around 25 by the mid-1960s.

In 1968, Napa was declared the 'Napa Valley Agricultural Preserve.' This succeeded in preserving the valley's natural beauty, but when Napa wines earned top honors at a 1976 blind tasting in Paris, the wine-drinking world noticed and land values skyrocketed. Only the very rich could afford to build. Hence, so many architecturally jaw-dropping wineries.

Because of strict county zoning laws, many Napa wineries cannot legally receive drop-in visitors; unless you've come strictly to buy, you'll have to call ahead. This is *not* the case with all wineries. We recommend booking one or two appointments, plus a lunch or dinner reservation, and planning your day around them.

LOCAL KNOWLEDGE: GETTING AROUND NAPA VALLEY

» Napa has an eponymous city, valley and county. The town of Napa is in Napa County, at the southern end of Napa Valley.

» Napa Valley is 30 miles long and 5 miles wide at its widest point (the city of Napa), 1 mile at its narrowest (Calistoga). Two roads run north–south: Hwy 29 (St Helena Hwy) and the more scenic Silverado Trail, a mile east. Drive up one, and down the other.

» The American Automobile Association determined Napa Valley to be America's eighth-most congested rural vacation destination. Summer and fall weekend traffic is unbearable, especially on Hwy 29 between Napa and St Helena. Plan accordingly.

» Cross-valley roads that link Silverado Trail with Hwy 29 – including Yountville, Oakville and Rutherford Cross Rds – are bucolic and get less traffic. For scenery, the Oakville Grade Rd and rural Trinity Rd (which leads southwest from Oakville on Hwy 29 to Hwy 12 near Glen Ellen in Sonoma Valley) are narrow, curvy and beautiful – but treacherous in rainstorms. Mt Veeder Rd leads through pristine countryside west of Yountville.

» Police watch like hawks for traffic violators. *Don't drink and drive.*

» You have the most flexibility by driving your own vehicle, but to drink and not drive, there are some tour options. Note that some wineries do not allow limousines (because the people in them are often obnoxious and don't buy anything); and limousine companies have set itineraries with little flexibility (ie, you'll have few choices about which wineries you visit).

» A cushy, if touristy, way to see Wine Country, the **Napa Valley Wine Train** (☎707-253-2111, 800-427-4124; http://winetrain.com; 1275 McKinstry St, Napa; tour from $129) offers three-hour daily trips in vintage Pullman dining cars, from Napa to St Helena and back, with an optional winery tour.

pairings on a vineyard-view stone patio. We especially love the olive-oil and wine-vinegar tastings, which are included with guided tours of the olive mill ($65).

The Drive » St Helena is another 4 miles north on Hwy 29, though you may be slowing to a crawl before hitting the first stoplight in the center of town.

5 St Helena

You'll know you're arriving here when traffic halts. St Helena (ha-*lee*-na) is the Rodeo Dr of Napa, with fancy boutiques lining Main St (Hwy 29). The historic downtown is good for a stroll, with great window-shopping, but parking is next to impossible on summer weekends.

Co-owned by Bill Clinton's former ambassador to Austria, **Hall** (☎707-967-2626; www.hallwines.com; 401 St Helena Hwy, St Helena; tasting & tour from $40; ◷10am-5:30pm; **P**) winery specializes in Sauvignon Blanc, Merlot and Cabernet Sauvignon, crafted in big-fruit California style. Its dramatic tasting room has a stand-up bar with 180-degree views of

WHY THIS IS A CLASSIC TRIP
SARA BENSON,
WRITER

It's the unique *terroir* – a French term to describe the character of a place's soil, climate and natural environment – that has made Napa Valley so famous. I always plan to get lost on back roads, where, while picnicking atop sun-dappled hillsides and among grapevines heavily laden with fruit, I can grab a hunk of earth and know firsthand the thing that gives meaning to the entire region.

Top: Oak barrels in the cellar of Robert Mondavi winery
Left: Relaxing at a spa in Calistoga
Right: Entrance to the fabulous Darioush winery

vineyards and mountains through floor-to-ceiling glass, and the glorious art collection includes a giant chrome rabbit leaping over the vines.

The **Robert Louis Stevenson Museum** (☎707-963-3757; http://stevensonmuseum.org; 1490 Library Lane; ☺noon-4pm Tue-Sat; P) contains a fascinating collection of the famous writer's memorabilia. In 1880, the author – then sick, penniless and unknown – stayed in an abandoned bunkhouse at the old Silverado Mine on Mt St Helena with his wife, Fanny Osbourne; his novel *The Silverado Squatters* is based on his time there. To reach Library Lane, turn east off Hwy 29 at the Adams St traffic light and cross the railroad tracks.

Hushed and regal, the 1889 stone château of the **Culinary Institute of America at Greystone** (☎707-967-2320; www.ciachef.edu/california; 2555 Main St; cooking demonstration $25, classes from $95; ☺cooking demonstrations 1:30pm Sat & Sun; ⬆) houses a gadget- and cookbook-filled culinary shop; an upscale restaurant and bakery-cafe; weekend cooking demonstrations; and wine-tasting classes by luminaries in the field, including Karen MacNeil, author of *The Wine Bible*.

✕ ⬛ p105

Classic Trip

The Drive » Trees begin to reappear on the landscape, breaking up the vineyard views as you head 8 miles northwest on Hwy 29 to Calistoga.

TRIP HIGHLIGHT

❻ Calistoga

The least gentrified town in Napa Valley feels refreshingly simple, with an old-fashioned main street lined with shops, not boutiques, and diverse characters wandering the sidewalks. Calistoga is synonymous with the mineral water bearing its name, bottled here since 1924, and its springs and geysers have earned it the nickname the 'hot springs of the West.' Plan to visit one of the town's spas, where you can indulge in the local specialty: a hot-mud bath, made of the volcanic ash from nearby Mt St Helena.

It took 14 years to build the perfectly replicated 13th-century Italian castle at winery **Castello di Amorosa** (📞707-967-6272; www. castellodiamorosa.com; 4045 Hwy 29, Calistoga; admission & tasting $25-35, incl guided tour $40-80; ⊙9:30am-6pm Mar-Oct, to 5pm Nov-Feb; 🅿️🚹), complete with moat, hand-cut stone walls, ceiling frescoes by Italian artisans, Roman-style cross-vault brick catacombs, and a torture chamber with period equipment. You can taste without an appointment, but this is one tour worth taking. Wines include some respectable Italian varietals, including a velvety Tuscan blend.

Calistoga's mini-version of Yellowstone, the **Old Faithful Geyser** (📞707-942-6463; www. oldfaithfulgeyser.com; 1299 Tubbs Lane; adult/child/under 4yr $14/8/free; ⊙8:30am-8pm, shorter hr Sep-Apr; 🅿️🚹) shoots boiling water about 60ft into the air, every 30 to 40 minutes. The vibe is pure roadside Americana, with folksy hand-painted interpretive exhibits, picnicking and a little petting zoo, where you can come nose-to-nose with llamas. It's 2 miles northwest of town, between Hwy 128 and Hwy 129.

✕ 🛏️ p105

The Drive » Backtrack southeast on Hwy 128 and go 4 miles west on forested and curvy Petrified Forest Rd.

---

❼ Petrified Forest & Safari West

Three million years ago, a volcanic eruption at nearby Mt St Helena blew down a stand of redwoods between Calistoga and Santa Rosa. The trees fell in the same direction, away from the blast, and were covered in ash and mud. Over the millennia, the mighty giants' trunks

---

> **DETOUR:**
> **ROBERT LOUIS STEVENSON STATE PARK**
>
> **Start: ❻ Calistoga**
>
> Eight miles north of Calistoga via curvaceous Hwy 29, the long-extinct volcanic cone of Mt St Helena marks the Napa Valley's end. Encircled within undeveloped **Robert Louis Stevenson State Park** (📞707-942-4575; www.parks.ca.gov; 3801 Hwy 29; ⊙sunrise-sunset; 🅿️), the crest often gets snow in winter. It's a strenuous 5-mile climb to the peak's 4343ft summit, but what a view – 200 miles on a clear winter's day. Check conditions before setting out. Also consider the 2.2-mile one-way Table Rock Trail (go south from the summit trailhead parking area) for drop-dead valley views. Temperatures are best in wildflower season, March to May; fall is prettiest, when the vineyards change colors.
>
> The park also includes the old Silverado Mine site where Stevenson and his wife honeymooned in 1880.

CALISTOGA SPAS

Calistoga is famous for hot-spring spas and mud-bath emporiums, where you're buried in hot mud and emerge feeling supple, detoxified and enlivened. (The mud is made with volcanic ash and peat; the higher the ash content, the better the bath.)

Packages take 60 to 90 minutes and cost $65 to $110. You start semisubmerged in hot mud, then soak in hot mineral water. A steam bath and blanket-wrap follow. The treatment can be extended with a massage, increasing the cost to $135 and up.

Baths can be taken solo or, at some spas, as couples. Variations include thin, painted-on clay-mud wraps (called 'fango' baths, good for those uncomfortable sitting in mud), herbal wraps, seaweed baths and various massage treatments.

Reservations are essential at all spas, especially on summer weekends. Most spas offer multi-treatment packages; some offer discounted spa-lodging packages. Discount coupons are sometimes available from the **Calistoga Visitors Center** (707-942-6333, 866-306-5588; www.calistogavisitors.com; 1133 Washington St; 9am-5pm).

Indian Springs (707-942-4913; www.indianspringscalistoga.com; 1712 Lincoln Ave; by appointment 9am-8pm) The longest continually operating spa and original Calistoga resort has concrete mud tubs and mines its own ash. Treatments include use of the huge, hot-spring-fed pool and a geyser-fed 'Buddha Pond' for relaxation and meditation.

Spa Solage (707-266-7531, 855-790-6023; www.solagecalistoga.com/spa; 755 Silverado Trail; by appointment 8am-8pm) Chichi, austere, top-end spa, with couples' rooms and a fango-mud bar for DIY paint-on treatments. Also has zero-gravity chairs for blanket wraps, and sex-segregated, clothing-optional mineral pools.

Dr Wilkinson's Hot Springs (707-942-4102; www.drwilkinson.com; 1507 Lincoln Ave; by appointment 8:30am-3:45pm) Operational for more than 60 years, 'the doc' uses more peat in its mud.

Mount View Spa (707-942-6877, 855-821-6668; www.mountviewhotel.com; 1457 Lincoln Ave; by appointment 8am-8pm) Traditional full-service, eight-room spa, good for those who prefer a mineral bath infused with lighter mud.

Calistoga Spa Hot Springs (707-942-6269, 866-822-5772; www.calistogaspa.com; 1006 Washington St; by appointment 8:30am-4:30pm Tue-Thu, to 9pm Fri Mon) Traditional mud baths and massage at a motel complex with two huge swimming pools, where you can invite one friend to join you (surcharge $25).

turned to stone. Gradually the overlay eroded, exposing them, and the first stumps of **Petrified Forest** (707-942-6667; www.petrifiedforest.org; 4100 Petrified Forest Rd; adult/youth 12-17yr/ child 6-11yr $10/9/5; 10am-7pm late May-early Sep, to 6pm Apr-late May & early Sep-Oct, to 5pm Nov-Mar; P) were discovered in 1870. A monument marks Robert Louis Stevenson's 1880 visit. He describes it in *The Silverado Squatters*.

Giraffes in Wine Country? Whadya know! Just 4 miles west (Petrified Forest Rd curves right onto Porter Creek Rd), **Safari West** (707-579-2551; www.safariwest.com; 3115 Porter Creek Rd, Santa Rosa; adult/child 4-12yr from $80/45; P) covers 400 acres and protects zebras, cheetahs and other exotic animals, which mostly roam free. See them on a guided 2½-hour safari in open-sided jeeps; reservations required. You'll also walk through an aviary and lemur condo. The

Classic Trip

reservations-only cafe serves lunch and dinner. If you're feeling adventurous, stay overnight in luxury canvas-sided tent cabins, right in the preserve.

The Drive » Return east via Petrified Forest Rd and drive 1 mile south on Hwy 29/128, then 1 mile north on Lincoln Ave to the Silverado Trail. Lined with row after row of grapevines, you'll journey almost 30 miles southeast along lovely Silverado Trail as you make your way back to Napa.

- - - - - - - - - - - - - -

TRIP HIGHLIGHT

❽ Silverado Trail

The Napa Valley winery jackpot, Silverado Trail runs from Calistoga to Napa and counts approximately three-dozen wineries along its bucolic path. At the northernmost reaches of the Silverado Trail, and breaking ranks with Napa snobbery, the party kids at **Lava Vine** (☎707-942-9500; www.lavavine.com; 965 Silverado Trail; tasting $15; ◷10am-5pm; P🚼🐾) take a lighthearted approach to their seriously good wines – don't be surprised if they bust out musical instruments and start jamming. Children and dogs play outside, while you let your guard down in the tiny tasting room. Bring a picnic.

One of Napa's oldest wineries, unfussy **Regusci** (☎707-254-0403; www.regusciwinery.com; 5584 Silverado Trail, Napa; tasting $30-50, incl tour $60; ◷10am-5pm; P) dates to the late 1870s, with 160 acres of vineyards unfurling around a century-old stone winery that makes Bordeaux-style blends. Located along the valley's quieter eastern side, it's a good bet when traffic up-valley is bad. Reservations are required, and the oak-shaded picnic area is lovely.

Like a modern-day Persian palace, **Darioush** (☎707-257-2345; www.darioush.com; 4240 Silverado Trail, Napa; tasting from $40; ◷10:30am-5pm; P) ranks high on the fabulosity scale, with towering columns, Le Corbusier furniture, Persian rugs and travertine walls. Though known for Cabernet Sauvignon, Darioush also bottles Chardonnay, Merlot and Shiraz, all made with 100% of their respective varietals. Reserve in advance for wine-and-cheese pairings ($75).

Eating & Sleeping

Napa ❶

✕ Alexis Baking Company and Cafe
Cafe $

(☎707-258-1827; www.abcnapa.com; 1517 3rd St; mains $7-17; ⊙7am-3pm Mon-Fri, 7:30am-3pm Sat, 8am-2pm Sun; ☀️ ♿) Our fave spot for quality egg scrambles, granola, focaccia sandwiches, big cups of joe and boxed lunches to go.

🛏 Andaz Napa
Hotel $$$

(☎707-687-1234; http://napa.andaz.hyatt. com; 1450 1st St; r from $400; P ♿ ✳️ @ 🛜) Smack downtown, the Andaz was constructed in 2009, and feels like a big-city hotel, with business-class-fancy rooms, styled in sexy contemporary style.

Yountville ❷

✕ French Laundry
Californian $$$

(☎707-944-2380; www.thomaskeller.com/ tfl; 6640 Washington St, Yountville; prix-fixe dinner $310; ⊙ seatings 11am-12:30pm Fri-Sun, 5:30-9:15pm daily) The pinnacle of California dining, Thomas Keller's French Laundry is epic, a high-wattage culinary experience on par with the world's best. Book one month ahead at 10am sharp, or log onto OpenTable.com precisely at midnight.

🛏 Napa Valley Railway Inn
Inn $$

(☎707-944-2000; www.napavalleyrailwayinn. com; 6523 Washington St; r $175-295; P ♿ ✳️ @ 🛜 ♨️) Sleep in a converted railroad car, part of two short trains parked at a central platform. They've little privacy, but come moderately priced. Bring earplugs.

Oakville ❸

✕ Oakville Grocery
Deli $$

(☎707-944-8802; www.oakvillegrocery.com; 7856 Hwy 29, Oakville; sandwiches $10-15; ⊙6:30am-5pm Sun-Thu, to 6pm Fri & Sat; ♿) The definitive Wine Country deli: excellent cheeses, charcuterie, bread, olives and wine – however pricey.

St Helena ❺

✕ Gott's Roadside
American $$

(☎707-963-3486; http://gotts.com; 933 Main St; mains $8-16; ⊙10am-10pm May-Sep, to 9pm Oct-Apr; ♿) Wiggle your toes in the grass and feast on quality burgers – of beef, turkey, ahi tuna or veggie – plus Cobb salads and fish tacos at this classic roadside drive-in. Avoid weekend waits by phoning ahead or ordering online. There's another at **Oxbow Public Market** (☎707-226-6529; www.oxbowpublicmarket. com; 610 & 644 1st St; items from $3; ⊙9am-7pm Wed-Mon, to 8pm Tue; 🛜 ♿).

🛏 Meadowood
Resort $$$

(☎707-963-3646, 877-963-3646; www. meadowood.com; 900 Meadowood Lane; r from $600; P ♿ ✳️ @ 🛜 ♨️) Hidden in a wooded dell with towering pines and miles of hiking, Napa's grandest resort has cottages and rooms in satellite buildings surrounding a croquet lawn. We most like the hillside fireplace suites; lawn-view rooms lack privacy but are good for families. Kids love the mammoth pool.

Calistoga ❻

✕ Calistoga Inn & Brewery
American $$$

(☎707-942-4101; www.calistogainn.com; 1250 Lincoln Ave; dinner mains $15-38; ⊙11:30am-9:30pm Mon-Fri, from 11am Sat & Sun) Locals crowd the outdoor beer garden on Sundays. Midweek we prefer the country dining room's big oakwood tables – a homey spot for simple American cooking.

🛏 Indian Springs Resort
Resort $$$

(☎707-942-4913; www.indianspringscalistoga. com; 1712 Lincoln Ave; r/cottage from $239/359; P ♿ ✳️ 🛜 ♨️) The definitive old-school Calistoga resort, Indian Springs has cottages facing a central lawn with palm trees, shuffleboard, bocce, hammocks and Weber grills – not unlike a vintage Florida resort. Some cottages sleep six. There are also top-end, motel-style lodge rooms (adults only). Huge hot-springs-fed swimming pool.

Sonoma Valley

7

Flanked by sun-drenched hills and vast vineyard landscapes, the bountiful roadside farms and unassuming top-notch wineries along this trip make for a relaxing excursion.

TRIP HIGHLIGHTS

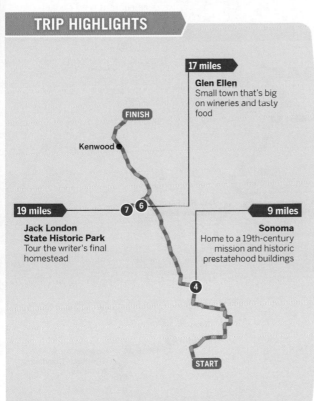

17 miles

Glen Ellen
Small town that's big on wineries and tasty food

FINISH

Kenwood

19 miles

Jack London State Historic Park
Tour the writer's final homestead

7 6

9 miles

Sonoma
Home to a 19th-century mission and historic prestatehood buildings

4

START

2 DAYS
30 MILES / 48KM

GREAT FOR...

BEST TIME TO GO
Witness 'the crush' in September and October and warm dry days from May through October.

ESSENTIAL PHOTO

Capture the past at the Mission San Francisco Solano de Sonoma.

BEST FOR OUTDOORS

Go hiking in Jack London State Historic Park.

7 Sonoma Valley

Locals call it 'Slow-noma.' Unlike fancy Napa, nobody in folksy Sonoma cares if you drive a clunker and vote Green. Anchoring the bucolic, 17-mile-long Sonoma Valley, the town of Sonoma makes a great jumping-off point for exploring Wine Country – it's only an hour from San Francisco. Rolling grass-covered hills rise alongside pastoral Hwy 12, peppered by vineyards, family farms and gardens.

❶ Cornerstone Gardens

There's nothing traditional about **Cornerstone Gardens** (📞707-933-3010; www.cornerstonesonoma.com; 23570 Arnold Dr, Sonoma; ⊘10am-5pm, gardens to 4pm; 🅿️ 👶), which showcases the work of renowned avant-garde landscape designers. Set aside an hour to stroll through the thought-provoking and conceptual plots, explore the garden shops and taste wine. Look for the enormous blue Adirondack chair at road's edge.

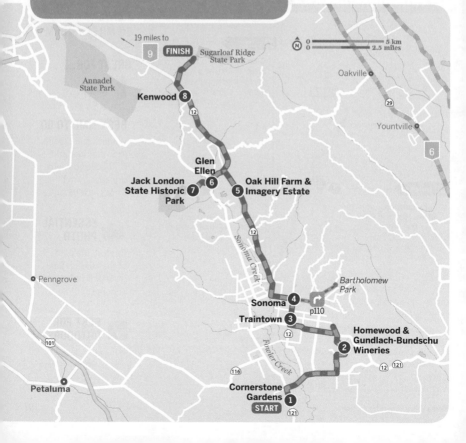

✕ p113

The Drive » Go north on Hwy 121 and follow it for 3 miles as it bears east. Turn south on Burndale Rd. Homewood winery is on your left, at the flagpole.

② Homewood & Gundlach-Bundschu Wineries

A stripy rooster named Steve chases dogs in the parking lot of **Homewood** (☏707-996-6353; www.homewoodwinery.com; 23120 Burndale Rd, Sonoma; tasting $5; ◷10am-4pm; 🅿), a down-home winery whose motto sums it up: 'Da redder, da better.' The tasting room is a garage, and the winemaker crafts standout Zinfandel

LINK YOUR TRIP

6 Napa Valley

For upscale wineries, spa resorts and top-notch restaurants, Hwy 12/121 is the main connector between the Napa and Sonoma Valleys.

9 Russian River & Bohemian Highway

From Kenwood, go west on Hwy 12 for summertime river dips, delightful wineries and rambles in redwood forest or by pristine beaches.

ports and Rhône-style Grenache, Mourvèdre and Syrah. Ask about 'vertical tastings,' and sample wines from the same vineyards but different years. From Homewood, go north on Burndale Rd, jog left briefly onto Napa Rd and then right onto Denmark St.

One of Sonoma Valley's oldest and prettiest wineries, **Gundlach-Bundschu** (☏707-938-5277; www.gunbun.com; 2000 Denmark St, Sonoma; tasting $20-30, incl tour $40-85; ◷11am-5:30pm Jun–Oct, to 4:30pm Nov-May; 🅿) looks like a storybook castle. Founded in 1858 by Bavarian immigrant Jacob Gundlach, it's now at the cutting edge of sustainability. Signature wines are Gewürztraminer and Pinot Noir, but 'Gun-Bun' was the first American winery to produce 100% Merlot. Tours of the vineyard and 1800-barrel cave ($40) are available by reservation. Down a winding lane and with a small lake, it's also pleasant for picnicking and hiking.

The Drive » Follow Denmark St back to Napa Rd, and go west to Hwy 12. Drive Hwy 12/ Broadway north one block to Traintown.

③ Traintown

If you're traveling with young children, make a beeline to **Traintown** (☏707-938-3912; www.

traintown.com; 20264 Broadway, Sonoma; ◷10am-5pm daily Jun-early Sep, Fri-Sun mid-Sep–May; 👫). A miniature steam engine makes 20-minute loops ($5.25), and there are vintage amusement-park rides ($2.75 per ride), including a carousel and a Ferris wheel.

The Drive » Drive north on Hwy 12/Broadway about one mile.

TRIP HIGHLIGHT

④ Sonoma

Kick back for a few hours in Sonoma's town square, with tree-lined paths and a playground, surrounded by shops, restaurants and tasting rooms. Comprising multiple sites, the **Sonoma State Historic Park** (☏707-938-9560; www.parks.ca.gov; adult/child $3/2; ◷10am-5pm) is a must-see for California history buffs. The **Mission San Francisco Solano de Sonoma** (☏707-938-9560; www.parks.ca.gov; 114 E Spain St; adult/child $3/2; ◷10am-5pm) at the plaza's northeast corner, was founded in 1823, in part to forestall the Russian coastal colony at Fort Ross from moving inland. The mission was the 21st and final California mission, and the only one built during the Mexican period (the rest were founded during the Spanish colonial era). The not-to-be-missed chapel dates from 1841.

The adobe **Sonoma Barracks** (☏707-939-9420; www.parks.ca.gov; 20 E Spain St; adult/child $3/2; ◷10am-5pm) was built by General Mariano Guadalupe Vallejo between 1836 and 1840 to house Mexican troops, but it became the capital of a rogue nation on June 14, 1846, when American settlers, of varying sobriety, surprised the guards and declared an independent 'California Republc' [sic] with a homemade flag featuring a grizzly bear. The US took over the republic a month later, but abandoned the barracks during the Gold Rush, leaving Vallejo to turn them into (what else?) a winery in 1860.

Walk just round the corner to stock up for an afternoon picnic. Known for its dry-jack cheeses (made here since the 1930s), **Vella Cheese Co** (☏707-938-3232; www.vellacheese.com; 315 2nd St E; ◷9:30am-6pm Mon-Fri, to 5pm Sat) also makes delectable Mezzo Secco with cocoa powder-dusted rind.

🍴 🛏 p71, p113

The Drive » Head north on Hwy 12 for about 5 miles to Oak Hill Farm along tree-lined vineyards.

❺ Oak Hill Farm & Imagery Estate

At the southern end of Glen Ellen, **Oak Hill Farm** (☏707-996-6643; www.oakhillfarm.net; 15101 Sonoma Hwy; ◷9am-3pm Sat May-Dec; P 🚻) contains acres upon acres of organic flowers and produce, hemmed in by lovely steep oak and manzanita woodland. The farm's Red Barn Store is a historic dairy barn filled with handmade wreaths, herbs and organic goods reaped from the surrounding fields. Try the heirloom tomatoes, pumpkins and blue plums.

Just further north on Sonoma Hwy, **Imagery Estate** (☏800-989-8890, 707-935-4515; www.imagerywinery.com; 14335 Sonoma Hwy; tasting $15; ◷10am-4:30pm Mon-Fri, to 5:30pm Sat

DETOUR: BARTHOLOMEW PARK

Start: ❹ Sonoma (p109)

Around Sonoma, the top, close-to-town outdoors destination is 400-acre **Bartholomew Park** (☏707-938-2244; www.bartholomewpark.org; 1000 Vineyard Lane; ◷10am-6pm; P 🚻), off Castle Rd to the east of town, where you can picnic beneath giant oaks and hike 3 miles of trails, with hilltop vistas to San Francisco. There's also a good **winery** (☏707-939-3026; www.bartpark.com; 1000 Vineyard Lane, Sonoma; tasting $10-20; ◷11am-4:30pm; P) and a small museum. The **Palladian Villa**, at the park's entrance, is a turn-of-the-20th-century replica of the original residence of Count Agoston Haraszthy, a pioneering Sonoma vintner. It's open noon to 3pm, Saturdays and Sundays, and managed by the Bartholomew Park Foundation.

Jack London State Historic Park Jack London's cottage

& Sun; **P** **♿**) boasts bottle labels designed by local artists; the art changes with each vintage and varietal. A gallery houses the entire collection of artwork – over 200 pieces with interpretations of the winery's signature Parthenon symbol. Imagery produces lesser-known varietals, biodynamically grown, that you often can't buy anywhere else.

The Drive » Continue a mile north on Hwy 12 before dipping 1.5 miles west and then south on Arnold Dr to the Jack London Village complex.

TRIP HIGHLIGHT

⑥ Glen Ellen

Try not to drool as you compare chocolates with varying percentages of cacao at **Wine Country Chocolates Tasting Bar** (☏707-996-1010; www.winecountrychocolates.com; 14301 Arnold Dr, Glen Ellen; ⊙10am-5pm). Pick up some champagne- or Cabernet-infused truffles for the drive, or do your best to save them for gifts. There's another tasting room back at Sonoma Plaza.

If you're new to wine, take a crash course in winemaking and biodynamic vineyard practices at **Benziger Winery** (☏707-935-3000, 888-490-2739; www.benziger.com; 1883 London Ranch Rd, Glen Ellen; tasting $20-40, tours $25-50; ⊙10am-5pm, tram tours 11am-3:30pm; **P** **♿**). Reserve ahead for the worthwhile tour, which includes an open-air tram ride through biodynamic vineyards, a stop in the barrel caves and a five-wine tasting. You'll also learn about the difference between organic and biodynamic farming – biodynamic systems work to achieve

111

a balance with the entire ecosystem, going beyond organic practices. Kids love the peacocks. The large-production wine is OK (head for the reserves), but the tour's the draw.

 p113

The Drive » From Benziger, go half a mile further west on London Ranch Rd to reach Jack London State Historic Park.

❼ Jack London State Historic Park

Napa has Robert Louis Stevenson, but Sonoma's got Jack London. This 1400-acre **park** (📞707-938-5216; www.jacklondon park.com; 2400 London Ranch Rd, Glen Ellen; per car $10, cottage adult/child $4/2; ⊙park 9:30am-5pm, museum 10am-5pm, cottage noon-4pm; P 🚻) frames the last years of the author's life.

Changing occupations from Oakland fisherman to Alaska gold prospector to Pacific yachtsman – and novelist on the side – London (1876–1916) ultimately took up farming. He bought Beauty Ranch in 1905 and moved there in 1911. With his second wife, Charmian, he lived and wrote in a small cottage while his mansion, Wolf House, was under construction. On the eve of its completion in 1913, it burned down. The disaster devastated London, and although he toyed with rebuilding, he died before construction got underway. His widow, Charmian, built the House of Happy Walls, which has been preserved as a museum. It's a half-mile walk from there to the remains of Wolf House, passing London's grave along the way. Other paths wind around the farm to the cottage where he lived and worked.

Miles of hiking trails (some open to mountain bikes) weave through oak-dotted woodlands.

The Drive » Drive east back to Hwy 12, and just over 3 miles north to Kenwood's Kunde winery on your right.

❽ Kenwood

It's worth making reservations in advance for the mountain-top tastings with impressive valley views and seasonal guided hikes at family-owned **Kunde** (📞707-833-5501; www. kunde.com; 9825 Hwy 12, Kenwood; tasting $15-50, tours free-$30; ⊙10:30am-5pm; P) winery. You can also just stop in for a tasting and a tour at this historic ranch with vineyards that are more than a century old. Elegant, 100% estate-grown wines include crisp Chardonnay and unfussy red blends, all made sustainably.

Further north along Hwy 12, turn off onto Adobe Canyon Rd and wind uphill to **Sugarloaf Ridge State Park** (📞707-833-5712; www.sugarloafpark. org; 2605 Adobe Canyon Rd, Kenwood; per car $8; P 🚻). There's fantastic hiking – when it's not blazingly hot. On clear days, Bald Mountain has drop-dead views to the sea, while the Brushy Peaks Trail peers into Napa Valley. Both are moderately strenuous hikes; plan on three hours round-trip.

Eating & Sleeping

Cornerstone Gardens ❶

✖ Fremont
Diner American, Southern **$$**

(☎707-938-7370; www.thefremontdiner.com; 2698 Fremont Dr, Sonoma; mains $9-22; ⊙8am-3pm Mon-Wed, to 9pm Thu-Sun; 🖼) Lines snake out the door peak times at this farm-to-table roadside diner. We prefer the indoor tables, but will happily accept a picnic table in the big outdoor tent to feast on ricotta pancakes with real maple syrup, chicken and waffles, oyster po' boys, finger-licking barbecue and skillet-baked cornbread. Arrive early, or late, to beat queues.

Sonoma ❹

✖ Della Santina's Italian **$$**

(☎707-935-0576; www.dellasantinas.com; 133 E Napa St; mains $14 26; ⊙11:30am-3pm & 5-9:30pm) The waiters have been here forever, and the 'specials' rarely change, but Della Santina's Italian American cooking – linguini pesto, veal parmigiana, rotisserie chickens – is consistently good.

🛏 Sonoma Chalet B&B **$$**

(☎707-938 3129, 800-938-3129; www.sonomachalet.com; 18935 5th St W; r with shared bath $140, r $160-190, cottage $210-235; 🅿️ ⊕ 🛜) On a historic farmstead surrounded by rolling hills, rooms in this Swiss chalet–style house are adorned with little balconies and country-style bric-a-brac. We love the freestanding cottages; Laura's has a wood burning fireplace. All rooms come with breakfast, which is served on a deck overlooking a nature preserve. No air-con in rooms with shared bath. No phones, no internet.

🛏 Sonoma Hotel Historic Hotel **$$**

(☎707-996-2996, 800-468-6016; www.sonomahotel.com; 110 W Spain St; r $160-270; ⊕ 🌸 🛜) Long on charm, this good-value, vintage-1920s hotel, decorated with country-style willow-wood furnishings, sits right on the plaza. Double-pane glass blocks the noise, but there's no elevator or parking lot.

Glen Ellen ❻

✖ fig cafe
& winebar French, Californian **$$**

(☎707-938-2130; www.thefigcafe.com; 13690 Arnold Dr, Glen Ellen; mains $12-24, 3-course dinner $36; ⊙10am-2:30pm Sat & Sun, 5-9pm Sun-Thu, to 9:30pm Fri & Sat) The fig's earthy California–Provençal comfort food includes flash-fried calamari with spicy lemon aioli, fig and arugula salad and *steak frites*. Good wine prices and weekend brunch give reasons to return. No reservations.

✖ Glen Ellen Village
Market Deli, Market **$**

(☎707 996 6728; www.sonoma-glenellenmkt.com; 13751 Arnold Dr, Glen Ellen; ⊙5am-8pm; 🖼) Fantastic market with a huge deli, ideal for picnickers.

🛏 Beltane Ranch B&B **$$**

(☎707-833-4233; www.beltaneranch.com; 11775 Hwy 12, Glen Ellen; d $185-295; 🅿️ ⊕ 🛜) Surrounded by horse pastures and vineyards, Beltane is a throwback to 19th-century Sonoma. The cheerful 1890s ranch house has double porches, lined with swinging chairs and white wicker. Though it's technically a B&B, each country-Americana-style room and the cottage has a private entrance – nobody will make you pet the cat. No phones or TVs mean zero distraction from pastoral bliss.

Healdsburg & Around

8

On this sojourn through Sonoma County's least crowded wine country, visit sun-drenched vineyards in the Dry Creek and Alexander Valleys before winding over the mountains to photogenic Clear Lake.

TRIP HIGHLIGHTS

100 miles

Clear Lake
Loop around Lake County's unfussy grape-growing region

Nice

6

FINISH

Hopland

Kelseyville

25 miles

Dry Creek Valley
Sun yourself on country lanes between vineyards

Geyserville

3

4

2

36 miles

Alexander Valley
Be wowed by hillside estate wineries' views

18 miles

Healdsburg
Upmarket wine-country living and stellar restaurants

Santa Rosa

START

2–3 DAYS
135 MILES / 170KM

GREAT FOR...

BEST TIME TO GO

April, May, September and October for dry, sunny days that aren't scorching hot.

ESSENTIAL PHOTO

Shimmering Clear Lake from atop Hopland Grade.

BEST FOR FOODIES

Eat, drink, shop and learn at Healdsburg's Shed.

Sonoma County A Dry Creek Valley vineyard

115

Healdsburg & Around

This is the California wine country you've always dreamed of: rustic wineries nestled beside wind-rustled vineyards; sunny Cal-Italian restaurants with patio trellises covered in grapevines; and more cyclists than limousines glimpsed on slow rural roads. Pull over for a picnic of artisanal cheeses, locally made olive oil and freshly baked bread, and toast your good fortune in finding this place with a bottle of old-vine Zinfandel.

❶ Santa Rosa

Wine Country's biggest city and the Sonoma County seat, Santa Rosa claims two famous native sons – a world-renowned cartoonist and a celebrated horticulturalist – whose legacies include museums and gardens enough to keep you busy for a couple of hours.

Charles Schulz, creator of *Peanuts* cartoons and Santa Rosa resident, was born in 1922, published his first drawing in 1937, introduced Snoopy and Charlie Brown in 1950,

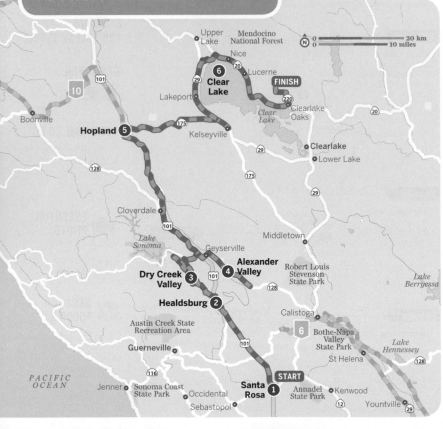

and produced *Peanuts* cartoons until his death in 2000. About 2 miles north of downtown, the modern **Charles M Schulz Museum** (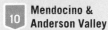707-579-4452; www.schulz museum.org; 2301 Hardies Lane; adult/child $10/5; ⊙11am-5pm Mon & Wed-Fri, from 10am Sat & Sun; P 🚻) honors the cartoonist's legacy with a Snoopy labyrinth, *Peanuts*-related art, and a recreation of Schulz's studio.

Downtown, **Railroad Square** possesses attractive turn-of-the-20th-century brick buildings that house shops, cafes, restaurants and bars. Just further east, stroll around the **Luther Burbank Home & Gardens** (707-524-5445; www.lutherburbank.org; 204 Santa Rosa Ave; grounds free, tour adult/child $10/5; ⊙gardens 8am-dusk, museum 10am-4pm Tue-Sun Apr-Oct, guided tours 10am-3:30pm Tue-Sun Apr-Oct). Pioneering horticulturist Luther Burbank (1849–1926) developed many hybrid plant species, including the Shasta daisy, here at his 19th-century, Greek Revival–style home, and the extensive gardens are lovely.

The Drive ›› Take Hwy 101 north from downtown Santa Rosa for about 14 miles to exit 503 (Healdsburg Ave). Traffic slows to a crawl as you roll over half a mile north to Healdsburg Plaza. Metered street parking around the plaza can be scarce on weekends. Go a few blocks east to find free (though often time-limited) parking in a residential neighborhood.

- - - - - - - - - - - - - - -

TRIP HIGHLIGHT

❷ Healdsburg

Once a sleepy agricultural town best known for its Future Farmers of America parade, Healdsburg has emerged as northern Sonoma County's culinary capital. Downtown's **Shed** (707 431 7433; www.healdsburgshed.com; 25 North St; dinner mains $15-28; ⊙8am-9pm Wed-Mon; 🚻) is foodie central, offering classes, workshops and lectures on food and sustainability, from cheese, wine and beer tasting to bee-keeping. The gourmands shop overflows with cookbooks, heritage seeds, high-quality homewares and more.

Foodie-scenester restaurants and cafes, wine-tasting rooms and upscale boutiques line 19th-century **Healdsburg Plaza**, the town's sun-dappled central square. Traffic grinds to a halt here on summer weekends. It's best visited on weekdays – stroll the surrounding tree-lined streets and soak up the genteel atmosphere.

On a hot summer day, take a dip in the Russian River at **Healdsburg Veterans Memorial Beach** (707 433-1625; www.sonomacountyparks.org; 13839 Old Redwood Hwy; per car $7; ⊙7am-30min before sunset; P 🚻). You could also cool off by paddling a canoe or kayak on the river, stopping at swimming holes and more secluded beaches. Watercraft rentals and shuttles are available seasonally from **Russian River Adventures** (800-280-7627, 707-433-5599; www.russianriveradventures.com; 20 Healdsburg Ave; canoe rental & shuttle adult/child from $45/25; 🚻) and **River's Edge Kayak & Canoe Trips** (707-433-7247; www.riversedgekayakandcanoe.com; 13840 Healdsburg Ave; kayak/canoe rental & shuttle from $50/100).

✕ 🛏 p121

The Drive ›› From Healdsburg Plaza, drive 1 mile north on Healdsburg Ave. Turn west onto

LINK YOUR TRIP

6 **Napa Valley**

From Geyserville, head 24 miles southeast on Hwy 128 toward Calistoga for the showcase wineries and destination restaurants of Napa Valley.

10 **Mendocino & Anderson Valley**

Hopland is the jumping-off point for a country drive through the Anderson Valley's wineries and apple orchards out to the Pacific Ocean.

Dry Creek Rd, a fast-moving thoroughfare; it's 5.5 miles to Truett Hurst. To reach wineries on West Dry Creek Rd, an undulating country lane with no center stripe – one of Sonoma's great back roads, ideal for cyclists – turn onto Lambert Bridge Rd by Dry Creek General Store.

TRIP HIGHLIGHT

❸ Dry Creek Valley

A wine-growing region hemmed in by 2000ft-high mountains, **Dry Creek Valley** (www.drycreek valley.org) is relatively warm, ideal for Sauvignon Blanc and Zinfandel, and in some places, Cabernet Sauvignon.

A welcoming, biodynamic winery, **Truett Hurst** (☎707-433-9545; www.truetthurst.com; 5610 Dry Creek Rd; tasting $5-10; ⊙10am-5pm; P) pours old-vine Zinfandel, standout Petite Sirah and Pinot Noir made from Russian River grapes inside a handsome, contemporary tasting room. Meander through the butterfly garden out back to the creek and sink into a red Adirondack chair.

An early leader in organics, **Preston** (☎707-433-3372; www.prestonvineyards.com; 9282 W Dry Creek Rd; tasting $10; ⊙11am-4:30pm; P 🚲) feels like old Sonoma County. Weathered picket fencing frames the 19th-century farm store and tasting room. The signature is citrusy Sauvignon Blanc, but try the Rhône varietals and small-lot wines. Buy some fresh-baked bread and cold-pressed olive oil for a picnic in the shade of a walnut tree.

Atop the valley's north end, cool caves are built into the hillside at **Bella** (☎707-473-9171; www.bella winery.com; 9711 West Dry Creek Rd; tasting $10; ⊙11am-4:30pm; P). The focus is on big reds, but your best bets are the dry rosé and sweet late-harvest Zinfandel dessert wine.

✗ p121

The Drive » Backtrack on West Dry Creek Rd for over a mile, turning left onto Yoakim Bridge Rd. Turn right onto Dry Creek Rd, then take a quick left onto Canyon Rd, which curves for 2 miles northeast and passes

underneath Hwy 101 before entering Alexander Valley. At the next T-intersection, hang a right on Geyserville Ave (Hwy 128).

TRIP HIGHLIGHT

❹ Alexander Valley

With postcard-perfect vistas and wide-open vineyards, the bucolic **Alexander Valley** (www.alexandervalley.org) flanks the Mayacamas Mountains that divide the Sonoma and Napa Valleys. Summers are hot, ideal for Cabernet Sauvignon, Merlot and warm-weather Chardonnay, but there's also fine Zinfandel and Sauvignon Blanc.

TOP TIP: CRUSH

Crush is autumn harvest, the most atmospheric time of year in Wine Country, when grapevine leaves turn brilliant colors and you can smell fermenting fruit in the breeze. Farmers throw big parties for the vineyard workers to celebrate their work. Everyone wants to be here then – that's why room rates skyrocket.

GEORGE ROSE / GETTY IMAGES ©

Alexander Valley Wine enthusiasts at Stryker Sonoma winery

A few miles south of the small farming town of **Geyserville**, named for nearby hot springs and other geothermal features, **Francis Ford Coppola Winery** (☏707-857-1471; www.francisford coppolawinery.com; 300 Via Archimedes, Geyserville; tasting free-$25; ⊘11am-6pm; P 🍴) has taken over the former Chateau Souverain estate. The famous movie director's hillside vineyard property is a self-described 'wine wonderland' of tasting flights, free movie-making memorabilia museum,

shameless gift shop and swimming pools.

From Geyserville, Hwy 128 trundles southeast through oak-studded hills, passing connoisseur-worthy wineries. The architecturally impressive glass-and-concrete tasting room at **Stryker Sonoma** (☏707-433-1944; www.strykersonoma.com; 5110 Hwy 128, Geyserville; tasting $30, incl tour $40; ⊘10.30am-5pm; P) delivers knock-out views, but the jury is out on the new winemaker. Further south along Hwy 128, which turns sharply left and then right just

past the landmark Jimtown Store, **Hanna** (☏707-431-4310, 800-854-3987; www.hannawinery.com; 9280 Hwy 128, Healdsburg; tasting $15-25; ⊘11am-4pm; P) winery crafts estate-grown Merlot and Cabernet Sauvignon and big-fruit Zinfandel.

✗ 🛏 p121

The Drive » Follow Hwy 128 back north through Geyserville and join Hwy 101 northbound. It's a 23-mile trip north via Cloverdale to the tiny town of Hopland, where all the whizzing traffic must brake for the stop sign at the main crossroads.

❺ Hopland

Cute little **Hopland** (www. destinationhopland.com) is the gateway to Mendocino County's wine country. Hops were first grown here in 1866, but Prohibition brought the industry temporarily to a halt. Today, booze drives the local economy again with wine tasting as the primary draw.

You'll find more than a dozen wine-tasting rooms on downtown's Main St, and many more in the surrounding countryside off Hwy 101. Pick up a free winery map from any local tasting room. Downtown, **Brutocao Cellars** (☏800-433-3689; www.brutocaocellars. com; 13500 S Hwy 101; ☺10am-5pm; P) has bocce courts, bold red wines and chocolate – a perfect combo. Three blocks north, **Graziano Family of Wines** (☏707-744-8466; www.grazianofamilyofwines. com; 13251 S Hwy 101; ☺10am-5pm; P) specializes in 'Cal-Ital' wines including Primitivo, Barbera, Dolcetto and Sangiovese.

A half-mile south of downtown lies the progressive, futuristic, 12-acre campus of the **Real Goods Solar Living Center** (☏707-742-2460; www.solarliving.org; 13771 S Hwy 101; self-guided tour free, guided tour per person/ family $3/5; ☺ center 9am-6pm daily, tours 11am & 3pm

Sat & Sun Apr-Oct; P ♿), largely responsible for the area's bold green initiatives. The Real Goods Store, run by the same company that sold the first solar panel in the US back in 1978, is a fascinating straw-bale house showroom.

🗡️ 🛏️ p121

The Drive » Get ready for a stunningly beautiful, yet gut-wrenchingly twisted trip on Hwy 175 east of Hopland. After ascending unnervingly steep Hopland Grade, panoramic views of Clear Lake and Mt Konocti open up below. Eighteen miles (about a 30-minute drive) from Hopland, turn right to stay on Hwy 175, which joins Hwy 29 south for an easy 5-mile coast into Kelseyville.

`TRIP HIGHLIGHT`

❻ Clear Lake

With over 100 miles of shoreline, Clear Lake is the largest naturally occurring freshwater lake entirely in California (Tahoe is bigger, but crosses the Nevada state line). In summer the warm water blooms with green algae, preventing humans (and dogs) from swimming but creating fabulous habitat for fish – especially bass – and tens of thousands of birds. Mt Konocti, a 4300ft-tall dormant volcano, lords over the lake.

Looking like a Hollywood Western movie set, downtown **Kelseyville** is where family-owned winery tasting rooms

such as **Wildhurst** (☏707-279-4302; www.wildhurst. com; 3855 Main St, Kelseyville; ☺10am-5pm; P) rustle beside hardware shops, soda fountains and cafes. Four miles northeast of town, **Clear Lake State Park** (☏707-279-4293, 707-279-2267; www.clearlake statepark.org; 5300 Soda Bay Rd, Kelseyville; per car $8; ☺ sunrise-sunset; P ♿) is idyllic, with hiking trails, fishing, boating and camping on the lake's south shore.

Follow Soda Bay Rd back west to Hwy 29, which heads north to Lakeport. Take the Nice-Lucerne Cutoff Rd for a scenic drive on Hwy 20 along the lake's north shore, passing the yesteryear cottage resorts of California's 'Little Switzerland.' About 10 miles east of Lucerne, turn off for a steep climb up High Valley Rd (which begins as Hwy 220) to peaceful **Brassfield Estate** (☏707-998-1895; www.brassfield estate.com; 10915 High Valley Rd, Clearlake Oaks; tasting $5; ☺11am-5pm Mar-Nov, from noon Dec-Apr; P), which pours estate-grown wines inside a peaceful Tuscan villa surrounded by 2500 acres of vineyards, cattle-ranch lands and wildlife reserve. Its proprietary Eruption red blend is made with grapes grown in volcanic soil on the slopes of an extinct cinder cone.

🛏️ p121

Eating & Sleeping

Healdsburg ❷

✖ Noble Folk Ice Cream
& Pie Bar
Desserts $

(☎707-395-4426; www.thenoblefolk.com; 116 Matheson St; items $3-6; ☻noon-9pm; 🖐) Handcrafted ice cream and classic American pie, made with top-quality, all-local ingredients.

🛏 H2 Hotel
Hotel $$$

(☎information 707-431-2202, reservations 707-922-5251; www.h2hotel.com; 219 Healdsburg Ave; r Mon-Fri $269-389, Sat & Sun $399-509; P ⊖ ✳ @ 🛜 ➰ 🛁) Little sister to **Hotel Healdsburg** (www.hotelhealdsburg.com), H2 has the same angular concrete style, but was built LEED-gold-certified from the ground up, with a living roof, reclaimed everything, and fresh-looking rooms.

Dry Creek Valley ❸

✖ Dry Creek
General Store
Deli, Market $

(☎707-433-4171; www.drycreekgeneralstore1881.com; 3495 Dry Creek Rd; sandwiches $7-13; ☻6:30am-5pm Mon-Thu, to 5:30pm Fri & Sat, 7am-5pm Sun) Before wine-tasting in Dry Creek Valley, stop at this vintage general store, where locals and bicyclists gather for coffee on the creaky front porch.

Alexander Valley ❹

✖ Diavola
Italian, Californian $$

(☎707-814-0111; www.diavolapizzera.com; 21021 Geyserville Ave, Geyserville; mains $15-26; ☻11:30am-9pm; 🖐) Ideal for lunch while wine-tasting in Alexander Valley, Diavola makes outstanding salumi (cold cuts) and thin-crust pizzas, served in an Old West, brick-walled space.

✖ Jimtown Store
Deli, Market $$

(☎707-433-1212; www.jimtown.com; 6706 Hwy 128; sandwiches $6-12; ☻7am-3pm Mon & Wed-Fri, 7:30am-5pm Sat & Sun) One of our favorite Alexander Valley stopovers, Jimtown is great for picnic supplies and sandwiches spread with housemade condiments.

🛏 Geyserville Inn
Motel $$

(☎707-857-4343, 877-857-4343; www.geyservilleinn.com; 21714 Geyserville Ave, Geyserville; r Mon-Fri $160-205, Sat & Sun $269-315; P ⊖ ✳ ➰ 🛁) Eight miles north of Healdsburg, this immaculately kept upmarket motel is surrounded by vineyards. Rooms have unexpectedly smart furnishings and quality extras, such as feather pillows.

Hopland ❺

✖ Bluebird Cafe
Diner $

(☎707-744-1633; 13340 S Hwy 101; mains $8-15; ☻7am-2pm Mon-Thu, to 7pm Fri-Sun; 🖐) Classic American diner serves hearty breakfasts and homemade pie (the summer selection of peach-blueberry pie is dreamy).

🛏 Piazza de Campovida
Inn $$$

(☎707-744-1977; www.piazzadecampovida.com; 13441 S Hwy 101; ste $175-285; P ⊖ 🛜) Modern Californian meets Italian at this very comfortable inn where all of the spacious suites have whirlpool tubs, fireplaces and private balconies. The homey taverna and pizzeria in front have big tables for communal dining and fantastic artisanal pizzas, craft beer and wine.

Clear Lake ❻

🛏 Sea Breeze Resort
Cottage $$

(☎707-998-3327; www.seabreezeresort.net; 9595 Harbor Dr, Glenhaven; cottages $125-180; ☻Apr-Oct; P ⊖ ✳ 🛜) Just south of Lucerne on a small peninsula, gardens surround seven lakeside cottages. All but one have full kitchens.

🛏 Tallman Hotel
Historic Hotel $$

(☎information 707-275-2244, reservations 707-275-2245; www.tallmanhotel.com; 9550 Main St, Upper Lake; cottages $169-259; P ⊖ ✳ 🛜 ➰) The centerpiece may be the smartly renovated historic hotel – tile bathrooms, warm lighting, thick linens – but the rest of the property's lodging, including the shady garden, walled-in swimming pool, brick patios and porches, exudes timeless elegance.

Russian River & Bohemian Highway

9

In western Sonoma County, tour organic wineries, stately redwood forests, ribbons of undulating road and the serene Russian River, and ogle seals and whales along the coast.

TRIP HIGHLIGHTS

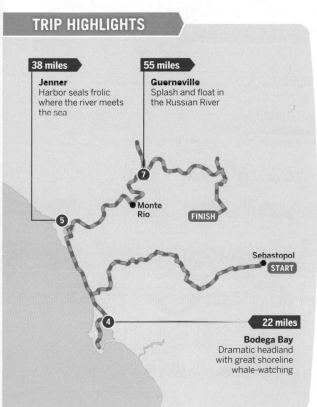

38 miles

Jenner
Harbor seals frolic where the river meets the sea

55 miles

Guerneville
Splash and float in the Russian River

Monte Rio

FINISH

5

7

Sebastopol
START

4

22 miles

Bodega Bay
Dramatic headland with great shoreline whale-watching

2 DAYS
75 MILES / 120KM

GREAT FOR...

BEST TIME TO GO
June to September for toasty days and idyllic river swimming.

 ESSENTIAL PHOTO
Catch the Russian River as it barrels into the Pacific in Jenner.

 BEST FOR WILDLIFE
Gray whales breaching just offshore at Bodega Head during winter and spring.

Russian River & Bohemian Highway

9

Sonoma's lesser-known western region was formerly famous for its apple farms. But vineyards have been replacing the orchards, and the Russian River has now taken its place among California's important wine appellations for superb Pinot Noir. 'The River,' as locals call it, has long been a summertime weekend destination for Northern Californians, who come to canoe, wander country lanes, taste wine, hike redwood forests and live at a lazy pace.

1 Sebastopol

Grapes have replaced apples as the new cash crop, but Sebastopol's farm-town identity remains rooted in the apple – evidenced by the much-heralded summertime **Gravenstein Apple Fair** (www.gravensteinapplefair. com), held in August. The town center feels suburban because of traffic, but a hippie tinge and quirky shops such as a beekeeping store give it color.

Just north off Bodega Ave, prepare to giggle at the wacky **Patrick**

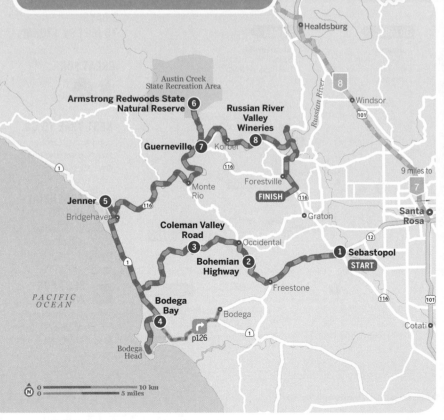

Amiot sculptures (www.patrickamiot.com; Florence Ave; P 🚻) gracing front yards along Florence Ave. Fashioned from recycled materials, a hot-rodding rat and a witch in mid-flight are a few of the oversized and demented lawn ornaments parading along the street.

✕ p129

The Drive ≫ From the central intersection of Hwys 116 and 12, head west on Bodega Ave (signed Bodega Bay) for 6 miles, passing apple orchards en route to tiny Freestone.

- - - - - - - - - - - -

❷ Bohemian Highway

Running north from the town of **Freestone**, the pastoral 10-mile Bohemian Hwy tours past farmland and then constricts as it

LINK YOUR TRIP

8 **Healdsburg & Around**

East of Guerneville, follow River Rd (which becomes Eastside Rd) or scenic Westside Rd for 18 country miles to Healdsburg.

7 **Sonoma Valley**

From Sebastopol, head east on Hwy 12 for less than 20 miles, passing through Santa Rosa and into the Sonoma Valley for more wine tasting.

passes through stands of redwoods, ending at the Russian River in tiny Monte Rio. At the highway's southern end, the crossroads of Freestone isn't much more than just that, though the former railway stop boasts a crazy-popular bakery (p129), a cute country store and **Osmosis** (📞707-823-8231; www.osmosis.com; 209 Bohemian Hwy, Freestone; ⊙by appointment 9am-8pm Thu-Mon, to 7pm Tue & Wed), a Japanese-inspired spa specializing in unique cedar treatments. Stop by for a tasting at **Joseph Phelps** (📞707-874-1010; www.josephphelps.com; 12747 El Camino Bodega; tasting $20-50; ⊙11am-5pm daily May-Dec, Thu-Mon Jan-Apr; P), a Napa-based winemaker that pours estate-grown Chardonnay and fog-kissed Pinot Noir from local vineyards.

Just over 3 miles north, **Occidental** is a haven of artists, back-to-the-landers and counter-culturalists. Historic 19th-century buildings line a single main street, easy to explore in an hour. On Fridays during summer and fall, meet the whole community at the detour-worthy **farmers market** (📞707-874-8478; www.occidentalfarmersmarket.com; 3611 Bohemian Hwy; ⊙4pm-dusk Fri Jun-Oct; 🚲 🚻), with musicians, craftspeople and – the star attraction – Gerard's paella of Food Network TV fame.

✕ p129

The Drive ≫ In the center of Occidental, turn west onto well-signed Coleman Valley Rd.

- - - - - - - - - - - -

❸ Coleman Valley Road

Sonoma County's most scenic drive isn't through the grapes, but along these 10 miles of winding byway from Occidental to the sea. It's best in the late morning, after the fog has cleared and the sun's behind you. First you'll pass through redwood forests and lush valleys where Douglas firs stand draped in sphagnum moss – an eerie sight in the fog. The real beauty shots lie further ahead, when the road ascends 1000ft hills, dotted with gnarled oaks and craggy rock formations, with the vast blue Pacific unfurling below.

The Drive ≫ The road ends at coastal Hwy 1 in the midst of Sonoma Coast State Park, which stretches 17 miles from Bodega Head to just north of Jenner. From Hwy 1, head 2.5 miles south, then west onto Eastshore Rd. Go right at the stop sign onto Bay Flat Rd and along the harbor until road's end.

- - - - - - - - - - - -

❹ Bodega Bay

The town of Bodega Bay sits at the southernmost section of the glorious **Sonoma Coast State Park** (📞707-875-3484; www.parks.ca.gov; off Hwy 1; per car

$8; ⊙ dawn-dusk; P 🚻), a series of beaches separated by several beautiful rocky headlands. Some beaches are tiny, hidden in little coves, while others stretch far and wide or are connected by vista-studded coastal hiking trails that wind along the bluffs. At the tip of a peninsula, the windy crown jewel of **Bodega Head** rises 265ft above sea level, with dreamy views out onto the open ocean and excellent whale-watching and kite-flying.

✗ p129

The Drive ≫ Return to Hwy 1 and trace the coastline 8 miles north toward Jenner, turning left onto Goat Rock Rd.

PHIL HABER PHOTOGRAPHY / GETTY IMAGES ©

TRIP HIGHLIGHT

⑤ Jenner

In the small village of Jenner, the Russian River merges with the ocean and the confluence turns brackish. At the end of Goat Rock Rd, bear left for **Blind Beach**, where the mass of Goat Rock looms above and splendid Arched Rock seems to hover offshore. Then double back and turn left (go north) to **Goat Rock Beach**, where a harbor seal colony sits at the river's mouth and pups are born from March to August. The best way to see the seals is by kayak, which you can rent at the river's edge in town from

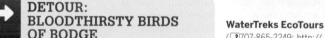

WaterTreks EcoTours
(📞707-865-2249; http://watertreks.com; kayak rental from $30; ⊙ hours vary).

✗ 🛏 p129

The Drive ≫ After crossing the last bridge over the Russian River before it joins the sea, go east on Hwy 116/River Rd, a well-paved country road sandwiched between the river and abrupt hills speckled with weather-beaten wooden barns. In Guerneville, turn left at the sign for Armstrong Woods Rd.

DETOUR: BLOODTHIRSTY BIRDS OF BODGE

Start: ④ Bodega Bay (p125)

Bodega Bay has the enduring claim to fame as the setting for Alfred Hitchcock's *The Birds* (1963). Although special effects radically altered the actual layout of the town, you still get a good feel for the supposed site of the farm owned by Mitch Brenner (played by Rod Taylor). The once-cozy Tides Restaurant, where much avian-caused havoc occurs in the movie, is still there, but it has been transformed into a vast restaurant complex. Venture 5 miles inland (south on Hwy 1) to the tiny town of **Bodega** and you'll find two icons from the film: the schoolhouse (now a private home – no trespassing) and St Teresa of Avila Church. Both stand just as they did in the movie – a crow overhead may make the hairs rise on your neck. Down the road, drop in at the **Bodega Country Store** (📞707-377-4056; www.bodegastore.com; 17190 Bodega Hwy; ⊙8am-8pm) to peruse a cache of Hitchcock movie memorabilia.

Jenner Goat Rock and Goat Rock Beach

⑥ Armstrong Redwoods State Natural Reserve

Soaring redwood trees and carpeted forest floor create a profound silence that spreads for 805 acres at **Armstrong Redwoods State Natural Reserve** (✆info 707-869-2015, visitor center 707-869-2958; www.parks.ca.gov; 17000 Armstrong Woods Rd; per car $8; ⊙8am-1hr after sunset; [P] [♿]), where you can walk between the columnar trunks of 30-story-high giants saved from the saw by a 19th-century lumber magnate. Equipped with a handheld rope and Braille signs, the tranquil Discovery Trail passes the Colonel Armstrong Tree, a 1400-year-old behemoth, and a tree-hugging platform. The self-guided Pioneer Nature Trail is wheelchair-accessible.

The Drive 》 Return 3 miles south to River Rd. Jog west one block to Church St and follow it one block south to the beach.

TRIP HIGHLIGHT

⑦ Guerneville

The colorful, oddball main street of Guerneville bustles with life, as tourists and locals alike cruise the storefronts and galleries and dip in to the cafes, restaurants and bars. There's nothing quite like floating in the cool river here on a scorching summer day. Head to **Johnson's Beach** (✆707-869-2022; www.johnsonsbeach.com; 16215 & 16217 First St, Guerneville; kayak & canoe rental per hr/day $15/40; ⊙10am-6pm mid-Jun–mid-Sep, 11am-6pm Sat & Sun only mid-May–mid-Jun & mid-late Sep; [♿]) to rent kayaks and canoes that you launch from and return to the beach.

✗ ⊨ p129

The Drive 》 Follow Main St east of central Guerneville onto River Rd and drive almost 3 miles to Korbel on your left.

8 Russian River Valley Wineries

The ivy-draped brick winery at **Korbel** (☎707-824-7000; www.korbel.com; 13250 River Rd, Guerneville; ☺10am-4:30pm; **P**) gets jammed on weekends as folks come from all around to sip the champagnes it's been making since 1882. No reservations are needed for the free, fascinating 50-minute tour that teaches you Champagne Making 101.

Continue east on River Rd, forking left onto Westside Rd just over 2 miles past Korbel. This two-lane road passes several wineries, and opens up views of Mt St Helena to the northeast. High on a hilltop, the tasting room at **Gary Farrell** (☎707-473-2909; www.garyfarrellwines.com; 10701 Westside Rd, Healdsburg; tasting from $20, incl tour $40; ☺10:30am-4:30pm Mon-Fri, by appointment Sat & Sun; **P**) sits perched among second-growth redwoods, where long-finish Pinot Noir is crafted by a big-name winemaker. Next up is solar-powered **Moshin** (☎707-433-5499; www.moshinvineyards.com; 10295 Westside Rd, Healdsburg; tasting $15; ☺11am-4:30pm; **P**), another Pinot Noir specialist. Two miles further along, **Porter Creek** (☎707-433-6321; www.portercreekvineyards.com; 8735 Westside Rd, Healdsburg; tasting fee $15; ☺10:30am-4:30pm; **P**) pours biodynamic Burgundian and Rhône-style wines on a former bowling-alley lane plunked atop wine barrels.

Backtrack south just over a mile on Westside Rd, turning left onto Wohler Rd. After almost 2 miles, turn right back onto River Rd, then take the next two lefts to end up on Covey Rd south toward the hamlet of Forestville. Turn left onto Front St, which is Hwy 116 E, and after a mile, turn left at Kozlowski Farms onto Ross Station Rd. A mile later, finally roll to a stop at **Iron Horse** (☎707-887-1507; www.ironhorsevineyards.com; 9786 Ross Station Rd, Sebastopol; tasting $20, incl tour $25-50; ☺10am-4:30pm; **P**), known for producing Pinot Noir and sparkling wines, which the White House often pours. Atop a hill with drop-dead views over the county, the outdoor tasting room is refreshingly unfussy.

Eating & Sleeping

Sebastopol ❶

✗ Mom's Apple Pie
Desserts $

(☎707-823-8330; www.momsapplepieusa.com; 4550 Gravenstein Hwy N; whole pies $7-17; ⊙10am-6pm; ⌖ 🖶) Pie's the thing at this roadside bakery – and yum, that flaky crust. Apple is predictably good, especially in autumn, but the blueberry is our fave, made better with vanilla ice cream.

Bohemian Highway ❷

✗ Howard Station Cafe
American $

(☎707-874-2838; www.howardstationcafe.com; 3611 Bohemian Hwy; mains $8-14; ⊙7am-2:30pm Mon-Fri, to 3pm Sat & Sun; 🖶 🖾) Big plates of comfort-food cooking and fresh-squeezed juices. Cash only.

✗ Wild Flour Bread
Bakery $

(☎707-874-2938; www.wildflourbread.com; 140 Bohemian Hwy, Freestone; items from $3; ⊙8.30am-6:30pm Fri Mon; 🖶) Organic brick-oven breads, giant sticky buns and good coffee.

Bodega Bay ❹

✗ Spud Point Crab Company
Seafood $

(☎707-875-9472; www.spudpointcrab.com; 1860 Westshore Rd; dishes $4-11; ⊙9am-5pm; 🖶) In the classic tradition of dockside crab shacks, Spud Point serves salty-sweet crab sandwiches and *real* clam chowder. Eat at picnic tables overlooking the marina. Take Bay Flat Rd to get here.

Jenner ❺

✗ Café Aquatica
Cafe $

(☎707-865-2251; 10439 Hwy 1, Jenner; items $3-10; ⊙8am-5pm; 🛜 ⌖) This is the kind of North Coast coffee shop you've been dreaming of: fresh pastries, fog-lifting organic coffee and chatty locals. The expansive view of the Russian River from the patio and gypsy sea-hut decor make it hard to leave.

✗ River's End Restaurant
Californian $$$

(☎707-865-2484; http://ilovesunsets.com; 11048 Hwy 1; lunch mains $15-26, dinner $26-42; ⊙noon-3:30pm & 5-9pm Fri-Mon) Unwind in style at this picture-perfect restaurant, perched on a cliff overlooking the river's mouth and the grand sweep of the Pacific Ocean.

🛏 River's End Inn
Cottage $$

(☎707-865-2484; http://ilovesunsets.com; 11048 Hwy 1; cottage $169-279; P ⌖) Ocean-view cottages are wood-paneled and have no TVs, wi-fi or phones, but many do come with fireplaces and breezy decks. Children under 12 years old not recommended.

Guerneville ❼

✗ Boon Eat + Drink
Californian $$$

(☎707-869-0780; http://eatatboon.com; 16248 Main St; lunch mains $14-18, dinner $15-26; ⊙11am-3pm & 5-9pm, from 10am Sat & Sun, to 10pm Fri & Sat, closed Wed; ⌖) Locally sourced ingredients inform the seasonal, Cali-smart cooking at this tiny, always-packed, New American bistro, with cheek-by-jowl tables that fill every night. Show up early or expect to wait.

✗ Seaside Metal Oyster Bar
Seafood $$

(☎707-604-7250; http://seasidemetal.com; 16222 Main St; dishes $8-16; ⊙5-9pm Wed & Thu, to 10pm Fri, 3-10pm Sat, 3-9pm Sun) Unexpectedly urban for Guerneville, this storefront raw bar is an offshoot of San Francisco's Bar Crudo – one of the city's best – and showcases oysters, clams, shrimp and exquisitely prepared raw-fish dishes. There's limited hot food, but it's overwrought: stick to raw.

🛏 Boon Hotel + Spa
Boutique Hotel $$

(☎707-869-2721; www.boonhotels.com; 14711 Armstrong Woods Rd; d $175-325; P ⌖ 🛜 🖾 🖾) Rooms surround a swimming-pool courtyard (with spa bath) at this 14-room motel resort, gussied up in minimalist modern style. The look is austere but fresh, with organic-cotton linens and spacious rooms; most have wood-burning fireplaces. It's a 15-minute walk north of downtown.

Mendocino & Anderson Valley

10

The uninitiated might roll their eyes at 'Mendocino Magic,' but spend a few days here cruising two-lane blacktop and you'll discover the enchantment of this place is undeniable.

TRIP HIGHLIGHTS

70 miles

Mendocino
A seaside gem of historic buildings and excellent B&Bs

100 miles

Orr Hot Springs
Soak among redwoods at this magical getaway

6

8
FINISH

Philo

2

Hopland
START

Boonville
Learn to speak Boontling and sip excellent local brew

25 miles

3–4 DAYS
100 MILES / 160KM

GREAT FOR...

BEST TIME TO GO
In fall, when skies are clear and apples harvested.

ESSENTIAL PHOTO
Otters swimming alongside your canoe on the Big River.

BEST DAY
Hike through pygmy forests in Van Damme State Park and canoe up the Big River.

Anderson Valley Apple cider for sale

131

10 Mendocino & Anderson Valley

This trip is about family-operated vineyards, hushed stands of redwoods and a string of idiosyncratic villages perched in the border area between California's rolling coastal hills and the jagged cliffs of the Pacific. Just far enough out of the Bay Area orbit to move to its own relaxed rhythm, this makes an unforgettable trip filled with low-key pampering, specialty Pinot Noir, sun-drenched days and romantic, foggy nights.

❶ Hopland

Tired of treading over the same ground with Napa and Sonoma? Make for adorable little Hopland, the wine hub of the Mendocino County. Less than 100 miles north of San Francisco, this unsung winemaking region offers a lighter, more delicate style of Pinot Noir and Chardonnay. You can taste the wines from many of the family farms you'll approach en route at the

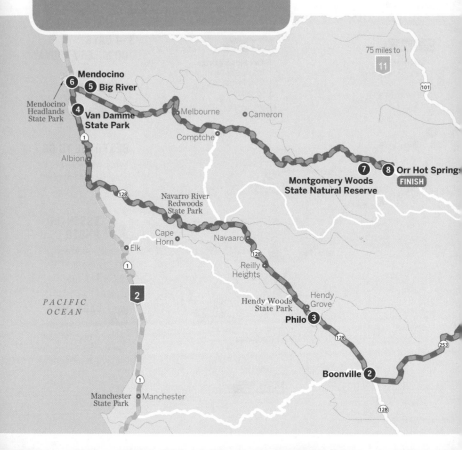

75 miles to 11

Mendocino
❻ ❺ Big River
Mendocino Headlands State Park
❹ Van Damme State Park
Melbourne   Cameron
Comptche
Albion
❼ ❽ Orr Hot Springs FINISH
Montgomery Woods State Natural Reserve
Navarro River Redwoods State Park
Cape Horn   Navaaro
Elk
Reilly Heights
2
Hendy Woods State Park   Hendy Grove
Philo ❸
PACIFIC OCEAN
Boonville ❷
Manchester State Park   Manchester

downtown wine shop **Sip Mendocino** (📞707-744-8375; www.sipmendocino.com; 13420 S Hwy 101; tasting $5-10; ⏰11am-6pm). Its expert staff pour hand-picked flights that include rare vintages you might not even taste at the wineries themselves.

✕ ⊨ p121

The Drive » Head north on Hwy 101 about 10 miles before exiting on Hwy 253, a beautiful, serpentine route southwest through the hills. Hwy 253 ends at Hwy 128, just south of Boonville by the brewery.

TRIP HIGHLIGHT

② Boonville

Descending from the hills, visitors spill out into the sun-washed village of Boonville, a short main street with historical buildings, boutiques and artisanal ice cream. Still, the town's most famous taste is just a mile down the road at the **Anderson Valley Brewing Company** (📞707-895-2337; www.avbc. com; 17700 Hwy 253, Boonville; tasting from $2, tours & disc-golf course free; ⏰11am-6pm Sat-Thu, to 7pm Fri; 🅿 ♿). The Bavarian-style brewhouse sits on a big corner lot overlooking the valley, and the grounds are complete with a sparsely furnished tasting room, copper-clad brewing vats and beefy draft horses that graze the grounds. The place also includes a disc-golf course, and players can buy beer inside the tasting room to drink as they play. The brewery's long-standing green

credentials include a solar array that generates much of its power.

✕ ⊨ p137

The Drive » Drive just north out of town on Hwy 128, passing a number of family wineries and fruit stands. The best fruit is ahead, in Philo, only 6 miles north of Boonville.

③ Philo

The gorgeous Philo Apple Farm (p137) is a bit like something out of a story-book: a dreamy patch of green run by warm-hearted staff and scented with apple blossoms. It's worth skipping over the other farm stands on the way here for its organic preserves, chutneys, heirloom apples and pears. (If you get here after hours, you're likely to be able to leave a few dollars in a jar and take some goodies along for the ride.) Those who linger can take cooking classes with some of the Wine Country's best chefs. For a swim, the

0 ——— 10 km
0 ——— 5 miles

● Redwood Valley

● Calpella 〔20〕

Lake Mendocino

The orks ○

〔101〕

○ kiah

🔗 LINK YOUR TRIP

2 Pacific Coast Highways

Can't get enough beachcombing and breathtaking cliffs? Join California's most epic drive along Hwy 1.

11 Lost Coast & Southern Redwoods

The northern edge of this trip nears California's wildest shores, perfect for travelers with sturdy hiking boots and a thirst for untouched wilds. Continue up Hwy 101 to connect with this trip.

START
① Hopland

rocky, shallow waters of the Navarro River are just a short stroll up the road.

📖 p137

The Drive » Take the twisting drive west along Hwy 128 though majestic fog-shrouded stands of redwood and you'll eventually emerge at Hwy 1. Go north on Hwy 1 through the seaside town of Albion and on toward Van Damme State Park.

4 Van Damme State Park

After emerging on one of California's most serene stretches of Hwy 1, a stroll along the waves seems mandatory. Three miles south of Mendocino, this sprawling 1831-acre **park** (📞707-937-5804; www.parks.ca.gov; 8001 N Hwy 1, Little River; per car $8; ⏰8am-9pm; P) draws beachcombers, divers and kayakers to its easy-access beach, and hikers to its pygmy forest. The latter is a unique and precious place, where acidic soil and an impenetrable layer of hardpan have created a miniature forest of decades-old trees. You can reach the forest on the moderate 3.5-mile Fern Canyon Scenic Trail, which crosses back and forth over Little River and past the Cabbage Patch, a bog of skunk cabbage that's rich with wildlife. The **visitor center** (📞707-937-4016; http://mendoparks.org/van-damme-state-park; Park

Rd; ⏰hours vary) has nature exhibits and programs.

📖 p137

The Drive » A short 2-mile drive north along Hwy 1 brings you to the bridge over the Big River. Just before the bridge, take a right on Comptche Ukiah Rd.

5 Big River

A lazy paddle up the Big River is a chance to get an intimate look at the border between land and sea – a place where otters, sea lions and majestic blue herons keep you company as you drift silently by. Although the area near the mouth of the river is an excellent place to watch the waves or catch the sunset, more adventurous travelers can check in at **Catch A Canoe & Bicycles, Too!** (📞707-937-0273; www.catchacanoe.com; Stanford Inn by the Sea, 44850 Comptche-Ukiah Rd; 3hr kayak, canoe or bicycle rental adult/child $28/14; ⏰9am-5pm; 🚲), a friendly riverside outfit that rents bikes, kayaks and canoes (including redwood outriggers) for trips up the 8-mile Big River tidal estuary, the longest undeveloped estuary in Northern California. Years of conservation efforts have protected this area from highways or buildings. Bring a picnic and a camera to enjoy the marshes, log-strewn beaches, abundant wildlife and

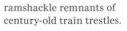

ramshackle remnants of century-old train trestles.

The Drive » The next stop, Mendocino, is just north of the bridge over the Big River.

TRIP HIGHLIGHT

6 Mendocino

Perched on a gorgeous headland, Mendocino is the North Coast's salt-washed gem, with B&Bs and rose gardens, white picket fences and New England–style redwood water towers. Bay Area weekenders walk along the headland among berry bramble and wildflowers, where

Mendocino Ford House Museum

cypress trees stand over dizzying cliffs. A stroll through this dreamy little village is a highlight of a trip through the region.

To get a sense for the village's thriving art scene, drop in at the **Mendocino Art Center** (☎800-653-3328, 707-937-5818; www.mendocinoart center.org; 45200 Little Lake St; ⊙10am-5pm Apr-Oct, to 4pm Tue-Sat Nov-Mar), a hub for visual, musical and theatrical arts. The center is also home to the **Mendocino Theatre Company** (http://mendocino theatre.org), which stages contemporary plays in the 81-seat Helen Schoeni Theatre.

The town itself is loaded with galleries, all of which host openings on the second Saturday evening of the month, when doors are thrown open to strolling connoisseurs of art and wine, and Mendocino buzzes with life. Of course, the natural setting here is a work of art itself. The spectacular **Mendocino Headlands State Park** (☎707-937-5804; www.parks.ca.gov) surrounds the village, with trails crisscross-ing the bluffs and rocky coves. Ask at the **Ford House Museum & Visitor Center** (☎707-537-5397; http://mendoparks.org; 45035 Main St; ⊙11am-4pm) about guided weekend walks, including spring wildflower walks and whale-watching jaunts.

✗ ⊨ p137

The Drive » Just south of town, turn inland at Comptche Ukiah Rd. It will make a loop taking you back toward the trip's beginning. All the turns make the next 30 miles eastbound slow going, but the views are impressive.

TOP ANDERSON VALLEY WINERIES

The valley's cool nights yield high-acid, fruit-forward, food-friendly wines. Pinot Noir, Chardonnay, Gewürtztraminer and Riesling grapes flourish.

Most **Anderson Valley wineries** (www.avwines.com) sit outside Philo. Many are family-owned and offer tastings, and some give tours. The following are particularly noteworthy:

Navarro Vineyards (☏800-537-9463, 707-895-3686; www.navarrowine.com; 5601 Hwy 128, Philo; ☺9am-6pm, to 5pm Nov-Mar; P) The best option with award-winning Pinot Noir and dry Gewürtzraminer, twice-daily tours (reservations accepted) and picnicking.

Husch Vineyards (☏707-462-5370, 800-554-8724; www.huschvineyards.com; 4400 Hwy 128, Philo; ☺10am-6pm, to 5pm Nov-Mar; P) The oldest vineyard in the valley serves exquisite tastings inside a rose-covered cottage.

Bink Wines (☏707-895-2940; http://binkwines.com; 9000 Hwy 128, Philo; ☺11am-5pm Wed-Mon; P) Small-batch artisanal wines that get rave reviews are poured inside the Madrones complex.

❼ Montgomery Woods State Natural Reserve

Two miles west of Orr, this 2743-acre **park** (☏707-937-5804; www.parks.ca.gov; 15825 Orr Springs Rd; P) protects five old-growth redwood groves, and some of the best groves within a day's drive from San Francisco. A 2-mile loop trail crosses the creek, winding through the serene groves, starting near the picnic tables and toilets. It's out of the way, so visitors are likely to have it mostly to themselves. The trees here are impressive – some are up to 14ft in diameter – but remember to admire them from the trail, both to protect the tree's root systems and to protect yourself from poison oak, which is all over the park.

The Drive ›› Continue 2 miles more east on Comptche Ukiah Rd (which may be called Orr Springs Rd on some maps) to reach Orr Hot Springs.

TRIP HIGHLIGHT

❽ Orr Hot Springs

After all the hiking, canoeing and beach-combing, a soak in the thermal waters of this rustic resort (p137) is heavenly, the ultimate zen-out to end the journey. While it's not for the bashful, the clothing-optional resort is beloved by locals, back-to-the-land hipsters, backpackers and liberal-minded tourists. Still, you don't have to let it all hang out to enjoy Orr Hot Springs. The place has private tubs; a sauna; a spring-fed, rock-bottomed swimming pool; a steam room; massage; and lovely, slightly shaggy gardens. Soaking in the rooftop stargazing tubs on a clear night is magical. Reservations are almost always necessary, even for day visits.

🛏 p137

Eating & Sleeping

Boonville ❷

✕ Table 128   Californian $$

(☎707-895-2210; www.boonvillehotel.com; 14050 Hwy 128, Boonville; lunch mains $10-14, dinner $19-31; ☺dinner Thu-Mon Apr-Oct) Food-savvy travelers love the constantly changing New American menu here, featuring simple dishes done well, such as roasted chicken, grilled local lamb and cheesecake. Opening hours vary.

🛏 Boonville Hotel   Boutique Hotel $$$

(☎707-895-2210; www.boonvillehotel.com; 14050 Hwy 128, Boonville; d $195-395; P ☺ ❄ ☎) Decked out in a contemporary American-country style with sea-grass flooring, pastel colors and fine linens that would make Martha Stewart proud, this historic hotel's rooms and suites are safe for urbanites who refuse to abandon style just because they've gone to the country. Some accommodations have air-con.

Philo ❸

🛏 Philo Apple Farm   Cottage $$$

(☎707-895-2333; www.philoapplefarm.com; 18501 Greenwood Rd, Philo; d $250-300; P ☺) Set within the orchard, guests of bucolic **Philo Apple Farm** (☺10am-6pm; P 🖐) choose from four exquisite cottages, each built with reclaimed materials. With bright, airy spaces, polished plank floors, simple furnishings and views of the surrounding trees, each one is an absolute dream.

Van Damme State Park ❹

🛏 Van Damme State Park Campgrounds   Campground $

(☎800-444-7275; www.reserveamerica.com; tent & RV sites $25-35; 🖐 ☎) Great for families, the main campground has lots of space and coin-operated hot showers. Some sites are just off Hwy 1, while others are in a meadow. Nine environmental campsites lie a 2-mile hike or bike ride up Fern Canyon.

Mendocino ❻

✕ Café Beaujolais   Californian $$$

(☎707-937-5614; http://cafebeaujolais.com; 961 Ukiah St; lunch mains $10-18, dinner $23-38; ☺11:30am-2:30pm Wed-Sun, dinner from 5:30pm daily) Mendocino's iconic, beloved country-Cal–French restaurant occupies an 1893 farmhouse restyled into a monochromatic urban-chic dining room. The refined, inspired cooking draws diners from San Francisco, who make this the centerpiece of their trip.

🛏 Andiron Seaside Inn & Cabins   Cabin $$

(☎800-955-6478, 707-937-1543; http://theandiron.com; 6051 N Hwy 1, Little River; d $109-299; P ☺ ☎ 🐾) Styled with hip vintage decor, this cluster of 1950s roadside cottages is a refreshingly playful option amid the cabbage-rose and lace aesthetic of Mendocino. Each cabin houses two rooms with complementing themes: 'Read' has old books and comfy vintage chairs while the adjoining 'Write' features a huge chalkboard and a ribbon typewriter.

🛏 MacCallum House Inn   B&B $$

(☎707-937-0289, 800-609-0492; www.maccallumhouse.com; 45020 Albion St; r & cottages from $149, water-tower ste $259-359; P ☺ @ ☎ 🐾) The finest B&B option in town with gardens in a riot of color. There are cheerful cottages, and a modern luxury home, but the most memorable space is within one of Mendocino's iconic water towers – living quarters fill the ground floor, a sauna is on the 2nd and there's a view of the coast from the top.

Orr Hot Springs ❽

🛏 Orr Hot Springs   Cabin, Campground $$

(☎707-462-6277; www.orrhotsprings.org; 13201 Orr Springs Rd, Ukiah; tent site per adult/child $70/25, r & yurt $210, cottage $280; P ☺ 🐾) Elegantly rustic rooms are a good match for this earthy **spa** (day-use adult/child $30/25; ☺by appointment 10am-10pm). Accommodations include use of the spa and communal kitchen, and some share bathrooms; cottages have their own kitchens.

Lost Coast & Southern Redwoods

11

Get lost along the empty shores of this pristine coastal area, then cruise under the ancient trees of the Avenue of the Giants, putting the charms of NorCal center stage.

TRIP HIGHLIGHTS

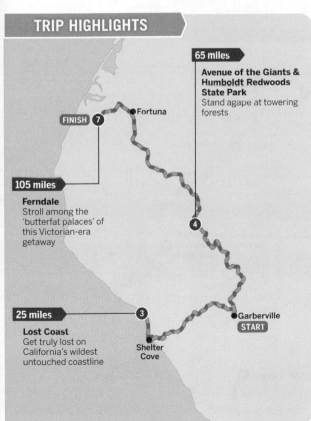

65 miles
Avenue of the Giants & Humboldt Redwoods State Park
Stand agape at towering forests

FINISH **7**

Fortuna

105 miles
Ferndale
Stroll among the 'butterfat palaces' of this Victorian-era getaway

4

25 miles
Lost Coast
Get truly lost on California's wildest untouched coastline

3

Shelter Cove

Garberville
START

3–4 DAYS
105 MILES / 170KM

GREAT FOR...

BEST TIME TO GO
May to August, when the temperamental weather is most manageable.

ESSENTIAL PHOTO
Hugging a redwood tree along the Avenue of the Giants.

BEST HIKE
Hiking out to Needle Rock on the Lost Coast to see what California's unspoiled coast used to look like.

Ferndale Victorian architecture adorns this small city

139

11 Lost Coast & Southern Redwoods

With its secluded trails and pristine beaches, the gorgeous 'Lost Coast' is one of the state's most untouched coastal areas and exciting hiking adventures. The region became 'lost' when the state highway system bypassed it early in the 20th century and it has since developed an outsider culture of political radicals, marijuana farmers and nature lovers. Inland, take a magical drive through the big trees of California's largest redwood park.

① Garberville

The first stop on a Lost Coast romp is scrappy little Garberville, the first town beyond the so-called 'Redwood Curtain' of Humboldt County. There's an uneasy relationship between the old-guard loggers and the hippies, many of whom came in the 1970s to grow marijuana after the feds chased them out of Santa Cruz. A visit to the three-block downtown should include browsing at **Brown's Sporting Goods** (☎707-923-2533;

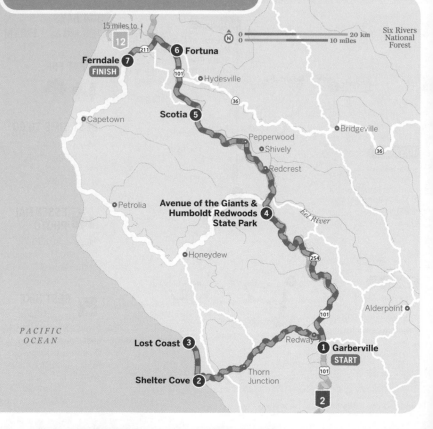

15 miles to 12

211

Ferndale ⑦ FINISH

⑥ **Fortuna**

101 ● Hydesville

36

● Capetown

Scotia ⑤

● Bridgeville

Pepperwood
● Shively
36

● Redcrest

Avenue of the Giants & Humboldt Redwoods State Park ④

Eel River

● Petrolia

● Honeydew

254

101

● Alderpoint

PACIFIC OCEAN

Lost Coast ③

Redway

① **Garberville** START

101

Shelter Cove ②

Thorn Junction

2

N 0 — 20 km / 0 — 10 miles

Six Rivers National Forest

797 Redwood Dr; ⏱9am-6pm Mon-Fri, to 5pm Sat). The Brown family has run the place for a couple generations and has encyclopedic knowledge of activities in the area. Those with extra time can spend part of the day south at **Benbow Lake State Recreation Area** (☎summer 707-923-3238, winter 707-923-3318; www.parks.ca.gov; Lake Benbow Dr, off Hwy 101; per car $8; P 🛱). The Eel River cuts through the park, which has a picnic area, hiking trails, and riverside sunbathing.

✕ 🛏 p145

The Drive » Take it easy and in a low gear on the steep and twisting drive down Briceland Thorn Rd (which becomes Shelter Cove Rd eventually) – driving the 21

LINK YOUR TRIP

12 Northern Redwood Coast

Link this trip with a jaunt to the forests of the Redwood National Park by continuing north past Ferndale on Hwy 101.

2 Pacific Coast Highways

Keep riding along the Pacific edge of California, either north toward Redwood National Park or south all the way to San Diego.

miles from Redway to Shelter Cove can be a challenge. Best to heed the 'No Trespassing' signs on this part of the drive, as the local marijuana farmers don't take kindly to strangers.

---

2 Shelter Cove

At the end of the road – and what seems like the end of the earth! – is the isolated community of Shelter Cove, the gateway to the Lost Coast. The tiny encampment of restaurants and shops sometimes seems equally populated by humans and Roosevelt elk. Although primarily used as a launching point for the nearby wilds, it makes a relaxing destination in its own right. From town, scan the water for migrating gray whales (look for mothers and their calves in early spring) and explore tidepools teeming with crabs, snails, sea stars and sponges; locals even spot an octopus on occasion.

✕ 🛏 p145

The Drive » There are trailheads for exploring the Lost Coast Trail both north and south of town. That's where the drive pauses; the trail has to be done on foot.

TRIP HIGHLIGHT

3 Lost Coast

The North Coast's superlative backpacking destination is a rugged, mystifying stretch of coast with trails crossing coastal peaks and

volcanic black-sand beaches. The King Range boldly rises 4000ft within 3 miles of the coast, which became 'lost' when the state's highway system deemed the region impassable in the early 20th century.

Made up of Sinkyone Wilderness State Park and the Kings Range National Conservation Area, the best way to explore is on a multiday hike. Leaving from Shelter Cove, a three-day hike north on the **Lost Coast Trail** ends at the mouth of the Mattole River. Equally challenging and rewarding, it passes the abandoned **Punta Gorda Lighthouse** near the end. You can arrange shuttle service back to your car through **Lost Coast Adventure Tours** (☎707-986-9895; http://lostcoastadventures.com). From Shelter Cove, you can take a day hike to **Black Sand Beach**, or overnight at **Needle Rock Campground** (☎/07-986-7711; www.parks.ca.gov; Country Road 435, off Briceland Rd; tent sites $35; P), about 9 miles south of the Hidden Valley Trailhead. The **visitor center** (☎707-986-7711; www.parks.ca.gov; County Rd 435, off Briceland Rd; per car $6; ⏱hours vary) there affords gorgeous coastal views.

The Drive » Retrace the twisting drive back to Garberville, then continue north on Hwy 101. Exit Hwy 101 when you see the 'Avenue of the Giants' sign, 6 miles north

TOP TIP:
ACCESSING THE
LOST COAST

Hikers who wish to hike the entirety of the Lost Coast often go from north to south in order to avoid northerly winds. Many hikers start at the Mattole Campground, just south of Petrolia, which is on the northern border of the Kings Range.

The Drive » From the Avenue of the Giants, follow signs to the groves in the park. You'll pass a number of small villages along the way that are ramshackle collections of mid-20th-century tourist traps, woodsy lodges and huge stands of trees. Avenue of the Giants ends at Hwy 101 near Pepperwood, from where it's a 5-mile drive north to Scotia.

of Garberville, near Phillipsville. This is the heart of the big-tree country.

TRIP HIGHLIGHT

④ Avenue of the Giants & Humboldt Redwoods State Park

The incredible, 32-mile, two-lane stretch of highway known as the **Avenue of the Giants** is one of the most justifiably celebrated drives in California, and a place where travelers stand with jaws agape and necks craned upward at the canopy. The route connects a number of small towns with mid-20th-century motels, diners serving 'lumberjack' meals and pull-offs parked with Harleys. Visitors would be remiss to drive right past these majestic groves along the Avenue without stopping at the **California Federation of Women's Clubs Grove**, home to an interesting four-sided hearth designed by renowned architect Julia Morgan, and the **Founders Grove**, where the 370ft **Dyerville Giant** was

knocked down in 1991 by another falling tree.

Much of the Avenue of the Giants snakes in and out of **Humboldt Redwoods State Park** (📞707-946-2409; www.parks.ca.gov; Hwy 101; [P] [🚻]). At 53,000 acres – 17,000 of which are old-growth – it boasts three-quarters of the world's tallest 100 trees. Tree huggers take note: these groves rival (and may surpass) those in Redwood National Park. The 100-plus miles of trails can be taken on foot, horse or bike and range in difficulty from the kid-friendly **Drury-Chaney Loop Trail** (with thimble berry picking in summer) to the rugged **Grasshopper Peak Trail**, which climbs to a fire lookout (3379ft). The primeval **Rockefeller Forest**, just over a mile west of the Avenue via Mattole Rd, is one of the park's most pristine stands. It's the world's largest remaining contiguous old-growth redwood forest.

🍴 🛏 p145

⑤ Scotia

For years, Scotia was California's last 'company town,' entirely owned and operated by the Pacific Lumber Company, which built cookie-cutter houses and had an open contempt for long-haired outsiders who liked to get between their saws and the big trees. The company went belly up in 2007, but the town is still in operation (and feels a bit like a scene from *The Twilight Zone*). A history of the town awaits visitors at the **Scotia Museum & Visitor Center** (📞707-764-4211; www.townofscotia.com; 122 Main St; ⏰ museum 8am-4pm Mon-Fri late May-early Sep, fisheries exhibit 8am-4:30pm Mon-Fri, also Sat late May-early Sep; [P]), at the town's southern end. But the real highlight of a stop is the museum's remarkably informative fisheries exhibit, which houses the largest freshwater aquarium on the North Coast.

The Drive » Follow Hwy 101 for almost 8 miles north to exit 687 for Kenmar Rd. At the south end of the town in Fortuna, turn right onto Alamar Way.

Avenue of the Giants

⑥ Fortuna

The penultimate stop is a cold, refreshing pint of beer at **Eel River Brewing Company** (📞702-725-2739; http://eelriverbrewing.com; 1777 Alamar Way, Fortuna; ⊙11am-11pm) in Fortuna. This place is completely in step with its amazing natural surroundings – it was the USA's first certified organic brewery and uses 100% renewable energy (there's a bit of irony in the fact that most of their beer is brewed in an old redwood mill that formerly belonged to the Pacific Lumber Company). The breezy beer garden and excellent burgers make it an ideal pit stop.

The Drive » Back on Hwy 101, go just over 2 miles north and take exit 691 for Fernbridge/Ferndale. Follow Hwy 211 for 5 miles southwest past rolling dairy farms to Ferndale.

TRIP HIGHLIGHT

⑦ Ferndale

The trip through the Lost Coast ends at one of the region's most charming towns, stuffed with impeccable Victorians – known locally as 'butterfat palaces' because of the dairy wealth that built them. The entire town is a state historical landmark with several nationally registered historic sites. Main St offers galleries, old-world emporiums and soda fountains and – of course – ice-cream parlors. To end the trip with whimsy, show up over Memorial Day weekend to see the fanciful, astounding, human-powered contraptions of the annual **Kinetic Grand Championship** (📞707-786-3443; www.kineticgrand championship.com; 🚴) race from Arcata to Ferndale. Shaped like giant fish and UFOs, these colorful piles of junk propel racers over roads, water and marsh in a three-day event.

🍴 🛏 p145

Eating & Sleeping

Garberville ❶

✕ Woodrose Café
Breakfast, American $

(☎707-923-3191; www.woodrosecafe.com; 911 Redwood Dr; mains $9-18; ⊗8am-2pm; 🌱 🐶) Garberville's beloved cafe serves organic omelets, veggie scrambles and buckwheat pancakes with *real* maple syrup in a cozy room. Lunch brings crunchy salads, sandwiches with all-natural meats and good burritos. Plenty of gluten-free options.

🛏 Benbow Historic Inn
Historic Hotel $$$

(☎800-355-3301, 707-923-2124; www.benbowinn.com; 445 Lake Benbow Dr, Garberville; d $160-455; P ⊛ ❄ 🤶 🐕 🐶) This inn is a monument to 1920s rustic elegance; the Redwood Empire's first luxury resort is a national historic landmark. Hollywood's elite once frolicked in the Tudor-style resort's lobby, where you can play chess by the crackling fire, and enjoy complimentary afternoon tea and scones.

Shelter Cove ❷

✕ Cove Restaurant
American $$$

(☎707-986-1197; http://theshelter cove restaurant.com; 10 Seal Ct; mains $10-44; ⊗5-9pm Thu-Sun) The first-choice place to eat, this place has everything from artichoke-mushroom lasagna to New York steaks.

🛏 Tides Inn
Hotel $$

(☎888-998-4337, 707-986-7900; www.sheltercovetidesinn.com; 59 Surf Pt; r $175, ste with kitchen $195-390; P ⊛ 🤶) Perched above tidepools teeming with starfish and sea urchins, the squeaky-clean rooms here offer excellent views (go for the mini suites on the 3rd floor).

Avenue of the Giants & Humboldt Redwoods State Park ❹

✕ Chimney Tree
American $

(☎707-923-2265; 1111 Avenue of the Giants, Phillipsville; mains $9-14; ⊗11am-7pm Thu-Sun;

🐶) If you're just passing through and want something quick, come here. It raises its own grass-fed beef. Alas, the fries are frozen, but those burgers...mmm-mmm!

🛏 Humboldt Redwoods State Park Campgrounds
Campground $

(☎information 707-946-2263, reservations 800-444-7275; www.reserveamerica.com; tent & RV sites $20-35; P 🐕) The park runs three seasonal campgrounds with hot showers, one environmental camp, a hike/bike camp and primitive trail camps. Of the developed spots, **Burlington Campground** is beside the visitor center and near a number of trailheads; **Hidden Springs Campground** is 5 miles south along Avenue of the Giants; and **Albee Creek Campground** is on Mattole Rd past Rockefeller Forest.

🛏 Miranda Gardens Resort
Resort $$

(☎707-943-3011; www.mirandagardens.com; 6766 Avenue of the Giants, Miranda; cottages $125-300; P ⊛ 🐕 🐶) The best indoor stay along the avenue. The cozy, dark, slightly rustic cottages have redwood paneling, some with fireplaces and kitchens, and are spotlessly clean. The grounds – replete with outdoor ping pong, a seasonal swimming pool and a play area for kids amid swaying redwoods – have wholesome appeal for families.

Ferndale ❼

✕ Lost Coast Cafe
Vegetarian $

(☎707-786-5330; 468 Main St; mains $7-10; ⊗10:30am-4pm Thu-Mon; 🌱) Step into a homey kitchen, where the soups, sandwiches, salads and baked goods are easily the best vegetarian choices north of Fort Bragg. Organic coffee is on the house. Cash only.

🛏 Francis Creek Inn
Motel $

(☎707-786-9611; www.franciscreekinn.com; 577 Main St; r from $90; P ⊛ 🤶) White picket balconies stand in front of this sweet little downtown motel, which is family owned and operated (you check in at the Red Front convenience store, right around the corner). Spartan rooms are basic, clean and furnished simply, and the value is outstanding.

Northern Redwood Coast

12

Hug a 700-year-old tree, stroll moody coastal bluffs and drop in on roadside attractions of yesteryear on this trip through verdant redwood parks and personality-packed villages.

TRIP HIGHLIGHTS

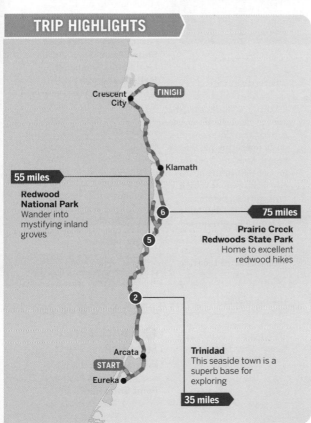

3–4 DAYS
150 MILES / 240KM

GREAT FOR...

BEST TIME TO GO

April to October for usually clear skies and the region's warmest weather.

ESSENTIAL PHOTO

Misty redwoods clinging to rocky Pacific cliffs at Del Norte Coast Redwoods State Park.

BEST SCENIC DRIVE

Howland Hill Rd through dense old-growth redwood forests.

Crescent City

FINISH

Klamath

55 miles

Redwood National Park
Wander into mystifying inland groves

6

5

75 miles

Prairie Creek Redwoods State Park
Home to excellent redwood hikes

2

Arcata

START

Eureka

Trinidad
This seaside town is a superb base for exploring

35 miles

Jedediah Smith Redwoods State Park A hiker gazes up at a giant tree

12 Northern Redwood Coast

This trip may have been charted in the glory days of the mid-20th-century American road trip – roadside attractions include a giant Paul Bunyan statue, drive-through trees and greasy burger stands – but that might as well be yesterday in this land of towering, mystical, ancient redwood forests. Curving roads and misty trails bring visitors to lush, spectacular natural wonders that are unlike any other place on earth. Prepare to be impressed.

❶ Samoa Peninsula

Even though this trip is about misty primeval forest, the beginning is a study of opposites: the grassy dunes and windswept beaches of the 10-mile long Samoa Peninsula. At the peninsula's south end is **Samoa Dunes Recreation Area** (☎707-825-2300; www.blm. gov; ☉sunrise-sunset; **P**), part of a 34-mile-long dune system that's the largest in Northern California. While it's great for picnicking or fishing, the wildlife viewing is excellent.

Or, leave the landlubbers behind and take a **Harbor Cruise** (☎707-445-1910; www.humboldtbay maritimemuseum.com; narrated cruise adult/child $18/10; ☉schedules vary; ⊕) aboard the 1910 *Madaket,* America's oldest continuously operating passenger vessel. Leaving from the foot of C St in the nearby city of Eureka, it ferried mill workers before the Samoa Bridge was built in 1972. The $10 sunset cocktail cruise serves drinks from the smallest licensed bar in the state.

🍴 p153

The Drive ≫ Head north on Hwy 101 from Eureka (see Eating & Sleeping options, p153), passing myriad views of Humboldt Bay. Fifteen miles north of Arcata, take the first Trinidad exit. Note that the corridor between Eureka and Arcata is a closely watched safety corridor (aka speed trap).

TRIP HIGHLIGHT

❷ Trinidad

Perched on an ocean bluff, cheery Trinidad somehow manages an off-the-beaten-path feel despite a constant flow of visitors. The free town map at the information kiosk will help you navigate the town's cute little shops and several fantastic hiking trails, most notably the **Trinidad Head Trail** with superb coastal views and excellent whale-watching (December to April). If the weather is nice, stroll the exceptionally beautiful cove at **Trinidad State Beach**; if not, make for the **HSU Telonicher Marine Laboratory** (☎707-826-3671; www.humboldt.edu/marinelab; 570 Ewing St; admission $1; ☉9am-4:30pm Mon-Fri year-round, also 10am-5pm Sat & Sun mid-Sep–mid-May; ⊕). It has a touch tank, several aquariums (look for the giant Pacific octopus), an enormous whale jaw and a cool three-dimensional map of the ocean floor.

🍴 🛏 p153

The Drive ≫ Head back north of town on Patrick's Point Dr to hug the shore for just over 5 miles.

❸ Patrick's Point State Park

Coastal bluffs jut out to sea at 640-acre **Patrick's Point State Park** (☎707-677-3570; www.parks.ca.gov;

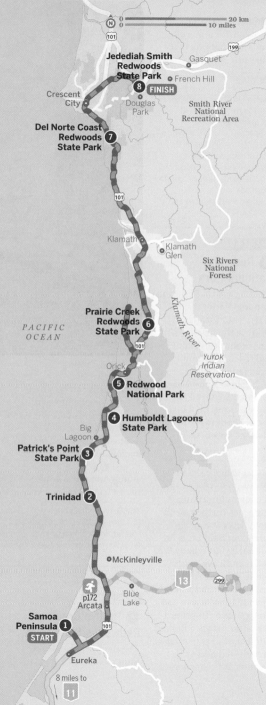

4150 Patrick's Point Dr; per car $8; P 🚻) where sandy beaches abut rocky headlands. Easy access to dramatic coastal bluffs makes this a best bet for families, but any age will find a feast for the senses as they climb rock formations, search for breaching whales, carefully navigate tidepools and listen to barking sea lions and singing birds. The park also has **Sumêg**, an authentic reproduction of a Yurok village, with hand-hewn redwood buildings. In the native plant garden you'll find species for making traditional baskets and medicines. The 2-mile **Rim Trail**, a former Yurok trail around the bluffs, circles the point with access to huge rocky outcrops. Don't miss

LINK YOUR TRIP

11 Lost Coast & Southern Redwoods

Head south on Hwy 101 from Arcata for more redwood wonders and the untouched Lost Coast, bringing on the North Coast's best hiking adventures.

13 Trinity Scenic Byway

Cut inland on Hwy 299 from Arcata and get lost in the wild country of California's northern mountains.

Wedding Rock, one of the park's most romantic spots, or **Agate Beach**, where lucky visitors spot (but don't take, since that's illegal) bits of jade and sea-polished agate.

🛏 p153

The Drive ≫ Make your way back out to Hwy 101 through thick stands of redwoods. North another 5 minutes will bring you to the sudden clearing of Big Lagoon, part of Humboldt Lagoons State Park. Continue 6 more miles north to the visitor center.

❹ Humboldt Lagoons State Park

Stretching out for miles along the coast, Humboldt Lagoons State Park has long, sandy beaches and a string of coastal lagoons. **Big Lagoon** and prettier **Stone Lagoon** are both excellent for kayaking and bird-watching. Sunsets are spectacular, with no structures in sight. At the Stone Lagoon Visitor Center, on Hwy 101, there are restrooms and a bulletin board displaying information. Just south of Stone Lagoon, tiny **Dry Lagoon** (a freshwater marsh) has a fantastic day hike. Park at Dry Lagoon's picnic area and hike north on the unmarked trail to Stone Lagoon; the trail skirts the southwestern shore and ends up at the ocean, passing through woods and marshland rich with

wildlife. Mostly flat, it's about 2.5 miles one way – and nobody takes it because it's unmarked.

🛏 p153

The Drive ≫ Keep driving north on Hwy 101. Now, at last, you'll start to lose all perspective among the world's tallest trees. This is likely the most scenic part of the entire trip; you'll emerge from curvy two-lane roads through redwood groves to stunning mist-shrouded shores dotted with rocky islets.

TRIP HIGHLIGHT

❺ Redwood National Park

Heading north, **Redwood National Park** (📞707-465-7335; www.nps.gov/redw; 🅿 ♿) is the first park in the patchwork of state and federally administered lands under the umbrella of Redwood National & State Parks. After picking up a map at the **Thomas H Kuchel Visitor Center** (📞707-465-7765; www.nps.gov/redw; Hwy 101, Orick; ⏰9am-5pm Apr-Oct, to 4pm Nov-Mar; ♿), you'll have a suite of choices for hiking. A few miles further north along Hwy 101, a trip inland on Bald Hills Rd will take you to **Lady Bird Johnson Grove**, with its 1-mile kid-friendly loop trail, or get you lost in the secluded serenity of **Tall Trees Grove**. To protect the latter grove, a limited number of cars per day are allowed access; get permits at the visitor

GARY CRABBE / AGEFOTOSTOCK ©

center. This can be a half-day trip itself, but you're well rewarded after the challenging approach (a 6-mile rumble on an old logging road behind a locked gate, then a moderately strenuous 4-mile round-trip hike).

The Drive ≫ Back on Hwy 101, less than 2 miles north of Bald Hills Rd, turn left onto Davison Rd, which trundles for 7 miles (mostly unpaved) out to Gold Bluffs Beach.

TRIP HIGHLIGHT

❻ Prairie Creek Redwoods State Park

The short stroll to **Gold Bluffs Beach** will lead

Prairie Creek Redwoods State Park Fern Canyon

you to the best spot for a picnic. Past the campground, you can take a longer hike beyond the end of the road into **Fern Canyon**, whose 60ft, fern-covered, sheer rock walls are seen in *The Lost World: Jurassic Park*. This is one of the most photographed spots on the North Coast – damp and lush, all emerald green – and totally worth getting your toes wet to see.

Back on Hwy 101, head two miles further north and exit onto the 8-mile **Newton B Drury Scenic Parkway**, which runs parallel to the highway through magnificent, untouched ancient redwood forests. Family-friendly nature trails branch off from roadside pullouts, including the wheelchair-accessible Big Tree Wayside, and also start outside the **Prairie Creek Redwoods State Park Visitor Center** (📞707-488-2039; www.parks. ca.gov; Newton B Drury Scenic Pkwy; ⏰9am-5pm May-Sep, to 4pm Wed-Sun Oct-Apr; 👪), including the Revelation Trail for visually impaired visitors.

The Drive ≫ Follow the winding Newton B Drury Scenic Parkway through beautiful inland forests with views of the east and its layers of ridges and valleys. On returning to Hwy 101, head north to Klamath (see Sleeping option, p153), with its bear bridge. Del Norte Coast Redwoods State Park is just a few minutes further north.

- - - - - - - - - - -

7 Del Norte Coast Redwoods State Park
Marked by steep canyons and dense woods, half the 6400 acres of this **park** (📞707 465 7335; www. parks.ca.gov; per car $8; P) are virgin redwood forest, crisscrossed by 15 miles of hiking trails. Even the most cynical of redwood-watchers can't help but be moved.

DRIVE-THRU TREES & GONDOLA RIDES

With lots of kitschy mid-20th-century appeal, the following destinations are a throwback to those bygone days of the great American road trip.

Trees of Mystery (☎800-638-3389, 707-482-2251; www.treesofmystery.net; 15500 Hwy 101; museum free, gondola adult/child $15/8; ☺8:30am-6:30pm Jun-Aug, 9am-6pm Sep & Oct, 9:30am-4:30pm Nov-May; P♿) In Klamath, it's hard to miss the giant statues of Paul Bunyan and Babe the Blue Ox towering over the parking lot at this shameless, if lovable, tourist trap. It has a gondola running through the redwood canopy.

Tour Thru Tree (430 Hwy 169; per car $5; ☺hours vary; P♿) In Klamath, squeeze through a tree and check out the emus.

Drive-Thru Tree Park (☎707-925-6464; www.drivethrutree.com; 67402 Drive Thru Tree Road; per car $5; ☺8:30am-9pm Jun-Aug, closes earlier Sep-May; P♿) Fold in your mirrors and inch forward, then cool off in the über-kitschy gift shop, in Leggett.

Shrine Drive Thru Tree (☎707-943-1975; 13078 Avenue of the Giants, Myers Flat; per car $6; ☺sunrise-sunset Apr-Oct; ♿) Look up to the sky as you roll through, on the Avenue of the Giants in Myers Flat. It's the least impressive of the three drive-thru trees.

Tall trees cling precipitously to canyon walls that drop to the rocky, timber-strewn coastline. It's almost impossible to get to the water, except via gorgeous but steep **Damnation Creek Trail** or **Footsteps Rock Trail**. The former may be only 4 miles long, but the 1100-ft elevation change and cliffside redwoods make it the park's best hike (temporarily closed since mid-2015). The trailhead is at an unmarked parking pull-out along Hwy 101 near mile marker 16.

The Drive » Leaving Del Norte Coast Redwoods State Park and continuing on Hwy 101, you'll enter dreary little Crescent City (see Eating & Sleeping options, p153), a fine enough place to gas up or grab a bite, but not worth stopping

long. About 4 miles northeast of town, Hwy 199 splits off from Hwy 101; follow it northeast for 6 miles to Hiouchi.

- - - - - - - - - - - - -

❽ Jedediah Smith Redwoods State Park

The final stop on the trip is loaded with worthy superlatives – the northernmost park has the densest population of redwoods and the last natural undammed, free-flowing river in California, the sparkling Smith. All in all **Jedediah Smith Redwoods State Park** (☎707-465-7335; www.parks.ca.gov; Hwy 199, Hiouchi; per car $8; ☺sunrise-sunset; P♿) is a jewel. The redwood stands here are so dense that few hiking trails penetrate the park, so drive the outstanding 10-mile **Howland Hill Rd**, which cuts through otherwise inaccessible areas, heading back toward Crescent City. It's a rough, unpaved road, and it can close if there are fallen trees or washouts, but you'll feel as if you're visiting from Lilliput as you cruise under the gargantuan trunks. To spend the night, reserve a site at the park's fabulous campground tucked along the banks of the Smith River.

Eating & Sleeping

Samoa Peninsula ❶

✖ Samoa Cookhouse American $

(☎707-442-1659; www.samoacookhouse.net; 908 Vance Ave; all-you-can-eat meals per adult $13-17, child $5-9; ⊙7am-3pm & 5-8pm; 🖮) On the Samoa Peninsula, the popular Samoa Cookhouse is the dining hall of an 1893 lumber camp.

Eureka

✖ Lost Coast Brewery
& Cafe Pub Food $

(☎707-445-4480; www.lostcoast.com; 617 4th St; mains $10-18; ⊙11am-10pm Sun-Thu, to 11pm Fri & Sat; 🛜🖮) The roster of the regular brews at Eureka's colorful brewery might not knock the socks off a serious beer snob (and can't hold a candle to some others on the North Coast).

Trinidad ❷

✖ Larrupin Cafe Californian $$$

(☎707-677-0230; www.thelarrupin.com; 1658 Patrick's Point Dr; mains $22-42; ⊙5-9pm) Everybody loves Larrupin, where Moroccan rugs, chocolate-brown walls, gravity-defying floral arrangements and deep-burgundy Oriental carpets create a moody atmosphere.

⮕ Trinidad Bay B&B B&B $$$

(☎707-677-0840; www.trinidadbaybnb.com; 560 Edwards St; r $200-350; 🅿️😊🛜) Opposite the lighthouse, this gorgeous light-filled Cape Cod–style home overlooks the harbor and Trinidad Head. Breakfast may be delivered to your uniquely styled room.

Patrick's Point State Park ❸

⮕ Patrick's Point State Park
Campgrounds Campground $

(☎information 707-677-3570, reservations 800-444-7275; www.reserveamerica.com; 4150 Patrick's Point Dr; tent & RV sites $35-45; 🅿️🐾)

Three well-tended campgrounds have coin-operated hot showers and clean bathrooms. Penn Creek and Abalone campgrounds are more sheltered than Agate Beach.

Humboldt Lagoons State Park ❹

⮕ Big Lagoon County Park
Campground Campground $

(☎707-445-7651; http://co.humboldt.ca.us; off Hwy 101; tent sites $20; 🅿️🐾) This county-run campground in a cypress grove beside Big Lagoon has first-come, first-served sites with flush toilets and cold water, but no showers.

Klamath

⮕ Historic Requa Inn Historic Hotel $$

(☎707-482-1425; www.requainn.com; 451 Requa Rd; r $119-199; 🅿️😊🛜) A woodsy country lodge on bluffs overlooking the mouth of the Klamath, the creaky and bright 1914 Requa Inn is a North Coast favorite and – even better – it's a carbon-neutral facility.

Crescent City

✖ Good Harvest Cafe American $

(☎707-465-6028; 575 Hwy 101 S; mains $7-16; ⊙7:30am-9pm Mon-Sat, from 8am Sun; 🖋️🖮) This popular local cafe is in a spacious location across from the harbor. It's got a bit of everything – all pretty good – from soups and sandwiches to full meals and smoothies.

⮕ Curly Redwood Lodge Motel $

(☎707-464-2137; www.curlyredwoodlodge.com; 701 Hwy 101 S; r $70-105; 🅿️😊❄️🛜) The motel is a marvel: it's entirely built and paneled from a single curly redwood tree which measured over 18ft thick in diameter. Progressively restored and polished into a gem of mid-20th-century kitsch, the inn is a delight for retro junkies. Rooms are clean, large and comfortable (request one away from the road). For truly modern accommodations, look elsewhere.

Trinity Scenic Byway

13

Cruising this secluded corner of California you'll pass majestic peaks, tranquil inland lakes and historic mountain towns, experiencing both rugged nature and plush hospitality.

TRIP HIGHLIGHTS

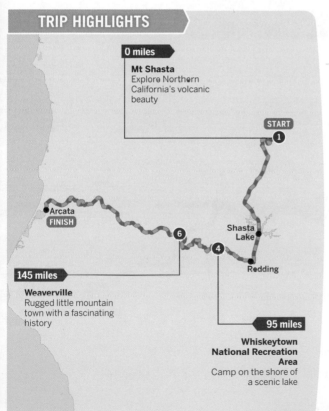

0 miles

Mt Shasta
Explore Northern California's volcanic beauty

START
1

Arcata
FINISH

6

Shasta Lake

4

Redding

145 miles

Weaverville
Rugged little mountain town with a fascinating history

95 miles

Whiskeytown National Recreation Area
Camp on the shore of a scenic lake

**3 DAYS
245 MILES / 395KM**

GREAT FOR...

BEST TIME TO GO
June through October, when the lakes and rivers are full and the air is crisp and clean.

ESSENTIAL PHOTO
Santiago Calatrava's futuristic Sundial Bridge.

BEST FOR FAMILIES
Lake Shasta Caverns admission includes a boat ride, wildlife-watching and a cave tour.

Mt Shasta A glimpse of the solitary peak

Trinity Scenic Byway

The back-to-landers, outdoorsy types and new-age escapists in this remote corner of Northern California proudly count the number of stoplights and fast-food joints in their counties on one hand. An epic cruise along the Trinity Scenic Byway takes visitors from one of California's most distinctive mountains to the Pacific shore, passing ample natural wonders and sophisticated small towns along the way.

TRIP HIGHLIGHT

❶ Mt Shasta

'When I first caught sight of it I was 50 miles away and afoot, alone and weary. Yet all my blood turned to wine, and I have not been weary since,' wrote naturalist John Muir in 1874 of **Mt Shasta** (☏530-926-4511; www.fs.fed.us/r5/shastatrinity; Everitt Memorial Hwy; 🅿 🚻). Though not California's highest (at 14,179ft it ranks fifth), the sight of this solitary peak is truly

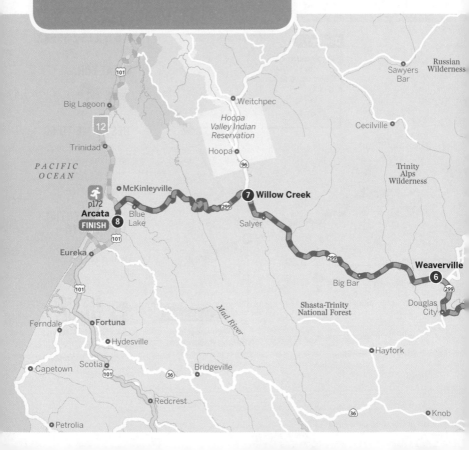

intoxicating. Start this trip near the top: you can drive almost all the way up via the Everitt Memorial Hwy (Hwy A10) to enjoy exquisite views any time of year. By the time you reach **Bunny Flat** (6860ft) you'll be gasping at the sights (and the thin air), but if the road is clear of snow continue the ascent for more amazing views. You'll see Lassen Peak to the south. Look west for a bird's-eye preview of the rest of this trip, towards the Marble Mountains and the green hills along the Trinity Scenic Byway. For information about hikes, contact the in-town **Mt Shasta Ranger Station** (✆530-926-4511; www.fs.usda.gov/stnf; 204 W Alma St; ⏱8am-4:30pm Mon-Fri), which issues permits and good advice.

🍴 🛏 p161, p169

The Drive » Follow Everitt Memorial Hwy back down the mountain. It'll take about 30 minutes to get down to Mt Shasta City, a new-agey town that's worth a look. Go south on I-5 for more than 40 miles to Shasta Lake.

❷ Shasta Lake

The largest reservoir in California, Shasta Lake has the state's biggest population of bald eagles, an endless network of hiking trails, and great fishing. On the north side, stop to tour the crystal-line caves of the **Lake Shasta Caverns** (✆530-238-2341, 800-795-2283; http://lakeshastacaverns.com; 20359 Shasta Caverns Rd, Lakehead; 2hr tour adult/child 3-15yr $26/15; ⏱tours every 30min 9am-4pm late May-early Sep; hourly 9am-3pm Apr-late May & early-late Sep; 10am, noon & 2pm Oct-Mar; P 🚻). Tours include a boat ride that's great for families (bring a sweater – it's chilly down there!). The **Shasta Dam visitors center** (✆530-275-4463; www.usbr.gov/mp/ncao/shasta-dam.html; 16349 Shasta

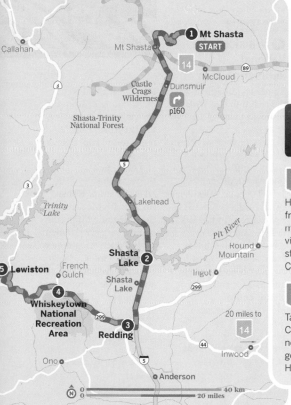

LINK YOUR TRIP

12 Northern Redwood Coast

Head north on Hwy 101 from Arcata to link this epic mountain journey with a visit to the proud redwood stands of the far North Coast.

14 Volcanic Legacy Scenic Byway

Take a trip around California's untouched northern volcanic wilds by going east of Redding on Hwy 44.

Dam Blvd; 😊 visitor center 8am-5pm, tours 9am, 11am, 1pm & 3pm; [P] [🚻]) to the south has maps of hiking trails and a picture-window view of the monstrous **Shasta Dam**. The colossal, 15-million-ton dam is second only in size to Hoover Dam in Nevada; its 487ft spillway is nearly three times as high as Niagara Falls. Woody Guthrie wrote 'This Land is Your Land' here. At the visitor center you can join a fascinating free guided tour of the structure's rumbling interior.

🛏 p161

The Drive ›› Retrace your path back to I-5 and head south about 9 miles to Redding.

❸ Redding

Redding's sprawl – malls, big-box stores and large housing developments – might be discordant with the north's natural wonders, but it's the launching point for the Trinity Scenic Byway, which starts west of town. Still, it's worth stopping for the **Turtle Bay Exploration Park** (📞800-887-8532; www.turtlebay.org; 844 Sundial Bridge Dr; adult/child $16/12, after 3:30pm $11/7; 😊9am-5pm Mon-Sat, from 10am Sun, closes 1hr earlier Nov–mid-Mar; 🚻). Situated on 300 acres, the complex has an art and natural-science museum with interactive exhibits for kids, extensive gardens, a butterfly conservatory

and a 22,000-gallon, walk-through river aquarium with regional aquatic life. Don't leave without a photo of the starkly futuristic **Sundial Bridge** that connects the park to the north bank of the Sacramento River and was designed by renowned Spanish architect Santiago Calatrava.

🍴 p161

The Drive ›› The banner stretch of the trip starts here: the Trinity Scenic Byway (Hwy 299) begins west of Redding and traces a winding path through the mountains to the Pacific Coast. Forests, mountain lakes, crumbling cabins and rushing rivers accompany the drive.

TRIP HIGHLIGHT

❹ Whiskeytown National Recreation Area

An old mining town lent the rich name to **Whiskeytown Lake** (📞530-242-3400; www.nps.gov/whis; off Hwy 299, Whiskeytown; 7-day pass per car $10; [P] [🚻]), a lovely, multi-use reservoir that was dedicated by John F Kennedy less than two months before his assassination. Today, folks descend on the lake's serene 36 miles of forested shoreline to camp, swim, sail, mountain bike and pan for gold. The **visitor center** (📞530-246-1225; www.nps.gov/whis; Hwy 299 at JFK Memorial Dr, Whiskeytown; 😊10am-4pm), on the northeast point of the lake, provides

information and free maps. The hike from the visitor center to roaring **Whiskeytown Falls** (3.4 miles round trip) follows a former logging road and is a quick trip. On the western side of the lake, the **Tower House Historic District** contains the El Dorado Mine ruins and the pioneer Camden House, open for summer tours. In winter, when the trees are bare, it's an atmospheric, quiet place to explore.

The Drive ›› Leaving Whiskeytown Lake, Hwy 299 enters more remote country – say goodbye to that cellphone service. About 10 miles west of

CHRISTIAN RICHARDS / EYEEM / GETTY IMAGES ©

Turtle Bay Exploration Park Crossing over Sundial Bridge

the lake the road becomes steep with white-knuckled turns and excellent lake vistas. Cut north on Trinity Dam Blvd for Lewiston.

- - - - - - - - - -

❺ Lewiston

Blink and you might miss Lewiston, a collection of buildings beside a rushing stretch of the Trinity River known for fishing. If you're passing through town, stop at the **Country Peddler** (4 Deadwood Rd; ⊙ hours vary), a drafty old barn filled with antiques that seem as if they have been plucked from some long-lost uncle's hunting cabin. The owners, avid outdoor enthusiasts,

know the area like the backs of their hands. **Lewiston Lake** is about 1.5 miles north of town and is a serene alternative to the other area lakes. Early in the evening you may see ospreys and bald eagles diving for fish. Still, the best natural sights are deeper afield – particularly the **Trinity Alps Wilderness**, west of Hwy 3. Look no further for rugged adventure: it hosts excellent hiking and backcountry camping, with over 600 miles of trails that cross granite peaks and skirt deep alpine lakes.

🛏 p161

The Drive » Take Lewiston Lake Rd back south to Hwy 299, then head west about 12 miles to Weaverville, the next village on this trip.

- - - - - - - - - -

TRIP HIGHLIGHT

❻ Weaverville

Of all California's historic parks, the walls of the **Weaverville Joss House State Historic Park** (☑530-623-5284; www.parks.ca.gov; 630 Main St; tour adult/child $4/2, ⊙ tours hourly 10am-4pm Thu-Sun; P) actually talk – they're papered inside with 150-year-old donation ledgers from the once-thriving Chinese community, a testament

DETOUR: DUNSMUIR

Start: ❶ Mt Shasta (p156)

Built by Central Pacific Railroad, Dunsmuir (population 1600) was originally named Pusher, for the auxiliary 'pusher' engines that muscled the heavy steam engines up the steep mountain grade. The town's reputation is still inseparable from the trains, making the stop essential for rail buffs. You can also stop here to quench your thirst; it could easily be – as locals claim – 'the best water on earth.' Maybe that water is what makes the beer at **Dunsmuir Brewery Works** (☎530-235-1900; www.dunsmuirbreweryworks. com; 5701 Dunsmuir Ave, Dunsmuir; mains $9-13; ⏰11am-10pm May-Sep, 11am-9pm Tue-Sun Oct-Apr; 🛜) so damn good. The crisp ales and malty porter are perfectly balanced. The IPA is apparently pretty good too, because patrons are always drinking it dry. Go south from Mt Shasta on I-5 for almost 8 miles and take exit 730 for central Dunsmuir.

to the rich culture of immigrants who built Northern California's infrastructure and then all but disappeared. The rich blue-and-gold Taoist shrine contains an ornate 3000-year-old altar, which was brought here from China. Sadly, state budget issues have made the future of this park uncertain, but it still makes a surprising gem within this far-flung mountain community.

✖️ 🛏️ p161

The Drive » Gas up and get ready for awe-inspiring views of granite mountains, the nationally designated Wild and Scenic Trinity River and sun-dappled forest in every direction. There are no turn-offs; simply continue west on Hwy 299.

❼ Willow Creek

Stay sharp as you navigate the road to Willow Creek – this remote little community was the site of some of the most convincing homemade footage ever captured of a Sasquatch. This makes an obligatory stop of the **Willow Creek–China Flat Museum** (☎530-629-2653; http://bigfootcountry.net; 38949 Hwy 299, Willow Creek; donations accepted; ⏰10am-4pm Wed-Sun May-Sep, from noon Fri-Sun Oct; 🅿️ 👶) for the fun, constantly changing Big Foot Exhibit that includes casts of very large footprints and some provocative (if blurry) photos. The 25ft-tall redwood sculpture

of the hairy beast in the parking lot is hard to miss. Willow Creek is also the beginning of the Bigfoot Scenic Byway (Hwy 96) – a route that winds north through breathtaking mountain and river country, taking you into the region with the most Bigfoot sightings in the country.

The Drive » About 10 miles west of Willow Creek, you'll pass the Berry Summit Vista Point (Mile 28.4) and then start to drop in elevation toward the Pacific. Continue just over 25 twisting miles on Hwy 299 to Hwy 101, turning south to Arcata.

❽ Arcata

Congratulations, road warrior, you've finally arrived in Arcata, an idiosyncratic college town on the sparkling shores of the Pacific and smack dab in the middle of California's majestic redwood country. Park the car at **Arcata Plaza** (www.humfarm.org; ⏰9am-2pm Sat Apr-Nov) and stroll around the historic downtown to find a bite to eat (the restaurants in Arcata are top-notch) or explore the campus of **Humboldt State University** (HSU; ☎707-826-3011; www.humboldt.edu; 1 Harpst St; 🅿️), home to a world-class environmental sustainability program.

✖️ 🛏️ p161

Eating & Sleeping

Mt Shasta ❶

✕ Trinity Café   Californian $$

(📞530-926-6200; www.trinitycafemountshasta.
com; 622 N Mt Shasta Blvd; mains $19-28;
🕐5-9pm Tue-Sat) Trinity Café has long rivaled
the Bay Area's best. The owners, who hail from
Napa, infuse the bistro with a wine country feel
and an extensive, excellent wine selection. The
organic menu ranges from delectable, perfectly
cooked steaks and herb-marinated chicken to
pan-seared scallops.

🛏 Shasta MountInn   B&B $$

(📞530-926-1810; www.shastamountinn.
com; 203 Birch St; r $150-175; 🅿😊🛜) Only
antique on the outside, this bright Victorian
1904 farmhouse on the inside is all relaxed
minimalism, bold colors and graceful decor.
Each airy room has a great bed and exquisite
views of the luminous mountain. Enjoy the
expansive garden, wraparound deck, outdoor
hot tub and sauna.

Shasta Lake ❷

🛏 US Forest Service
Campgrounds   Campground $

(📞info 530-275-1587, reservations 877-444-
6777; www.recreation.gov; tent sites free-$35;
🅿😊) About half of the campgrounds around
Shasta Lake are open year-round. The lake's
many fingers have a huge range of camping
options, with lake and mountain views.

Redding ❸

✕ Moonstone Bistro   Californian $$$

(📞530-241-3663; www.moonstonebistro.
com; 3425 Placer St; lunch mains $14-22, dinner
$22-44; 🕐11am-9pm Tue-Thu, to 10pm Fri &
Sat, 10am-2pm Sun; 😊) Organic, local, free
range, line-caught, you name it, if the word is
associated with sustainable food, you can use it
to describe this place.

Lewiston ❺

🛏 Lewiston Hotel   Historic Hotel $

(📞530-778-3823; www.lewistonhotel.biz; 125
Deadwood Rd; r with shared bath $60; 🅿😊🛜)

This 1862 rambling, ramshackle hotel has small,
rustic rooms with quilts, historic photos and river
views – all have tons of character but none have
attached bathrooms. Ask (or don't ask) for the
room haunted by George.

Weaverville ❻

✕ Trinideli   Deli $

(📞530-623-5856; www.trinideli.com; 201 Trinity
Lakes Blvd; sandwiches $5-10; 🕐6:30am-4pm
Mon-Fri, 10am-3pm Sat; 🚻) Cheerful staff
prepare decadent sandwiches stuffed with fresh
goodness. The one-and-a-half-pound 'Trinideli'
with four types of meat and three types of
cheese will fill the ravenous, while simple turkey
and ham standards explode with fresh veggies.

🛏 Weaverville Hotel   Historic Hotel $$

(📞530-623-2222, 800-750-8957; www.
weavervillehotel.com; 481 Main St; r $110-390;
🅿😊❄🛜) Play like you're in the Old West
at this upscale hotel and historic landmark,
refurbished in grand Victorian style. It's
luxurious but not stuffy, and the very gracious
owners take great care in looking after you.
Guests may use the local gym, and $10 credit at
local restaurants is included in the rates. Kids
under 12 years are not allowed.

Arcata ❽

✕ Folie Douce   Modern American $$$

(📞707-822-1042; www.foliedoucearcata.com;
1551 G St; dinner mains $28-37, pizzas $17-24;
🕐11am-2pm Mon, 11am-2pm & 5:30-9pm Tue-
Thu, to 10pm Fri & Sat; 😊) Just a slip of a place,
but with an enormous reputation. The short but
inventive menu features seasonally inspired
bistro cooking, from Asian to Mediterranean, with
an emphasis on local organics. Wood-fired pizzas
are renowned. Dinner reservations essential.

🛏 Hotel Arcata   Historic Hotel $

(📞800-344-1221, 707-826-0217; www.
hotelarcata.com; 708 9th St; r $100-170;
🅿😊🛜🐾) Anchoring the plaza, this
renovated 1915 brick landmark has friendly
staff, high ceilings and comfortable, old-world
rooms of mixed quality. The rooms in front are
an excellent perch for people-watching on the
square, but the quietest face the back.

Volcanic Legacy Byway

14

Even at the peak of summer, the byways of Northern California's wilderness are largely empty. This loop skirts the edge of Lassen Peak, the southernmost active volcano in the Cascades.

TRIP HIGHLIGHTS

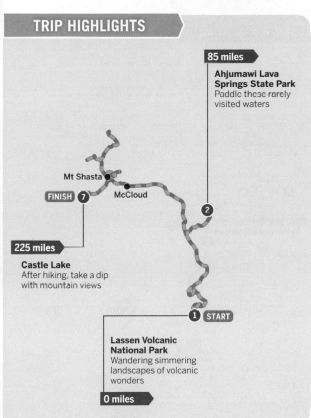

85 miles

Ahjumawi Lava Springs State Park
Paddle these rarely visited waters

Mt Shasta

FINISH 7 McCloud

2

225 miles

Castle Lake
After hiking, take a dip with mountain views

1 **START**

Lassen Volcanic National Park
Wandering simmering landscapes of volcanic wonders

0 miles

3 DAYS
225 MILES / 360KM

GREAT FOR...

BEST TIME TO GO
July and August when the snow finally clears from the highest passes.

 ESSENTIAL PHOTO
Snow-capped Mt Shasta at sunset.

 BEST ADVENTURE
Renting a boat and making the trip to Ahjumawi Lava Springs State Park.

Lassen Volcanic National Park Clouds of steam emerge from this geothermal area

163

Volcanic Legacy Byway

Looping the big, green patches of the map is perfect for hiking, fishing, camping or getting lost. This is a place where few people venture, but those who do come back with stories. Settlements in this neck of the woods are mostly just places to gas up and buy some jerky, but adventurers are drawn here for just that reason. This is the deeply satisfying final frontier of California's wilderness.

① Lassen Volcanic National Park

Driving through the surrounding fields studded with volcanic boulders, **Lassen Volcanic National Park** (📞530-595-4480; www.nps.gov/lavo; 38050 Hwy 36 E, Mineral; 7-day entry per car mid-Apr–Nov $20, Dec–mid-Apr $10; P 🚹) glowers in the distance. Lassen Peak rises 2000 dramatic feet over the surrounding landscape to 10,457ft above sea level. Lassen's dome has a volume of

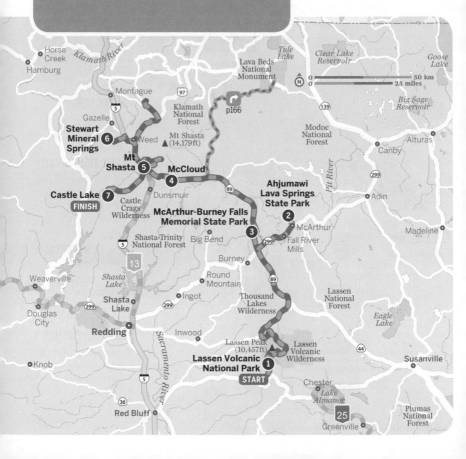

half a cubic mile, making it one of the world's largest plug-dome volcanoes – its most recent eruption took place in 1915, when it blew a giant billow of smoke, steam and ash many miles high into the atmosphere.

Approaching the park, the road begins to climb, entering corridors of dense forest and emerging at the LEED platinum-certified **Kohm Yah-mah-nee Visitor Facility**. Stop in to pick up maps and the handy park newspaper, which outlines campsites and over 150 miles of hiking trails. Heading north, you can roam through the tawny stone slopes of burbling **Sulphur Works** – you'll know it by the ripe scent in the air and the gaseous bursts hissing

LINK YOUR TRIP

25 **Feather River Scenic Byway**

Join this epic mountain journey 10 miles southeast of Lassen National Park in Chester for an inland trip along Hwy 70 and the river.

13 **Trinity Scenic Byway**

From Mt Shasta, go via the rugged Trinity Alps to the sparkling sea, following Hwy 299 past pristine wilderness.

over the roadway. The moderate 1.5-mile hike to **Bumpass Hell** traverses an active geothermal area festooned with otherworldly colored pools and billowing clouds of steam.

🛏 p169

The Drive » Follow Hwy 89 for 29 miles through the park, looping east of Lassen Peak. Go right on Hwy 299 for Fall River Mills, where you may be able to rent a kayak or canoe. Entering McArthur, turn left onto Main St by the Inter-Mountain fairgrounds, cross a canal and continue on a dirt road to the Rat Farm boat launch.

- - - - - - - - - - -

TRIP HIGHLIGHT

❷ Ahjumawi Lava Springs State Park

Of all the stops along this trip, none is more remote and more rewarding than the **Ahjumawi Lava Springs State Park** (📞530-335-2777; www.parks. ca.gov; ☉ sunrise-sunset). A visit here comes with serious bragging rights as the abundant springs, aquamarine bays and islets, and jagged flows of black basalt lava are truly off the beaten path, and can be reached only by boat. The best way to visit is to silently glide across these waters in a canoe or kayak. These can often be rented in nearby towns such as Fall River Mills. After you paddle out, the hikes are glorious: there are basalt outcroppings, lava tubes, cold springs

bubbling and all kinds of volcanic features. For more information about boat rentals and primitive camping, contact McArthur-Burney Falls Memorial State Park.

The Drive » Backtrack more than 20 miles west of McArthur on Hwy 299, then turn right on Hwy 89 and take it 6 miles north to McArthur-Burney Falls Memorial State Park.

- - - - - - - - - - -

❸ McArthur-Burney Falls Memorial State Park

After all the volcanic rock and sulfur fields, there's a soothing stop up the road in **McArthur-Burney Falls Memorial State Park** (📞530-335-2777; www.parks ca.gov; Hwy 89, Burney; per car $8; P 🚻). Fed by a spring, the splashing 129ft-tall waterfalls flow at the same temperature, 42°F, year-round. Rangers are quick to point out that it might not be California's highest waterfall, but it may be the most beautiful (Teddy Roosevelt called it the 'eighth wonder of the world.') Clear, lava-filtered water surges over the top and also from springs in the waterfall's face. Hiking trails include a portion of the Pacific Crest Trail, which continues north to Castle Crags State Park. The 1.3-mile **Burney Falls Trail** is the one you shouldn't miss. Upgraded with guardrails, it's an easy loop for families and allows close-up views of water rushing right out of the rock.

🛏 p169

The Drive ⟫ Continue northwest on Hwy 89 for about 40 miles to McCloud.

🛏 p169

❹ **McCloud**

An old logging town, McCloud sits serenely on the southern slopes of Mt Shasta (14,179ft), with the peak looming in the distance. It is a mellow, comfortable place from which to explore the pristine wilderness that surrounds it. Bump along the tiny, partially paved **McCloud River Loop**, which begins off Hwy 89 about 11 miles east of McCloud, to find the lovely **McCloud River Trail**, which passes three waterfalls on the lower reaches

of Mt Shasta. The easy, 1.8-mile trail passes gorgeous, secluded falls, and you'll discover a lovely habitat for bird-watching in Bigelow Meadow. Other good hiking trails include the **Squaw Valley Creek Trail** (not to be confused with the ski area near Lake Tahoe), an easy 5-mile loop trail south of town, with options for swimming, fishing and picnicking.

🛏 p169

The Drive ⟫ Hwy 89 climbs steeply to reach the city of Mt Shasta. Along the way you'll pass Mt Shasta Ski Park, which has ski and snowboard trails that are converted into awesome mountain biking runs in summer.

❺ **Mt Shasta**

Still classified as an active volcano, **Mt Shasta**

🠖 **DETOUR: LAVA BEDS NATIONAL MONUMENT**

Start: ❹ **McCloud**

Lava Beds National Monument (☏530-667-8113; www.nps.gov/labe; 1 Indian Well HQ, Tulelake; 7-day entry per car $15; P♿), perched on a shield volcano, is a truly remarkable 72-sq-mile landscape of geological features – lava flows, craters, cinder cones, spatter cones and amazing lava tubes. Nearly 750 caves have been found in the monument and they average a comfortable 55°F no matter what the outside temperature. Spy Native American petroglyphs throughout the park too. From McCloud, go southeast several miles on Hwy 89, then take Harris Spring Rd northeast; the one-way drive takes about 2¼ hours.

(☏530-926-4511; www.fs.fed.us/r5/shastatrinity; Everitt Memorial Hwy; P♿) remains a mecca for mystics. Seekers are attracted to the peak's reported cosmic properties, but this reverence for the great mountain is nothing new: for centuries Native Americans have honored it as sacred, considering it to be no less than the Great Spirit's wigwam. Reach its highest drivable point by heading through Mt Shasta City to Everitt Memorial Hwy, which leads to **Bunny Flat**, one of the lower access points on the mountain for excellent hikes. An amble around the town at the base of the mountain will provide you with an opportunity to duck into book shops and excellent eateries. Visitors can also fill their water bottles at the **Sacramento River Headwaters** off Mt Shasta Blvd, about a mile north of downtown. Pure water gurgles up from the ground in a large, cool spring amid a city park with walking trails, picnic spots and a children's playground.

✕ 🛏 p161, p169

The Drive ⟫ From the north side of Mt Shasta City go 10 miles north on I-5, past Weed to the Edgewood exit, then turn left at Stewart Springs Rd and follow the signs.

KEN BROWN / GETTY IMAGES ©

McArthur-Burney Falls Memorial State Park Burney Falls

⑥ Stewart Mineral Springs

Make all the jokes you want about the name of the little town of Weed, but a visit to **Stewart Mineral Springs** (☑530-938-2222; http:// stewartmineralsprings.com; 4617 Stewart Springs Rd, Weed; sauna/mineral baths $18/30; ⊘10am-6pm Thu-Sun, from noon Mon) will only inspire a satisfied sigh. At this popular alternative (read: clothing optional) hangout on the banks of a clear mountain stream guests soak in a private claw-foot tub or cook in the dry-wood sauna. There's also massage, body wraps, a Native American–style sweat lodge and a riverside sunbathing deck. You'll want to call ahead to be sure there is space in the steam and soaking rooms, especially on busy weekends.

While in the area, tickle your other senses at **Mt Shasta Lavender Farms** (☑530-926-2651; www.mtshastalavenderfarms. com; 9706 Harry Cash Rd, Montague; ⊘9am-4pm mid-Jun–early Aug; Ⓟ), about 19 miles northeast of Weed off Hwy 97. You can harvest your own sweet French lavender during the June and July blooming season.

✕ 🛏 p169

The Drive » Castle Lake can be reached by driving south on I-5 and taking exit 736. Go under the highway and the service road to the north on the west side of the highway to connect with Castle Lake Rd. The lake is approximately 7 miles beyond Lake Siskiyou. En route you'll pass Ney Springs and the short hike to Faery Falls.

TRIP HIGHLIGHT

⑦ Castle Lake

Castle Lake is an easily accessible yet pristine mountain pool surrounded by granite formations and pine forest. In the distance you'll see two of Northern California's most recognizable rocks: Castle Crags and Mt Shasta. Swimming, fishing, picnicking and camping are popular in summer.

🛏 p169

Eating & Sleeping

Lassen Volcanic National Park ❶

🛏 Lassen Volcanic National Park Campgrounds
Campground $

(📞518-885-3639, reservations 877-444-6777; www.recreation.gov; tent & RV sites $12-24; Ⓟ) The park has eight developed campgrounds that are variably open between late May and late October, depending on snow conditions. Manzanita Lake is the only one with hot showers.

🛏 Manzanita Lake Camping Cabins
Cabin $

(📞May-Oct 530-335-7557, Nov-Apr 530-840-6140; www.lassenrecreation.com; Hwy 89, near Manzanita Lake; cabins $69-95; Ⓟ ⊖) These log cabins enjoy a lovely position on one of Lassen's lakes, and they come in one- and two-bedroom options and slightly more basic eight-bunk configurations, which are a bargain for groups. They all have bear boxes, propane heaters and fire rings, but no bedding, electricity or running water. Shared bathrooms and coin-op hot showers are nearby.

McArthur-Burney Falls Memorial State Park ❸

🛏 McArthur-Burney Falls Memorial State Park Campground
Cabin, Campground $

(📞information 530-335-2777, summer reservations 800-444-7275; www.reserveamerica.com; off Hwy 89, Burney; tent & RV sites $35, cabins $83-105; Ⓟ🐾) The park campground has hot showers, bunk-bed cabins (bring your own sleeping bags) and campsites. It's open year-round.

McCloud ❹

🛏 McCloud River Mercantile Hotel
Inn $$

(📞530-964-2330; www.mccloudmercantile.com; 241 Main St; r $129-250; Ⓟ ⊖ 🛜) Stroll upstairs to the 2nd floor of McCloud's central Mercantile Hotel and try not to fall in love; it's all high ceilings, exposed brick and a perfect marriage of preservationist class and modern panache. Antique-furnished rooms have open floor plans. Guests are greeted with fresh flowers and can drift to sleep on feather beds after soaking in claw-foot tubs.

Mt Shasta ❺

🍴 Berryvale Grocery
Market, Cafe $

(📞530-926-1576; www.berryvale.com; 305 S Mt Shasta Blvd; cafe items $4-11; ⏰ store 8am-8pm, cafe to 7pm; 🅿 ⬆) This market sells groceries and organic produce to health-conscious eaters. The excellent cafe serves good coffee and an array of tasty – mostly veggie – salads, sandwiches and wraps.

🛏 Swiss Holiday Lodge
Motel $

(📞530-926-3446; www.swissholidaylodge.com; 2400 S Mt Shasta Blvd; r from $90; Ⓟ ⊖ ❄ 🛜 🦽 🐾) Run by a friendly family and a small, energetic dog, you get a peek of the mountain from the back windows of these clean, well-priced rooms.

Stewart Mineral Springs ❻

🍴 Mt Shasta Brewing Company Alehouse & Bistro
Pub Food $

(📞530-938-2394; www.weedales.com; 360 College Ave, Weed; mains $11-18; ⏰11am-9pm or 10pm) Try a tasty Shastafarian Porter or the rich, amber-colored Mountain High IPA. Brats, flatbread pizzas and grilled panini round out the brewpub menu. the kitchen closes an hour before the pub.

🛏 Stewart Mineral Springs
Cabin, Campground $

(📞530-938-2222; http://stewartmineralsprings.com; 4617 Stewart Springs Rd, Weed; tent & RV sites $35, tipis $45, d $80 120; Ⓟ ⊖) Basic accommodations available at the springs include a rough-cut lodge, rustic cabins and canvas tipis. Book ahead.

Castle Lake ❼

🛏 Castle Lake Campground
Campground $

(📞530-926-4511; www.fs.usda.gov/main/stnf/home; tent sites free; ⏰May-Oct; Ⓟ) There are six primitive campsites with picnic tables and fire pits about a quarter mile below the lake. Bring your own water.

STRETCH YOUR LEGS SAN FRANCISCO

Start/Finish Chinatown Gate

Distance 3.3 miles

Duration 4–5 hours

Limber up and look sharp: on this walk, you'll pass hidden architectural gems, navigate the winding alleys of Chinatown and catch shimmering views of the bay. Along the way, enjoy controversial art, savory street snacks and a flock of parrots.

Take this walk on Trips

Chinatown Gate

The elaborate threshold of the **Dragon's Gate** (cnr Grant Ave & Bush St; 1, 8, 30, 45, California St), which was donated by Taiwan in 1970, announces the entrance to Chinatown. The street, beyond the gate, was once a notorious red-light district, but forward-thinking Chinatown businessmen reinvented the area in the 1920s, hiring architects to create a signature 'Chinatown Deco' look. The jumble of glittering shops is the perfect place to pick up a cheap souvenir.

The Walk >> Huff it uphill from Chinatown Gate, past gilded dragon lamps on Grant Ave to Old St Mary's Square. Two blocks beyond the noble Old St Mary's Church take a left on Clay St.

Chinese Historical Society of America Museum

At this intimate museum, visitors picture what it was like to be Chinese during the Gold Rush, the transcontinental railroad construction and the Beat heyday. The **Chinese Historical Society of America Museum** (CHSA; 415-391-1188; www.chsa.org; 965 Clay St; noon-5pm Tue-Fri, 11am-4pm Sat; 1, 8, 30, 45, California St, Powell-Mason, Mason-Hyde) hosts rotating exhibits across the courtyard in a graceful building, built as Chinatown's YWCA in 1932.

The Walk >> Backtrack past Stockton St and turn left down Spofford Alley where mah-jongg tiles click and Sun Yat-sen plotted the 1911 overthrow of China's last dynasty. At Washington St, take a right. Then go left on Ross Alley.

Golden Gate Fortune Cookie Factory

Ross Alley (sometimes marked as Old Chinatown Alley) might seem familiar to movie buffs; it's been the backdrop for flicks like *Karate Kid, Part II* and *Indiana Jones and the Temple of Doom*. The humble little warehouse at No 56 is where to get your fortune while it's hot, folded into warm cookies at the **Golden Gate Fortune Cookie Factory** (415-781-3956; 56 Ross Alley; 9am-6pm; 8, 30, 45, Powell-Mason, Powell-Hyde). For a small fee you can even write custom fortunes.

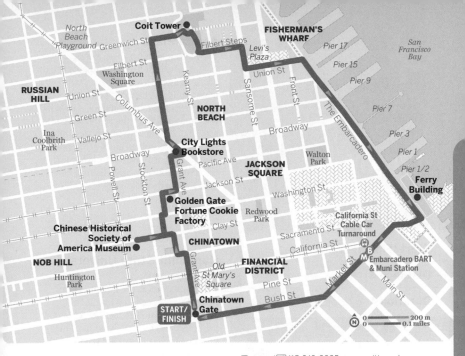

The Walk » Go right on Jackson St and left on Grant Ave. You'll pass a number of Chinese bakeries with piping hot *char siu bao* (BBQ pork buns). Take a shortcut through Jack Kerouac Alley, where the poetic vagabond once strolled.

City Lights Bookstore

Ever since manager Shigeyoshi Murao and Beat poet Lawrence Ferlinghetti successfully defended their right to 'willfully and lewdly print' Allen Ginsberg's magnificent *Howl and Other Poems* in 1957, **City Lights Bookstore** (☎415-362-8193; www.citylights.com; 261 Columbus Ave; ◷10am-midnight) has been a free-speech landmark. Snuggle into the Poet's Chair upstairs overlooking Jack Kerouac Alley. If reading makes you thirsty, grab a pint at Vesuvio next door.

The Walk » Go left on Columbus Ave. Make a slight right on Grant Ave and walk for five blocks, then take a right and head up the Greenwich St steps.

Coit Tower

Adding an exclamation mark to San Francisco's landscape, a visit to **Coit Tower** (☎415-249-0995; www.coittowertours. com; Telegraph Hill Blvd; nonresident elevator fee adult/child $8/5; ◷10am-6pm May-Oct. to 5pm Nov-Apr; ◻39) is the high point of the walk atop Telegraph Hill. This peculiar 210ft-projectile is a monument to San Francisco firefighters. When it was completed in 1934, the Diego Rivera–style murals lining the lobby were denounced as Communist. To see more murals hidden inside Coit Tower's stairwell, take a free guided tour at 11am on Wednesday or Saturday.

The Walk » Take the Filbert Steps downhill past wild parrots and hidden cottages to Levi's Plaza. Head right on Embarcadero to the Ferry Building.

Ferry Building

The historic **Ferry Building** (p36) is a transit hub that has transformed itself into a destination for foodies. Artisan food producers, boutique vendors, famous-name restaurants and a thrice-weekly **farmers market** (p37).

The Walk » Walk down Market St. Turn right on Bush St back to Chinatown Gate.

STRETCH YOUR LEGS
ARCATA

Start/Finish Arcata Plaza

Distance 4 miles

Duration 4–6 hours

The North Coast's colorful college town offers a stroll on the most progressive edge of America, an artsy community – with visionary sustainability practices, excellent parks, amazing food and a wealth of historic buildings – that marches proudly to its own beat.

Take this walk on Trips

Arcata Plaza

The buzzing **hub** (www.humfarm.org; ⊙9am-2pm Sat Apr-Nov) of Arcata is a place where young students toss Frisbees, farmers hawk crops and bearded professors saunter by dreadlocked vagabonds. Lined by boutiques and bars, the centerpiece is a bronze of President William McKinley who sternly observes one festival after another. The 1915 **Hotel Arcata** (p161) on the National Register of Historic Places, is on the northeast corner.

The Walk ≫ Walk up G St past a number of excellent, cheap restaurants and take the pedestrian bridge over the highway at 17th St, which brings you to campus.

Humboldt State University

The **university** (HSU; ☎707-826-3011; www.humboldt.edu; 1 Harpst St; Ⓟ) is the North Coast's secluded intellectual center. In addition to a clutch of leading environmentalists its alumni also include novelist Raymond Carver and Stephen Hillenburg, creator of Sponge-Bob SquarePants. The **Campus Center for Appropriate Technology** (CCAT; www.ccathsu.com) is a world leader in developing sustainable technologies; on Tuesdays at 10am and Fridays at 3pm you can take a tour of CCAT's house, a converted residence that uses only 4% of the energy of a comparably sized dwelling.

The Walk ≫ Walk south through campus to reach 14th St. Take a left to enter Redwood Park.

Arcata Community Forest

Few city parks hold a candle to **Redwood Park**, adjacent to 790 acres of community forest crossed by trails for biking, hiking and horseback riding. Without the big stands of trees common to the region, it doesn't have an untamed feel, but trail No 1 is a 0.9-mile loop that's an enjoyable hike for kids. Despite a few scruffy, semipermanent residents, whose tents flout the 'no camping' ordinance, the place feels magical, particularly during a performance on the park's stage.

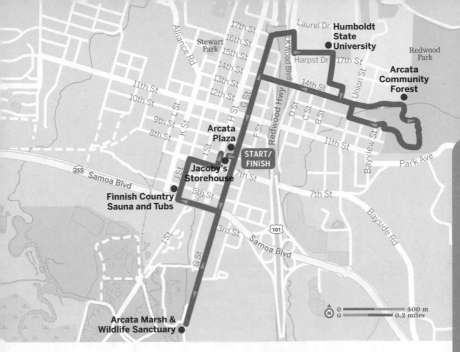

The Walk » Retrace your path on 14th St and continue, crossing over the highway. When you reach G St, take a left. Eventually, this will cross Samoa Blvd and take you onward to an interpretive center and trailhead for Arcata Marsh.

Arcata Marsh & Wildlife Sanctuary

On the shores of Humboldt Bay, the Arcata Marsh & Wildlife Sanctuary has 5 miles of walking trails and outstanding bird-watching – during sunset it can be arrestingly beautiful – particularly when you consider that it was once the site of lumber mills and that the water originates at Arcata's water treatment system. Two organizations – **Redwood Region Audubon Society** (www.rras. org; donation welcome) and the Friends of Arcata Marsh at the **Arcata Marsh Interpretive Center** (707-826-2359; www2.humboldt.edu/arcatamarsh; 569 South G St; 9am-5pm Tue-Sun, from 1pm Mon;) – offer guided walks on Saturdays.

The Walk » Trails through the marshes will bring you near a colorful array of migratory and shore birds. Walk north from the marsh, take a left on Samoa Blvd and then a right on J St.

Finnish Country Sauna & Tubs

The private, open-air redwood tubs at the **Finnish Country Sauna and Tubs** (707-822-2228; http://cafemokkaarcata. com; 495 J St; 30min per adult/child $9.75/2; noon-11pm Sun-Thu, to 1am Fri & Sat;) make an ideal place to rest your legs. The hot tubs and sauna are situated around a frog pond, and birds flutter in the redwood branches above. The attached coffeehouse has a mellow, old-world vibe.

The Walk » Continue north on J St and take a right at 7th St, then a left on H St.

Jacoby's Storehouse

The final stop returns to another corner of Arcata Plaza and another nationally registered historic place, **Jacoby's Storehouse** (780 7th St). The creaking halls of this 1857 mercantile building have received a handsome upgrade and now lead to restaurants, some tasteful history displays and – importantly for any traveling stop – an ice-cream parlor.

173

Central California Trips

The fairy-tale stretch of coast between San Francisco and LA is too often dismissed as 'flyover country.' But it's packed with beautiful beaches, historic lighthouses and tall redwood forests that hide magical waterfalls and hot springs, especially in bohemian Big Sur.

Get acquainted with central California's agricultural heartland while driving along inland highways. Lazily roll past vineyards and farms where you can taste the goodness of the land, from juicy strawberries to prickly artichokes to wine, including around Santa Barbara and Santa Cruz.

Further east rises the Sierra Nevada, uplifted along faultlines and weathered by glaciers, wind and rain. Soothe your soul with natural wonders, from Yosemite Valley to Lake Tahoe. Then drop into the foothills to trace California's gold-rush history and take a dip in summertime swimming holes.

Sequoia National Park Hiking amid giant sequoia trees
NEALE CLARK / GETTY IMAGES ©

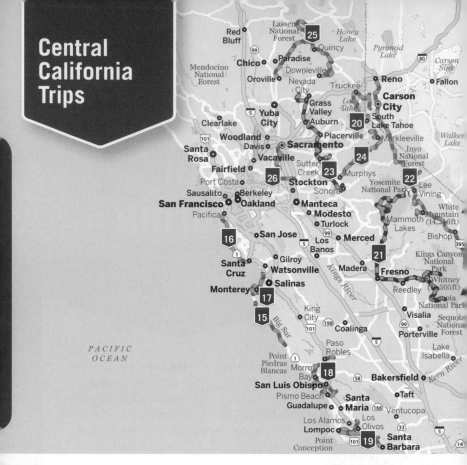

Central California Trips

 DON'T MISS

Pfeiffer Beach

Catch sunset shining through a sea arch in the Pacific and dig down into the purple-tinged sand on Trip **15**

Vikingsholm Castle

Tour this Scandinavian-style mansion at Emerald Bay, Lake Tahoe's most captivating shoreline, which you can also hike along on Trip **20**

Kings Canyon Scenic Byway

Wind down into one of the USA's deepest canyons, carved by glaciers and the mighty Kings River, on Trip **21**

Alabama Hills

Explore the terrain where Hollywood Western movies and TV shows have been filmed outside Lone Pine, just below Mt Whitney, on Trip **22**

South Yuba River State Park

Swim, hike and photograph the USA's longest covered wooden bridge, near the 19th-century mining town of Nevada City, on Trip **23**

Big Sur

Nestled up against mossy redwood forests, the rocky Big Sur coast is a secretive place. Get to know it like locals do, visiting wild beaches, waterfalls and hot springs.

TRIP HIGHLIGHTS

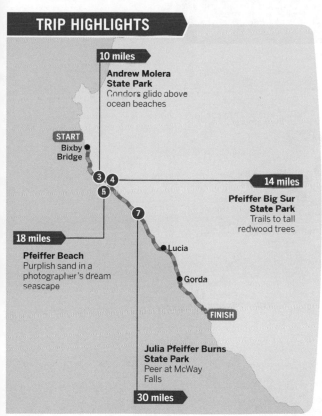

10 miles

Andrew Molera State Park
Condors glide above ocean beaches

START
Bixby Bridge

14 miles

Pfeiffer Big Sur State Park
Trails to tall redwood trees

Lucia

Gorda

FINISH

18 miles

Pfeiffer Beach
Purplish sand in a photographer's dream seascape

Julia Pfeiffer Burns State Park
Peer at McWay Falls

30 miles

2–3 DAYS
60 MILES / 95KM

GREAT FOR...

BEST TIME TO GO
April to May for waterfalls and wildflowers; September to October for sunny, cloudless days.

ESSENTIAL PHOTO
McWay Falls dropping into the Pacific.

BEST FOR FAMILIES
Pfeiffer Big Sur State Park for camping, cabins and easy hikes.

Bixby Bridge Wildflowers bloom near this photogenic bridge

15 | Big Sur

Much ink has been spilled extolling the raw beauty of this craggy land shoehorned between the Santa Lucia Mountains and the Pacific. Yet nothing quite prepares you for that first glimpse through the windshield of Big Sur's wild, unspoiled coastline. There are no traffic lights, banks or strip malls, and when the sun goes down, the moon and the stars are the only streetlights – if coastal fog hasn't extinguished them.

➊ Bixby Bridge

To tell the truth, Big Sur is more a state of mind than a place you can pinpoint on a map. But the photogenic Bixby Bridge lets you know you've finally arrived. Arching above Rainbow Canyon, this landmark is one of the world's highest single-span bridges, completed in 1932 by prisoners eager to lop time off their sentences. Stop on the north side of the bridge for an irresistible photo op.

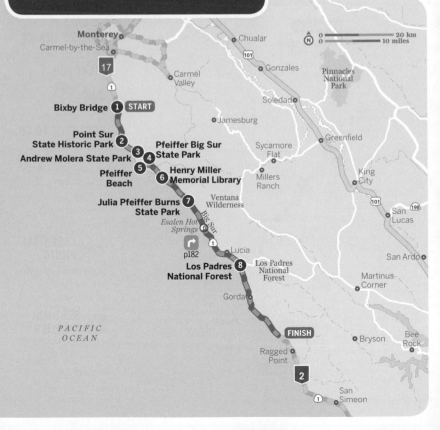

The Drive » From Bixby Bridge, it's about 6 miles south along Hwy 1, rolling beside pasture lands, to Point Sur State Historic Park. Like everywhere else along Big Sur's coast, watch out for cyclists and use signposted roadside pullouts to let fast-moving traffic pass by.

❷ Point Sur State Historic Park

Rising like a velvety green fortress out of the sea, **Point Sur State Historic Park** (☎831-625-4419; www.pointsur.org; off Hwy 1; adult/child 6-17yr from $12/5; ☾ tours usually at 1pm Wed, 10am Sat & Sun Oct-Mar; 10am & 2pm Wed & Sat, 10am Sun Apr-Sep, also 10am Thu Jul & Aug) looks like an island, but is actually connected to the mainland by a

LINK YOUR TRIP

2 Pacific Coast Highways

Big Sur is just one famous stretch of Hwy 1 along the California coast, which you can drive along from Mexico to Oregon.

17 Around Monterey & Carmel

From Bixby Bridge, drive almost 20 miles north on Hwy 1 to Monterey for maritime history lessons and California's top-ranked aquarium.

sandbar. On the volcanic rock sits California's only turn-of-the-20th-century lightstation that's still open to the public. Ocean views and tales of the lighthouse-keepers' family lives are engrossing, especially during spooky moonlight tours. Call ahead to confirm schedules; arrive early because space is limited (no reservations).

The Drive » Lighthouse tours meet at the locked farm gate a quarter-mile north of Point Sur Naval Facility. Afterwards, drive south on Hwy 1 another 2 miles along the coast to Andrew Molera State Park.

❸ Andrew Molera State Park

With ocean vistas beckoning along Hwy 1, you'll be eager to put your feet on a beach by now. Named after the farmer who first planted artichokes in California, **Andrew Molera State Park** (☎831-667-2315; www.parks.ca.gov; Hwy 1; per car $10; ☾30min before sunrise-30min after sunset; Ⓟ ♿) is a trail-laced pastiche of grassy meadows, ocean bluffs and sandy beaches, all offering excellent wildlife-watching. Hike for about a mile out to where the Big Sur River meets the rocky driftwood-strewn beach, whipped by strong winds and the surf. Back at the parking lot, walk south to the **Big Sur Discovery**

Center (☎831-624-1202; www.ventanaws.org/discovery_center; ☾10am-4pm Sat & Sun late May-early Sep; Ⓟ ♿) to learn all about endangered California condors that sometimes soar overhead.

The Drive » Speeds rarely top 35mph along Hwy 1, which narrows and becomes curvier the further south you go. Slow down a few miles beyond the state park and watch for pedestrians in 'the village,' Big Sur's hub for shops, services, motels and cafes (see Eating & Sleeping options, p184). About 5 miles south of Andrew Molera State Park, you'll see the entrance for Pfeiffer Big Sur State Park on the inland side of the highway.

❹ Pfeiffer Big Sur State Park

The biggest all-natural draw on the Big Sur coast is **Pfeiffer Big Sur State Park** (☎831-667-2315; www.parks.ca.gov; 47225 Hwy 1; per car $10; ☾30min before sunrise-30min after sunset; Ⓟ ♿). Named after Big Sur's first European settlers, who arrived here in 1869, it's also the largest state park along this coast. Hiking trails loop through tall redwood groves and run uphill to 60ft-high **Pfeiffer Falls**, a delicate cascade that's hidden in the forest and usually flows between December and May. Near the park entrance, inside a rustic lodge built in the 1930s by the Civilian Conservation

Corps (CCC), you'll find a convenient general store selling cold drinks, ice cream, snacks, camping supplies and road-trip souvenirs.

 p184

The Drive » Just 2 miles south of Pfeiffer Big Sur State Park, about half a mile past ranger-staffed Big Sur Station, make a sharp right turn off Hwy 1 onto Sycamore Canyon Rd, marked only by a small yellow sign saying 'Narrow Road.' Partly unpaved, this road (RVs and trailers prohibited) corkscrews down for over 2 miles to Pfeiffer Beach.

TRIP HIGHLIGHT

⑤ Pfeiffer Beach

Hidden down a side road to the sea, **Pfeiffer Beach** (☎831-667-2315; www.fs.usda.gov/lpnf; end of Sycamore Canyon Rd; per car $10; ☺9am-8pm; Ⓟ ♿) is worth the trouble it takes to reach it. This

phenomenal, crescent-shaped strand is known for its huge double rock formation, through which waves crash with life-affirming power. It's often windy, and the surf is too dangerous for swimming. But dig down into the wet sand – it's purple! That's because manganese garnet washes down from the craggy hillsides above.

The Drive » Backtrack up narrow, winding Sycamore Canyon Rd for more than 2 miles, then turn right onto Hwy 1 southbound. After two more twisting, slow-moving miles, look for Nepenthe restaurant on your right. The Henry Miller Library is another 0.4 miles south, at a hairpin turn on your left.

---

⑥ Henry Miller Memorial Library

'It was here at Big Sur that I first learned to

say Amen!' wrote Henry Miller in *Big Sur and the Oranges of Hieronymus Bosch*. A surrealist novelist, Miller was a local resident from 1944 to 1962. A beatnik memorial, alt-cultural venue and bookshop, the **Henry Miller Memorial Library** (☎831-667-2574; www. henrymiller.org; 48603 Hwy 1; donations accepted; ☺11am-6pm; Ⓟ) was never actually the writer's home. The house belonged to Miller's friend, painter Emil White. Inside are copies of all of Miller's published books, many of his paintings and a collection of Big Sur and Beat Generation material. Stop by to browse and hang out on the front deck with coffee, or join the bohemian carnival of live music, open-mic nights and independent-film screenings.

✕ ▣ p184, p185

The Drive » You'll leave most of the traffic behind as Hwy 1 continues southbound, curving slowly along the vertiginous cliffs, occasionally opening up for ocean panoramas. It's fewer than 8 miles to Julia Pfeiffer Burns State Park; the entrance is on the inland side of Hwy 1.

TRIP HIGHLIGHT

⑦ Julia Pfeiffer Burns State Park

If you've got an appetite for chasing waterfalls, swing into **Julia Pfeiffer Burns State Park** (☎831-667-2315; www.parks.ca.gov;

↱ DETOUR: ESALEN HOT SPRINGS

Start ⑦ Julia Pfeiffer Burns State Park

Ocean beaches and waterfalls aren't the only places to get wet in Big Sur. At private Esalen Institute, clothing-optional **baths** (☎831-667-3047; www.esalen. org; 55000 Hwy 1; per person $30; ☺by reservation 1pm-3am) fed by a natural hot spring sit on a ledge high above the ocean. Dollars to donuts you'll never take another dip that compares scenery-wise, especially on stormy winter nights. Only two small outdoor pools perch directly over the waves, so once you've stripped and taken a quick shower, head outside immediately. Advance reservations are required. The signposted entrance is on Hwy 1, about 3 miles south of Julia Pfeiffer Burns State Park.

Pfeiffer Beach Rock arch at sunset

Hwy 1; per car $10; ☺30min before sunrise-30min after sunset; P 🚻). From the parking lot, the short Overlook Trail rushes downhill towards the sea, passing through a tunnel underneath Hwy 1. Everyone is in a hurry to see **McWay Falls**, which tumbles year-round over granite cliffs and free-falls into the ocean or onto the beach, depending on the tide. This is the classic Big Sur postcard shot, with tree-topped rocks jutting above a golden beach next to swirling blue pools and crashing white surf. During winter, watch for migrating whales offshore.

The Drive » The tortuously winding stretch of Hwy 1 southbound is sparsely populated, rugged and remote, running through national forest. Make sure you've got enough fuel in the tank to at least reach the expensive gas station at Gorda, over 20 miles south of Julia Pfeiffer Burns State Park.

- - - - - - - - - - -

8 Los Padres National Forest

If you have any slivers of sunlight left, keep trucking down Hwy 1 approximately 8 miles past Gorda to **Salmon Creek Falls** (www.fs.usda.gov/lpnf; Hwy 1; P 🚻), which usually runs from December through May. Take a short hike to splash around in the pools at the base of this double-drop waterfall, tucked uphill in a forested canyon. In a hairpin turn of Hwy 1, the roadside turnoff is marked only by a small brown trailhead sign.

🛏 p185

Eating & Sleeping

Big Sur Village

✕ Big Sur Burrito Bar & General Store   Deli $

(☎831-667-2700; www.bigsurriverinn.com; 46840 Hwy 1; mains $8-10; ⊙11am-7pm; 🚻) Order a San Francisco–sized burrito or wrap sandwich with a fresh-fruit smoothie from the back of the Big Sur River Inn's well-stocked general store, which carries snacks, drinks and camping supplies.

🛌 Big Sur Campground & Cabins   Cabin, Campground $$

(☎831-667-2322; www.bigsurcamp.com; 47000 Hwy 1; tent/RV sites from $60/70, cabins $170-425; P ⊖ 🐾) On the Big Sur River and shaded by redwoods, cozy housekeeping cabins sport full kitchens and fireplaces, while canvas-sided tent cabins are dog-friendly (pet fee $20). The riverside campground, where neighboring sites have little privacy, is popular with RVs. There are hot showers, a coin-op laundry, playground and general store.

🛌 Glen Oaks Motel   Motel, Cabin $$$

(☎831-667-2105; www.glenoaksbigsur.com; 47080 Hwy 1; d $275-425; P ⊖ 📶) At this 1950s redwood-and-adobe motor lodge, rustic rooms and cabins seem effortlessly chic. Dramatically transformed by eco-conscious design, snug romantic hideaway rooms all have gas fireplaces. Woodsy cabins in a redwood grove have kitchenettes and share outdoor fire pits, or retreat to the one-bedroom house with a full kitchen.

Pfeiffer Big Sur State Park ❹

🛌 Big Sur Lodge   Lodge $$$

(☎831-667-3100, 800-424-4787; www. bigsurlodge.com; 47225 Hwy 1; d $215-415; P ⊖ 📶 🏊) What you're really paying for is a peaceful location, right inside Pfeiffer Big Sur State Park. Fairly rustic duplexes each have a deck or balcony looking out into the redwood forest, while family-sized rooms may have a kitchenette or wood-burning fireplace. The outdoor swimming pool is closed in winter.

🛌 Pfeiffer Big Sur State Park Campground   Campground $

(☎reservations 800-444-7275; www. reserveamerica.com; 47225 Hwy 1; tent & RV sites $35-50; P 🐾) Best for novice campers and families with young kids, here over 200 campsites nestle in a redwood-shaded valley. Facilities include drinking water, fire pits and coin-op hot showers and laundry.

Henry Miller Memorial Library ❻

✕ Big Sur Deli & General Store   Deli $

(☎831-667-2225; www.bigsurdeli.com; 47520 Hwy 1; items $2-10; ⊙7am-8pm) With the most reasonable prices in Big Sur, this family-owned deli slices custom-made sandwiches and piles up tortillas with carne asada, pork *carnitas*, veggies or beans and cheese. The small market carries camping food, snacks and beer and wine.

✕ Nepenthe   Californian $$$

(☎831-667-2345; www.nepenthebigsur.com; 48510 Hwy 1; mains $17-48; ⊙11:30am-4:30pm & 5-10pm; 📶 🚻) Nepenthe comes from a Greek word meaning 'isle of no sorrow,' and indeed, it's hard to feel blue while sitting by the fire pit on this aerial terrace. Just-okay California cuisine (try the renowned Ambrosia burger) takes a backseat to the views and Nepenthe's history – Orson Welles and Rita Hayworth briefly owned a cabin here in the 1940s. Reservations essential.

✕ Restaurant at Ventana   Californian $$$

(☎831-667-4242; www.ventanainn.com; 48123 Hwy 1; lunch mains $16-28, 4-course dinner menu $75; ⊙7-10:30am, 11:30am-4:30pm & 6-9pm; 📶) The old truism about the better the views, the worse the food just doesn't seem to apply here. The resort's clifftop terrace restaurant and cocktail bar are Big Sur's gathering spot for foodies and bon vivants. Feast on squid-ink ravioli, a house-smoked brisket sandwich or salads flavored with herbs grown in the garden right outside. Reservations essential.

🛏 Post Ranch Inn
Resort $$$

(📞800-527-2200, 831-667-2200; www.
postranchinn.com; 47900 Hwy 1; d incl breakfast
from $675; P 🚗 ❄ @ 🛜 🐾) The last word
in luxurious coastal getaways, the exclusive
Post Ranch pampers demanding guests with
slate spa tubs, wood-burning fireplaces, private
decks and walking sticks for coastal hikes.
Ocean-view rooms celebrate the sea, while
treehouses lack views and have a bit of sway.
Paddle around the clifftop infinity pool after a
shamanic-healing session or yoga class in the
spa. No children allowed.

Los Padres National Forest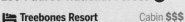

🛏 Treebones Resort
Cabin $$$

(📞877-424-4787; www.treebonesresort.
com; 71895 Hwy 1; d with shared bath incl
breakfast from $265; P 🚗 🛜 🐾) Don't let
the word 'resort' throw you. Yes, they've got an
ocean-view hot tub, heated pool and massage
treatments. But a unique woven 'human
nest' and canvas-sided yurts with polished
pine floors, quilt-covered beds, sink vanities
and redwood decks are more like glamping,
with little privacy. Communal bathrooms and
showers are a short stroll away. Wi-fi in main
lodge only. Children must be at least six years
old. Look for the signposted turnoff a mile north
of Gorda, at the southern end of Big Sur.

Along Highway 1 to Santa Cruz

16

South of San Francisco to Santa Cruz, you'll travel one of the most jaw-dropping stretches of scenic highway on California's coast, passing farmstands, lighthouses and beaches.

TRIP HIGHLIGHTS

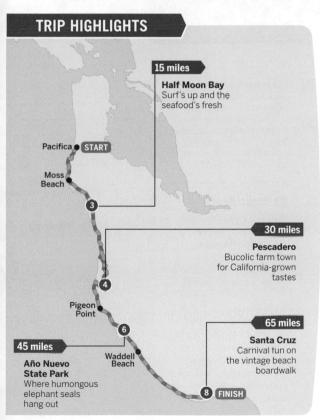

15 miles

Half Moon Bay
Surf's up and the seafood's fresh

Pacifica • START

Moss Beach

3

30 miles

Pescadero
Bucolic farm town for California-grown tastes

Pigeon Point

6

45 miles

Año Nuevo State Park
Where humongous elephant seals hang out

Waddell Beach

65 miles

Santa Cruz
Carnival fun on the vintage beach boardwalk

8 FINISH

2–3 DAYS
65 MILES / 105KM

GREAT FOR...

BEST TIME TO GO
July to October gives you the best chance of sunshine.

 ESSENTIAL PHOTO
Elephant seal antics at Año Nuevo's beaches.

☑ **BEST FOR FOODIES**
Pescadero's bakery, goat dairy and roadside farms.

Pigeon Point Light Station State Historic Park Pigeon Point lighthouse

16 Along Highway 1 to Santa Cruz

A lazily flowing river of tourism, serpentine Hwy 1 is most celebrated for its scenic charms along the Big Sur coast. But some locals says that the most enchanting stretch of this iconic road starts just south of San Francisco, winding its way slowly down to Santa Cruz. Most beaches are buffeted by wild and unpredictable surf, making them better for tidepooling than swimming or sunbathing. But, oh, the views!

❶ Pacifica

In often fog-bound Pacifica, the divided four-lane highway from San Francisco peters out at an intersection overlooking pounding waves, a portent of things to come. Narrowing to two lanes, Hwy 1 jogs inland through thick eucalyptus groves before turning back to the coast. Downhill at **Pacifica State Beach**, stretch your legs or surf, and breathe the sea-salted air. Then swerve up through the new tunnels to **Devil's Slide**, where a stretch of the old highway has been converted into a popular hiking and cycling path.

The Drive » As Hwy 1 keeps heading south, you'll be enjoying the sea views. In the next 6 miles, you'll pass Gray Whale Cove and Montara State Beaches. In Moss Beach, turn right onto Vermont Ave, then follow Lake St to its end.

❷ Moss Beach

South of Point Montara Lighthouse, **Fitzgerald Marine Reserve** (☎650-728-3584; www. fitzgeraldreserve.org; 200 Nevada Ave; ☺8am-sunset; **P** **♿**) is a thriving habitat for harbor seals and natural tidepools. Walk out among the pools at low tide to observe (but never pick up) myriad crabs, sea stars, mollusks and rainbow-colored sea anemones. Note it's

illegal to remove any creatures, shells or even rocks.

Back on Hwy 1 southbound, take the next right onto Cypress Ave, turning left onto Beach Way to find **Moss Beach Distillery** (📞650-728-5595; www.mossbeachdistillery.com; 140 Beach Way; 🕑noon-9pm Mon-Sat, from 11am Sun). Overlooking the cove where bootleggers used to unload Prohibition-era liquor, the heated ocean-view deck is perfectly positioned for sunset cocktails. Head elsewhere for a meal if you're hungry.

The Drive » Continue south on Hwy 1 past the airport. Pillar Point Harbor is on the right after 2 miles. For downtown Half Moon Bay, go four more miles south on Hwy 1, turn left onto Hwy 92, then right onto Main St.

LINK YOUR TRIP

4 **Marin County**
Starting in San Francisco, follow Hwy 1 in the other direction by crossing north over the Golden Gate Bridge to find redwood groves, beaches and lighthouses.

17 **Around Monterey & Carmel**
From Santa Cruz, Hwy 1 winds 40 miles south to Monterey, passing more beaches, fishing ports and farms.

TRIP HIGHLIGHT

❸ Half Moon Bay

Offshore from the western end of Pillar Point Harbor lies **Mavericks** (http://titansofmavericks. com/event), a serious surf break, where an annual contest attracts the world's pro big-wave riders to battle huge, steep wintertime swells over 50ft high. Not feeling that brave? Paddle in calmer waters with **Half Moon Bay Kayak** (☏650-773-6101; www.hmbkayak.com; 2 Johnson Pier; kayak/SUP rental per hr from $25; ⏰9am-5pm Wed-Mon; 🚻), which rents kayaks and guides tours. Further south down Hwy 1, detour inland to amble down this Victorian-era seaside resort's quaint Main St, its tree-lined blocks overstuffed with knick-knackeries, bookstores, antiques shops and cafes.

✖ 🛏 p193

The Drive ≫ For the next 11 miles heading south, Hwy 1 gently follows the contours of the coast. Vistas of pounding surf, unspoiled shores and dramatic rock outcrops seem boundless. Turn inland onto Hwy 84 at San Gregorio, then right after less than a mile onto Stage Rd, which narrowly winds through the hills for 7 miles south to Pescadero.

TRIP HIGHLIGHT

❹ Pescadero

With its long coastline, mild weather and abundant fresh water, Pescadero has always been prime real estate. Spanish for 'fishmonger,' Pescadero was formally established in 1856, when it was mostly a farming and dairy settlement with a key location along the stagecoach route. Munch on a freshly baked, pull-apart loaf of Italian garlic-and-herb bread stuffed with juicy artichokes from **Arcangeli Grocery Co** (Norm's Market; ☏650-879-0147; www. normsmarket.com; 287 Stage Rd; ⏰10am-6pm; 🅿 🚻) before traipsing around downtown's art galleries and antiques shops. At the north end of the main drag, turn right onto North St and drive a mile to steal-your-heart **Harley Farms Goat Dairy** (☏605-879-0480; www.harleyfarms. com; 205 North St; ⏰10am-5pm Mar-Dec, 11am-4pm Thu-Mon Jan & Feb; 🚻). The farm shop sells creamy artisanal goat cheeses festooned with fruit, nuts and a rainbow of edible flowers. Call ahead for a weekend farm tour or show up anytime to pat the heads of the goats in the pens out back.

✖ 🛏 p193

The Drive ≫ Continue driving past the goat farm on North St to Pescadero Rd. Turn right and head west 2 miles to Pescadero State Beach, passing marshlands where bird-watchers spot waterfowl. Turn left back onto Hwy 1, driving south beside pocket beaches and coves for almost 6 miles to the Pigeon Point turnoff on your right.

❺ Pigeon Point

One of West Coast's tallest lighthouses stands in **Pigeon Point Light Station State Historic Park** (☏650-879-2120; www.parks. ca.gov; 210 Pigeon Point Rd;

Año Nuevo State Park Northern elephant seals

⊙8am-sunset, visitor center 10am-4pm Thu-Mon; P ♦).
The 1872 landmark had to close access to its Fresnel lens when chunks of its cornice began to rain from the sky, but the beam still flashes brightly and the bluff is a prime, though blustery, spot to scan for breaching gray whales.

🛏 p193

The Drive » Back at Hwy 1, turn right and cruise south along the coastline, curving slightly inland as the wind howls all around you, for about 5 miles to Año Nuevo State Park's main entrance.

TRIP HIGHLIGHT

6 Año Nuevo State Park

During winter and early spring, thousands of enormous northern elephant seals noisily mate, give birth, learn to swim, battle for dominance or just laze around on the sands at **Año Nuevo State Park** (☎information 650-879-0227, tour reservations 800-444-4445; www.parks.ca.gov; off Hwy 1, per car $10, 2½-hr tour per person $7; ⊙8:30am-5pm Apr-Nov, tours only mid-Dec–Mar; P ♦). Join park rangers for a guided hike (reservations required)

through the sand dunes for up-close views of the huge pinnipeds – a mature male weighs twice as much as your car!

The Drive » Over the next 6 miles, Hwy 1 southbound traces the coast. As you descend a long hill bordered by a sheer cliff face that recalls Devil's Slide, look for Waddell Beach on your right.

7 Waddell Beach

These thrilling breaks are usually alive with windsurfers, kitesurfers and other daredevils. Wander the chilly sands and get blasted by the winds and you'll quickly

DETOUR: SANTA CRUZ MOUNTAINS

Start: ❽ Santa Cruz

Hwy 9 is a sun-dappled backwoods byway into the Santa Cruz Mountains, passing towering redwood forests and a few fog-blessed vineyards (estate-bottled Pinot Noir is a specialty). Seven miles north of Santa Cruz, **Henry Cowell Redwoods State Park** (info 831-335-4598, reservations 800-444-7275; www.parks.ca.gov; 101 N Big Trees Park Rd, Felton; entry per car $10, campsites $35; sunrise-sunset;) has hiking trails through old-growth redwood trees. Nearby in Felton, **Roaring Camp Railroads** (831-335-4484; www.roaringcamp.com; 5401 Graham Hill Rd, Felton; adult/child 2-12yr from $27/20, parking $8;) operates narrow-gauge steam trains up into the redwoods. It's another 7 miles up to Boulder Creek, a tiny mountain town with simple cafes and a grocery store for picnic supplies. Take Hwy 236 northwest for 10 more twisty miles to **Big Basin Redwoods State Park** (831-338-8860; www.parks.ca.gov; 21600 Big Basin Way, Boulder Creek; entry per car $10, campsites $35; sunrise-sunset;), where misty nature trails loop past skyscraping redwoods.

understand that without a wet suit, you won't be hankering to swim here. Across Hwy 1 is the end of the popular Skyline-to-the-Sea Trail that descends from the redwoods of Big Basin State Park. Just inland, **Rancho del Oso Nature and History Center** (831-427-2288; http://ranchodeloso.org; 3600 Hwy 1, Davenport; noon-4pm Sat & Sun;) has two kid-friendly nature trails, both open daily, through the marshlands behind the beach.

The Drive » Hwy 1 begins slowly moving away from the rocky shoreline as the coast's limestone and sandstone cliffs regularly shed chunks into the white-capped waters below. Motor past roadside farmstands and barns and more pocket beaches before rolling into Santa Cruz after 15 miles.

- - - - - - - - - - - - - - -

TRIP HIGHLIGHT

❽ Santa Cruz

SoCal beach culture meets NorCal counter-culture in Santa Cruz. Witness the old-school radical and freak-show weirdness along **Pacific Ave**, downtown's main drag. Tumble downhill to the West Coast's oldest oceanfront amusement park, **Santa Cruz Beach Boardwalk** (831-423-5590; www.beachboardwalk.com; 400 Beach St; per ride $3-6, all-day pass $34-45; daily Apr-early Sep, seasonal hours vary;), where the smell of cotton candy mixes with the salt air. Continue up W Cliff Dr, which winds for a mile to Lighthouse Point. Join the gawkers on the cliffs peering down at the floating kelp beds, hulking sea lions, playful sea otters and black wet-suit-clad surfers riding **Steamer Lane** surf break. Inside the 1960s-era lighthouse is the memorabilia-packed **Santa Cruz Surfing Museum** (831-420-6289; www.santacruzsurfingmuseum.org; 701 W Cliff Dr; by donation; 10am-5pm Wed-Mon Jul 4-early Sep, noon-4pm Thu-Mon early Sep-Jul 3;). Almost 2 miles further west, W Cliff Dr dead-ends at **Natural Bridges State Beach** (831-423-4609; www.parks.ca.gov; 2531 W Cliff Dr; per car $10; 8am-sunset;), named for its sea arches. Starfish, anemones, crabs and more inhabit myriad tidepools carved into the limestone rocks. Find out about sea creatures both great (look at that blue-whale skeleton!) and small at the nearby **Seymour Marine Discovery Center** (831-459-3800; http://seymourcenter.ucsc.edu; 100 Shaffer Rd; adult/child 3-16yr $8/6; 10am-5pm Tue-Sun Sep-Jun, daily Jul & Aug;).

p61, p193

Eating & Sleeping

Half Moon Bay ③

✕ Half Moon Bay Brewing Company
Pub Food $$

(☎650-728-2739; www.hmbbrewingco.com; 390 Capistrano Rd; mains $14-24; ⏱11:30am-9pm Mon-Thu, to 10pm Fri, 10am-10pm Sat, 10am-9pm Sun; 🐕♿🅿) Serves seafood, burgers and a tantalizing menu of local brews from a sheltered and heated outdoor patio looking out over the bay.

🛏 Beach House at Half Moon Bay
Hotel $$$

(☎800-315-9366, 650-712-0220; www.beach-house.com/half-moon-bay; 4100 N Cabrillo Hwy/Hwy 1; r $225-375; 🅿♿🐕♨) Overlooking the bay from the oceanfront bluffs near Pillar Point Harbor, all of these loft-style suites have down comforters and gas fireplaces to keep you toasty in the fog.

Pescadero ④

✕ Duarte's Tavern
American $$

(☎650-879-0464; www.duartestavern.com; 202 Stage Rd; mains $12-45; ⏱7am-8pm; ♿) You'll rub shoulders with fancy-pants foodies, spandex-swathed cyclists and dusty cowboys at this casual, surprisingly unpretentious fourth-generation family restaurant.

🛏 Costanoa
Cabin, Campground $$

(☎650-879-1100, 877-262-7848; www.costanoa.com; 2001 Rossi Rd; tent/cabin with shared bath from $100/200, lodge r from $200; 🅿♿🐕) Even though the resort includes a **campground** (☎800-562-9867; www.koa.com/campgrounds/santa-cruz-north; tent site $30-34, RV site from $69; 🐕♨), no one can pull a straight face to declare they're actually roughing it here. Down bedding swaddles guests in cushy canvas tent cabins, and chill-averse tent campers can use communal 'comfort stations' with 24-hour dry saunas, fireside patio seating, heated floors and hot showers.

Pigeon Point ⑤

🛏 HI Pigeon Point Lighthouse Hostel
Hostel $

(☎650-879-0633; www.norcalhostels.org/pigeon; 210 Pigeon Point Rd; d/tr with shared bath from $78/107, dm $26-32; ⏱reception 7:30am-10:30pm; 🅿♿@🐕) Not your workaday HI outpost, this highly coveted coastside hostel is all about location. Check in early to snag a spot in the outdoor hot tub, and contemplate roaring waves as the lighthouse beacon races through a starburst sky. Book ahead.

Santa Cruz ⑧

✕ Picnic Basket
Deli $

(☎831-427-9946; http://thepicnicbasketsc.com; 125 Beach St; dishes $3-11; ⏱7am-9pm; ✈♿) Across the street from the beach boardwalk, this locavarian kitchen puts together creative sandwiches such as beet with lemony couscous or 'fancy pants' grilled cheese with fruit chutney, plus homemade soups, breakfast burritos and baked goods.

🛏 Dream Inn
Hotel $$$

(☎831-426-4330, 866-774-7735; www.dreaminnsantacruz.com; 175 W Cliff Dr; r $329-509; 🅿♿❄@🐕♨) Overlooking the wharf from a spectacular hillside perch, this chic boutique hotel is as stylish as Santa Cruz gets. Rooms have all mod cons, while the beach is just steps away.

🛏 Pacific Blue Inn
B&B $$$

(☎831-600-8880; www.pacificblueinn.com; 636 Pacific Ave; r incl breakfast $229-339; 🅿♿🐕♨) This downtown courtyard B&B is an eco-conscious gem, with water-saving fixtures and renewable and recycled building materials. Refreshingly elemental rooms have pillowtop beds, electric fireplaces and flat-screen TVs with DVD players. Free parking and loaner bikes.

Around Monterey & Carmel

17

Briny sea air and drifting fog define Monterey, a fishing village holding relics of California's Spanish and Mexican past. As you explore, witness the scenery lauded by artists and writers.

TRIP HIGHLIGHTS

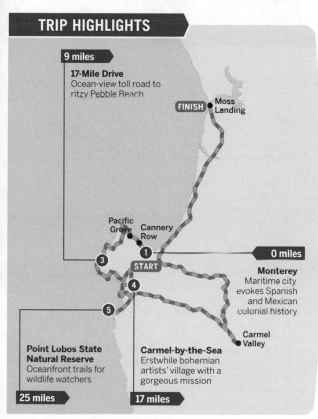

9 miles

17-Mile Drive
Ocean-view toll road to ritzy Pebble Beach

FINISH • **Moss Landing**

Pacific Grove **Cannery Row**

1 **START**

3

4

5

0 miles

Monterey
Maritime city evokes Spanish and Mexican colonial history

Carmel Valley

Point Lobos State Natural Reserve
Oceanfront trails for wildlife watchers

25 miles

Carmel-by-the-Sea
Erstwhile bohemian artists' village with a gorgeous mission

17 miles

**2–3 DAYS
70 MILES / 115KM**

GREAT FOR...

BEST TIME TO GO

August to October for sunniest skies; December to April for whale-watching.

ESSENTIAL PHOTO

Pebble Beach's trademarked lone cypress tree.

BEST FOR FAMILIES

Spend the day at the Monterey Bay Aquarium.

Monterey A lone cypress tree on the coast along 17-Mile Drive

17 Around Monterey & Carmel

Tourist-choked Cannery Row isn't actually the star attraction on the Monterey Peninsula. Much more memorable are ocean panoramas caught from roadside pull-offs on the edge of the bay, on the hiking trails of Point Lobos or from the open-air decks of a winter whale-watching boat. Historical roots show all along this drive, from well-preserved Spanish Colonial adobe buildings in downtown Monterey to Carmel's jewel-box Catholic mission.

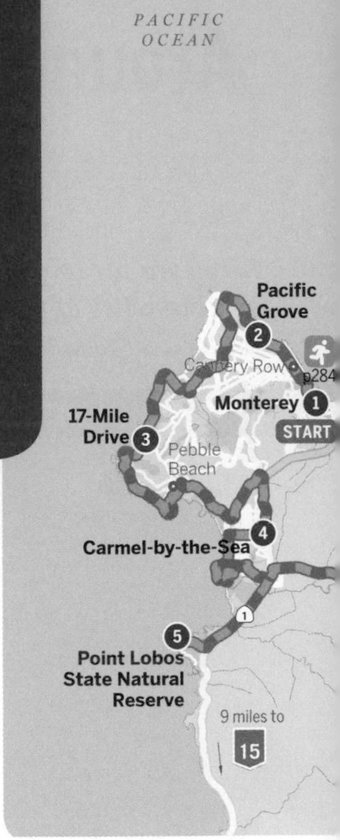

PACIFIC OCEAN

Pacific Grove ②
Cannery Row ✦ p284
Monterey ① START
17-Mile Drive ③
Pebble Beach
Carmel-by-the-Sea ④
Point Lobos ⑤ State Natural Reserve
9 miles to 15

TRIP HIGHLIGHT

① Monterey

Working-class Monterey is all about the sea. Start exploring by walking around **Old Monterey** (p284), downtown's historic quarter, which preserves California's Mexican and Spanish Colonial roots. It's just inland from the salt-sprayed **Municipal Wharf II**, overlooking Monterey Bay National Marine Sanctuary, which protects kelp forests, seals, sea lions, dolphins and whales.

Less than 2 miles northwest of downtown via Lighthouse Ave, was the hectic, smelly epicenter of the sardine-canning industry, Monterey's lifeblood till the 1950s, as immortalized by novelist John Steinbeck. Today, the ecoconscious **Monterey Bay Aquarium** (info 831-648-4800, tickets 866-963-9645; www.monterey bayaquarium.org; 886 Cannery Row; adult/youth 13-17yr/child 3-12yr $40/30/25; 9:30am-6pm Jun, to 6pm Mon-Fri, to 8pm Sat & Sun Jul-Aug, 10am-5pm or 6pm Sep-May;) puts aquatic creatures on educational display, from touch-tolerant sea stars to slimy sea slugs to animated sea otters.

Walking south along Cannery Row, take a few steps up Bruce Ariss Way to peek into the one-room shacks of former cannery workers. Further south along Cannery Row, stop at **Steinbeck Plaza** (Cannery Row) to soak up bay views and snap a photo of yourself with a bronze bust of the famous writer.

p61, p201

The Drive » From Cannery Row, Ocean View Blvd slowly traces the bayfront coastline for 2.5 miles west to Point Pinos,

196

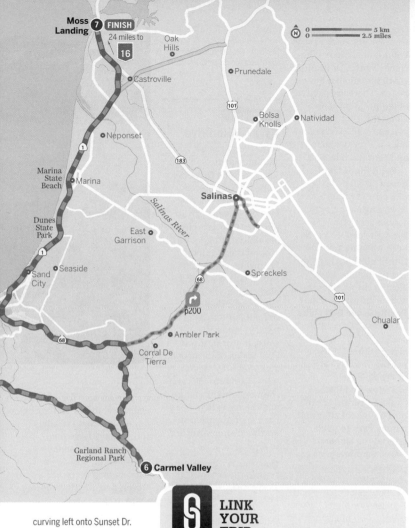

Moss Landing **7** FINISH
24 miles to **16**

Oak Hills

Castroville

Prunedale

101

Bolsa Knolls

Natividad

Neponset

183

Salinas

Marina State Beach

Marina

Salinas River

Dunes State Park

East Garrison

Seaside

Sand City

Spreckels

68

101

Chualar

p200

Ambler Park

68

Corral De Tierra

Garland Ranch Regional Park

6 Carmel Valley

N   0 ——————— 5 km
    0 ——————— 2.5 miles

curving left onto Sunset Dr.
Watch out for cyclists along
this route.

- - - - - - - - - -

❷ Pacific Grove

Founded as a tranquil
Methodist retreat in 1875,
Pacific Grove was where
John Steinbeck's family
once had a summer
cottage. Aptly named

 LINK YOUR TRIP

15 **Big Sur**
Big Sur's
vertiginous coastal
cliffs, hippie-beatnik
retreats and redwood
forests alongside Hwy 1
start 15 miles south of
Carmel-by-the-Sea.

16 **Along Highway 1 to Santa Cruz**
Santa Cruz's 'Surf City'
beaches are about
25 miles north of Moss
Landing via Hwy 1,
which curves around
Monterey Bay.

Ocean View Blvd runs from Lovers Point west to Point Pinos, where it becomes Sunset Dr heading south to Asilomar State Beach. There are plenty of tempting turnoffs along this route where you can walk past pounding surf, rocky outcrops and teeming tidepools.

Point Pinos Lighthouse (☎831-648-3176; www.pointpinoslighthouse.org; 80 Asilomar Ave; suggested donation adult/child 7-12yr $2/1; ☉1-4pm Thu-Mon) has been warning ships off this peninsula's hazardous point since 1855. Next to the lighthouse, golfers crowd the windy **Pacific Grove Golf Links** (☎831-648-5775; www.play pacificgrove.com; 77 Asilomar Blvd; green fees $29-69), a penny-pincher's version of Pebble Beach.

Follow Lighthouse Ave east, turning right onto Ridge Rd after half a mile. Park to stroll around the **Monarch Grove Sanctuary** (www. cityofpacificgrove.org/visiting; 250 Ridge Rd; ☉dawn-dusk; 👫) between October and February or March, when over 25,000 migratory monarch butterflies cluster in this thicket of tall eucalyptus trees – watch out for falling branches!

🍴 🛏 p201

The Drive » Drive back north on Ridge Rd to Lighthouse Ave, which heads east toward leafy downtown Pacific Grove, with its shops, cafes and a natural-history museum for kids. To bypass downtown PG, take the next right after Ridge Rd onto 17-Mile Drive. Drive another mile southwest, crossing Sunset Dr/ Hwy 68, to the Pacific Grove toll gate.

- - - - - - - - - -

TRIP HIGHLIGHT

③ 17-Mile Drive

Once promoted as 'Mother Nature's Drive-Thru,' **17-Mile Drive** (www. pebblebeach.com; per car/ bicycle $10/free) is a spectacularly scenic private toll road (motorcyclists prohibited) that loops around the Monterey Peninsula, connecting Pacific Grove with Pebble Beach and Carmel-by-the-Sea. Using the self-guided tour map handed out at the toll gates, motor past postcard vistas of the ocean and Monterey cypress trees, world-famous golf courses, a luxury lodge and the bay where Spanish explorer Gaspar de Portolá dropped anchor in 1769.

The Drive » If you follow the coastal road heading south and then wrap around back east again, the 17-Mile Drive is only 9 miles long between the Pacific Grove and Carmel toll gates. After exiting the toll road, continue south to Ocean Ave, then turn left for downtown Carmel-by-the-Sea.

- - - - - - - - - -

TRIP HIGHLIGHT

④ Carmel-by-the-Sea

Once an artists' beach colony, this quaint village now has the

GERALD FRENCH / GETTY IMAGES ©

well-manicured feel of a country club. Watch the parade of behatted ladies toting fancy-label shopping bags, and dapper gents driving top-down convertibles along **Ocean Ave**, the slow-mo main drag.

On the west side of town, **Carmel Beach City Park** (off Scenic Rd; 👫 🐕) is a gorgeous white-sand strand, where pampered pups excitedly run off-leash. Just inland, 20th-century poet Robinson Jeffers' **Tor House** (☎831-624-1813; www. torhouse.org; 26304 Ocean View Ave; adult/child 12-17yr $10/5; ☉tours hourly

Pebble Beach Golfers enjoying the game and the scenery

10am-3pm Fri & Sat) **offers fascinating insights into bohemian Old Carmel.**

✕ 🛏 p201

The Drive ≫ From the mission, continue southeast down Rio Rd to the intersection with Hwy 1. Turn right and drive about 2 miles south to the turn-off for Point Lobos State Natural Reserve on your right.

TRIP HIGHLIGHT

⑤ Point Lobos State Natural Reserve

They bark, they bathe and they're fun to watch – sea lions are the stars here at Punta de los Lobos Marinos (Point of the Sea Wolves), where

a dramatically rocky coastline offers excellent tidepooling. Short walks around **Point Lobos State Natural Reserve** (📞831-624-4909; www. pointlobos.org; Hwy 1; per car $10; ☺8am-7pm, closes 5pm early Nov–mid-Mar; **P** 🚹) take in wild scenery and wildlife-watching, including Bird Island, shady cypress groves, the historic Whaler's Cabin and the Devil's Cauldron, a whirlpool that gets splashy at high tide.

The Drive ≫ Back at the park entrance, turn left onto Hwy 1 northbound. Wind 2.5 miles uphill away from the coast to the stoplight intersection

with Carmel Valley Rd. Turn right and drive east through farmlands and vineyards toward Carmel Valley village, about 11.5 miles away.

----

⑥ Carmel Valley

Where sun-kissed vineyards and farm fields rustle beside one another, Carmel Valley is a peaceful side trip. At organic **Earthbound Farm** (📞805-625-6219; www. ebfarm.com; 7250 Carmel Valley Rd; ☺8am-6:30pm Mon-Sat, 9am-6pm Sun; **P** 🚹), sample the fresh-fruit smoothies and home-made soups, or cut your own herbs in the garden. Several wineries further

DETOUR: SALINAS

Start: ❻ Carmel Valley (p199)

From Salinas farmhands to Monterey cannery workers, the sun-baked Central Valley hills to the fishing coastline, Nobel Prize–winning author John Steinbeck drew a perfect picture of the landscapes and communities he knew. See the land and people of his hometown Salinas, a 25-minute drive east of Monterey via Hwy 68. Downtown, the **National Steinbeck Center** (☎831-775-4721; www.steinbeck.org; 1 Main St; adult/child 6-17yr $13/7; ⏰10am-5pm; 🚼) brings his novels to life with interactive exhibits and short movie clips. Look for Rocinante, the camper Steinbeck drove across America while writing *Travels with Charley*. Take a moment and listen to Steinbeck's Nobel acceptance speech – it's grace and power combined.

A few blocks west, **Steinbeck House** (☎831-424-2735; www.steinbeckhouse.com; 132 Central Ave; ⏰restaurant 11:30am-2pm Tue-Sat, gift shop to 3pm) is the author's childhood home. A classic Queen Anne Victorian with dainty bird-patterned lace curtains, it's both a minimuseum and a twee restaurant, where waitstaff in quasi-period dress serve lunch and high tea.

Two miles southeast of downtown, Steinbeck pilgrims can pay their last respects at **Garden of Memories Memorial Park** (850 Abbott St; Ⓟ). An iron sign points the way to the Hamilton family plot, where a simple grave marker identifies where some of Steinbeck's ashes were buried.

---

east offer tastings – don't miss the Pinot Noir bottled by **Boekenoogen** (☎831-659-4215; www.boekenoogenwines.com; 24 W Carmel Valley Rd; tasting fee $10-15; ⏰11am-5pm; Ⓟ). Afterwards, stretch your legs in Carmel Valley village, chock-a-block with genteel cafes and whimsical shops.

The Drive » Backtrack 2 miles west of the village along Carmel Valley Rd, then turn right onto Laureles Grade. After 6 miles, turn left on Hwy 68, driving west to join Hwy 1 northbound. After passing sand dunes, suburbs and artichoke and strawberry fields, Hwy 1 swings back towards the coast. Turn left onto Moss Landing Rd.

- - - - - - - - - - -

❼ Moss Landing

Here's your last chance to get out of the car and meet the local wildlife. Rent a kayak from outfitters on Hwy 1 and paddle past harbor seals into **Elkhorn Slough National Estuarine Research Reserve** (☎831-728-2822; www.elkhornslough.org; 1700 Elkhorn Rd, Watsonville; adult/child 16yr & under $4/free; ⏰9am-5pm Wed-Sun; Ⓟ 🚼), or take a guided weekend hike and go bird-watching. From the fishing harbor at the ocean end of Moss Landing Rd, **Sanctuary Cruises** (☎info 831-917-1042, tickets 888-394-7810; www.sanctuarycruises.com; 7881 Sandholdt Rd; tours $45-55; 🚼) operates year-round whale-watching and dolphin-spotting cruises aboard biodiesel-fueled boats (make advance reservations).

🍴 p201

Eating & Sleeping

Monterey ❶

✖ Sandbar & Grill · Seafood $$

(📞831-373-2818; www.sandbarandgrill
monterey.com; Municipal Wharf 2; mains $10-30;
⏱11am-9pm; 👶) Watch otters play outside
the bay-view windows at this floating seafood
kitchen on the wharf. Stick with the classics
like creamy clam chowder, grilled sand dabs
and jumbo crab club sandwiches. Reservations
strongly recommended.

🛏 Casa Munras · Boutique Hotel $$

(📞831-375-2411, 800-222-2446; www.
hotelcasamunras.com; 700 Munras Ave; r from
$150; P ⊗ @ 🛜 ❄ 👶) Built around an adobe
hacienda once owned by a 19th-century Spanish
colonial don, chic modern rooms come with
lofty beds and some gas fireplaces, all inside
two-story motel-esque buildings. Splash in a
heated outdoor pool, unwind at the tapas bar or
take a sea-salt scrub in the tiny spa. Pet fee $50.

🛏 InterContinental–Clement · Hotel $$$

(📞831-375-4500, 866-781-2406; www.
ictheclementmonterey.com; 750 Cannery Row; r
from $235; P ⊗ ❄ @ 🛜 ❄) Like an upscale
version of a New England millionaire's seaside
mansion, this all-encompassing resort presides
over Cannery Row. For the utmost luxury and
romance, book an ocean-view suite with a
balcony and a private fireplace, then breakfast
in bayfront C Restaurant downstairs.

Pacific Grove ❷

✖ Passionfish · Seafood $$$

(📞831-655-3311; www.passionfish.net; 701
Lighthouse Ave, Pacific Grove; mains $15-36;
⏱5-9pm Sun-Thu, to 10pm Fri & Sat) Fresh,
sustainable seafood is artfully presented in
any number of inventive ways, and a seasonally
inspired menu also carries slow-cooked meats
and vegetarian dishes spotlighting local farms.

🛏 Sunset Inn · Motel $$

(📞831-375-3529; www.gosunsetinn.com;
133 Asilomar Blvd; r incl breakfast $120-239;
P ⊗ 🛜) At this small motor lodge near the
golf course and the beach, attentive staff hand
out keys to crisply redesigned rooms that have
hardwood floors, king-sized beds with cheery
floral-print comforters and sometimes a hot tub
and a fireplace.

Carmel-by-the-Sea ❹

✖ La Bicyclette · French, Italian $$

(📞831-622-9899; www.labicycletterestaurant.
com; Dolores St, at 7th Ave; dinner mains $17-29;
⏱8-10:45am, 11:45am-3:30pm & 5-10pm) Rustic
European comfort food using seasonal local
ingredients packs canoodling couples into this
bistro, with an open kitchen baking wood-fired
oven pizzas. Excellent local wines by the glass.

✖ Mundaka · Tapas $$

(📞831-624-7400; www.mundakacarmel.com;
San Carlos St, btwn Ocean & 7th Aves; small
plates $7-23; ⏱5:30-10pm Sun-Wed, to 11pm
Thu-Sat) This stone courtyard hideaway is a
svelte escape from Carmel's stuffy 'newly wed
and nearly dead' crowd. Taste Spanish tapas
and house-made sangria while world beats spin.

🛏 Cypress Inn · Boutique Hotel $$$

(📞800-443-7443, 831-624-3871; www.cypress-
inn.com; Lincoln St, at 7th Ave; r incl breakfast from
$265; P ⊗ 🛜 👶) Done up in Spanish Colonial
style, this 1929 inn is co-owned by movie star
Doris Day. Airy terracotta hallways with colorful
tiles give it a Mediterranean feel, while sunny
rooms face the courtyard. Pet fee $30.

Moss Landing ❼

✖ Phil's Fish Market · Seafood $$

(📞831-633-2152; www.philsfishmarket.com;
7600 Sandholdt Rd; mains $9-23; ⏱10am-
8pm Sun-Thu, to 9pm Fri & Sat; P 👶) Devour
buckets of crab, mussels, squid, scallops and
prawns covered in San Francisco–style cioppino
sauce at this warehouse-sized eatery right by
the harbor.

Around San Luis Obispo

18

It's nothing but all-natural fun in SLO County, with sunny beaches and rolling vineyard roads. Slow down – this idyllic coast deserves to be savored, not gulped.

TRIP HIGHLIGHTS

95 miles

Paso Robles Wine Country
Rural vineyards off Hwy 46

Paso Robles

FINISH

7

33 miles

Avila Beach
Sunny shores by an old fishing port

Cayucos

Morro Bay

San Luis Obispo
START

55 miles

5

Montaña de Oro State Park
Peak hikes and tidepooling coves

4

3

Arroyo Grande

Pismo Beach
Rockin' retro California beach town

25 miles

2–3 DAYS
115 MILES / 185KM

GREAT FOR...

BEST TIME TO GO
July through October brings sunniest skies.

 ESSENTIAL PHOTO
Morro Rock silhouetted at sunset.

 BEST FOR WINERIES
Hwy 46 east and west of Paso Robles.

Pismo Beach Monarch butterflies clustered in a eucalyptus tree

18 Around San Luis Obispo

Halfway between San Francisco and LA, the laid-back college town of San Luis Obispo (aka 'SLO') is a gateway to coastal adventures. Beach towns and fishing villages offer a bucketful of outdoor pursuits, both on land and at sea – and wherever there's natural beauty, it's never too far from Hwy 1. Farm-to-table locavorian restaurants and vineyards abound, especially in Paso Robles' wine country, ideal for lazy weekend or weekday drives.

❶ San Luis Obispo

Oprah called it 'the happiest city in America,' and once you spend a few hours downtown, you might agree. CalPoly university students inject a healthy dose of hubbub into the streets, shops, pubs and cafes, especially during the weekly **farmers market** (☏805-541-0286; http://downtownslo.com; Higuera St; ⏰6-9pm Thu; 🅿 👫), which turns downtown's Higuera St into a street festival with live music and sidewalk food stalls. Like many

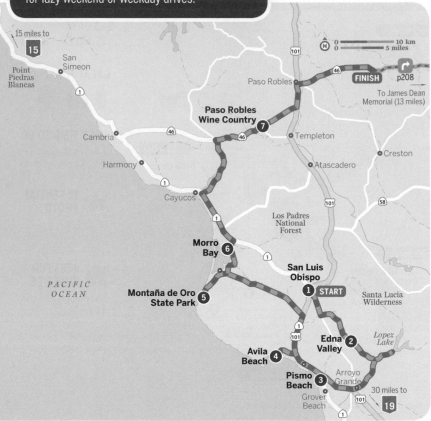

other California towns, SLO grew up around a Spanish Catholic mission, **Mission San Luis Obispo de Tolosa** (☎805-543-6850; www.missionsanluisobispo. org; 751 Palm St; donation $2; ☺9am-5pm late Mar-Oct, to 4pm Nov–mid-Mar; ⏶), founded in 1772 by missionary Junípero Serra. The creek that once used to irrigate mission orchards still flows through downtown, beside tranquil, shaded walking paths.

✖ ⏟ p209

The Drive » From downtown SLO, follow Broad St/Hwy 227 for 2.5 stop-and-go miles southeast, turning left before the airport onto Tank Farm Rd. After a mile, curve right and continue onto Orcutt Rd, which rolls up and down past vineyards into Edna Valley

LINK YOUR TRIP

19 **Santa Barbara Wine Country**

Want more good grapes? Follow Hwy 101 south of Pismo Beach for 45 miles to the Santa Ynez Valley.

15 **Big Sur**

From Cayucos, cruise Hwy 1 north for 45 miles to the southern Big Sur coast, passing Hearst Castle halfway along.

---

❷ Edna Valley

Cradled by the rich volcanic soil of the Santa Lucia foothills, thriving **Edna Valley wineries** (www.slowine.com) are known for their crisp, often unoaked Chardonnay and subtle Syrah and Pinot Noir. Pick up a free map from any tasting room. All are signposted along Orcutt Rd and Edna Rd/Hwy 227. These roads run parallel through the peaceful valley, which is cooled by drifting coastal fog in the morning before being brightened by afternoon sunshine. **Niven Family Wine Estates** (☎805-269-8200; www.nivenfamilywines. com; 5828 Orcutt Rd; tasting fee $12; ☺10am-5pm; P) pours inside a 20th-century wooden schoolhouse, while **Edna Valley Vineyard** (☎805-544-5855; www.ednavalleyvineyard.com; 2585 Biddle Ranch Rd; tasting fee $10-15; ☺10am-5pm; P) has panoramic windows, which overlook vineyards. Further southeast, **Talley Vineyards** (☎805-489-0446; www.talleyvineyards. com; 3031 Lopez Dr, Arroyo Grande; tasting fee $10-18; ☺10:30am-4:30pm; P) offers winery tours by appointment.

The Drive » From Talley Vineyards, Lopez Rd winds west toward Arroyo Grande, just over 6 miles away. Turn left onto Branch St, then merge onto Hwy 101 north to Pismo Beach. Exit at Price St, which enters

downtown Pismo Beach. Turn left onto Pomeroy Ave and roll downhill to the ocean.

TRIP HIGHLIGHT

❸ Pismo Beach

By a wooden pier that stretches towards the setting sun, James Dean once trysted with Pier Angeli. Today, this classic California beach town feels like somewhere straight out of a 1950s hot-rod dream. Pismo likes to call itself the 'Clam Capital of the World,' but these days the wide, sandy beach is pretty much clammed out. You'll have better luck catching something fishy off the pier. To ride the waves, rent a wet suit and board from any surf shop. After dark, go bar hopping or knock down pins at the retro bowling alley. The next day, drive a mile south of downtown to the **Monarch Butterfly Grove** (☎805-773-5301; www. monarchbutterfly.org; Hwy 1, ☺sunrise-sunset, ⏶), where migratory monarchs roost by the thousands in eucalyptus trees, usually from November through February.

✖ ⏟ p60, p209

The Drive » Follow Hwy 1 north through downtown Pismo Beach, then follow the signs to rejoin Hwy 101 northbound for almost 4 miles to exit 195 for Avila Beach Dr. Keep left at the fork, then wind slowly west downhill to Avila Beach, about 3 miles away.

DANITA DELIMONT / GETTY IMAGES ©

❹ Avila Beach

For a perfectly lazy summer day at the beach, rent beach chairs and umbrellas underneath Avila Pier, off downtown's sparkling new waterfront promenade. Two miles further west, the coastal road dead-ends at Port San Luis. The barking of sea lions echoes as you stroll past seafood markets and shacks to the end of creaky weather-worn **Harford Pier**, where you while away time gazing out over the choppy waters. If you'd like to visit 1890 **Point San Luis Lighthouse** (✐ guided hike reservations 805-528-8758, trolley tour reservations 800-838-3006; www.sanluislight house.org; lighthouse $5, incl trolley tour adult/child 3-12yr $20/15; ☺ guided hikes 8:45am-1pm Wed & Sat, trolley tours noon & 1pm Wed, noon, 1pm & 2pm Sat Mar-Jul), guided tour reservations are required.

Back uphill near Hwy 101, you can pick your own fruit and feed the goats at **Avila Valley Barn** (✐805-595-2816; www.avilavalleybarn.com; 560 Avila Beach Dr; ☺9am-6pm mid-Mar–late Dec, to 5pm Thu-Mon Jan–mid-Mar; P ✸) farmstand, or do some stargazing from a private redwood hot tub at **Sycamore Mineral Springs** (✐805-595-7302; www.sycamoresprings.com; 1215 Avila Beach Dr; 1hr per person $14.50-18.50; ☺8am-midnight).

The Drive » Take Hwy 101 back northbound toward San Luis Obispo. Exit after 4.5 miles at Los Osos Valley Rd, which leaves behind stop-and-go strip-mall traffic to slowly roll past rural farmlands for about 11 miles. After passing through downtown Los Osos, curve left onto Pecho Valley Rd, which enters Montaña de Oro State Park a few miles later.

❺ Montaña de Oro State Park

In spring, the hillsides of **Montaña de Oro State Park** (✐805-772-7434; www.parks.ca.gov; 3550 Pecho Valley Rd, Los Osos; ☺6am-10pm; P ✸) are blanketed by bright California native poppies, wild mustard

Montaña de Oro State Park Yellow flowers cover the coastline

and other wildflowers, giving this park its Spanish name, meaning 'mountain of gold.' Along the winding access road, sand dunes and the wind-tossed bluffs of the Pacific appear. Pull over at Spooner's Cove, a postcard-perfect sandy beach once used by smugglers. Here the grinding of the Pacific and

North American plates has uplifted and tilted sedimentary layers of submarine rock, visible from shore. Hike along the beach and the park's grassy ocean bluffs, or drive uphill past the visitor center to tackle the 4-mile round-trip trail up rocky Valencia Peak – the summit views are exhilarating.

The Drive » Backtrack on Pecho Rd out of the park, curving right onto Los Osos Valley Rd. East of Los Osos, turn left onto Bay Blvd, winding north alongside Morro Bay's estuary. Before reaching Hwy 101, turn left onto Morro Bay State Park Rd, continuing on Main St into downtown Morro Bay. Turn left on Marina St and drive downhill to the Embarcadero.

DETOUR: JAMES DEAN MEMORIAL

Start: ❼ Paso Robles Wine Country

On Hwy 46 about 25 miles east of Paso Robles, there's a monument near the spot where *Rebel Without a Cause* star James Dean fatally crashed his Porsche on September 30, 1955, at the age of 24. Ironically, the actor had recently filmed a public-safety campaign TV spot against drag racing and speeding on US highways. Look for the shiny brushed-steel memorial wrapped around an oak tree outside the Jack Ranch Cafe truck stop, which has a few old photographs and some dusty movie-star memorabilia inside.

❻ Morro Bay

This fishing village is home to **Morro Rock**, a volcanic peak jutting up from the ocean floor. (Too bad about those power-plant smokestacks obscuring the views, though.) You're likely to spot harbor seals and sea otters as you paddle around the bay in a kayak rented from the waterfront Embarcadero, crowded with seafood shacks. Or drive a mile north of the marina to walk partway around the base of the landmark rock. West of downtown in **Morro Bay State Park** (☏805-772-2694; www.parks.ca.gov; 60 State Park Rd; park entry free, museum adult/child under 17yr $3/free; ⏱museum 10am-5pm; 🅿♿) at the **Museum of Natural History**, kids can touch interactive models of the bay's ecosystem and stuffed wildlife mounts.

🍴 🛏 p209

The Drive » Follow Main St north to Hwy 1. For 4 miles, Hwy 1 northbound rides above ocean beaches. In Cayucos, turn right onto Old Creek Rd, a winding, narrow back road, passing citrus farms and cattle ranches. Turn right after 9 miles onto Hwy 46, which heads east through wine country for 11 miles to meet Hwy 101 in Paso Robles.

TRIP HIGHLIGHT

❼ Paso Robles Wine Country

Franciscan missionaries brought the first grapes to this region in the late 18th century, but it wasn't until the 1920s that the now-famous Zinfandel vines took root in Paso Robles. Coasting through golden-brown hills and grassy pasture lands, Hwy 46 passes family-owned vineyards, olive orchards and rustic farmstands. Pick up a free **winery tour map** (www.pasowine.com) from any tasting room and sniff out boutique winemakers such as Adelaida and Linne Calodo, as well as established big-name producers like Justin, Eberle and Tobin James. Or trust serendipity and follow rural side roads to discover the region's next break-out winery. After a long afternoon spent in sun-drenched vineyards, retreat to leafy downtown Paso Robles. Just off the central park square, you'll find dozens more wine-tasting rooms and bars, restaurants and urbane boutiques.

🍴 p209

Eating & Sleeping

San Luis Obispo ❶

✖ Big Sky Café
Californian $$

(📞805-545-5401; www.bigskycafe.com; 1121 Broad St; dinner mains $11-25; ⏱7am-9pm Mon-Thu, to 10pm Fri, 8am-9pm Sat, 8am-9pm Sun; 🅿 👪) Big Sky is a big room, and still the wait can be long – its tagline is 'analog food for a digital world.' Vegetarians have almost as many options as carnivores, and many of the ingredients are sourced locally.

✖ Firestone Grill
Barbecue $

(📞805-783-1001; www.firestonegrill.com; 1001 Higuera St; dishes $4-11; ⏱11am-10pm Sun-Wed, to 11pm Thu-Sat; 👪) If you can stomach huge lines, long waits for a table, and sports-bar-style service, you'll get to sink your teeth into an authentic Santa Maria–style tri-tip steak sandwich on a toasted garlic roll and a basket of super-crispy fries.

🛏 Peach Tree Inn
Motel $$

(📞805-543-3170, 800-227-6396; http://peachtreeinn.com; 2001 Monterey St; r incl breakfast $89-149; ⏱office 7am-10pm; 🅿 ☕ @ 🛜) The folksy, nothing-fancy motel rooms here are inviting, especially those right by the creek or with rocking chairs on wooden porches overlooking grassy lawns, eucalyptus trees and rose gardens. Continental breakfast features homemade breads.

Pismo Beach ❸

✖ Old West Cinnamon Rolls
Bakery $

(📞805-773-1428; http://oldwestcinnamonrolls.com; 861 Dolliver St; snacks $3-6; ⏱6:30am-5:30pm; 🅿 👪) The name says it all at this gob-smacking bakery by the beach.

🛏 Pismo Lighthouse Suites
Hotel $$

(📞805-773-2411, 800-245-2411; www.pismolighthousesuites.com; 2411 Price St; ste incl breakfast from $179; 🅿 ☕ @ 🛜 ♿ 👪) With everything a vacationing family needs – from kitchenettes to a life-sized outdoor chessboard, a putting green, table tennis and badminton

courts – this contemporary all-suites hotel right on the beach is hard to tear yourself away from. Ask about off-season discounts. Pet fee $30.

Morro Bay ❻

✖ Giovanni's Fish Market & Galley
Seafood $$

(📞877-521-4467; www.giovannisfishmarket.com; 1001 Front St; mains $5-15; ⏱market 9am-6pm, restaurant from 11am; 👪) At this family-run joint on the Embarcadero, folks line up for batter-fried fish and chips and killer garlic fries. You'll have to dodge beggar birds on the outdoor deck. Inside there's a market with all the fixin's for a beach campground fish-fry.

✖ Taco Temple
Californian, Seafood $$

(📞805-772-4965; 2680 Main St; mains $10-20; ⏱11am-9pm Wed-Mon; 👪) Overlook the Hwy 1 frontage-road location for huge helpings of Cal Mex fusion flavor. At the next table, there might be fishers talking about the good ol' days or starving surfers. Cash only.

🛏 Beach Bungalow Inn & Suites
Motel $$

(📞805-772-9700; www.morrobaybeachbungalow.com; 1050 Morro Ave; d $130-230; 🅿 ☕ 🛜 👪) This butter-yellow motor court's chic, contemporary rooms are dressed up with hardwood floors, plush rugs, pillowtop mattresses and down comforters for foggy nights. Pet fee $30.

Paso Robles Wine Country ❼

✖ Artisan
Californian $$$

(📞805-237-8084; www.artisanpasorobles.com; 843 12th St; shared plates $8-19, mains $19-39; ⏱3-9pm Mon-Thu, to 10pm Fri, 10am-2pm & 5:30-10pm Sat, 10am-2pm & 5:30-9pm Sun) Chef Chris Kobayashi often ducks out of the kitchen just to make sure you're loving his impeccable contemporary renditions of modern American cuisine, featuring sustainably farmed meats, wild-caught seafood and artisan California cheeses. Impressive wine, beer and cocktail menus. Reservations essential.

Santa Barbara Wine Country

19

Oak-dotted hillsides, winding country roads, rows of sweetly heavy grapevines stretching into the distance – let yourself be seduced sideways by the Santa Maria and Santa Ynez Valleys.

TRIP HIGHLIGHTS

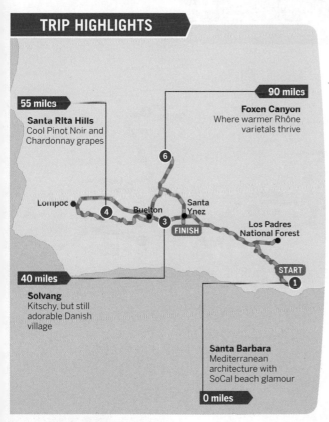

90 miles

Foxen Canyon
Where warmer Rhône varietals thrive

55 miles

Santa Rita Hills
Cool Pinot Noir and Chardonnay grapes

Lompoc

Buelton

Santa Ynez

FINISH

Los Padres National Forest

40 miles

Solvang
Kitschy, but still adorable Danish village

START

Santa Barbara
Mediterranean architecture with SoCal beach glamour

0 miles

2–3 DAYS
145 MILES / 235KM

GREAT FOR...

BEST TIME TO GO
April to October for optimal sunshine.

 ESSENTIAL PHOTO

Danish windmills in Solvang.

 BEST FOR WALKING

Los Olivos' wine-tasting rooms and boutique shops.

19 Santa Barbara Wine Country

The 2004 Oscar-winning film *Sideways*, an ode to wine-country living as seen through the misadventures of middle-aged buddies Miles and Jack, may have gotten the party started. But passionate vintners, ecominded entrepreneurs and gorgeous wine trails are what's keeping Santa Barbara in the juice. More than 100 wineries spread out across the pastoral landscape, with five small towns all clustered prettily within a 10-mile drive of one another.

TRIP HIGHLIGHT

1 Santa Barbara

Start pretending to live the luxe life in Santa Barbara, a coastal Shangri-la where the air is redolent with citrus and flowery bougainvillea drapes whitewashed buildings with Spanish Colonial-style red-tiled roofs, all cradled by pearly beaches. Before heading out of town into the wine country for the day or the weekend, make time to visit landmark **Mission**

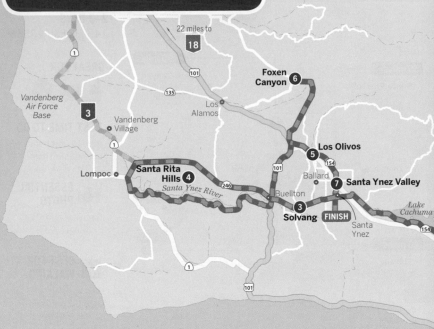

Santa Barbara (☎805-682-4713; www.santa barbaramission.org; 2201 Laguna St; adult/child 5-17yr $8/3; ☺9am-5pm, last entry 4:15pm; P 👤), California's 'Queen of the Missions.' Then walk around downtown's historical buildings and museums (p286), all on or just off **State St**, which leads downhill to the ocean and splintered wooden **Stearns Wharf** (www. stearnswharf.org; ☺ open daily, hours vary; P 👤), the West Coast's oldest continuously operating pier. A few blocks inland from the beach, follow Santa Barbara's **Urban Wine Trail** (www.urbanwinetrailsb. com), where boutique wine-tasting rooms are typically open from noon to 6pm daily (tasting fees $5 to $15).

✕ 🛏 p60, p70, p217, p319

The Drive ›› In the morning, take a short drive north on Hwy 101, then follow winding, narrow Hwy 154 up into the Santa Ynez Mountains and over San Marcos Pass. About 9 miles from Hwy 101, turn left onto Stagecoach Rd, passing the 1860s Cold Springs Tavern. After 2 miles, turn right on Paradise Rd.

- - - - - - - - - - - - -

❷ Los Padres National Forest

Off Paradise Rd, the tall-treed **Los Padres National Forest** (☎805-967-3481; www.fs.usda. gov/lpnf; 3505 Paradise Rd; daily pass per car $5; ☺8am-4:30pm Mon-Fri, also 8am-4:30pm Sat late May-early Sep; 👤) contains several good hiking trails for all ages, all easily accessed off Hwy 154. Starting beyond the family campgrounds and river crossing on Paradise Rd, the creek-side Red Rock Trail leads for a mile to rocky pools and waterfalls where you can sunbathe or swim.

The Drive ›› Backtrack along Paradise Rd, then turn right and follow Hwy 154 northbound past Lake Cachuma and the rolling hillsides for over 13 miles. Turn left onto Hwy 246 and keep motoring five more flat miles through the Santa Ynez Valley west to Solvang.

- - - - - - - - - - - - -

TRIP HIGHLIGHT

❸ Solvang

Loosely translated as 'sunny fields,' this touristy Danish village was founded in 1911 on what was once a Mexican *rancho* land grant. Filled with knick-knack stores and storybook-esque motels, the town is almost as sticky-sweet as the Scandinavian bakery pastries gobbled by day-trippers. Wine-tasting rooms and windmills decorate the village's pedestrian-friendly streets. **Tocatta**

San Rafael Wilderness

0 —— 10 km
0 —— 5 miles

Los Padres National Forest ❷

154
Goleta
101
p286
START ❶
Santa Barbara

LINK YOUR TRIP

18 Around San Luis Obispo

Want more wine, but beaches too? Drive Hwy 101 north of the Santa Ynez Valley for 45 miles to Pismo Beach.

3 Mission Trail

Trace the path of Spanish colonial history at La Purísima Mission, 18 miles northwest of Solvang via Hwy 246.

Tasting Room (☎805-685-5506; www.llwine.com; 1665 Copenhagen Dr; tasting fee $8-15; ⏰11am-5:30pm Sun-Thu, usually open later Fri & Sat), where locals gather for after-work drinks, specializes in Italian varietals and robust Tuscan blends. For a break from the grapes, the pint-sized **Wildling Museum** (☎805-688-1082; www.wildlingmuseum.org; 1511 Mission Dr; adult/child under 17yr $5/free; ⏰11am-5pm Mon & Wed-Fri, from 10am Sat & Sun; P 👶) exhibits nature-themed California and American Western art. On a residential side street, the tiny **Elverhøj Museum of History & Art** (☎805-686-1211; www.elverhoj.org; 1624 Elverhoy Way; suggested donation adult/child under 13yr $5/free; ⏰11am-4pm Wed-Sun; 👶) uncovers the real roots of Danish life in Solvang. Tranquil today, **Old Mission Santa Inés** (☎805-688-4815; www.missionsantaines.org; 1760 Mission Dr; adult/child under 12yr $5/free; ⏰9am-4:30pm; P 👶) witnessed an 1824 Chumash revolt against Spanish colonial cruelty.

✕ 🍴 p217

The Drive » Continue west on Hwy 246 past equestrian ranches and the famous ostrich farm (as seen during Jack's predawn run in *Sideways*) for just a few miles to Buellton. Continue across Hwy 101 and drive west toward Lompoc.

TRIP HIGHLIGHT

❹ Santa Rita Hills

When it comes to rolling scenery, ecoconscious farming practices and top-notch Pinot Noir and Chardonnay grapes kissed by coastal fog, the **Santa Rita Hills** (www.staritahills.com) undoubtedly hold their own. Almost a dozen tasting rooms open their doors daily along this 36-mile scenic loop west of Hwy 101. Be prepared to share these slow-moving roads with sweaty cyclists, Harley Davidson bikers and an occasional John Deere tractor. Heading west of Buellton into the countryside, **Babcock Winery** (☎805-736-1455; www.babcockwinery.com; 5175 E Hwy 146, Lompoc; tasting fee $15-18; ⏰10:30am-5pm Sun-Wed, to 6pm Thu-Sat; P) and **Melville Vineyards and Winery** (☎805-735-7030; www.melvillewinery.com; 5185 E Hwy 146, Lompoc; tasting fee $10-20; ⏰11am-4pm Sun-Thu, to 5pm Fri & Sat; P) are neighboring small-lot estate winemakers who talk about pounds per plant, not tons per acre. Turn left onto Hwy 1 south, then left again on Santa Rosa Rd. Just west of Hwy 101 by a hillside olive orchard, **Mosby Winery** (☎805-688-2415; www.mosbywines.com; 9496 Santa Rosa Rd, Buellton; tasting fee $10; ⏰10am-4pm

NIK WHEELER / GETTY IMAGES ©

Mon-Thu, to 4:30pm Fri-Sun; P) pours unusual Cal-Italian varietals inside a red carriage house.

The Drive » At the eastern end of Santa Rosa Rd, merge onto fast-tracked Hwy 101 northbound. After 6 miles, take the Hwy 154 exit for Los Olivos, driving another 3 miles further east past more rolling vineyards.

❺ Los Olivos

Strutting in cowboy hats and high heels, the ranching town of 'The Olives' has a four-block-long main street lined with wine bars and

Santa Ynez Valley Rows of vines near Los Olivos

restaurants, art galleries, cafes and fashionable shops seemingly airlifted straight out of Napa Valley. To make it all the more perfect, you can easily walk between downtown's inviting wine-tasting rooms on a long, lazy afternoon. Chat with the family winemakers inside the wooden shack at **Carhartt Vineyard Tasting Room** (☎805-693-5100; www.carharttvineyard.com; 2990A Grand Ave; tasting fee $10; ☺11am-6pm). Wine snobs are given the boot at **Saarloos + Sons** (☎805-688-1200; http://saarloosandsons.com; 2971

Grand Ave; tasting fee $10-15; ☺11am-5pm, last pour 4:30pm), a shabby-chic tasting room where wine flights can be paired with mini cupcakes.

✗ p217

The Drive » From Los Olivos, drive west on Hwy 154 for 3 miles. Before reaching Hwy 101, turn right onto Zaca Station Rd, then follow it for 3 winding miles northwest onto Foxen Canyon Rd.

- - - - - - - - - -

TRIP HIGHLIGHT

6 Foxen Canyon

On the celebrated wine trail through **Foxen Canyon** (www.foxencanyon-winetrail.com), tidy rows of

grapevines border some of Santa Barbara County's prettiest wineries. This country lane meanders north all the way to the Santa Maria Valley before finally reaching the 1875 **San Ramon Chapel** (www.sanramonchapel.org; Foxen Canyon Rd; P), a good turnaround point after about 15 miles.

Furthest south, tour buses crowd **Firestone Vineyard** (☎805 688 3940; www.firestonewine.com; 5017 Zaca Station Rd, Los Olivos; tasting fee $10-15, incl tour $20; ☺10am-5pm; P), Santa Barbara's oldest estate winery (it's where Miles, Jack and their dates

LOCAL KNOWLEDGE: WINE TASTING TIPS

To make the most of your wine tour, travel the wine country in small groups and with an itinerary focused on just a handful of wineries. Keep an open mind: don't tell the staff you never drink Chardonnay or Merlot – who knows, the wine you try that day may change your mind. Picnicking is usually welcome, and you'll be considered especially cool if you complement your lunch with a bottle of just-purchased wine. Not so cool? Heavy perfume and smoking. Otherwise, enjoy yourself and don't be afraid to ask questions – most tasting rooms welcome novices.

sneak into the barrel room in *Sideways*). At hidden **Demetria Estate** (☏805-686-2345; www.demetriaestate.com; 6701 Foxen Canyon Rd, Los Olivos; tasting fee $20; ☺ by appt only; P), Rhône varietals and pinot grapes are farmed biodynamically. On a former cattle ranch, sustainable **Foxen Winery** (☏805-937-4251; www.foxenvineyard.com; 7200 & 7600 Foxen Canyon Rd, Santa Maria; tasting fee $10-15; ☺11am-4pm; P) cracks open steel-cut Chardonnay and full-fruited Pinot Noir in a solar-powered tasting room. Up the road, Foxen's old 'shack' – with a corrugated-metal roof and funky decor – pours Bordeaux-style and Italian varietals that are award-winning.

The Drive » Backtrack just over 17 miles along Foxen Canyon Rd, keeping left at the intersection with Zaca Station Rd to return to Los Olivos. Turn left onto Hwy 154 southbound for 2 miles, then turn right onto Roblar Ave for Ontiveros Rd.

- - - - - - - - - - -

❼ Santa Ynez Valley

Further inland in the warm Santa Ynez Valley, Rhône-style grapes do best, including Syrah and Viognier. Some of the most popular tasting rooms cluster between Los Olivos, Solvang and Santa Ynez, but noisy tour groups, harried staff and stingy pours too often disappoint.

Thankfully that's not the case at **Beckmen Vineyards** (☏805-688-8664; www.beckmenvineyards. com; 2670 Ontiveros Rd, Solvang; tasting fee $20-28, incl tour $25; ☺11am-5pm; P 🍴), where biodynamically farmed, estate-grown varietals flourish on the unique terroir of Purisima Mountain. For more natural beauty, backtrack east on Roblar Ave to family-owned **Clairmont Farms** (☏805-688-7505; www.clairmontfarms.com; 2480 Roblar Ave; ☺10am-4pm; P 🍴), where purple lavender fields bloom like a Monet masterpiece in early summer.

Turn right onto Refugio Rd, which flows south past more vineyards, fruit orchards and farms and straight across Hwy 154 to **Kalyra Winery** (☏805-693-8864; www.kalyrawinery.com; 343 N Refugio Rd, Santa Ynez; tasting fee $12-14; ☺11am-5pm Mon-Fri, from 10am Sat & Sun; P), where an Australian traveled halfway around the world to combine two loves: surfing and wine making. Try his Shiraz made with imported Australian grapes or locally grown varietals, all in bottles with Aboriginal art–inspired labels.

Eating & Sleeping

Santa Barbara ❶

✖ Olio Pizzeria   Italian $$

(☎805-899-2699; www.oliopizzeria.com; 11 W Victoria St; shared plates $5-24, lunch mains $11-16; ⏱11:30am-10pm; ✈) Just around the corner from State St, this high-ceilinged pizzeria with a happening wine bar proffers crispy, wood-oven-baked pizzas, platters of imported cheeses and meats, garden-fresh *insalate* (salads), savory traditional Italian *antipasti* and sweet *dolci* (desserts).

▥ Agave Inn   Motel $

(☎805-687-6009; http://agaveinnsb.com; 3222 State St; r from $119; P⊖❄️🛜) While it's still just a motel at heart, this boutique-on-a-budget property's 'Mexican pop meets modern' motif livens things up with a color palette from a Frieda Kahlo painting. Flat-screen TVs, microwaves, minifridges and air-con make it a standout option. Family-sized rooms have kitchenettes and pull-out sofa beds. Continental breakfast included.

▥ Harbor House Inn   Motel $$

(☎805-962-9745, 888-474-6789; www.harborhouseinn.com; 104 Bath St; r from $180; P⊖🛜) Down by the harbor, this converted motel offers brightly lit studios with hardwood floors and a beachy design scheme. A few have full kitchens and fireplaces, but there's no air-con. Rates include a welcome basket of breakfast goodies (with a two-night minimum stay) and beach towels, chairs and umbrellas and three-speed bicycles to borrow.

Solvang ❸

✖ El Rancho Market   Supermarket $

(☎805-688-4300; http://elranchomarket.com; 2886 Mission Dr; ⏱6am-11pm; ♿) East of downtown, this upscale supermarket – with a full deli, smokin' barbecued meats, a wine shop and an espresso bar – is the best place to fill your picnic basket before heading out to the wineries.

▥ Hadsten House   Boutique Hotel $$

(☎805-688-3210, 800-457-5373; www.hadstenhouse.com; 1450 Mission Dr; r $99-225; P⊖❄️🛜🏊) This revamped motel has luxuriously updated just about everything, except for its routine exterior. Inside, rooms are surprisingly plush, with flat-screen TVs, comfy duvets and high-end bath products. Spa suites come with jetted tubs.

▥ Hamlet Inn   Motel $$

(☎805-688-4413; http://thehamletinn.com; 1532 Mission Dr; r $99-229; P⊖❄️🛜) This remodeled motel is to wine-country lodging what IKEA is to interior design: a budget-friendly, trendy alternative. Crisp, modern rooms have bright Danish-flag bedspreads and iPod docking stations.

Los Olivos ❺

✖ Los Olivos Wine Merchant
& Café   Californian, Mediterranean $$

(☎805-688-7265; www.losolivoscafe.com; 2879 Grand Ave; mains breakfast $9-12, lunch & dinner $13-29; ⏱11:30am-8.30pm daily, also 8-10:30am Sat & Sun) With white canopies and a wisteria-covered trellis, this wine-country landmark (as seen in *Sideways*) swirls up a casual-chic SoCal ambience. It stays open between lunch and dinner for antipasto platters, hearty salads and crispy pizzas and wine flights at the bar.

✖ Petros   Greek $$$

(☎805-686-5455; www.petrosrestaurant.com; Fess Parker Wine Country Inn & Spa, 2860 Grand Ave, shared plates $8-20, dinner mains $22-36; ⏱7am-10pm Sun-Thu, to 11pm Fri & Sat; ✈) In a sunny dining room, sophisticated Greek cuisine makes a refreshing change from Italianate wine-country kitsch. Housemade *meze* (appetizers) will satisfy even picky foodies.

✖ Sides Hardware
& Shoes   American $$$

(☎805-688-4820; http://sidesrestaurant.com; 2375 Alamo Pintado Ave; mains lunch $14-18, dinner $26-35; ⏱11am-2:30pm daily, 5-8:30pm Sun-Thu, to 9pm Fri & Sat; ♿) Inside a historic storefront, this bistro delivers haute country cooking like 'hammered pig' sandwiches topped by apple slaw, fried chicken with garlicky kale and Colorado lamb sirloin alongside goat-cheese gnocchi. Book ahead for dinner.

Lake Tahoe Loop

20

Shimmering in myriad blues and greens, and astounding in its clarity, Lake Tahoe is the USA's second-deepest lake. Drive around its spellbinding 72-mile shoreline.

TRIP HIGHLIGHTS

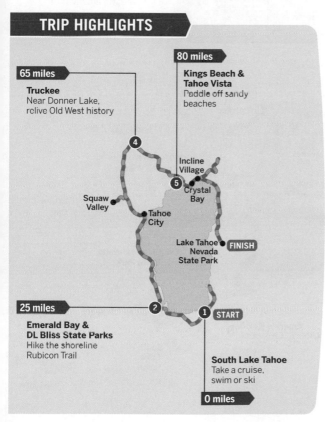

65 miles

Truckee
Near Donner Lake, relive Old West history

80 miles

Kings Beach & Tahoe Vista
Paddle off sandy beaches

Squaw Valley

Incline Village

Crystal Bay

Tahoe City

Lake Tahoe Nevada State Park **FINISH**

25 miles

Emerald Bay & DL Bliss State Parks
Hike the shoreline Rubicon Trail

START

South Lake Tahoe
Take a cruise, swim or ski

0 miles

2–3 DAYS
105 MILES / 170KM

GREAT FOR...

BEST TIME TO GO
May to September for sunshine; January to March for snow.

 ESSENTIAL PHOTO

Inspiration Point above Emerald Bay.

 BEST ROADSIDE VIEWS

South Lake Tahoe to Tahoe City.

Lake Tahoe Skier overlooking the lake from the ski slope of Heavenly

20 Lake Tahoe Loop

The horned peaks surrounding Lake Tahoe, straddling the California–Nevada state line, are four-seasons playgrounds. During summer hit the cool sapphire waters fringed by sandy beaches or trek and mountain-bike forest trails. In winter, Lake Tahoe woos powder-hungry skiers and boarders with scores of slopes. Year-round, the north shore is quiet and upscale; the west shore, rugged and old-timey; the east shore, blissfully undeveloped; and the south shore, always busy.

TRIP HIGHLIGHT

① South Lake Tahoe

South Lake Tahoe is a chock-a-block commercial strip bordering the lake framed by postcard-perfect mountains. In winter, go swooshing down the double-black diamond runs and monster vertical drops of **Heavenly** (☎775-586-7000; www.skiheavenly.com; 4080 Lake Tahoe Blvd, South Lake Tahoe; adult/youth 13-18yr/child 5-12yr $125/103/69; ☺9am-4pm Mon-Fri, from 8:30am Sat, Sun & holidays; 🚡), a behemoth

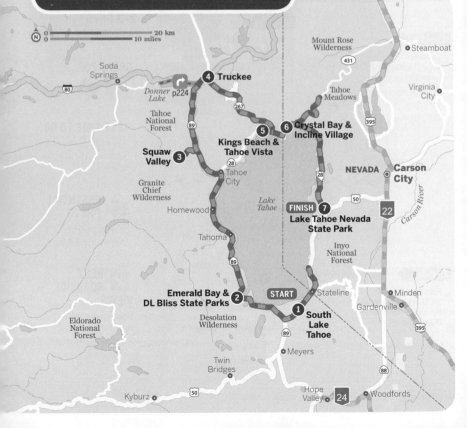

ski resort. From the top, you're on the spine of the Sierra Nevada between mountains and desert flatlands. For killer lake views in summer, ascend the gondola from Heavenly Village, or board the paddle wheelers of **Lake Tahoe Cruises** (☏800-238-2463; www.zephyrcove. com; 900 Ski Run Blvd; adult/child from $55/20; 👪) that ply the 'Big Blue.' Survey the azure expanse of the lake at eye level from in-town beaches or aboard a kayak launched from **Zephyr Cove** (☏775-589-4901; www.zephyrcove.com; 760 Hwy 50; per car $10; 👪), which also has sandy swimming beaches. It's about 3 miles north of Stateline, NV, where you can bet a stack of chips at the hulking casinos, all buzzing with bars, nightclubs and 24-hour restaurants.

LINK YOUR TRIP

22 **Eastern Sierra Scenic Byway**

Downtown Reno's casinos are just over 30 miles northeast of Truckee via the I-80 Fwy.

24 **Ebbetts Pass Scenic Byway**

From South Lake Tahoe, it's 20 miles south along Hwy 89 to Hope Valley, although Ebbetts Pass is closed during winter and spring.

✖ 🛏 p225

The Drive ›› Unless the road has been closed by heavy snowfall, set a course heading northwest from South Lake Tahoe's 'The Y' intersection onto scenic lakeside Hwy 89. You'll pass USFS Tallac Historic Site and Taylor Creek Visitor Center, both of which have nature trails and educational exhibits, before reaching Inspiration Point and, further along, the parking lot of Vikingsholm Castle.

- - - - - - - - - - - - -

TRIP HIGHLIGHT

② Emerald Bay & DL Bliss State Parks

Sheer granite cliffs and a jagged shoreline mark glacier-carved **Emerald Bay** (☏530-541-6498; www. parks.ca.gov; per car $10; ☺late May-Sep; P 👪), a teardrop cove that will get you digging for your camera. Panoramic pullouts all along Hwy 89 peer over the uninhabited granite speck of **Fannette Island**, which harbors the vandalized remains of a 1920s teahouse once belonging to heiress Lora Knight. She also built **Vikingsholm Castle** (tour adult/child 7-17yr $10/8; ☺10:30am-3:30pm or 4pm late May-Sep; P 👪), a Scandinavian-style mansion on the bay that's reached via a steep 2-mile round-trip hiking trail. Heading north, the 4.5-mile **Rubicon Trail** ribbons along the lakeshore past hidden coves to **DL Bliss State Park** (☏530-525-7277; www.parks. ca.gov; per car $10; ☺late

May-Sep; P 👪), with its old lighthouse and sandy beaches. In summer, the **Emerald Bay Trolley** (☏531-541-7149; www.tahoetransportation. org; fare $2; 👪) shuttles between the parks.

The Drive ›› Head north on Hwy 89 past the sandy beach at Meeks Bay, forested Ed Z'berg Sugar Pine Point State Park and the lakeshore hamlets of Tahoma and Homewood. At the intersection with N Lake Blvd/Hwy 28, Tahoe City's commercial strip, turn left to stay on Hwy 89 for another 5 miles northwest to Squaw Valley Rd.

- - - - - - - - - - - - -

③ Squaw Valley

After stopping in Tahoe City for supplies and to refuel your stomach and the car, it's a short drive up to **Squaw Valley** (☏530-452-4331, 800-403-0206; www.squaw.com; 1960 Squaw Valley Rd, off Hwy 89, Olympic Valley; adult/youth 13-22yr/child 5-12yr $139/87/60; ☺9am-4pm Mon Fri, from 8:30am Sat, Sun & holidays; 👪), a megasized ski resort that hosted the 1960 Winter Olympics. You could spend a whole winter weekend here and not ski the same run twice. Hold on tight as the aerial tram rises over granite ledges to High Camp at a lofty 8200ft, where you can take a spin around the ice rink while being mesmerized by vistas of the lake so very far below. In summer, families crowd the outdoor swimming pool, disc-golf course, zip lines and the hiking and mountain-biking trails radiating out from High Camp.

The Drive » Backtrack out of Squaw Valley, turning left onto Hwy 89 and driving north for about 8 miles. Before reaching I-80, turn right onto W River St for another mile to downtown Truckee.

TRIP HIGHLIGHT

❹ Truckee

Cradled by mountains and forests, this speck of a town is steeped in Old West history. Truckee was put on the map by the railroad, grew rich on logging and ice harvesting, and found Hollywood fame with the 1924 filming of Charlie Chaplin's *The Gold Rush*.

The aura of the Old West still lingers over Truckee's teensy one-horse downtown, where railroad workers and lumberjacks once milled about in raucous saloons, bawdy brothels and shady gambling halls. Most of the late-19th-century buildings now contain restaurants and upscale boutiques.

Truckee is also close to a dozen downhill and cross-country ski resorts, most famously **Northstar California** (📞800-466-6784, 530-562-1010; www.northstarcalifornia.com; 5001 Northstar Dr, off Hwy 267, Truckee; adult/youth 13-18yr/child 5-12yr $130/107/77; ⏰8am-4pm; 🚡), where

ski lifts also transport summer hikers and mountain-bikers into the highlands.

🍴 🛏 p225

The Drive » In downtown Truckee, cross over the railroad tracks and the river, following Brockway Rd southeast for 1.5 miles. Turn right onto Hwy 267 back toward Lake Tahoe, passing Northstar ski resort before cruising downhill to the lakeshore town of Kings Beach, 10 miles away.

TRIP HIGHLIGHT

❺ Kings Beach & Tahoe Vista

On summer weekends, picturesque **Kings Beach State Recreation Area** (📞530-583-3074; www.parks.ca.gov; off Hwy 28; per car $10; ⏰6am-10pm; 🅿 👫 🐕) gets deluged with sun-seekers, especially the picnic tables, barbecue grills and boat rentals. **Adrift Tahoe** (📞530-546-1112; www.standuppaddletahoe.com; 8338 N Lake Blvd, Kings Beach; rentals per hr $20-40, per day from $75; 👫) handles kayak, outrigger canoe and stand-up paddle boarding (SUP) rentals, paddling lessons and tours. Just inland, the 1920s **Old Brockway Golf Course** (📞530-546-9909; www.oldbrockwaygolf.com; 400 Brassie Ave, cnr Hwys 267 & 28; green fees $30-50, club/cart rental from $25/18) runs along pine-bordered fairways where Hollywood celebs once hobnobbed. Spread southeast along Hwy 28, **Tahoe Vista** has

more public beaches than any other lakeshore town. Lose the crowds on the hiking and mountain-biking trails or disc-golf course at **North Tahoe Regional Park** (📞530-546-4212; www.northtahoeparks.com; 6600 Donner Rd, off National Ave; per car $5; ⏰7am-9pm Jun-Sep, to 7pm Sep & Oct, to 5pm Nov-May; 🅿 👫), which also has a snow-sledding hill and

Lake Tahoe People enjoying a day at the beach

cross-country ski and snowshoe trails in winter. In summer, local hikers, picnickers and disc-golf fans keep the park just as busy.

✗ 🛏 p225

The Drive » East of Kings Beach, Hwy 28 barrels uphill across the California–Nevada border past the small-potatoes casinos of Crystal Bay before reaching Incline Village just a few miles later.

- - - - - - - - - -

❻ Crystal Bay & Incline Village

Crossing into Nevada, the neon starts to flash and old-school gambling palaces appear. You can try your luck at the gambling tables or catch a live-music show at the **Crystal Bay Casino** (📞775-833-6333; www.crystalbaycasino.com; 14 Hwy 28; ℗). Straddling

the state border, the **Cal Neva Resort & Casino** (www.calnevaresort.com; 2 Stateline Rd; ℗) evokes a colorful history of ghosts, mobsters and ex-owner Frank Sinatra.

One of Lake Tahoe's ritziest communities, **Incline Village** is a gateway to winter ski resorts. During summer, you can tour the eccentric **Thunderbird**

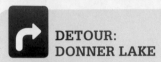

DETOUR:
DONNER LAKE

Start: ❹ Truckee (p222)

Donner Summit is where the infamous Donner Party became trapped during the fierce winter of 1846–47. Their grisly tale of survival – and cannibalism – is chronicled inside the visitor center at **Donner Memorial State Park** (📞530-582-7892; www.parks. ca.gov; Donner Pass Rd; per car $8; ⏱10am-5pm; 🅿🚹), where tree-lined **Donner Lake** (www.donnerlakemarina. com; 🅿🚹) offers sandy beaches. Further west, popular municipal **West End Beach** (📞530-582-7720; www.tdrpd.com; off Donner Pass Rd; adult/child 2-17yr $4/3; 🚹) has a roped-off swimming area for kids, and kayak, paddleboat and stand-up paddle boarding (SUP) rentals. The state park and lakeshore are just a few miles east of Truckee via Donner Pass Rd.

Lodge (📞800-468-2463; http://thunderbirdtahoe.org; adult/child 6-12yr from $39/19; ⏱Tue-Sat mid-May–mid-Oct; 🚹), a historical mansion only accessible by bus, boat or kayak. Or drive northeast up Hwy 431 into the Mt Rose Wilderness, a gateway to miles of unspoiled terrain, including easy wildflower walks at **Tahoe Meadows**.

The Drive » Beyond the stop-and-go traffic of Incline Village, Hwy 28 winds south, staying high above Lake Tahoe's east shore, offering peekaboo lake views and roadside pull-offs, from where locals scramble down the cliffs to hidden beaches. It's a slow-moving 13 miles south to Spooner Lake.

❼ Lake Tahoe Nevada State Park

With pristine beaches and miles of wilderness trails for hikers, mountain-bikers, skiers and snowshoers, **Lake Tahoe Nevada State Park** (📞775-831-0494; www.parks. nv.gov; per car $7-12; 🅿🚹) is the east shore's big draw. Summer crowds splash in the warm, turquoise waters and sun themselves on the white, boulder-strewn beaches of **Sand Harbor**, a few miles south of Incline Village. The 15-mile **Flume Trail** (📞775-298-2501; http://flumetrail tahoe.com; 1115 Tunnel Creek Rd, Incline Village; mountain bike rental per day $40-75, shuttle $15), a mountain-biker's holy grail, starts further south at **Spooner Lake**, where anglers fish along the shore (no swimming – too many leeches!). It's just north of the Hwy 50 junction.

Eating & Sleeping

South Lake Tahoe ①

✕ Burger Lounge
Fast Food $

(📞530-542-2010; 717 Emerald Bay Rd; dishes $4-10; ⏰10am-8pm daily Jun-Sep, 11am-7pm Thu-Mon Oct-May; 👪) You can't miss that giant beer mug standing outside a shingled cabin. Step inside for the south shore's tastiest burgers, including the crazy 'Jiffy burger' (with peanut butter and cheddar cheese), the zingy pesto fries or the knockout ice-cream shakes.

✕ Ernie's Coffee Shop
Diner $

(📞530-541-2161; http://erniescoffeeshop.com; 1207 Hwy 50; mains $8-14; ⏰6am-2pm; 👪) A sun-filled local institution, Ernie's dishes out filling three-egg omelets, hearty biscuits with gravy, fruity and nutty waffles and bottomless cups of locally roasted coffee. Breakfast is served all day.

🛏 968 Park Hotel
Boutique Hotel $$

(📞855-544-0968, 530-544-0968; www.968parkhotel.com; 968 Park Ave; r $129-279; P🐶@📶🏊) A refashioned motel with hipster edge, here recycled, rescued and re-envisioned building materials have made an LEED-certified property an aesthetically pleasing eco-haven near the lake. The lobby CoffeePub offers free wine tastings on Friday evenings.

🛏 Alder Inn
Motel $

(📞530-544-4485; www.alderinn.com; 1072 Ski Run Blvd; r $89-149; P🐶📶🏊) Even better than staying at your best friend's house by the lake, this hospitable inn on the Heavenly ski-shuttle route charms with color schemes that really pop, pillow-top mattresses, organic bath goodies, mini-fridges, microwaves and flat-screen TVs. Dip your toes in the kidney-shaped pool in summer.

Truckee ④

✕ Coffeebar
Cafe $

(📞530-587-2000; www.coffeebartruckee.com; 10120 Jiboom St; items $3-9; ⏰6am-6pm Sun-Thu, to 7pm Fri & Sat; 📶) This beatnik, bare-bones industrial coffee shop serves Italian gelato, delectable pastries and home-brewed kombucha. Go for tantalizing breakfast crepes and overstuffed panini on herbed focaccia bread, or for a jolt of organic espresso or flavored tea lattes.

🛏 Cedar House Sport Hotel
Boutique Hotel $$$

(📞866-582-5655, 530-582-5655; www.cedarhousesporthotel.com; 10918 Brockway Rd; r incl breakfast $170-295; P🐶@📶🏊) This chic, environmentally conscious contemporary lodge aims at getting folks out into nature. It boasts countertops made from recycled paper, 'rain chains' that redistribute water from the green roof garden, low-flow plumbing and in-room recycling.

🛏 Clair Tappaan Lodge
Hostel $

(📞530-426-3632; http://clairtappaanlodge.com/; 19940 Donner Pass Rd, Norden; dm/r from $40/80; P🐶📶) About 2 miles west of Sugar Bowl, this cozy Sierra Club–owned rustic mountain lodge puts you near major ski resorts and sleeps up to 140 people in dorms and private rooms. You're expected to do small chores and bring your own sleeping bag, towel and swimsuit (for the hot tub!). Family-style meals cost extra.

Kings Beach & Tahoe Vista ⑤

✕ Old Post Office Cafe
American $

(📞530-546-3205; 5245 N Lake Blvd, Tahoe Vista; mains $8-12; ⏰6:30am-2pm; 👪) Head west of the town of Tahoe Vista toward Carnelian Bay, where this always-packed, cheery wooden shack serves scrumptious breakfasts – buttery potatoes, eggs Benedict, biscuits with gravy, fluffy omelets with lotsa fillings and fresh-fruit smoothies.

🛏 Franciscan Lakeside Lodge
Cabin $$

(📞800-564-6754, 530-546-6300; www.franciscanlodge.com; 6944 N Lake Blvd; cabin $109-399; P🐶📶🏊) Spend the day on a private sandy beach or in the outdoor pool, then light the barbecue grill after sunset – ah, now that's relaxation. All of the simple cabins, cottages and suites have kitchenettes. Lakeside lodgings have better beach access and views, but roomier cabins near the back of the complex tend to be quieter and will appeal to families.

Classic Trip

Yosemite, Sequoia & Kings Canyon National Parks

Drive up into the lofty Sierra Nevada, where glacial valleys and ancient forests overfill the windshield scenery. Go climb a rock, pitch a tent or photograph wildflowers and wildlife.

TRIP HIGHLIGHTS

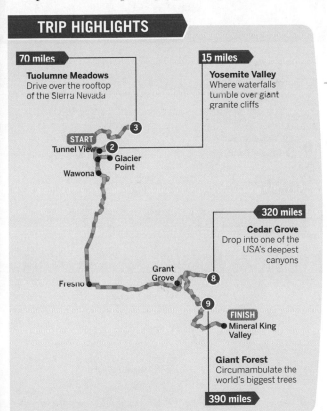

70 miles

Tuolumne Meadows
Drive over the rooftop of the Sierra Nevada

15 miles

Yosemite Valley
Where waterfalls tumble over giant granite cliffs

320 miles

Cedar Grove
Drop into one of the USA's deepest canyons

Giant Forest
Circumambulate the world's biggest trees

390 miles

START
Tunnel View
Glacier Point
Wawona
Grant Grove
Fresno
FINISH
Mineral King Valley

5–7 DAYS
450 MILES / 725KM

GREAT FOR...

BEST TIME TO GO
April and May for waterfalls; June to August for mountain highlands.

ESSENTIAL PHOTO
Yosemite Valley from panoramic Tunnel View.

BEST SCENIC DRIVE
Kings Canyon Scenic Byway to Cedar Grove.

21

Yosemite, Sequoia & Kings Canyon National Parks

Glacier-carved valleys resting below dramatic peaks make Yosemite an all-ages playground. Here you can witness earth-shaking waterfalls, clamber up granite domes and camp out by high-country meadows where wildflowers bloom in summer. Home to the USA's deepest canyon and the biggest tree on the planet, Sequoia and Kings Canyon National Parks justify detouring further south into the Sierra Nevada, which conservationist John Muir called 'The Range of Light.'

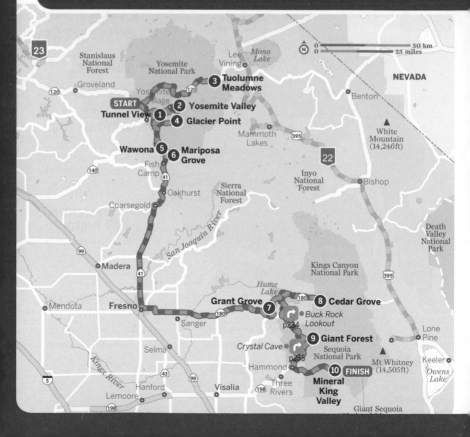

❶ Tunnel View

Arriving in **Yosemite National Park** (📞209-372-0200; www.nps.gov/yose; 7-day entry per car $30; **P** 🚻) at the Arch Rock entrance station, follow Hwy 140 east, then backtrack west about 1.5 miles on Wawona Rd/Hwy 41. Pull over at **Tunnel View** for your first look into Yosemite Valley, which has inspired painters, poets, naturalists and adventurers for centuries. On the right, Bridalveil Fall swells with snowmelt in late spring, but by late summer, it's a mere whisper, often lifted and blown aloft by the wind. Spread below you are the pine forests and meadows of the valley floor, with the sheer face of El Capitan rising on the left and, in the distance straight ahead, iconic granite Half Dome.

The Drive » Merge carefully back onto eastbound Wawona Rd, which continues downhill into Yosemite Valley, full of confusingly intersecting one-way roads. Drive east along the Merced River on Southside Dr past the Bridalveil Fall turnoff. Almost 6 miles from Tunnel View, turn left and drive across Sentinel Bridge to Yosemite Village's day-use parking lots. Ride free shuttle buses that circle the valley.

- - - - - - - - - - -

TRIP HIGHLIGHT

❷ Yosemite Valley

From the bottom looking up, this dramatic valley cut by the meandering Merced River is song-inspiring, and not just for birds: rippling meadow grasses; tall pines; cool, impassive pools reflecting granite monoliths; and cascading, glacier-cold whitewater ribbons.

At busy **Yosemite Village**, start inside the **Yosemite Valley Visitor Center** (📞209-372-0200; 9035 Village Dr, Yosemite Village; ⏱9am-5pm; 🚻), with its thought-provoking history and nature displays and free *Spirit of Yosemite* film screenings. At the nearby **Yosemite Museum** (www.nps.gov/yose; 9037 Village Dr, Yosemite Village; ⏱9am-5pm summer, 10am-4pm winter), Western landscape paintings are hung beside Native American baskets and beaded clothing.

The valley's famous waterfalls are thunderous cataracts in May, but mere trickles by late July. Triple-tiered **Yosemite Falls** is North America's tallest, while **Bridalveil Fall** is hardly less impressive. A strenuous, often slippery staircase beside **Vernal Fall** leads you, gasping, right to the top edge of the waterfall, where rainbows pop in clouds of mist. Keep hiking up the same Mist Trail to the top of **Nevada Fall** for a heady 5.5-mile round-trip trek.

In midsummer, you can rent a raft at Curry Village and float down the **Merced River**. The serene stretch between Stoneman Bridge and Sentinel Beach is gentle enough for kids. Or take the whole family to see the stuffed wildlife mounts at the hands-on **Nature Center at Happy Isles** (www.nps.gov/yose; off Southside Dr, Yosemite Valley; ⏱9am-5pm late May-Sep; 🚻), east of Half Dome Village.

✗ 🍴 p236

The Drive » From Yosemite Village, drive west on Northside Dr, passing Yosemite Falls and El Capitan. After 6 miles, turn right onto Big Oak Flat Rd/Hwy 120. For almost 10 miles, the road curves above the valley into the forest. Near Crane Flat gas station, turn right to follow Tioga Rd/Hwy 120 east (open summer and fall only).

LINK YOUR TRIP

22 **Eastern Sierra Scenic Byway**

From Yosemite's Tuolumne Meadows, roll over high-elevation Tioga Pass and downhill towards Mono Lake, a 20-mile trip.

23 **Highway 49 Through Gold Country**

En route between Yosemite Valley and Tuolumne Meadows, turn west onto Hwy 120, then follow Hwy 49 north to Sonora, a 70-mile drive away.

CENTRAL CALIFORNIA **21** YOSEMITE, SEQUOIA & KINGS CANYON NATIONAL PARKS

❸ Tuolumne Meadows

Leave the crushing crowds of Yosemite Valley behind and escape to the Sierra Nevada high country along Tioga Rd, which follows a 19th-century wagon road and Native American trading route. Warning! Completely closed by snow in winter, Tioga Rd is usually open *only* from May or June until October or November.

About 45 miles from Yosemite Valley, stop at **Olmsted Point**. Overlooking a lunar-type landscape of glaciated granite, gaze deeply down Tenaya Canyon to Half Dome's backside. A few miles further east, a sandy half-moon beach wraps around **Tenaya Lake**, tempting you to brave some of the park's coldest swimming. Sunbathers lie upon rocks that rim the lake's northern shore.

About a 90-minute drive from Yosemite Valley, Tuolumne Meadows is the Sierra Nevada's largest subalpine meadow, with fields of wildflowers, bubbling streams, ragged granite peaks and cooler temperatures at an elevation of 8600ft. Hikers find a paradise of trails to tackle, or unpack a picnic basket by the stream-fed meadows.

🛏 p236

The Drive » From Tuolumne Meadows, backtrack 50 miles to Yosemite Valley, turning left on El Portal Rd, then right on Northside Dr and right again on Wawona Rd. Follow narrow Wawona Rd/Hwy 41 up out of the valley. After 9 miles, turn left onto Glacier Point Rd at the Chinquapin intersection, driving 15 more miles to the Glacier Point parking lot.

HIKING HALF DOME & AROUND YOSEMITE VALLEY

Over 800 miles of hiking trails in Yosemite National Park fit hikers of all abilities. Take an easy half-mile stroll on the valley floor or underneath giant sequoia trees, or venture out all day on a quest for viewpoints, waterfalls and lakes in the mountainous high country.

Some of the park's most popular hikes start right in Yosemite Valley, including to the top of **Half Dome** (16-mile round-trip), the most famous of all. It follows a section of the John Muir Trail and is strenuous, difficult and best tackled in two days with an overnight in Little Yosemite Valley. Reaching the top can only be done in summer after park rangers have installed fixed cables; depending on snow conditions, this may occur as early as late May and the cables usually come down in mid-October. To limit the cables' notorious human logjams, the park now requires permits for day hikers, but the route is still nerve-wracking because hikers must share the cables. Advance permits go on sale by a preseason lottery in early spring, with a limited number available via another daily lottery two days in advance during the hiking season. Permit regulations and prices keep changing; check the park website (http://www.nps.gov/yose) for current details.

The less ambitious or physically fit will still have a ball following the **Mist Trail** as far as Vernal Fall (2.5-mile round-trip), the top of Nevada Fall (5.5-mile round-trip) or idyllic Little Yosemite Valley (8-mile round-trip). The **Four Mile Trail** (9-mile round-trip) up to Glacier Point is a strenuous but satisfying climb to a glorious viewpoint. If you've got the kids in tow, nice and easy valley walks include to **Mirror Lake** (2-mile round-trip) and viewpoints at the base of thundering **Yosemite Falls** (1-mile round-trip) and lacy **Bridalveil Fall** (0.5-mile round-trip).

④ Glacier Point

In just over an hour, you can zip from Yosemite Valley up to head-spinning Glacier Point. Warning! The final 10 miles of Glacier Point Rd is closed by snow in winter, usually from November through April or May. During winter, the road remains open as far as the Yosemite Ski & Snowboard Area, but snow tires and tire chains may be required.

Rising over 3000ft above the valley floor, dramatic Glacier Point (7214ft) practically puts you at eye level with Half Dome. Glimpse what John Muir and US President Teddy Roosevelt saw when they camped here in 1903: the waterfall-strewn Yosemite Valley below and the distant peaks ringing Tuolumne Meadows. To get away from the crowds, hike a little way down the Panorama Trail, just south of the crowded main viewpoint.

On your way back from Glacier Point, take time out for a 2-mile hike up **Sentinel Dome** or out to **Taft Point** for incredible 360-degree valley views.

The Drive » Drive back downhill past Badger Pass, turning left at the Chinquapin intersection and winding south through thick forest on Wawona Rd/Hwy 41. After almost 13 curvy miles, you'll reach Wawona, with its lodge, visitor center, general store and gas station, all on your left.

WINTER WONDERLANDS

When the temperature drops and the white stuff falls, there are still tons of fun outdoor activities around the Sierra Nevada's national parks. In Yosemite, strap on some skis or a snowboard or go tubing downhill off Glacier Point Rd; plod around Yosemite Valley on a ranger-led snowshoe tour; or just try to stay upright on ice skates at Half Dome Village. Further south in Sequoia and Kings Canyon National Parks, the whole family can go snowshoeing or cross-country skiing among groves of giant sequoias. Before embarking on a winter trip to the parks, check road conditions on the official park websites or by calling ahead. Don't forget to put snow tires on your car, and always carry tire chains too.

⑤ Wawona

At Wawona, a 45-minute drive south of the valley, drop by the **Pioneer Yosemite History Center** (www.nps.gov/yose; off Wawona Rd, Wawona; rides adult/child $5/4; ⊙24hr, rides Wed-Sun Jun-Sep; P ♿), with its covered bridge, pioneer-era buildings and historic Wells Fargo office. In summer take the short, bumpy stage-coach ride and really feel like you're living in the past. Peek inside the **Wawona Visitor Center** (☎209-375-9531; www.nps.gov/yose; off Wawona Rd, Wawona; ⊙8:30am-5pm May-Sep) at 19th-century artist Thomas Hill's re-created studio, hung with romantic Sierra Nevada landscape paintings. On summer evenings, imbibe a civilized cocktail in the lobby lounge of the Big Trees Lodge, where pianist Tom Bopp often plays tunes from Yosemite's bygone days.

🛏 p237

The Drive » In summer, you must leave your car at Wawona and take a free shuttle bus to Mariposa Grove. By car, follow Wawona Rd/Hwy 41 south for 4.5 miles to the four-way stop by the park's south entrance. Continue straight ahead on Mariposa Rd (closed in winter) for 3.5 miles to the parking lot – when it's full, drivers are turned away.

⑥ Mariposa Grove

Wander giddily around the Mariposa Grove (closed for restoration until spring 2017), home of the 1800-year-old Grizzly Giant and 500 other giant sequoias that tower above your head. Nature trails wind through this popular grove, but you can only hear yourself think above the noise of vacationing crowds during the early morning or

WHY THIS IS A CLASSIC TRIP
SARA BENSON, WRITER

The Sierra Nevada Mountains encompass three of the USA's oldest and grandest national parks. This trip follows scenic roads right up to the base of towering waterfalls, skyscraping granite peaks and the biggest trees on earth. To escape the most crushing crowds in summer, I head to Cedar Grove near Road's End in Kings Canyon and the remote, high-elevation Mineral King Valley of Sequoia National Park.

Top: Tunnel View, Yosemite National Park
Left: Cycling through Sentinel Meadow, Yosemite National Park
Right: General Sherman Tree, Sequoia National Park

evening. Notwithstanding a cruel hack job back in 1895, the walk-through California Tunnel Tree continues to survive, so pose your family in front and snap away. If you've got the energy, make a round-trip pilgrimage on foot to the fallen Wawona Tunnel Tree in the upper grove.

The Drive » From Yosemite's south entrance station, it's a 115-mile, three-hour trip to Kings Canyon National Park (see Sleeping options, p237). Follow Hwy 41 south 60 miles to Fresno, then slingshot east on Hwy 180 for another 50 miles, climbing out of the Central Valley back into the mountains. Keep left at the Hwy 198 intersection, staying on Hwy 180 towards Grant Grove.

- - - - - - - - - - - - - - -

❼ Grant Grove

Through **Sequoia and Kings Canyon National Parks** (☏559-565-3341; www.nps.gov/seki; 7-day entry per car $30; P 🚶), roads seem barely to scratch the surface of the twin parks' beauty. To see real treasures, you'll need to get out and stretch your legs. North of Big Stump entrance station in Grant Grove Village, turn left and wind downhill to **General Grant Grove**, where you'll see some of the park's landmark giant sequoia trees along a paved path. You can walk right through the Fallen Monarch, a massive, fire-hollowed trunk that's done duty as a cabin,

hotel, saloon and horse stable. For views of Kings Canyon and the peaks of the Great Western Divide, follow a narrow, winding side road (closed in winter, no RVs or trailers) starting behind the John Muir Lodge for more than 2 miles up to **Panoramic Point**.

 p237

The Drive » Kings Canyon National Park's main visitor areas, Grant Grove and Cedar Grove, are linked by the narrow, twisting Kings Canyon Scenic Byway (Hwy 180), which dramatically descends into the canyon. Expect spectacular views all along this outstandingly scenic 30-mile drive. **Warning!** Hwy 180 from the Hume Lake turnoff to Cedar

Grove is closed during winter (usually mid-November through mid-April).

- - - - - - - - - - - - -

TRIP HIGHLIGHT

⑧ Cedar Grove

Serpentining past chiseled rock walls laced with waterfalls, Hwy 180 plunges down to the Kings River, where roaring white water ricochets off the granite cliffs of North America's deepest canyon, technically speaking. Pull over partway down at **Junction View** overlook for an eyeful, then keep rolling down along the river to **Cedar Grove Village**. East of the village, **Zumwalt Meadow** is the place for spotting birds, mule deer and black bears. If the day is hot and your swimming gear is handy, stroll from Road's End to **Muir Rock**, a large flat-top river

boulder where John Muir once gave outdoor talks, now a popular summer swimming hole. Starting from **Road's End**, a very popular day hike climbs 4 miles each way to **Mist Falls**, which thunders in late spring.

 p237

The Drive » Backtrack from Road's End nearly 30 miles up Hwy 180. Turn left onto Hume Lake Rd. Curve around the lake past swimming beaches and campgrounds, turning right onto 10 Mile Rd. At Hwy 198, turn left and follow the Generals Hwy (sometimes closed in winter) south for about 23 miles to the Wolverton Rd turn-off on your left.

- - - - - - - - - - - - -

TRIP HIGHLIGHT

⑨ Giant Forest

We dare you to try hugging the trees in **Giant Forest**, a 3-sq-mile grove protecting the park's most gargantuan specimens. Park off Wolverton Rd and walk downhill to reach the world's biggest living tree, the **General Sherman Tree**, which towers 275ft into the sky. With sore arms and sticky sap fingers, you can lose the crowds on any of many forested trails nearby. The trail network stretches all the way south to Crescent Meadow, a 5-mile one-way ramble.

By car, drive 2.5 miles south along the Generals Hwy to get schooled on sequoia ecology and fire cycles at the **Giant Forest**

↪ DETOUR: BUCK ROCK LOOKOUT

Start: ⑧ Cedar Grove

To climb one of California's most evocative fire lookouts, drive east of the Generals Hwy on Big Meadows Rd into the Sequoia National Forest between Grant Grove and the Giant Forest. Follow the signs to staffed **Buck Rock Fire Lookout** (www. buckrock.org; FR-13S04, off Big Meadows Rd; ⊙9:30am-6pm May-Oct). Constructed in 1923, this active fire lookout allows panoramic views from a dollhouse-sized cab lording it over the horizon from 8500ft atop a granite rise, reached by 172 spindly stairs. It's not for anyone with vertigo! Opening hours may vary seasonally, and the lookout closes during lightning storms and fire emergencies.

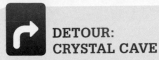

DETOUR: CRYSTAL CAVE

Start: ❾ Giant Forest (p234)

Off the Generals Hwy, about 2 miles south of the Giant Forest Museum, turn right (west) onto twisting 6.5-mile-long Crystal Cave Rd for a fantastical walk inside 10,000-year-old **Crystal Cave** (www. explorecrystalcave.com; Crystal Cave Rd, off Generals Hwy; tours adult/youth/child from $16/8/5; ☻May-Nov; [P][♿]), carved by an underground river. Stalactites hang like daggers from the ceiling, and milky-white marble formations take the shape of ethereal curtains, domes, columns and shields. Bring a light jacket – it's 50°F (10°C) inside the cave. Buy tour tickets a month or more in advance online at www.recreation.gov; during October and November, tickets are only sold in person at the Giant Forest Museum and Foothills Visitor Center. Tour tickets are *not* available at the cave itself.

Museum ([☏]559-565-4480; www.nps.gov/seki; Generals Hwy, at Crescent Meadow Rd; ☻9am–4:30pm; [P][♿]). Starting outside the museum, Crescent Meadow Rd makes a 6-mile loop into the Giant Forest, passing right through **Tunnel Log**. For 360-degree views of the Great Western Divide, climb the steep quarter-mile staircase up **Moro Rock**. Warning! Crescent Meadow Rd is closed to traffic by winter snow;

during summer, ride the free shuttle buses around the loop road.

The Drive » Narrowing, the Generals Hwy drops for more than 15 miles into the Sierra Nevada foothills, passing Amphitheater Point and exiting the park beyond Foothills Visitor Center. Before reaching the town of Three Rivers, turn left on Mineral King Rd, a dizzyingly scenic 25-mile road (partly unpaved, no trailers or RVs allowed) that switchbacks up to Mineral King Valley.

❿ Mineral King Valley

Navigating over 700 hairpin turns, it's a winding 1½-hour drive up to the glacially sculpted Mineral King Valley (7500ft), a 19th-century silver-mining camp and lumber settlement, and later a mountain retreat. Trailheads into the high country begin at the end of Mineral King Rd, where historic private cabins dot the valley floor flanked by massive mountains. Your final destination is just over a mile past the ranger station, where the valley unfolds all of its hidden beauty, and hikes to granite peaks and alpine lakes beckon.

Warning! Mineral King Rd is typically open only from late May through late October. In summer, Mineral King's marmots like to chew on parked cars, so wrap the undercarriage of your vehicle with a tarp and rope (which can be bought, though not cheaply, at the hardware store in Three Rivers).

Eating & Sleeping

Yosemite Valley ❷

✖ Degnan's Deli   Deli $

(www.travelyosemite.com; off Village Dr, Yosemite Village; items $3-10; ⊙7am-5pm; 🖉 🛒) Excellent made-to-order sandwiches, breakfast items and snack foods.

✖ Mountain Room Restaurant   American $$$

(🖀209-372-1403; www.travelyosemite. com; Yosemite Valley Lodge; mains $20-36; ⊙5:30-8pm or 9pm; 🖉 🛒) With a killer view of Yosemite Falls, the window tables at this casual yet elegant contemporary restaurant are a hot commodity. Plates of flat-iron steak, cider-brined pork chops and locally caught mountain trout woo diners, who are seated beside gallery-quality nature photographs. Reservations accepted only for groups larger than eight.

🛏 Half Dome Village   Cabin $$

(🖀reservations 888-413-8869; www. travelyosemite.com; off Southside Dr, Yosemite Valley; tent cabin from $100, r from $135, cabin with shared/private bath from $160/220; ⊙daily mid-Mar–late Nov, Sat & Sun early Jan–mid-Mar; ℗ 🖨 🛜 📺) Founded in 1899 as summertime Camp Curry, hundreds of units are squished tightly together here beneath towering evergreens. The canvas cabins (heated or unheated) are basically glorified tents, so for more comfort, quiet and privacy get one of the cozy wood cabins, which have vintage posters. There are 18 motel-style rooms in Stoneman House, including a loft suite that sleeps six.

🛏 Majestic Yosemite Hotel   Historic Hotel $$$

(🖀reservations 888-413-8869; www. travelyosemite.com; 1 Ahwahnee Dr, Yosemite Valley; r from $450; ℗ 🖨 @ 🛜 📺) The crème de la crème of Yosemite's lodging, this sumptuous historic property (formerly called the Ahwahnee) dazzles with soaring ceilings and atmospheric lounges with mammoth stone fireplaces. It's the gold standard for upscale lodges, though if you're not blessed with bullion, you can still soak up the ambiance during afternoon tea, a drink in the bar or a gourmet meal.

🛏 Yosemite Valley Campground Reservation Office   Accommodation Services $

(🖀877-444-6777, information 209-372-8502, reservations 518-885-3639; www.nps.gov/ yose; off Southside Dr, Yosemite Valley; tent & RV sites $26; ⊙8am-5pm; ℗ 🖨) The main campground reservation office for Yosemite Valley can be found in the Half Dome Village parking lot. If you couldn't reserve a site in advance (go online to www.recreation.gov), head here first thing in the morning to get on the list for available valley campsites from no-shows and cancellations.

🛏 Yosemite Valley Lodge   Motel $$$

(🖀reservations 888-413-8869; www. travelyosemite.com; 9006 Yosemite Lodge Dr, Yosemite Valley; r from $220; ℗ 🖨 @ 🛜 📺) Situated a short walk from Yosemite Falls, this multibuilding complex contains a wide range of eateries, a lively bar, big pool and other handy amenities. Delightful rooms, thanks to a recent eco-conscious renovation, now feel properly lodge-like, with rustic wooden furniture and striking nature photography. All have cable TV, telephone, fridge and coffeemaker, and great patio or balcony panoramas.

Tuolumne Meadows ❸

🛏 Tuolumne Meadows Lodge   Cabin $$

(🖀reservations 888-413-8869; www. travelyosemite.com; off Tioga Rd; tent cabin $125; ⊙ mid-Jun–mid-Sep; ℗ 🖨) In the high country, about 50 miles from Yosemite Valley, this option attracts hikers to its 69 canvas tent cabins with two or four beds each, a wood-burning stove and candles (no electricity). Breakfast and dinner available (surcharge applies, dinner reservations required).

Wawona ⑤

🛏 Big Trees Lodge   Historic Hotel $$

(☑reservations 888-413-8869; www.travelyosemite.com; 8308 Wawona Rd, Wawona; r with shared/private bath from $150/220; ☺mid-Mar–late Nov & mid-Dec–early Jan; P ⊖ 🛜 🎞) This National Historic Landmark, dating from 1879, is a collection of six graceful, whitewashed New England–style buildings flanked by wide porches. The 104 rooms – with no phone or TV – come with Victorian-style furniture and other period items, and about half the rooms share bathrooms, with nice robes provided for the walk there. Wi-fi available in annex building only.

Grant Grove ⑦

🛏 John Muir Lodge   Lodge $$

(☑877-436-9615, 559 335-5500; www.visitsequoia.com; off Hwy 180, Grant Grove Village; r from $180; P ⊖ 🛜) An atmospheric wooden building hung with historical black-and-white photographs, this year-round hotel is a place to lay your head and still feel like you're in the forest. Wide porches have wooden rocking chairs, and homespun rooms contain rough-hewn wood furniture and patchwork bedspreads. Cozy up to the big stone fireplace on chilly nights with a board game.

Cedar Grove ⑧

🛏 Sentinel Campground   Campground $

(www.nps.gov/seki; Hwy 180, Cedar Grove Village; tent & RV sites $18; ☺late Apr–mid-Nov; P 🎯) It's Cedar Grove's busiest and most centrally located campground, near the visitor center and campfire ranger programs in summer. Premier riverside sites at the beginning of the first loop fill fastest.

Sequoia National Park

🛏 Lodgepole Campground   Campground $

(☑877-444-6777, 518-885-3639; www.recreation.gov; Lodgepole Rd, off Generals Hwy; tent & RV sites $22; ☺late Apr-Nov; P 🎯) Closest to the Giant Forest area with over 200 closely packed sites, this place fills quickly because of proximity to Kaweah River swimming holes and Lodgepole Village amenities. The 16 walk-in sites are more private. Reservations available (and strongly recommended) from late May through late September.

🛏 Wuksachi Lodge   Lodge $$

(☑866-807-3598, information 559-565-4070, reservations 801-559-4340; www.visitsequoia.com; 64740 Wuksachi Way, off Generals Hwy; r $215-290; P ⊖ 🛜) Built in 1999, Wuksachi Lodge is the park's most upscale lodging and dining option. But don't get too excited – the wood-paneled atrium lobby has an inviting stone fireplace and forest views, but charmless motel-style rooms with coffee makers, mini fridges, oak furniture and thin walls have an institutional feel. The lodge's location nearby Lodgepole Village, however, can't be beaten.

Eastern Sierra Scenic Byway

A straight shot north along California's arched geological backbone, Hwy 395 dazzles with high-altitude vistas, crumbling Old West ghost towns and limitless recreational distractions.

TRIP HIGHLIGHTS

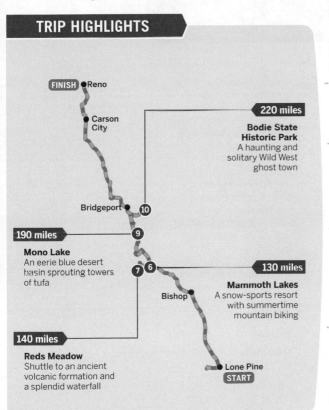

FINISH ● Reno

● Carson City

220 miles

Bodie State Historic Park
A haunting and solitary Wild West ghost town

Bridgeport ● **10**

190 miles **9**

Mono Lake
An eerie blue desert basin sprouting towers of tufa

7 6

Bishop ●

130 miles

Mammoth Lakes
A snow-sports resort with summertime mountain biking

140 miles

Reds Meadow
Shuttle to an ancient volcanic formation and a splendid waterfall

● Lone Pine
START

3–5 DAYS
360 MILES / 580KM

GREAT FOR...

BEST TIME TO GO

June to September for warm days and (mostly) snow-free mountain ramblings.

 ESSENTIAL PHOTO

Sunrise or sunset at the Alabama Hills, framed by the snowy Sierra Nevada.

 BEST FOR OUTDOORS

Hike tranquil mountain trails and camp in Mammoth Lakes.

Reds Meadow Rainbow Falls, Devils Postpile National Monument

22

❶ Lone Pine

The diminutive town of Lone Pine stands as the southern gateway to the craggy jewels of the Eastern Sierra. At the southern end of town, drop by the **Museum of Western Film History** (☏760-876-9909; www.museumofwestern filmhistory.org; 701 S Main St; adult/child under 12yr $5/ free; ⊙10am-6pm Mon-Wed, to 7pm Thu-Sat, to 4pm Sun Apr-Oct, 10am-5pm Mon-Sat, to 4pm Sun Nov-Mar; P 🚻), which contains exhibits of paraphernalia from the over 450 movies shot in the area. Don't miss the occasional screenings in its theater or the tricked-out Cadillac convertible in its foyer.

Just outside the center of town on Whitney Portal Rd, an orange otherworldly alpenglow makes the **Alabama Hills** a must for watching a slow-motion sunset. A frequent backdrop for movie Westerns and the *Lone Ranger* TV series, the rounded earthen-colored mounds stand out against the steely gray foothills and jagged pinnacles of the Sierra range, and a number of graceful rock arches are within easy hiking distance of the roads.

🍴 🛏 p247

The Drive 》 From Lone Pine, the jagged incisors of the Sierra surge skyward in all their raw and fierce glory. Continue west past the Alabama Hills and then brace yourself for the dizzying

240

ascent to road's end – a total of 13 miles from Hwy 395. The White Mountains soar to the east, and the dramatic Owens Valley spreads below.

- - - - - - - - - - -

➋ Whitney Portal

At 14,505ft, the celestial granite giant of **Mt Whitney** (www.fs.usda.gov/inyo) stands as the loftiest peak in the Lower 48 and the obsession of thousands of high-country hikers every summer. Desperately coveted permits (assigned by advance lottery) are your only passport to the summit, though drop-in day-trippers can swan up the mountain as far as Lone Pine Lake – about 6 miles round-trip – to kick up some dust on the iconic Whitney Trail. Back in town, ravenous hikers can stop by the **Whitney Portal Store** (☏760-876-0030; www.whitneyportalstore.com; ☺May–Oct; ☉) for

LINK YOUR TRIP

21 Yosemite, Sequoia & Kings Canyon National Parks

In Lee Vining, go west on Hwy 120 to enter Yosemite National Park via the 9945ft Tioga Pass.

31 Life in Death Valley

From Lone Pine, head southeast on Hwys 136 and 190 to reach Panamint Springs, a western access point for Death Valley.

enormous burgers and plate-sized pancakes.

As you get a fix on this majestic megalith cradled by scores of smaller pinnacles, remember that the country's lowest point is only 80 miles (as the crow flies) east of here: Badwater in Death Valley.

The Drive » Double back to Lone Pine and drive 9 miles north on divided Hwy 395. Scrub brush and tumbleweed desert occupy the valley between the copper-colored foothills of the Sierra Nevada and the White Mountain range. Well-signed Manzanar sits along the west side of the highway.

③ Manzanar National Historic Site

A monument to one of the darkest chapters in US history, the Manzanar unfolds across a barren and windy sweep of land cradled by snow-dipped peaks. During the height of WWII, the federal government interned more than 10,000 people of Japanese ancestry here following the attack on Pearl Harbor. Though little remains of the infamous war concentration camp, the camp's former high-school auditorium houses a superb

DETOUR: ANCIENT BRISTLECONE PINE FOREST

Start: ④ Independence

For encounters with some of the earth's oldest living things, plan at least a half-day trip to the Ancient Bristlecone Pine Forest. These gnarled, otherworldly looking trees thrive above 10,000ft on the slopes of the seemingly inhospitable White Mountains, a parched and stark range that once stood even higher than the Sierra. One of the oldest trees – called Methuselah – is estimated to be over 4700 years old, beating even the Great Sphinx of Giza by about two centuries.

To reach the groves, take Hwy 168 east 12 miles from Big Pine to White Mountain Rd, then turn left (north) and climb the curvy road 10 miles to **Schulman Grove**, named for the scientist who first discovered the trees' biblical age in the 1950s. The entire trip takes about one hour one-way from Independence. There's access to self-guided trails near the solar-powered **Schulman Grove Visitor Center** (☏760-873-2500; www.fs.usda.gov/inyo; White Mountain Rd; per person/car $3/6; ⊙10am-4pm Fri-Mon mid-May–early Nov). White Mountain Rd is usually closed from November to April.

interpretive center

(☏760-878-2194; www.nps. gov/manz; 5001 Hwy 395, Independence; ⊙9am-5:30pm Apr–mid-Oct, 10am-4:30pm mid-Oct–Mar; P ♿). Watch the 22-minute documentary film, then explore the thought-provoking exhibits chronicling the stories of the families that languished here yet built a vibrant community. Afterwards, take a self-guided 3.2-mile driving tour around the grounds, which include a re-created mess hall and barracks, vestiges of buildings and gardens, as well as the haunting camp cemetery.

Often mistaken for Mt Whitney, 14,375ft Mt Williamson looms above this flat, dusty plain, a lonely expanse that bursts with wildflowers in spring.

The Drive » Continue north 6 miles on Hwy 395 to the small town of Independence. In the center of town, look for the columned Inyo County Courthouse and turn left onto W Center St. Drive six blocks through a residential area to the end of the road.

④ Independence

This sleepy highway town has been a county seat since 1866 and is home to the **Eastern California Museum** (☏760-878-0364; www. inyocounty.us/ecmsite; 155 N Grant St; donation requested; ⊙10am-5pm; P ♿). An excellent archive of Eastern Sierra history

Bodie Old horse-drawn wagon

and culture, it contains one of the most complete collections of Paiute and Shoshone baskets in the country, as well as historic photographs of local rock climbers scaling Sierra peaks – including Mt Whitney – with huge packs and no harnesses. Other highlights include artifacts from Manzanar and an exhibit about the fight to keep the region's water supply from being diverted to Los Angeles.

Fans of Mary Austin (1868–1934), renowned author of *The Land of Little Rain* and vocal foe of the desertification of the Owens Valley, can follow signs leading to her former house at **253 Market St**.

The Drive » Depart north along Hwy 395 as civilization again recedes amid a buffer of dreamy granite mountains, midsized foothills and (most of the year) an expanse of bright blue sky. Tuffs of blackened volcanic rock occasionally appear roadside. Pass through the blink-and-you-missed-it town of Big Pine, and enter Bishop.

- - - - - - - - - - -

5 Bishop

The second-largest town in the Eastern Sierra and about a third of the way north from Lone Pine to Reno, Bishop is a major hub for hikers, cyclists, anglers and climbers. To see what draws them here, visit the **Mountain Light Gallery** (☎760-873-7700; www.mountainlight.com; 106 S Main St; ☺10am-5pm Mon-Sat, 11am-4pm Sun), featuring the stunning outdoor photography of the late Galen Rowell, whose High Sierra images are some of the best in existence.

Where Hwy 395 swings west, continue northeast for 4.5 miles on Hwy 6 to reach the **Laws Railroad Museum & Historic Site** (☎760-873-5950; www.lawsmuseum.org; Silver Canyon Rd, off Hwy 6; donation $5; ☺9:30am-4pm late May-early Sep, 10am-4pm early Sep-late

May; P 🚶), a remnant of the narrow-gauge Carson and Colorado rail line that closed in 1960. Train buffs will hyperventilate over the collection of antique railcars, and kids love exploring the 1883 depot and clanging the brass bell. Dozens of historic buildings from the region have been reassembled with period artifacts to create a time-capsule village.

🍴 p247

The Drive » Back on Hwy 395, continue over 40 miles north to Hwy 203, passing Lake Crowley and the southern reaches of the Long Valley Caldera seismic hot spot. On Hwy 203 before the center of town, stop in at the Mammoth Lakes Welcome Center for excellent local and regional information.

- - - - - - - - - - - -

TRIP HIGHLIGHT

❻ Mammoth Lakes

Splendidly situated at a breathless 8000ft, Mammoth Lakes is an active year-round outdoor-recreation town buffered by alpine wilderness and punctuated by its signature 11,053ft peak, **Mammoth Mountain** (☎800-626-6684, 760-934-2571, 24hr snow report 888-766-9778; www.mammothmountain. com; adult/youth 13-18yr/child 7-12yr $125/98/35; 🚶). This ever-burgeoning resort complex has 3100 vertical feet – enough to whet any snow-sports appetite – and an enviably long season that may last from November to June.

When the snow finally melts, the ski and snowboard resort does a quick costume change and becomes the massive Mammoth Mountain Bike Park, and with a slew of mountain-bikers decked out in body armor, it could be mistaken for the movie set of an apocalyptic *Mad Max* sequel. With more than 80 miles of well-tended single-track trails and a crazy terrain park, it draws those who know their knobby tires.

Year-round, a vertiginous **gondola** (☎800-626-6684; www.mammoth mountain.com; adult/youth 13-18yr/child 5-12yr $23/18/11; 🕐hours vary; P 🚶) whisks sightseers to the apex for breathless views of snow-speckled mountaintops.

🍴 🛏 p247

The Drive » Keep the car parked at Mammoth Mountain and catch the mandatory Reds Meadow shuttle bus from the Gondola Building. However, you may want to drive up 1.5 miles west and back on Hwy 203 as far as Minaret Vista to contemplate eye-popping views of the Ritter Range, the serrated Minarets and the remote reaches of Yosemite National Park.

- - - - - - - - - - - -

TRIP HIGHLIGHT

❼ Reds Meadow

One of the most beautiful and varied landscapes near Mammoth is the Reds Meadow Valley, west of Mammoth Mountain. The most fascinating attraction in Reds Meadow is the surreal 10,000-year-old volcanic formation of **Devils Postpile National Monument**. The 60ft curtains of near-vertical, six-sided basalt columns formed when rivers of molten lava slowed, cooled and cracked with perplexing symmetry. This honeycomb design is best appreciated from atop the columns, reached by a short trail. The columns are an easy, half-mile hike from the **Devils Postpile Ranger Station** (☎760-934-2289; www.nps.gov/depo; 🕐9am-5pm mid-Jun–mid-Oct).

From the monument, a 2.5-mile hike passing through fire-scarred forest leads to the spectacular **Rainbow Falls**, where the San Joaquin River gushes over a 101ft basalt cliff. Chances of actually seeing a rainbow forming in the billowing mist are greatest at midday. The falls can also be reached via an easy 1.5-mile walk from the Reds Meadow shuttle stop.

The Drive » Back on Hwy 395, continue north to Hwy 158 and pull out the camera for the alpine lake and peak vistas of the June Lake Loop.

- - - - - - - - - - - -

❽ June Lake Loop

Under the shadow of massive Carson Peak (10,909ft), the stunning 16-mile June Lake Loop (Hwy 158) meanders through a picture-perfect horseshoe canyon, past the relaxed resort town of June Lake and four sparkling, fish-rich lakes: Grant, Silver, Gull and June. It's especially scenic in fall when the basin is ablaze with golden aspens. Hardy ice climbers scale its frozen waterfalls in winter.

June Lake is backed by the Ansel Adams Wilderness, which runs into Yosemite National Park. From Silver Lake, Gem and Agnew Lakes make spectacular day hikes, and boat rentals and horseback rides are available.

The Drive » Rejoin Hwy 395 heading north, where the rounded Mono Craters dot the dry and scrubby eastern landscape and the Mono Lake Basin unfolds into view.

TRIP HIGHLIGHT

⑨ Mono Lake

North America's second-oldest lake is a quiet and mysterious expanse of deep blue water, whose glassy surface reflects jagged Sierra peaks, young volcanic cones and the unearthly tufa (*too*-fah) towers that make the lake so distinctive. Protruding from the water like drip sand castles, tufas form when calcium bubbles up from subterranean springs and combines with carbonate in the alkaline lake waters.

The salinity and alkaline levels are unfortunately too high for a pleasant swim. Instead, paddle a kayak or canoe

EASTERN SIERRA HOT SPRINGS

Nestled between the White Mountains and the Sierra Nevada near Mammoth is a tantalizing slew of natural pools with snow-capped panoramic views. When the high-altitude summer nights turn chilly and the coyotes cry, you'll never want to towel off. About 9 miles southeast of Mammoth Lakes, Benton Crossing Rd juts east off Hwy 395, accessing a delicious bounty of hot springs. For detailed directions and maps, pick up Matt Bischoff's excellent *Touring California and Nevada Hot Springs* or see www.mammothweb.com/recreation/hottubbing.cfm for directions to a few.

around the weathered towers of tufa, drink in wide-open views of the Mono Craters volcanic field, and discreetly spy on the water birds that live in this unique habitat.

The **Mono Basin Scenic Area Visitor Center** (☏760-647-3044; www.fs.usda.gov/inyo; 1 Visitor Center Dr, Lee Vining; ☺8am-5pm, hours vary, closed Dec-Mar; ♿), a half a mile north of Lee Vining, has interpretive displays, a bookstore and a 20-minute movie about Mono Lake.

✗ ⌂ p247

The Drive » About 10 miles north of Lee Vining, Hwy 395 arrives at its highest point, Conway Summit (8148ft). Pull off at the vista point for awe-inspiring panoramas of Mono Lake, backed by the Mono Craters and June and Mammoth Mountains. Continue approximately 8 miles north, and go 13 miles east on Hwy 270; the last 3 miles are unpaved.

TRIP HIGHLIGHT

⑩ Bodie State Historic Park

For a time warp back to the gold-rush era, swing by **Bodie** (☏760-647-6445; www.parks.ca.gov/bodie; Hwy 270, adult/child $7/5; ☺9am-6pm mid-Mar–Oct, to 4pm Nov–mid-Mar; P ♿), one of the West's most authentic and best-preserved ghost towns. Gold was discovered here in 1859, and the place grew from a bare-bones mining camp to a lawless boomtown of 10,000. Fights and murders occurred almost daily, fueled by liquor from 65 saloons, some of which doubled as brothels, gambling halls or opium dens.

The hills disgorged some $35 million worth of gold and silver in the 1870s and '80s, but when production plummeted, Bodie was abandoned, and about 200 weather-beaten

DETOUR: VIRGINIA CITY

Start: ⑩ Bodie State Historic Park (p245)

During the 1860s gold rush, Virginia City was a high-flying, rip-roaring Wild West boomtown. It was the site of the legendary Comstock Lode, a massive silver bonanza that began in 1859 and stands as one of the world's richest strikes. Some of the silver barons went on to become major players in California history, and much of San Francisco was built with the treasure dug up from the soil beneath the town. Mark Twain spent time in this raucous place during its heyday, and his eyewitness descriptions of mining life were published in *Roughing It*.

The high-elevation town is a National Historic Landmark, with a main street of Victorian buildings, wooden sidewalks, wacky saloons and small museums ranging from hokey to intriguing. On the main drag, C St, you'll find the **visitor center** (📞800-718-7587, 775-847-7500; www.visitvirginiacitynv. com; 86 S C St; ⏰9am-5pm Mon-Sat, 10am-4pm Sun). To see how the mining elite lived, stop by the **Mackay Mansion** (📞775-847-7500; 291 South D St; adult/child $5/ free; ⏰10am-4:30pm, winter hours vary) and the **Castle** (cnr Taylor & B Sts).

From Carson City on Hwy 395, go east on Hwy 50, and then another 7 miles via Hwy 341 and Hwy 342. Continuing on to Reno, wind through a spectacular 13 miles of high desert along Hwy 341 to rejoin Hwy 395, with another 7 miles to reach Reno.

The Drive » Retrace your way back to Hwy 395, where you'll soon come to the big-sky settlement of Bridgeport. From there, it's approximately two hours to Reno along a lovely two-lane section of the highway that traces the bank of the snaking Walker River.

- - - - - - - - - - - -

⑪ Reno

Nevada's second-largest city has steadily carved a noncasino niche as an all-season outdoor-recreation spot. The Truckee River bisects the heart of the high mountain-ringed city, and in the heat of summer, the **Truckee River Whitewater Park** teems with urban kayakers and swimmers bobbing along on inner tubes. Two kayak courses wrap around Wingfield Park, a small river island that hosts free concerts in summertime. **Tahoe Whitewater Tours** (📞775-787-5000; www.truckeewhitewater rafting.com; 400 Island Ave; 2-hr kayak rental/tour $48/68) and **Sierra Adventures** (📞775-323-8928, 866-323-8928; www.wildsierra.com; Truckee River Lane; kayak rental from $19) offer kayak rentals, tours and lessons.

🍴 🛏 p247

buildings now sit frozen in time in this cold, barren and windswept valley. Peering through dusty windows you'll see stocked stores, furnished homes, a schoolhouse with desks and books, the jail and many other buildings. The former Miners' Union Hall now houses a **museum** and **visitor center** (⏰9am to one hour before park closes), and rangers conduct free tours in summer.

Eating & Sleeping

Lone Pine ❶

✗ Alabama Hills Cafe
Diner $

(✆760-876-4675; 111 W Post St; mains $8-14; ⏰7am-2pm; ✈ 🚹) Everyone's favorite breakfast joint, the portions here are big, the bread fresh-baked, and the hearty soups, sandwiches and fruit pies make lunch an attractive option, too.

🛏 Dow Hotel & Dow Villa Motel
Hotel, Motel $

(✆800-824-9317, 760-876-5521; www.dowvillamotel.com; 310 S Main St; hotel r with/without bath from $89/70, motel r $117-158; P 🚻 ❄ @ 🛜 🖾 🐾) John Wayne and Errol Flynn are among the stars who have stayed at this venerable hotel. Built in 1922, the place has been restored but retains much of its rustic charm.

Bishop ❺

✗ Great Basin Bakery
Bakery, Cafe $

(✆760-873-9828; www.greatbasinbakerybishop.com; 275D S Main St, entrance on Lagoon St; salads & sandwiches $5-8; ⏰6am-4pm Mon-Sat, from 6:30am Sun; ✈ 🚹) On a side street in the southern part of town, this excellent bakery serves locally roasted coffee, breakfast sandwiches on freshly baked bagels with local eggs, homemade soups and lots of delectable baked goods (with vegan and gluten-free options).

Mammoth Lakes ❻

✗ Toomey's
Modern American $$

(✆760-924-4408, http://toomeyscatering.com; 6085 Minaret Rd; mains $10-33; ⏰7am-9pm; 🚹) The legendary chef from Whoa Nellie Deli in Lee Vining has decamped here, along with his eclectic menu of wild-buffalo meatloaf, seafood jambalaya and lobster taquitos with mango salsa – plus a lifetime's worth of baseball paraphernalia.

🛏 Alpenhof Lodge
Hotel $

(✆800-828-0371, 760-934-6330; www.alpenhof-lodge.com; 6080 Minaret Rd; r $99-199;

P 🚻 @ 🛜 🖾) A snowball's toss from the Village, this Euro-flavored inn has updated lodge rooms with tasteful accent walls and ski racks, plus more luxurious accommodations with gas fireplaces or kitchens.

Mono Lake ❾

✗ Whoa Nellie Deli
American $$

(✆760-647-1088; www.whoanelliedeli.com; Tioga Gas Mart, 22 Vista Point Dr, off Hwy 120; mains $10-25; ⏰6:30am-8:30pm late Apr-Oct; 🚹) After putting this unexpected gas station restaurant on the map, its famed chef has moved on to Mammoth, but locals think the food is still damn good. Stop in for delicious burgers, BBQ chicken pizza and other tasty morsels, and live bands some nights.

🛏 Yosemite Gateway Motel
Motel $$

(✆760-647-6467; http://yosemitegatewaymotel.com; 51340 Hwy 395; r $139-209; P 🚻 🛜) Think vistas. This is the only motel on the east side of the highway, and the views from some of the rooms are phenomenal. Its somewhat tired rooms have comfortable beds with thick duvets and big bathrooms.

Reno ⓫

✗ Silver Peak Restaurant & Brewery
Pub Food $$

(✆775-324-1864; www.silverpeakbrewery.com; 124 Wonder St; dinner mains $15-25; ⏰restaurant 11am-10pm Sun-Thu, to 11pm Sat & Sun, pub open 1hr later; 🚹) Casual and pretense-free, this place hums with the chatter of happy locals settling in for a night of microbrews and great eats, from pizza with barbecue chicken to filet mignon.

🛏 Peppermill
Casino Hotel $$

(✆775-826-2121, 866-821-9996; www.peppermillreno.com; 2707 S Virginia St; r Sun-Thu from $69, Fri & Sat from $149; P ❄ @ 🛜 🖾) With a dash of Vegas-style opulence, the ever-popular Peppermill boasts Tuscan-themed suites in its newest 600-room tower, and plush remodeled rooms throughout the rest of the property.

Classic Trip

Highway 49 Through Gold Country

There's plenty to see on winding Hwy 49. A trip through Gold Country shows off California's early days, when hell-raising prospectors and ruffians rushed helter-skelter into the West.

TRIP HIGHLIGHTS

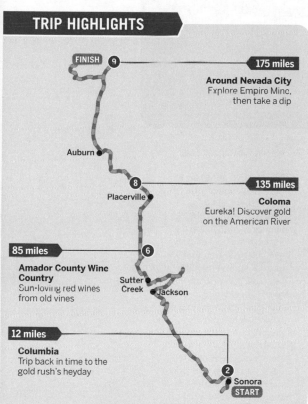

FINISH — 9 — **175 miles**

Around Nevada City
Explore Empire Mine, then take a dip

Auburn

— 8 — **135 miles**

Placerville

Coloma
Eureka! Discover gold on the American River

85 miles — 6

Amador County Wine Country
Sun-loving red wines from old vines

Sutter Creek · Jackson

12 miles

Columbia
Trip back in time to the gold rush's heyday

2 — Sonora
START

3–4 DAYS
175 MILES / 281KM

GREAT FOR...

BEST TIME TO GO
May to October for sunny skies.

📷 **ESSENTIAL PHOTO**

Sutter's Mill, California's original gold discovery site.

✓ **BEST FOR SWIMMING**
South Yuba River State Park.

Angels Camp Gold-Rush-era buildings

Classic Trip

23 Highway 49 Through Gold Country

When you roll into Gold Country on a sunny afternoon, the promise of adventure recalls the days when newspaper headlines screamed about gold discoveries and the Golden State was born. Today this rural region offers different cultural riches: exploring crumbling false-front saloons, rusting machines that once moved mountains and an endless parade of patinaed bronze historical markers along Hwy 49, one of California's most enchantingly scenic byways.

① Sonora

Settled in 1848 by Mexican miners, Sonora soon became a cosmopolitan center with ornate saloons patronized by gamblers, drunkards and gold diggers. Its downtown district is so well preserved that it's frequently a location for Hollywood films such as Clint Eastwood's *Unforgiven*. Likewise, **Railtown 1897 State Historic Park** (☎20 9-984-3953; www.railtown1897. org; 10501 Reservoir Rd, Jamestown; adult/child $5/3, incl train ride $15/10; ☻9:30am-4:30pm Apr-Oct, 10am-3pm Nov-Mar, train rides 10:30am-3pm Sat & Sun Apr-Oct; ℙ 🚻) and the surrounding hills of **Jamestown**, about 4 miles southwest of Sonora along Hwy 49, have been a backdrop for over 200 Western movies and TV shows, including *High Noon*. There's a lyrical romance to the historical railway yard, where orange poppies bloom among the rusting shells of steel goliaths. On some weekends and holidays, you can board the narrow-gauge railroad that once transported ore,

lumber and miners. Making a 45-minute, 6-mile circuit, it's the best train ride in Gold Country. The park is five blocks east of Jamestown's pint-sized Main St.

✗ ⊨ p258

The Drive » Follow Hwy 49 just over 2 miles north of Sonora, then turn right onto Parrots Ferry Rd at the sign for Columbia. The state historic park is 2 miles further along this two-lane country road.

TRIP HIGHLIGHT

2 Columbia

Grab some suspenders and a floppy hat for **Columbia State Historic Park** (📞209-588-9128; www.parks.ca.gov; 11255 Jackson St, Columbia; ⊙most businesses 10am-5pm; P ♿), near the so-called 'Gem of the Southern Mines.'

LINK YOUR TRIP

24 Ebbetts Pass Scenic Byway

From Columbia, wind 13 miles northwest on Parrots Ferry Rd and Hwy 4 to Murphys, in Calaveras County wine country.

26 Sacramento Delta & Lodi

Sacramento is an hour's drive or less from such Gold Country towns as Placerville via Hwy 50 or Auburn via I-80.

It's like a miniature gold-rush Disneyland, but with more authenticity and heart. Four blocks of town have been preserved, where volunteers perambulate in 19th-century dress and demonstrate gold panning. The blacksmith's shop, theater, hotels and saloon are all carefully framed windows into California's past. The yesteryear illusion of Main St is shaken only a bit by fudge shops and the occasional banjo picker or play-acting '49er whose cell phone rings. Stop by the **Columbia Museum** (209-532-3184; www.parks.ca.gov; cnr Main & State Sts; 10am-5pm Apr-Sep, to 4pm Oct-Mar) inside Knapp's Store to learn more about historical mining techniques.

p258

The Drive Backtrack south on Parrots Ferry Rd, veering right and then turning right to stay on Springfield Rd for just over a mile. Rejoin Hwy 49 northbound, which crosses a long bridge over an artificial reservoir. After a dozen miles or so, Hwy 49 becomes Main St through the small town of Angels Camp.

---

3 Angels Camp

On the southern stretch of Hwy 49, one literary giant looms over all other Western tall-tale tellers: Samuel Clemens, aka Mark Twain, who got his first big break with the short story *The Celebrated Jumping Frog of Calaveras County*, written in 1865 and set in Angels Camp. With a mix of Victorian and art-deco buildings that shelter antiques shops and cafes, this 19th-century mining town makes the most of its Twain connection. The annual **Calaveras County Fair & Jumping Frog Jubilee** (www.frogtown.org; 2465 Gun Club Rd; admission from $8; May;) is held at the fairgrounds just south of town on the third weekend in May. You could win $5000 if your frog beats the world-record jump (over 21ft) set by 'Rosie the Ribeter' back in 1986.

The Drive Hwy 49 heads north of Angels Camp through rolling hillside farms and ranches. Past San Andreas, make a short detour through Mokelumne ('Moke') Hill, another historic mining town. In Jackson, turn right onto Hwy 88 east. After 9 miles, turn left on Pine Grove-Volcano Rd for 3 miles to reach Volcano, passing Indian Grinding Rock State Historic Park en route.

---

4 Volcano

Although the village of Volcano once yielded tons of gold and saw Civil War intrigue, today it slumbers away in solitude. Huge sandstone rocks lining Sutter Creek were blasted from the

DETOUR: CALIFORNIA CAVERN

Start: 3 Angels Camp

A 20-minute drive east of San Andreas via Mountain Ranch Rd, off Hwy 49 about 12 miles north of Angels Camp, **California Cavern State Historical Landmark** (866-762-2837, 209-736-2708; www.caverntours.com; 9565 Cave City Rd, Mountain Ranch; adult/child from $17.50/9.50; 10am-5pm, to 4pm early Sep–mid-May;) has the Gold Country's most extensive system of natural underground caverns. John Muir described them as 'graceful flowing folds deeply plicated like stiff silken drapery.' The family-friendly walking tours take 60 to 80 minutes, or get a group together and reserve ahead for a three-hour 'Mammoth Expedition' ($99) or a five-hour 'Middle Earth Expedition' ($130), which include some serious spelunking (no children under age 16 allowed). The Trail of Lakes walking tour, available only during the wet season in winter and spring, is magical.

Sutter Creek Taking a break at a local shop

surrounding hills using a hydraulic process before being scraped clean of gold-bearing dirt. Hydraulic mining had dire environmental consequences, but at its peak, miners raked in nearly $100 a day. Less than a mile southeast of town, **Black Chasm Cavern** (☎888-762-2837; www.caverntours.com; 15701 Pioneer Volcano Rd, Pine Grove; adult/child $17.50/9.50; ⊙9am-5pm mid-May–early Sep, 10am-4pm early Sep–mid-May; P⚐) has the whiff of a tourist trap, but one look at the helictite crystals – sparkling white formations resembling giant snowflakes – makes the crowds bearable.

Two miles southwest of town at **Indian Grinding Rock State Historic Park** (☎209-296-7488; parks.ca.gov; 14881 Pine Grove-Volcano Rd; per car $8; ⊙museum 11am-2:30pm Fri-Sun), a limestone outcrop is covered with petroglyphs and over 1000 *chaw'se* (mortar holes) used for grinding acorns into meal. Learn more about the Sierra Nevada's indigenous tribes inside the park's museum shaped like a Native American *hun'ge* (roundhouse).

🛏 p258

The Drive » Backtrack along Pine Grove-Volcano Rd, turning right onto Hwy 88 for about half a mile, then turn right onto Ridge Rd, which winds for around 8 miles back to Hwy 49. Turn right and head north about a mile to Sutter Creek.

- - - - - - - - - - - -

❺ Sutter Creek

Perch on the balcony of one of Main St's gracefully restored buildings and view this gem of a Gold Country town, boasting raised, arcaded sidewalks and high-balconied, false-fronted buildings that exemplify California's 19th-century frontier architecture. Pick up self-guided walking- and driving-tour maps at the **visitor center** (☎209-267-1344; www.suttercreek.org; 71a Main St). The nearby **Monteverde General Store Museum** (☎209-267-0493; www.suttercreek.org; 11 Randolph St; entry by donation; ⊙by appointment) is a trip back in time, as is the **Sutter Creek Theatre** (☎916-425-0077; www.suttercreektheater.com; 44 Main St; tickets $15-40), an 1860s saloon and billiards hall, now hosting live-music concerts and, occasionally, plays, films and cultural events. The rest of the town's four-block-long Main St is crowded with antiques shops, county boutiques, cafes and tasting bars pouring regional wines and craft spirits.

253

Classic Trip

WHY THIS IS A CLASSIC TRIP
SARA BENSON, WRITER

Even some well-traveled Californians haven't made the journey to see where the Golden State was born. A long weekend spent driving the roller-coaster hills of twisting Hwy 49 feels removed not just in space, but also in time from modern life. Slow down to savor the most captivating two-lane stretches of this historic byway among the vineyards north of Sutter Creek and between Placerville, Coloma and Auburn.

Top: Autumn colors along the highway near Nevada City
Left: Artifacts from Marshall Gold Discovery State Historic Park
Right: Vineyards in Amador County

JOHN ALVES / GETTY IMAGES ©

p258

The Drive » Follow Main St north of Sutter Creek for 3 miles through quaint Amador City. Back at Hwy 49, turn right and continue north toward Plymouth.

TRIP HIGHLIGHT

6 Amador County Wine Country

Amador County might be something of an underdog among California's wine-making regions, but a circuit of welcoming wineries and local characters make for great sipping without any pretension. Planted with California's oldest surviving zinfandel vines, the countryside has a lot in common with its most celebrated grape varietal – bold, richly colored and earthy. North of tiny Amador City, **Drytown Cellars** (209-245-3500; www.drytowncellars.com; 16030 Hwy 49, Drytown; 11am-5pm; P) has a gregarious host and an array of big red blends and single-varietal wines. Drive further north to the one-horse town of Plymouth, then head east on Shenandoah Rd, where rolling hills are covered with rocky rows of neatly pruned vines, soaking up gallons of sunshine. Pause at modern **Andis Wines** (209-245-6177; www.andiswines.com; 11000 Shenandoah Rd, Plymouth; tasting fee $5; 11am-4:30pm; P) for a rich array of reds, particularly Barbera, and

CHASING THE ELEPHANT

Every gold prospector in the Sierra Nevada foothills came to 'see the elephant,' a phrase that captured the adventurous rush for gold, and a colloquialism of the '49ers. Those on the overland California Trail were 'following the elephant's tracks,' and when they hit it rich, they'd seen the beast from 'trunk to tail.' Like hunting a rare wild animal, rushing Gold Country's hills was a once-in-a-lifetime risk, with potential for a jumbo reward.

picnic tables with vineyard views. Further along, turn left onto Steiner Rd toward **Renwood Winery** (☑209-245-6979; www.renwoodwinery.com; 12225 Steiner Rd, Plymouth; tasting fee $5-10, incl tour $15; ☺11am-6pm; **P**), crafting outstanding Zinfandel. Backtrack and continue straight across Shenandoah Rd, bending south towards hilltop estate **Wilderotter Vineyard** (☑209-245-6016; www.wilderottervineyard.com; 19890 Shenandoah School Rd, Plymouth; tasting fee $10; ☺10:30am-5pm; **P**), which pours Sauvignon Blanc and smoothly balanced reds.

✖ p258

The Drive 》 Follow Shenandoah School Rd briefly west until it ends. Turn left back onto Shenandoah Rd for 1.5 miles, then turn right onto Hwy 49 northbound. Less than 20 miles later, after up-and-down roller-coaster stretches, you'll arrive in downtown Placerville, south of Hwy 50.

❼ Placerville

Things get livelier in 'Old Hangtown,' a nickname Placerville earned for the vigilante-justice hangings that happened here in 1849. Most buildings along Placerville's Main St date from the 1850s.

Poke around antiques shops or ho-hum **Placerville Hardware** (☑530-622-1151; 441 Main St; ☺8am-6pm Mon-Sat, 9am-5pm Sun), the oldest continuously operating hardware store west of the Mississippi River. Downtown dive bars get an annual cleaning at Christmas and are great for knocking elbows with odd birds. For family-friendly shenanigans, head 1 mile north of town via Bedford Ave to **Hangtown's Gold Bug Park & Mine** (☑530-642-5207; www.goldbugpark.org; 2635 Goldbug Ln; adult/child $7/4; ☺10am-4pm Apr-Oct, from noon Sat & Sun Nov-Mar; **P** 🛉), where hard-hatted visitors can descend into a 19th-century mine shaft, or try gem panning (per hour $2).

Around Placerville, El Dorado County's mountainous terrain and volcanic soil combine with intense summertime heat and cooling night breezes off the Sierra Nevada to produce some noteworthy wines. Welcoming wineries on Apple Hill north

of Hwy 50 include **Lava Cap Winery** (☑530-621-0175; www.lavacap.com; 2221 Fruitridge Rd, Placerville; tasting fee free-$5; ☺10am-5pm; **P**), which sells well-stocked picnic baskets, and **Boeger Winery** (☑530-622-8094; www.boegerwinery.com; 1709 Carson Rd, Placerville; tasting $5-15; ☺10am-5pm; **P**), whose vineyards were first planted during the gold rush.

✖ p259

The Drive 》 Back on Hwy 49 northbound, you'll ride along one of the most scenic stretches of the Golden Country's historic route. Patched with shade from oak and pine trees, Hwy 49 drifts beside Sierra Nevada foothills for the next 9 miles to Coloma.

TRIP HIGHLIGHT

❽ Coloma

At pastoral, low-key **Marshall Gold Discovery State Historic Park** (☑530-622-3470; www.parks.ca.gov; Hwy 49, Coloma; per car $8; ☺8am-8pm late May-early Sep, to 6pm early Sep-Oct & Mar-late May, to 5pm Nov-Feb; **P** 🛉), a simple dirt path leads to the place along the banks of the American River where James Marshall made his famous discovery of gold flecks below Sutter's Mill on January 24, 1848. Today, several reconstructed and restored historical buildings are all within a short stroll along grassy trails that pass mining artifacts, a blacksmith's shop, pioneer emigrant houses and the **Gold Discovery Museum** (530-622-3470; http://marshallgold.org; 310 Back St, Coloma; guided tour adult/child $3/2; 10am-5pm Mar-Oct, 9am-4pm Nov-Feb, guided tours 11am & 1pm year-round;), which is also the park's visitor center. Panning for gold is always popular at **Bekeart's Gun Shop** (329 Hwy 49, Coloma; per person $7; 10am-3pm Sat & Sun;). Opposite the pioneer cemetery, you can walk or drive up Hwy 153 – the sign says it's California's shortest state highway (but it's not really) – to where the **James Marshall Monument** marks Marshall's final resting place. Ironically, he died bankrupt, penniless and a ward of the state.

 p259

The Drive » Rolling northbound, Hwy 49 unfolds more of the region's historical beauty over the next 17 miles. In Auburn, drive across I-80 and stay on Hwy 49 north for another 22 miles, gaining elevation while heading toward Grass Valley. Exit onto Empire St, turning right to follow the signs for Empire Mine State Historic Park's visitor center.

TRIP HIGHLIGHT

9 Around Nevada City

You've hit the biggest bonanza of the mother lode: **Empire Mine State Historic Park** (530-273-8522; www.empiremine.org; 10791 Empire St, Grass Valley; adult/child $7/3; 10am-5pm;), where California's richest hard-rock mine produced 5.8 million ounces of gold between 1850 and 1956. The mine yard is littered with the massive mining equipment and buildings constructed from waste rock.

Backtrack west, then follow the Golden Chain Hwy (Hwy 49) about 5 miles further north to Nevada City. On the town's quaint main drag, hilly Broad St, the

National Hotel (530-265-4551; www.thenational hotel.com; 211 Broad St; r with shared bath $80-125;) purports to be the oldest continuously operating hotel west of the Rockies. Mosey around the block to **Historic Firehouse No 1 Museum** (530-265-3937; www.nevadacounty history.org; 214 Main St; admission by donation; 1-4pm Tue-Sun May-Oct, by appointment Nov-Apr), where Native American artifacts join displays about Chinese laborers and creepy Donner Party relics.

Last, cool off with a dip at **South Yuba River State Park** (530-432-2546; www.parks.ca.gov; 17660 Pleasant Valley Rd, Penn Valley; park sunrise-sunset, visitor center 11am-4pm May-Sep, to 3pm Thu-Sun Oct-Apr;), which has popular swimming holes and forest hiking trails near Bridgeport, the USA's longest covered wooden bridge (temporarily closed for restoration at the time of research). It's a 30-minute drive northwest of Nevada City or Grass Valley.

p259

Classic Trip

Eating & Sleeping

Sonora ❶

✖ Diamondback Grill American $

(📞209-532-6661; www.thediamondbackgrill.com; 93 S Washington St, Sonora; mains $7-18; ⊙11am-9pm Mon-Thu, to 9:30pm Fri & Sat, to 8pm Sun; 🏄) With exposed brick and modern fixtures, the fresh menu and contemporary details at this cafe and wine bar are a reprieve from occasionally overbearing Victorian frill. Sandwiches dominate the menu (the salmon and eggplant-mozzarella are both great) and everything is homemade.

🛏 Gunn House Hotel Historic Hotel $$

(📞209-532-3421; www.gunnhousehotel.com; 286 S Washington St, Sonora; r incl breakfast $85-140; 🅿 ⊛ ❄ 🛜 🏊) For a lovable alternative to Gold Country's cookie-cut chains, this historic hotel hits the sweet spot. Rooms feature period decor and guests take to rocking chairs on the wide porches in the evening. A nice pool and a breakfast buffet also make it a hit with families.

Columbia ❷

🛏 City Hotel Historic Hotel $$

(📞information 209-532-1479, reservations 800-444-7275; www.reserveamerica.com; 22768 Main St, Columbia; r $85-115; 🅿 ⊛ ❄ 🛜) Among a handful of restored Victorian hotels in the area, the City Hotel is the most elegant, with rooms that overlook a shady stretch of Main St. Adjoining the on-site restaurant Christophers at the City Hotel (mains $10 to $30), What Cheer Saloon is an atmospheric Gold Country joint with oil paintings of lusty ladies and stripped wallpaper.

Volcano ❹

🛏 Union Inn Historic Hotel $$

(📞209-296-7711; www.volcanounion.com; 21375 Consolation St, Volcano; r incl breakfast $125-145; 🅿 ⊛ ❄ 🛜) The preferred of two historic hotels in Volcano, there are four lovingly updated rooms with crooked floors: two have street-facing balconies. Flat-screen TVs and modern touches are a bit incongruous with the old building, but it's a comfortable place to stay. The on-site **Union Pub** (mains $10-30; ⊙5-8pm Mon & Thu, to 9pm Fri, noon-9pm Sat, noon-8pm Sun) has a superb menu.

Sutter Creek ❺

🛏 Hanford House Inn B&B $$

(📞209-267-0747; www.hanfordhouse.com; 61 Hanford St; d incl breakfast $145-245; 🅿 ⊛ ❄ @ 🛜 🐾) Nod off on platform beds in contemporary rooms or fireplace cottage suites. Chef-prepared breakfasts are harvested from the inn's garden, freshly baked goods appear every afternoon and evening brings wine tasting.

Amador County Wine Country ❻

✖ Taste Californian $$$

(📞209-245-3463; www.restauranttaste.com; 9402 Main St, Plymouth; small plates $5-16, dinner mains $24-41; ⊙11:30am-2pm Fri-Sun, also from 5pm Mon, Tue, Thu & Fri, from 4:30pm Sat & Sun) Book a table at Taste, where excellent Amador County wines are paired with a fine menu of California-style cooking. There's open seating in the wine bar.

Placerville ❼

✖ Cozmic Café
Health Food $

(☎530-642-8481; http://ourcoz.com; 594 Main St; mains $6-13; ⏲cafe 7am-8pm Tue-Sun, pub 6pm-midnight Thu-Sun; 🛜🏍🚻) In the historic Placerville Soda Works building attached to an authentic mine shaft, this feel-good cafe spotlights organic, vegetarian and healthy fare backed by fresh-fruit smoothies. There's a good selection of wine and craft beer at night, often with live music.

Coloma ❽

✖ Argonaut Farm to Fork Cafe
American $

(☎530-626-7345; www.argonautcafe.com; 331 Hwy 49, Coloma; items $3-10; ⏲8am-4pm; 🛜🏍🚻) Truly delicious soups, sandwiches and coffee from well-known Sacramento and local purveyors find their way to this little wooden house in Marshall Gold Discovery State Historic Park. Crowds of schoolkids waiting for gelato can slow things down.

Around Nevada City ❾

✖ Ike's Quarter Cafe
Creole, Breakfast $$

(☎530-265-6138; www.ikesquartercafe.com; 401 Commercial St; mains $11-15; ⏲8am-3pm Thu-Mon; 🏍🚻) Right out of New Orleans' Garden District, Ike's serves splendid brunch fare with a sassy charm. There's eggs Sardou, jambalaya, vegetarian po' boy sandwiches and more. It's an excellent place to get 'Hangtown Fry' – a cornmeal-crusted mess of cornmeal-crusted oysters, bacon, caramelized onions and spinach.

🛏 Broad Street Inn
Inn $$

(☎530-265-2239; www.broadstreetinn.com; 517 W Broad St, Nevada City; r $115-125; ❄🛜🐾) This six-room inn is a favorite because it keeps things simple. (No weird old dolls, no yellowing lace doilies.) The good-value rooms are modern, brightly furnished and elegant.

Ebbetts Pass Scenic Byway

Follow this winding road over the rooftop of the Sierra Nevada, crossing from Gold Country to Lake Tahoe, passing lakes, giant sequoia groves, hot springs and all-seasons resorts.

TRIP HIGHLIGHTS

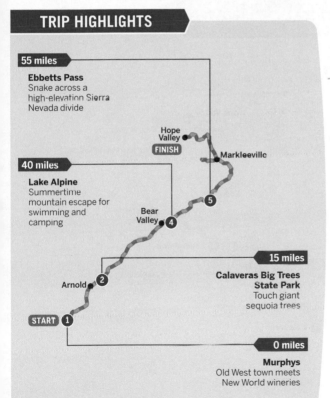

55 miles

Ebbetts Pass
Snake across a high-elevation Sierra Nevada divide

40 miles

Lake Alpine
Summertime mountain escape for swimming and camping

Hope Valley

FINISH

Markleeville

Bear Valley ④

⑤

15 miles

Calaveras Big Trees State Park
Touch giant sequoia trees

Arnold ②

START ①

0 miles

Murphys
Old West town meets New World wineries

2 DAYS
95 MILES / 155KM

GREAT FOR...

BEST TIME TO GO
June to October, when the pass is open.

ESSENTIAL PHOTO

Sierra Nevada peaks from Ebbetts Pass.

BEST FOR FAMILIES

Bear Valley's ski resort and summertime trails and lakes.

24

- - - - - - - - - - -
TRIP HIGHLIGHT

❶ Murphys

With its white-picket fences, the 19th-century 'Queen of the Sierra' is one of the most picturesque towns along the southern stretch of California's Gold Country. Amble along Main St, which shows off plenty of historical charm alongside its wine-tasting rooms, art galleries, boutiques and cafes. These rocky, volcanic Sierra Nevada foothills are known for making

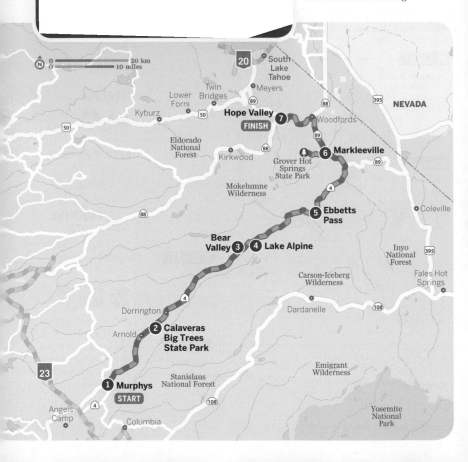

brambly Zinfandel and spicy Syrah, which you can sample at a dozen wineries all crowded together on a four-block stretch downtown. It's best to arrive early if you're visiting on the weekend. Start at **Tanner** (🗘209-728-8229; www.tannervineyards.com; 202 Main St; tasting $5; ☺noon-5pm Mon-Fri, 11am-6pm Sat, 11am-5:30pm Sun), whose family was the first to plant grapes and pay an alcohol tax in Calaveras County in the 1860s. Don't miss the 'Train Wreck' red blend at **Newsome Harlowe** (🗘209-728-9817; www.nhvino.com; 403 Main St; tasting $10; ☺noon-5pm Mon-Thu, 11am-5:30pm Fri-Sun; 👪) or the %#&@! (rhymes with 'duck') Rhône red blend at tongue-in-cheek

LINK YOUR TRIP

20 Lake Tahoe Loop

From Hope Valley, it's a 20-mile drive northwest on Hwy 89 past stream-fed meadows to South Lake Tahoe's beaches and ski resorts.

23 Highway 49 Through Gold Country

From Murphys, mosey 13 miles along Hwy 4 and Parrots Ferry Rd to old-time Columbia State Historic Park.

Twisted Oak (🗘209-728-3000; www.twistedoak.com; 363 Main St; tasting fee $5; ☺11:30am-5:30pm Sun-Fri, from 10:30am Sat).

✕ 🛏 p267

The Drive » Hwy 4 ascends through the workaday small town of Arnold, which has a few cafes and motels strung along the roadside 12 miles east of Murphys. After motoring another 3 miles uphill, turn right into Calaveras Big Trees State Park.

TRIP HIGHLIGHT

② Calaveras Big Trees State Park

Truthfully named **Calaveras Big Trees State Park** (🗘209-795-2334; www.parks.ca.gov; 1170 Hwy 4, Arnold, per car $10; ☺sunrise-sunset; P 👪) is home to giant sequoias The most massive trees on earth, they grow only in the western Sierra Nevada range. Reaching up to 275ft tall here and with trunk diameters over 35ft, these leftovers from the Mesozoic era are thought to weigh upwards of 2000 tons, or more than 10 blue whales. Close to the park entrance, the **North Grove Big Trees Trail** is a 1.5-mile self-guided loop, where the air is scented with fresh pine, fir and incense cedar. To escape some of the crowds, drive 8.5 miles along the curving park road to the start of the **South Grove Trail**. This 3.5-mile loop as-

cends to a peaceful grove that protects 10 times as many giant sequoias; a 1.5-mile round-trip spur trail leads to the Agassiz Tree, the big daddy of them all. Afterward, cool off with a summertime dip in Beaver Creek below the trail's footbridge or in the Stanislaus River along the main park road.

🛏 p267

The Drive » Back at Hwy 4, turn right and drive uphill past Dorrington, a 19th-century stagecoach stop and toll-water station, stopping at Hell's Kitchen Vista Point for panoramas of the glaciated volcanic landscape. About 22 miles northeast of the state park lies Bear Valley.

---

③ Bear Valley

It's all about outdoor family fun here. Sniff out anything from rock climbing to mountain biking and hiking all within a short distance of Bear Valley Village, which has a gas station, shops and casual restaurants. In winter, **Bear Valley Mountain** (🗘209-753-2301; www.bearvalley.com; 2280 Hwy 207, Bear Valley; ski lift ticket adult/youth 13-19yr/child 6-12yr $74/64/30; ☺hours vary; 👪) ski area will get your brain buzzing with 2000ft of vertical rise and 12 lifts. The resort's somewhat off-the-beaten-track location gives it a beginner-friendly, locals-only feel. On your left as you pull into Bear Valley

CANDIA BAXTER / SHUTTERSTOCK ©

Village, **Bear Valley Adventure Company** (📞209-753-2834; www.bearvalleyxc.com; 1 Bear Valley Rd, Bear Valley; ⏰hours vary; 🅿) is a one-stop shop for outdoor gear and supplies – kayak, stand-up paddle boarding (SUP), mountain bike and cross-country ski rentals – plus insider information on just about everything there is to do in the area. Staff also arrange mountain-bike shuttles and sell helpful maps.

The Drive » From the Bear Valley Village turnoff, it's less than 4 miles up Hwy 4 to Lake Alpine's beaches, campgrounds and day-use parking lots.

- - - - - - - - - - - -

TRIP HIGHLIGHT

4 Lake Alpine

Suddenly Hwy 4 reaches the shores of gasp-worthy Lake Alpine, a reservoir skirted by slabs of granite and offering several sandy beaches and a handful of rustic US Forest Service (USFS) campgrounds. Paddling, swimming and fishing opportunities abound, which means that it's always jammed with people on summer weekends. No matter how many folks descend upon the lake (and there are far fewer midweek), it's still hard to beat the gorgeous Sierra Nevada setting, 7350ft above sea level. Of several nearby hiking trailheads, the scramble to Inspiration Point gets you spectacular views of lakes

and the Dardanelles; this 3-mile round-trip hike starts from the lakeshore trail near Pine Marten Campground. Next to the boat ramp on the lake's northern shore, Lake Alpine Resort's summertime kiosk rents rowboats, paddleboats, kayaks and canoes.

🛏 p267

The Drive » Make sure you've got plenty of gas in the tank before embarking on the 33-mile drive over Ebbetts Pass downhill to Markleeville. There are campgrounds, but no services, gas stations, motels or places to eat along this high-elevation, twisting mountain road, which is only open seasonally during summer and fall.

- - - - - - - - - - - -

TRIP HIGHLIGHT

5 Ebbetts Pass

Ebbetts Pass National Scenic Byway officially runs from Arnold to Markleeville, yet it's the dramatic stretch east of Lake Alpine that really gets drivers' hearts pumping. Narrowing, the highway continues 4 miles past **Cape Horn Vista** to **Mosquito Lakes** and over Pacific Grade Summit before slaloming through historic **Hermit Valley**, where the Mokelumne River meadow blooms with summer wildflowers. Finally, Hwy 4 winds up and over the actual summit of Ebbetts Pass (elevation 8736ft), where the top-of-the-world scenery encompasses snaggletoothed granite

peaks rising above the tree line. About 0.4 miles east of the signposted pass, the highway crosses the **Pacific Crest Trail** (PCT), which zigzags from Mexico to Canada. For wildflowers, volcanic cliffs and granite canyon views, take an 8-mile round-trip hike to Nobel Lake. Or park the car and have a picnic beside **Kinney Reservoir**, just over another mile east.

Kinney Reservoir View of the lake from near Ebbetts Pass

The Drive » With a maximum 24% grade (no vehicles with trailers or over 25ft long), Hwy 4 loses elevation via dozens of steep hairpin turns, crossing multiple creek and river bridges as forested valley views open up below bald granite peaks. After 13 miles, turn left onto Hwy 89 and drive almost 5 miles northwest to Markleeville.

⑥ Markleeville

Breathlessly coming down from Ebbetts Pass, Hwy 4 winds past remnants of old mining communities long gone bust, including a pioneer cemetery, ghost towns and cattle ranches. From the junction below Monitor Pass, Hwy 89 runs gently north alongside the Carson River, where anglers fish for trout from pebble-washed beaches that kids love. Crossing Hangman's Bridge, Hwy 89 threads through Markleeville, a historic toll-road outpost that boomed with silver mining in the 1860s.

TOP TIP: CROSSING EBBETTS PASS

Hwy 4 is usually plowed from the west as far as Lake Alpine year-round, but Ebbetts Pass closes completely after the first major snowfall in November, December or January. The pass typically doesn't open again until April, May or June. Check current road conditions with the **California Department of Transportation** (CalTrans; ☎800-427-7623; www.dot.ca.gov/cgi-bin/roads.cgi).

Today it's a quiet spot to refuel and relax. Downtown, turn left onto Hot Springs Rd, then head up School St to **Alpine County Museum** (☎530-694-2317; www.alpinecounty museum.com; 1 School St, Markleeville; suggested donation $2; ⊙10am-4pm Thu-Sun late May-Oct; P), with its one-room 1882 schoolhouse, log-cabin jail and tiny museum displaying Native American baskets and pioneer-era artifacts. Back on Hot Springs Rd, drive 4 miles west through pine forests to **Grover Hot Springs State Park** (☎530-694-2249, 530-694-2248; www.parks. ca.gov; 3415 Hot Springs Rd,

Markleeville; per car $8, pool adult/child $7/5; ⊙hours vary; ♿), which has a shady picnic area, campground and natural spring-fed swimming pool. Carry tire chains in winter.

✕ ⌂ p267

The Drive ≫ Drive north out of Markleeville for 6 miles to the unremarkable junction of Hwys 88 and 89 at Woodfords. Turn left and continue lazily west another 6 miles, crossing the bridge over the Carson River to Hope Valley, where Hwys 88 and 89 split at Picketts Junction.

– – – – – – – – – – – – –

➐ Hope Valley

After all the fantastical scenery leading up to and over Ebbetts Pass,

what's left? Hope Valley, where wildflowers, grassy meadows and burbling streams are bordered by evergreen pines and aspen trees that turn brilliant yellow in fall. This panoramic valley is ringed by Sierra Nevada peaks, which remain dusted with snow even in early summer. Incidentally, the historic Pony Express route once ran through this way. Today, whether you want to dangle a fishing pole or splash around in the chilly mountain waters, or just take a bird-watching stroll or snowshoe trek in winter around the meadows, Hope Valley can feel like the most magical place in Alpine County. Start exploring on the nature trails of **Hope Valley Wildlife Area** (☎916-358-2900; www.wildlife.ca.gov; off Hwy 88; P).

⌂ p267

Eating & Sleeping

Murphys ❶

✗ Firewood
American, Pizza **$$**

(☎209-728-3248; www.firewoodeats.com; 420 Main St; mains $8-15; ⏰11am-9pm Sun-Thu, to 9:30pm Fri & Sat; 🛋) A rarity in a town with so much historical frill, Firewood's exposed-concrete walls and corrugated metal offer a minimalist respite. When the weather's nice, they open the front wall for al-fresco dining. There are wines by the glass, half a dozen beers on tap and basic pub fare, but the wood-fired pizzas are the hallmark.

🛏 Murphys Historic Hotel
Inn **$$**

(☎209-728-3444, 800-532-7684; www.murphyshotel.com; 457 Main St; d $130-205, with shared bath $95-215; 🅿😀) Since 1856, this hotel has anchored Main St. A must-stop on the Mark Twain slept here tour, the original structure is a little rough around the edges. The adjoining buildings have bland, modern rooms that cost more.

🛏 Victoria Inn
B&B **$$**

(☎209-728-8933; www.victoriainn-murphys.com; 402 Main St; r $135-320, cottages from $295; 🅿😀📶) This newly built B&B has elegant rooms with claw-foot slipper tubs, sleigh beds and balconies. The common spaces, like the long verandah for enjoying tapas and wine from the **restaurant and bar** (http://vrestaurantandbar-murphys.com), have chic, modern country appeal.

Calaveras Big Trees State Park ❷

🛏 Calaveras Big Trees State Park Campgrounds & Cabins
Campground, Cabin **$**

(☎reservations 800-444-7275; www.reserveamerica.com; off Hwy 4; tent & RV sites $25-35, cabins $165-185; 🅿) At the park entrance is busy **North Grove Campground**. Less crowded, hillside **Oak**

Hollow Campground is about 4 miles further along the park's main road. Rustic two-bedroom cabins with kitchens are also rented.

Lake Alpine ❹

🛏 Lake Alpine Resort
Cabins **$$**

(☎209-753-6350; www.lakealpineresort.com; 4000 Hwy 4, Bear Valley; tent cabins $65-70, cabins with kitchenette or kitchen $130-280; ⏰May-Oct; 🅿😀🍴) If you're not ready to rough it at rustic lakeshore campgrounds, this lodge with a general store, lake-view restaurant and bar has a handful of wooden and canvas-tent cabins for families.

Markleeville ❻

✗ Stone Fly
Californian **$$**

(☎530-694-9999; www.stoneflyrestaurant.com; 14821 Hwy 89, Markleeville; mains $15-24; ⏰5-9pm Fri & Sat) Meaty mains like braised lamb shank with creamy polenta take a back seat to wood-fired pizzas and homemade desserts, all delivered to an open-air patio in summer. Reservations recommended.

🛏 Creekside Lodge
Inn **$**

(☎866-802-7335; www.markleevilleusa.com; 14820 Hwy 89, Markleeville; r $85-115; 🅿😀) Beside busy Wolf Creek restaurant, this quaint white-shingled inn has a dozen tidy little rooms with pedestal sinks, high-end mattresses and country quilts covering the beds.

Hope Valley ❼

🛏 Sorensen's Resort
B&B, Cabins **$$**

(☎800-423-9949, 530-694-2203; www.sorensensresort.com; 14255 Hwy 88, Hope Valley; r incl breakfast $135-210, cabins $125-325; 🅿😀🍴) A year-round, outdoor-adventure base camp, Sorensen's rents charming cabins with kitchenettes and cottages in the woods, not far from the Carson River. The cozy country cafe serves three square meals a day (dinner reservations recommended).

Feather River Scenic Byway

Get ready for an icy plunge into a Feather River swimming hole. This trip visits unexplored forests, and is rich with wildlife, awesome hiking and views of volcanic peaks.

TRIP HIGHLIGHTS

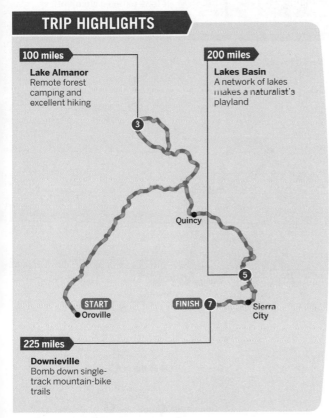

100 miles

Lake Almanor
Remote forest camping and excellent hiking

200 miles

Lakes Basin
A network of lakes makes a naturalist's playland

Quincy

START
● Oroville

FINISH 7

5

Sierra City

225 miles

Downieville
Bomb down single-track mountain-bike trails

3–4 DAYS
225 MILES / 360KM

GREAT FOR...

BEST TIME TO GO
April to June when hills are green, and September to October when oak leaves turn.

 ESSENTIAL PHOTO
The crags of the Sierra Buttes.

BEST SWIMMING HOLE
Just before Grizzly Dome tunnel on Hwy 70, it's a 10-minute scramble above the second tunnel.

25

❶ Oroville

This journey begins in Oroville, a little town that shares a name with the nearby lake that's filled by the Feather River. There's not much to see in Oroville, save the stunning **Chinese Temple & Museum Complex** (☎530-538-2496; 1500 Broderick St; adult/child $3/free; ☸noon-4pm; Ⓟ), a quiet monument to the 10,000 Chinese people who once lived here. During the 19th century, theater troupes from China toured a circuit of

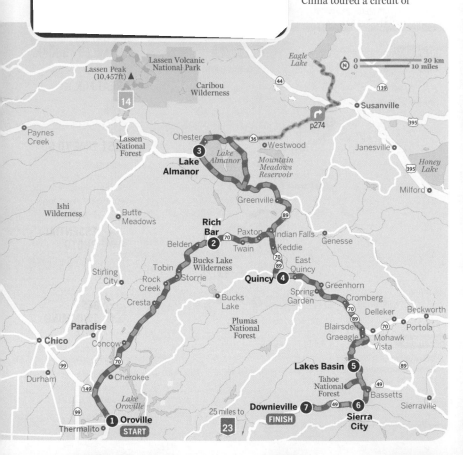

Chinatowns in California, and Oroville was the end of the line, which explains the unrivaled collection of 19th-century Chinese stage finery. The **Feather River Ranger District** (Plumas National Forest; ☑530-534-6500; http://www.fs.usda.gov; 875 Mitchell Ave; ⊙8am-4:30pm Mon-Fri) office is also in town; it issues permits and has a handout detailing historic stops along the byway. The nearby **Lake Oroville State Recreation Area** (☑530-538-2219; www.parks.ca.gov; 917 Kelly Ridge Rd; ⊙park 8am-8pm, visitor center 9am-5pm; P 🚻) is an excellent place to hike, camp and hook bass. Climb the 47ft-observation tower and look west at the smallest mountain range in the world, the Sutter Buttes.

LINK YOUR TRIP

23 **Highway 49 Through Gold Country**

More swimming holes, wild history lessons and winding byways await on the 'Golden Chain.' Link to Hwy 49 in Downieville.

14 **Volcanic Legacy Scenic Byway**

Skirt the volcanic domes of Mt Shasta and Mt Lassen, starting 30 miles northwest of Chester via Hwys 36 and 89.

🛏 p275

The Drive » Take Hwy 70 into the granite gorge, passing hydroelectric plants, mountain tunnels and historic bridges, including the Pulga Bridge. Four miles past the red bridge to Belden turn off Hwy 70 onto Rich Bar Rd, on your right.

❷ Rich Bar

Although the so-called Golden Chain, Hwy 49, is still further up the road, the Feather River area was dotted with its own rough-and-ready encampments of fortune hunters. One of the most successful of these was the aptly named **Rich Bar**, where little remains today except a crumbling graveyard and a historic marker. This quiet place wasn't so tame in the 1850s, when a resident named Dame Shirley chronicled life at Rich Bar as a part of her fascinating diary of life in California gold towns. Published as *The Shirley Letters,* her letters paint Rich Bar as a chaotic place of bloody accidents, a couple of murders, mob rule enforced by horse-whipping and hanging, an attempted suicide and a fatal duel. And she was only here a single month!

The Drive » Continue the lovely drive on Hwy 70, catching quick views of Lassen and Shasta peaks in the rearview mirror. Go north on Hwy 89 to reach the south shore of Lake Almanor. Follow the shore around the lake clockwise.

❸ Lake Almanor

This artificial lake is a crystalline example of California's beautiful, if sometimes awkward, conservation and land-management policy: the lake was created by the now-defunct Great Western Power Company and is now ostensibly owned by the Pacific Gas & Electric (PG&E) Company. The lake is surrounded by lush meadows and tall pines, most of it in the **Lassen National Forest** and **Caribou Wilderness** area. Both offer quiet camping with a free permit from the **Almanor Ranger District** (Lassen National Forest; ☑530-258-2141; www.fs.usda.gov; 900 E Hwy 36, Chester; ⊙8am-4:30pm Mon-Fri) office. The main town near the lake is **Chester**, and though you could whiz right by and dismiss it as a few blocks of nondescript roadside storefronts, don't – it's not. This robust little community has a fledgling art scene, decent restaurants and some comfy places to stay. You can rent bicycles for a cruise along the lakeshore at **Bodfish Bicycles & Quiet Mountain Sports** (☑530-258-2338; www.bodfishbicycles.com; 149 Main St, Chester; bicycle rental per hr/day $10/33; ⊙10am-5pm Tue-Sat, noon-4pm Sun, shorter off-season hours).

✕ ⊨ p275

The Drive » Continue around the lake and retrace the route south on Hwy 89, which will bring you back to the Feather River Scenic Byway. You'll hit Quincy when the road makes a T-junction.

④ Quincy

Idyllic Quincy (population 1728) is a mountain community that teeters on the edge of becoming an incorporated town. It's no metropolis, but after the route along the Feather River it may feel like one: it boasts a large grocery and even a fast-food franchise. Three streets make up Quincy's low-key commercial district. One of the nicest community museums in the state is also located here, amid flowering gardens. Visit the **Plumas County Museum** (⏿530-283-6320; www.plumas museum.org; 500 Jackson St, at Coburn St; adult/child $2/1; ⏱9am-4:30pm Tue-Sat, 10am-3pm Sun; ⓟ ♿) and you'll find that the building houses hundreds of historical photos and relics from the county's pioneer and Maidu days, early mining and timber industries, and construction of the Western Pacific Railroad.

✕ ⊨ p275

The Drive » Continue down Hwy 70/89 passing horse pastures and distant mountain views. At Graeagle take the right fork in the road to follow Hwy 89 south, then after less than 3 miles take a right on Gold Lake Hwy and start climbing.

TRIP HIGHLIGHT

⑤ Lakes Basin

Haven Lake, Gold Lake, Rock Lake, Deer Lake: dotted with crystalline alpine waters, this area is a secluded corner of paradise. Over a dozen of these gems can be reached only on foot, and great trails are virtually endless – you can even connect to the Pacific Crest Trail. The most scenic hike in the area is the **Haskell Peak Trail**, which affords views of both Lassen and Shasta

Downieville A small town in the remote Sierra County

and, on a clear day, Mt Rose in Nevada. To reach the trailhead, turn right from Gold Lake Hwy at Haskell Peak Rd (Forest Rd 9) and follow it for 8.5 miles. The hike is only 4.5 miles round-trip, but it's not for the faint of heart – you'll climb more than 1000ft through dense forest before it opens on an expansive view. From there you can see the rugged Sierra Buttes, distinguished from their surrounding mountains by jagged peaks, which look like a miniature version of the Alps.

🛏 p275

The Drive » Gold Lake Hwy will now descend and connect to Hwy 49 in Bassetts (a town that consists of little more than a gas station). Go right on Hwy 49 for 5 miles to reach Sierra City.

- - - - - - - - - - - - - -

⑥ Sierra City

Sierra City is the primary supply station for people headed to the **Sierra Buttes** and offers more chances at amazing short hikes to summits with panoramic views. From the **Sierra Country Store**

DETOUR:
EAGLE LAKE

Start: ❸ Lake Almanor (p271)

Those who have the time to get all the way out to Eagle Lake, California's second-largest natural lake, are rewarded with one of the most striking sights in the region: a stunningly blue jewel on the high plateau. From late spring until early fall, this lovely lake, over 15 miles northwest of Susanville, attracts a smattering of visitors who come to cool off, swim, fish, boat and camp. On the south shore, you'll find a pristine 5-mile paved recreational trail for cycling and hiking and several busy federal **campgrounds** (📞information 530-257-4188, reservations 877-444-6777; www.recreation.gov; tent/RV sites from $20/30) managed by **Eagle Lake Marina** (www.eaglelakerecreationarea.com), which offers hot showers, laundry and boat rentals. It also can help you get out onto the lake with a fishing license. To get to Eagle Lake, take Hwy 36 northeast of Lake Almanor toward Susanville, then continue north on Eagle Lake Rd to the south shore.

(📞530-862-1560; www.sierracountrystore.com; 213 Main St; ⏱8am-8pm May-Sep, 10am-6pm Oct-Apr; 🛜), there's a vast network of trails that is ideal for backpacking and casual hikes. They are listed in the *Lakes Basin, Downieville–Sierra City* map ($2), which is on sale at the store. Sierra City's local museum, the **Kentucky Mine** (📞530-862-1310; www.sierracountyhistory.org; 100 Kentucky Mine Rd; museum $1, tour adult/child $7/3.50; ⏱10am-4pm Wed-Sun late May-early Sep; 🅿️ ♿), is a worthy stop that introduces the famed 'Golden Chain Highway.' Its gold mine and stamp mill are just northeast of town.

🛏 p275

The Drive » Head west on Hwy 49 along the North Yuba River for a dozen miles to Downieville.

- - - - - - - - - - -

TRIP HIGHLIGHT

❼ Downieville

Even with a population smaller than 300, Downieville is the biggest town in the remote Sierra County, located at the junction of the North Yuba and Downie Rivers. With a reputation that quietly rivals Moab, Utah (before it got big), the town is the premiere place for trail riding in the state, and a staging area for true

wilderness adventures. Brave souls bomb down the **Downieville Downhill**, a molar-rattling 4000ft vertical descent, which is rated among the best mountain-bike routes in the USA. **Downieville Outfitters** (📞530-289-0155; www.downievilleoutfitters.com; 114 Main St; bike rental per day $60-65, shuttle $20; ⏱8:30am-5pm Mon-Thu, 8am-6pm Fri-Sun, shuttles May-Oct) is a good place to rent a bike and arrange a shuttle to make the one-way trip, which makes a thrilling end to this journey.

🛏 p275

Eating & Sleeping

Oroville ❶

🛏 Lake Oroville State Recreation Area Campground
Campground $

(📞information 530-538-2219, reservations 800-444-7275; www.reserveamerica.com; tent & RV sites $20-45; P) Drive-in campgrounds aren't the most rustic choice, but there are good primitive sites if you're willing to hike or – perhaps the coolest feature of the park – boat. There's a cove of floating platform campsites (per night $175).

Lake Almanor ❸

✕ Red Onion Grill
Modern American $$$

(📞530-258-1800; www.rdoniongrill.com; 303 Peninsula Dr, Westwood; meals $12-36; ⏱11am-9pm, shorter hours Oct-Apr) Head here for the finest dining on the lake with upscale New American, Italian-influenced cuisine (like the simply prepared shrimp scampi), and bar food that's executed with real panache. The setting is casual and fun, made all the more warm by the wine list.

🛏 PG&E Recreational Area Campgrounds
Campground $

(📞916-386-5164; http://recreation.pge.com; tent & RV sites $14-22; ⏱May-Sep; P 🐾) A favorite for tents and RVs, **Rocky Point Campground** is right on the lake, with some sites basically on the beach. For something more remote, try **Cool Springs Campground** or **Ponderosa Flat Campground**, both at Butt Reservoir near the lake's south shore, at the end of Prattville Butt Reservoir Rd.

Quincy ❹

✕ Pangaea Cafe & Pub
Cafe $

(📞530-283 0426; www.pangaeapub.com; 461 W Main St; mains $10-13; ⏱11am-9pm Mon-Fri; 🛜🔧♿) Like a stranger you feel you've met before, this earthy spot feels warmly familiar, all the more lovable when you consider its commitment to serving local produce. Choose from regional beef burgers, salmon sushi, a slew of panini sandwiches (many veggie), burritos and rice bowls.

🛏 Quincy Courtyard Suites
Apartment $$

(📞530-283-1401; www.quincycourtyardsuites. com; 436 Main St; apt $129-169; P 🐾🛜) Staying in this beautifully renovated 1908 Clinch building, overlooking the small main drag of Quincy's downtown, feels just right, like renting the village's cutest apartment. The warmly decorated rooms are modern – no fussy clutter – and apartments have spacious, modern kitchens, claw-foot tubs and gas fireplaces.

Lakes Basin ❺

🛏 Salmon Creek Campground
Campground $

(📞information 530-994-3401, reservations 877-444-6777; www.recreation.gov; Gold Lake Hwy, Calpine; tent & RV sites $24; ⏱mid-May–late Sep; P 🐾) With dramatic views of the Sierra Buttes, this USFS campground in the Tahoe National Forest is 2 miles north of Bassetts on Gold Lake Hwy, off Hwy 49. It has vault toilets, running water and sites for tents and RVs, but no hook-ups.

Sierra City ❻

🛏 Buttes Resort
Cabin, Lodge $$

(📞530-862-1170; www.buttesresort.citymax. com; 230 Main St; d $90-155; P 🐾) In the heart of Sierra City, the small Buttes Resort occupies a lovely spot overlooking the river and is a favorite with hikers looking to recharge. Most cabins have a private deck and barbecue, and some have full kitchens. You can borrow bikes and games from the wilderness-loving owners.

Downieville ❼

🛏 Riverside Inn
Hotel $

(📞888-883-5100, 530-289-1000; www. downieville.us; 206 Commercial St; r incl breakfast $90-125, ste $180-190; P 🐾🛜) There is a secluded, rustic charm to these 11 stove-warmed rooms and a suite overlooking the river. About half have kitchens and all have balconies for enjoying the river. Delightful innkeepers Nancy and Mike share excellent information about hiking and biking in the area, and in winter lend snowshoes.

Sacramento Delta & Lodi

Shady levy roads on the river delta bring you to an eccentric string of one-horse towns, where surprises are around every bend. Then meander east into Lodi's family-owned vineyards.

TRIP HIGHLIGHTS

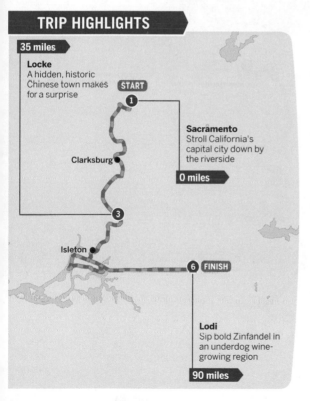

35 miles

Locke
A hidden, historic Chinese town makes for a surprise **START**

1

Sacramento
Stroll California's capital city down by the riverside

0 miles

Clarksburg

3

Isleton

6 **FINISH**

Lodi
Sip bold Zinfandel in an underdog wine-growing region

90 miles

---

2 DAYS
90 MILES / 144KM

GREAT FOR...

- - - - - - - - - - - - - - - -

BEST TIME TO GO

May to October when the 'Delta Breeze' keeps the sweltering heat at bay.

- - - - - - - - - - - - - - - -

ESSENTIAL PHOTO

One of the many colored metal bridges along S River Rd.

- - - - - - - - - - - - - - - -

BEST FOR CULTURE

The tiny town of Locke, California's last remaining rural Chinese American community.

Sacramento Statue of Queen Isabella and Christopher Columbus in the California State Capitol

277

26

TRIP HIGHLIGHT

❶ Sacramento

At the confluence of two of California's most powerful waterways – the American and Sacramento Rivers – lies the tidy grid of streets that make up the state capital. With invitingly cool marble corridors, the impressive **California State Capitol** (☏916-324-0333; http://capitolmuseum.ca.gov; 1315 10th St; ⏰8am-5pm Mon-Fri, from 9am Sat & Sun; 🚻) is a mandatory stop, as is

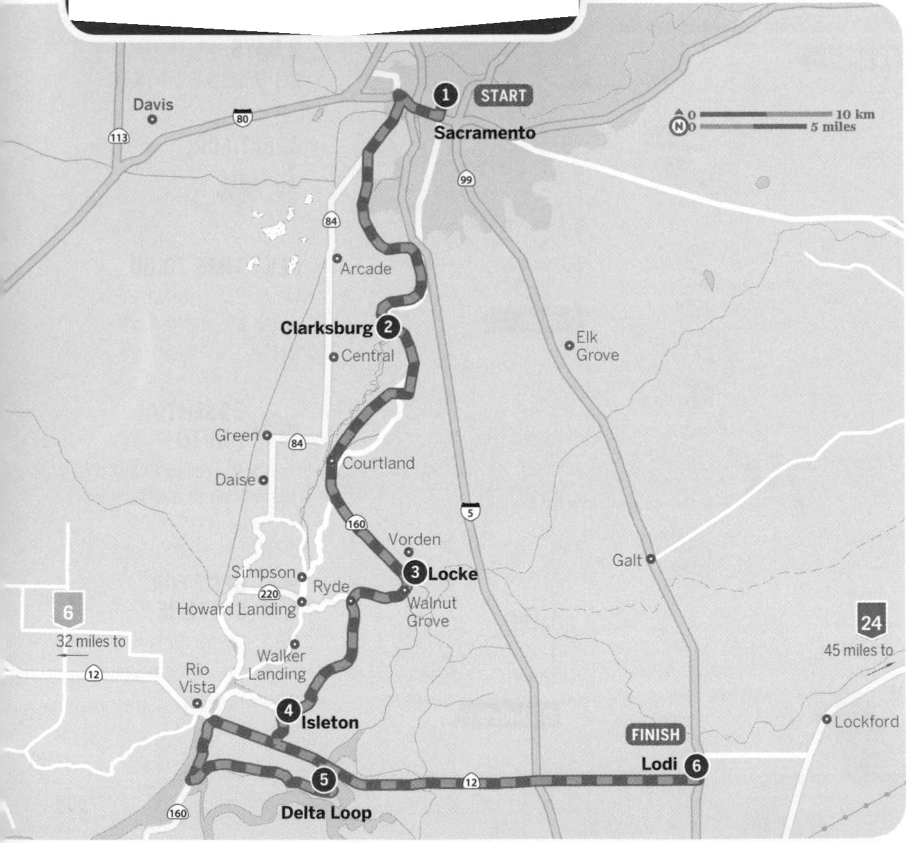

Capitol Park, the 40-acre garden surrounding the dome.

At the river port neighboring downtown, **Old Sacramento State Historic Park** (916-445-7387; http://oldsacramento.com; 922 2nd St; P) remains the city's stalwart tourist draw. The old-fashioned gold-rush atmosphere and the pervasive aroma of saltwater taffy make it good for a stroll, especially on summer evenings. California's largest concentration of buildings on the National Register of Historic Places is found here. At the north end, the **California State Railroad Museum** (916-323-9280; www.csrmf.org; 125 I St; adult/child museum $10/5, train ride $12/6; 10am-5pm; P) displays a sizeable

LINK YOUR TRIP

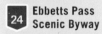

24 Ebbetts Pass Scenic Byway

Ready for another off-the-beaten-path excursion? Head east from Lodi via Hwys 12, 49 and 4 for 55 miles to Murphys in Gold Country.

6 Napa Valley

Contrasting with Lodi's humble charms, Northern California's most celebrated wine circuit is off Hwy 12, which runs west from Rio Vista.

collection of railcars and locomotives, including a fully outfitted Pullman sleeper and vintage dining cars. Board a restored passenger train for a 45-minute jaunt along the river; weather permitting, train rides run hourly from 11am to 4pm on weekends from April to September.

🍴 🛏 p283

The Drive » Point the car west from over the golden Tower Bridge, a landmark on the Sacramento River that opened in 1935. Across the bridge, turn left by Raley Field onto 5th St, following it south until it connects with S River Rd. It's less than 20 miles to Clarksburg.

- - - - - - - - - - - -

② Clarksburg

The fields and arid heat surrounding West Sacramento offer little clue that the 'Thousand Miles of Waterways' is near. But as you follow River Rd into Clarksburg, the breeze begins to blow. Travelers can't miss the **Old Sugar Mill** (916-744-1615; www.oldsugarmill. com; 35265 Willow Ave, Clarksburg; 11am-5pm; P), the hub of a thriving community of local winemakers. Live music often echoes through the space to complement the wines of the Carvalho family, who own this custom crushing facility. The wines made in the Clarksburg region of the Sacramento Valley have developed a lot over the

last decades, benefiting from the blazing sun and cool breezes. A few miles southwest of town via County Rds 141 and 144, the region's best-known winery, **Bogle** (916-744-1092; www.boglewinery. com; 37783 Country Rd 144, Clarksburg; 10am-5pm Mon-Fri, from 11am Sat & Sun; P), is prettily set among the vineyards of a sixth-generation family farm.

The Drive » Just over a mile south of Bogle, turn east on County Rd 142 to return to S River Rd, which winds beside a wide stretch of the Sacramento River. At the next bridge you come to, cross over to the river's eastern side and continue south another 6 miles. Turn left onto Locke Rd to enter Locke's historic district.

- - - - - - - - - - - -

TRIP HIGHLIGHT

③ Locke

Locke was founded by Chinese laborers, who built the levies that line nearly every inch of this Delta drive. In its heyday, Locke had a fairly wild reputation; during Prohibition (1920–33) the town's lack of a police force and quiet nearby waterways made it a hotbed of boozing and gambling. As you drop off the main road that parallels the river down into the old town, the view is unlike anywhere else in the country: tightly packed rows of wooden structures with creaking balconies and architecture that blends

Western and Chinese details. Locke's wild days are in evidence at the **Dai Loy Museum** (☎916-776-1661; http://www.locke-foundation.org; 13951 Main St, Locke; donations appreciated; ⏰noon-4pm Fri-Sun; 🚻), a former gambling house with exhibits on regional history. Its humble displays are worth a peek, but the best part is the atmospheric building itself. Nearby, the Chinese cultural shop sells souvenirs, crafts, games, imported teas and books including *Bitter Melon: Inside America's Last Rural Chinese Town*, which contains luminous photographs and oral histories.

✖ p283

The Drive » Immediately south of Locke in Walnut Grove, cross west over the bridge, then keep motoring south on gently curving Hwy 160, running alongside the Sacramento River.

As you approach Isleton, look for the yellow swing bridge, which turns on a pivot so that large ships can pass. Drive east over the bridge, then continue south on Hwy 160 into town.

- - - - - - - - - - - - -

④ Isleton

So-called 'Crawdad Town USA' seems more like the Mississippi Delta than California. Once it also boasted a thriving Chinese community, which is evident in the historic storefronts that line its main drag. The town is a regular stop for weekend Harley cruisers and Delta boaters, who lend the streets an amiably scruffy atmosphere and ensure the bars are always busy. Fishers should drop in to **Bob's Bait Shop** (☎916-777-6666; http://themasterbaiter.tripod.com; 302 2nd St, Isleton; ⏰6am-5pm Sun-Thu, to 6pm Fri-Sat) for advice from the self-described, ahem,

'Master Baiter.' As well as dispensing expert information on fishing in the area, he sells live crayfish that you can take along for a picnic.

✖ p283

The Drive » Take Jackson Slough Rd south out of town and go left on Hwy 12. Just before the next big bridge, go right on Brannan Island Rd and follow it along the Delta Loop for views of bird-filled skies and marshy lowlands. With the air-conditioning off, the rush of heat through the open window smells of tilled earth and sea salt.

- - - - - - - - - - - - -

⑤ Delta Loop

The drive along the Delta Loop is best taken at an unhurried pace – proof that sometimes the journey itself is as important as the destination. This is the heart of the Delta: marinas line the southern stretch where you can charter anything that floats, migratory birds fill the skies and cruisers meander the uncrowded roads. The loop ends at **Brannan Island State Recreation Area** (☎916-777-6671; www.parks.ca.gov; 17645 Hwy 160, Rio Vista; per car $10; ⏰sunrise-sunset; P🚻), where sandy picnic areas and grassy barbecue spots draw hard-partying campers. By day, it's a great place for families: it has lots of space in which to run around and a beach where little ones can wade into the reeds. The park offers excellent

LOCAL KNOWLEDGE: CALIFORNIA STATE FAIR

For two weeks every July, the **California State Fair** (☎916-263-3247; www.castatefair.org/home; 1600 Exposition Blvd; adult/child $12/8; 🚻) fills the Cal-Expo fairgrounds, east of I-80 on the north side of the American River, with a small city of cows and carnival rides. It's likely the only place on earth where you can plant a redwood tree, watch a pig give birth, ride a roller coaster, catch some barrel racing and taste exquisite Napa vintages and California craft beers all in one (exhausting) afternoon. Make time to see some of the auctions ($500 for a dozen eggs!) and the interactive agricultural exhibits run by the University of California, Davis.

Lodi Clusters of Zinfandel wine grapes

bird-watching at **Little Franks Tract**, a protected wetland marsh and riparian habitat, where keen-eyed visitors might also spot mink, beavers or river otters.

🛏 p283

The Drive ›› Take Hwy 160 north to connect with Hwy 12, just across the bridge from Rio Vista, a place to stop and grab a bite. Otherwise, turn right and head east on Hwy 12 for 17 miles toward Lodi, usually a 30-minute drive away. Less than 2 miles east of the I-5 Fwy, look for Michael David Winery on your right.

- - - - - - - - - - - -

6 Lodi

Although Lodi used to be the 'Watermelon Capital of the World,' today

vineyards rule this patch of the valley. Breezes from the Delta soothe the area's intensely hot vineyards, where more Zinfandel grapes are grown than anywhere else in the world. Some particularly old vines have been tended by the same families for more than a century.

On the way into town, **Michael David Winery** (📞209-368-7384; www. michaeldavidwinery.com; 4580 W Hwy 12; tasting $5-10; ⌚10am-5pm; P) scoops up the most awards, including for its '7 Deadly Zins.' A few miles northeast at the **Lodi Wine & Visitor Center** (📞20 9-367-4727; www.lodiwine. com; 2545 W Turner Rd; tasting fee $7; ⌚10am-5pm), local

vintages are poured at the tasting bar and there's a demonstration vineyard outside. Free maps are available for making a circuit of Lodi's rural wineries on country lanes. Or head straight downtown to sip some of the region's boutique wines and more famous labels at several tasting rooms within a few blocks of one another. **Jessie's Grove at Old Ice House Cellars** (📞209-368-0880; www.jessiesgrovewinery. com; 27 E Locust St; tasting fee $5; ⌚noon-5pm Fri & Sat, from 1pm Sun; P) is by the railroad tracks, north of the Lodi Arch.

🍴 🛏 p283

CENTRAL CALIFORNIA **26** SACRAMENTO DELTA & LODI

TRIP HIGHLIGHT

Eating & Sleeping

Sacramento ❶

✕ Gunther's
Ice Cream $

(☎916-457-6646; www.gunthersicecream.com; 2801 Franklin Blvd; sundaes $4; ⊙10am-10pm; 🖤) Always popular, this vintage 1940s soda fountain makes its own ice cream and frozen novelties.

✕ Mulvaney's B&L
Modern American $$$

(☎916-441-6022; www.mulvaneysbl.com; 1215 19th St; dinner mains $33-44; ⊙11:30am-2:30pm & 5-10pm Tue-Fri, 5-10pm Sat) With an obsessive commitment to seasonality, the menu at this swank, converted 19th-century firehouse includes delicate pastas and grilled meats that change every day.

🛏 Citizen Hotel
Boutique Hotel $$

(☎877-829-2429, 916-442-2700; www.thecitizenhotel.com; 926 J St; r from $180; P ⊛ ❄ @ 🛜 🐾) After an elegant, ultra-hip upgrade, this long vacant 1927 beaux-arts tower downtown became one of the city's coolest stays. Rooms look sumptuous, with luxe linens and striped wallpaper. There's an upscale farm-to-fork **restaurant** (☎916-492-4450; www.grangesacramento.com; dinner mains $19-39; ⊙6:30-10:30am, 11:30am-2pm & 5:30-10pm Mon-Thu, to 11pm Fri, 8am-2pm & 5:30-11pm Sat, to 10pm Sun; 🛜) on the ground floor. Valet parking is $25.

🛏 Delta King
B&B $$

(☎916-444-5464, 800-825-5464; www.deltaking.com; 1000 Front St; d from $145; P ⊛ ❄ 🛜) It's a treat to sleep aboard the *Delta King*, a 1927 paddle wheeler docked on the river in Old Sacramento. It lights up like a Christmas tree at night.

Locke ❸

✕ Al's Place
American $

(☎916-776-1800; 13943 Main St, Walnut Grove; mains $7-21; ⊙11am-9pm) Aka 'Al the Wop's,' this is a magnet for amiable Harley crews. The draw isn't the food (the special is a peanut butter-slathered hamburger) so much as the ambience. Above the creaking floorboards, the ceiling's covered in wrinkled dollar bills.

Isleton ❹

✕ Rogelio's
Fusion $$

(☎916-777-5878; http://rogelios.net; 34 Main St, Isleton; mains $8-15; ⊙4-8pm Wed & Thu, from noon Fri-Sun) Making the most of the Delta's multiethnic history, Rogelio's hotel and casino restaurant serves a mash-up of Mexican and Chinese dishes, with a few Italian and American standards mixed in. But nothing beats the carnitas chow mein.

Delta Loop ❺

🛏 Brannan Island State Park Recreation Area Campgrounds
Campground, Cabin $

(☎800-444-7275; www.reserveamerica.com, 17645 Hwy 160, Rio Vista; tent & RV sites $31-49, cabin $56; P 🐾) A tidy facility in a protected wetland marsh provides drive-in and walk-in campsites. There's a hike-in log cabin with electricity that sleeps four; bring sleeping bags.

Lodi ❻

✕ Farm Cafe
American $

(☎209-368-7384; www.michaeldavidwinery.com; 4580 W Hwy 12; mains $7-14; ⊙7:30am-3pm; 🖤) On the outskirts of town at Michael David Winery, this farmstand cafe slings big breakfast plates of fluffy omelets with country potatoes, cinnamon pancakes and homemade breads with strawberry jam.

🛏 Wine & Roses
Hotel $$$

(☎209-334-6988; http://winerose.com; 2505 W Turner Rd, r $179-240, ste from $335; P ⊛ ❄ @ 🛜 🐾) Surrounded by a vast rose garden, this is the most luxurious offering to spring up amid Lodi's vineyards. Tasteful and romantic, the rooms have slate bathrooms, high-quality toiletries and lots of square footage. There's an acclaimed restaurant and spa, too.

STRETCH YOUR LEGS
MONTEREY

Start/Finish Municipal Wharf II

Distance 2 miles

Duration 3–4 hours

Old Monterey holds California's most extraordinary collection of 19th-century brick and adobe buildings, all located along the self-guided Path of History. Museums and hidden gardens are also within a fishing line's cast of Monterey Bay.

Take this walk on Trips

Municipal Wharf II

For an authentic look at seaside life in Monterey, start by walking out onto Municipal Wharf II. There, fishing boats bob and sway, plein-air landscape painters work on their canvases and seafood purveyors hawk fresh catches.

The Walk » From the foot of the wharf, walk south and join the paved recreational trail heading west. Before reaching Fisherman's Wharf, turn south toward Custom House Plaza.

Pacific House

A beautifully preserved 1847 adobe, **Pacific House** (☏831-649-7118; www.parks. ca.gov; 20 Custom House Plaza; ☉10am-4pm Fri-Mon; 👪) has in-depth museum exhibits on California's complex multicultural history. Grab a free Path of History map, find out what other historical houses are currently open by asking state-park staff, and buy guided-tour tickets here.

The Walk » It's a quick stroll north across the plaza to the Custom House.

Custom House

In 1846 when the US flag was raised over the **Custom House** (☏831-649-7111; www.parks.ca.gov; Custom House Plaza; ☉10am-4pm; 👪), California was formally annexed from Mexico. Today, this restored adobe building displays an exotic selection of goods that traders once brought to exchange for local cowhides. The gift shop sells nostalgic toys, household goods, artisan crafts and books.

The Walk » Head south through Portola Plaza onto Alvarado St, passing the historical Monterey Hotel, theaters, shops, bars and cafes. Turn right onto Jefferson St, then left onto Pacific St. Ahead on your right is Colton Hall.

Colton Hall & Old Monterey Jail

Peek inside brick **Colton Hall** (☏831-646-5640; www.monterey.org/museums; 570 Pacific St; ☉10am-4pm), where California's first constitutional convention took place in 1849. Once the capitol of Alta (Upper) California, today this two-story white stone building houses a small historical museum that's free to poke around.

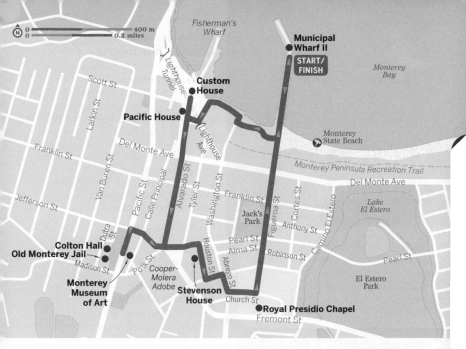

Just south is the **Old Monterey Jail** ([☎]831-646-5640; www.monterey.org; Dutra St; ⏰10am-4pm), which featured in John Steinbeck's classic novel *Tortilla Flat*.

The Walk » On the opposite side of Pacific St is the art museum.

Monterey Museum of Art

Downtown's **Monterey Museum of Art – Pacific Street** ([☎]831-372-5477, www.montereyart.org; 559 Pacific St; adult/child $10/free; ⏰11am-5pm Thu-Mon, to 8pm 1st Fri of month; [P] [♿]) is small, but is particularly strong in California contemporary art and modern landscape painters and photographers, including famous names such as Ansel Adams and Edward Weston.

The Walk » Retrace your steps up Pacific St, turning right onto Jefferson St back to Munras Ave, passing the Cooper-Molera Adobe on your right. Follow Pearl St two blocks east, then turn right onto Houston St.

Stevenson House

Writer Robert Louis Stevenson came to Monterey in 1879 to court his wife-to-be, Fanny Osbourne. **Stevenson House** ([☎]831-649-7118; www.parks.ca.gov; 530 Houston St; ⏰10am-4pm Thu-Sun), then called the French Hotel, was where he stayed while reputedly devising the novel *Treasure Island*. The restored interior is filled with memorabilia, including from the writer's later years in Polynesia.

The Walk » Continue down Houston St, then zigzag southeast by turning left on Webster St, right on Abrego St and finally left on Church St.

Royal Presidio Chapel

Today known as San Carlos Cathedral, graceful **Royal Presidio Chapel** ([☎]831-373-2628; www.sancarloscathedral.org; 500 Church St; ⏰10am-noon Wed, to 3pm Fri, to 2pm Sat, 1-3pm Sun, also 10am-noon & 1:15-3:15pm 2nd & 4th Mon of month; [P] [♿]) is California's oldest continuously functioning church. As Monterey expanded under Mexican rule in the 1820s, older buildings were destroyed, leaving behind this National Historic Landmark as a reminder of the defeated Spanish colonial presence.

The Walk » Head north up Figueroa St for eight blocks back to the foot of Municipal Wharf II.

STRETCH YOUR LEGS
SANTA BARBARA

Start/Finish Santa Barbara County Courthouse

Distance 1.6 miles

Duration 3–4 hours

Frankly put, this chic SoCal city is damn pleasant to putter around. Low-slung between lofty mountains and the sparkling Pacific, downtown's red-tiled roofs, white stucco buildings and Mediterranean vibe make this an irresistible ramble on any sunny afternoon.

Take this walk on Trips

Santa Barbara County Courthouse

Built in Spanish-Moorish Revival style, the **county courthouse** (📞805-962-6464; http://sbcourthouse.org; 1100 Anacapa St; ⏰8am-4:45pm Mon-Fri, 10am-4:45pm Sat & Sun) is an absurdly beautiful place to stand trial. The magnificent 1929 courthouse features hand-painted ceilings, wrought-iron chandeliers and Tunisian and Spanish tiles. Step into the 2nd-floor mural room, then climb the *Vertigo*-esque clocktower for arch-framed panoramas of the city, ocean and mountains.

The Walk » Exit the courthouse and head southwest along Anapamu St, passing the striking Italianate 1924 Santa Barbara Public Library. Turn left onto State St, downtown's main drag.

Santa Barbara Museum of Art

This petite **museum** (📞805-963-4364; www.sbmuseart.org; 1130 State St; adult/child 6-17yr $10/6, all free 5-8pm Thu; ⏰11am-5pm Tue-Wed & Fri-Sun, to 8pm Thu; ♿) holds a nevertheless impressive collection of contemporary California artists, modern European and American masters such as Matisse and O'Keeffe, 20th-century photography and classical antiquities. Traipse up to the 2nd floor, where Asian art exhibits include an intricate Tibetan sand mandala and the armor of a Japanese samurai.

The Walk » Walk three blocks southeast on State St, jam-packed with cafes, restaurants and boutiques. Turn left on Cañon Perdido St, passing the 1873 Lobero Theatre, then cross Anacapa St.

El Presidio de Santa Barbara State Historic Park

Built to defend Santa Barbara's mission, this 18th-century **fort** (📞805-965-0093; www.sbthp.org; 123 E Cañon Perdido St; adult/child under 17yr $5/free; ⏰10:30am-4:30pm) was colonial Spain's last military stronghold in Alta California. Today, this small park encloses several reconstructed adobe buildings. Be sure to peek inside the chapel, its interior radiant with gold and scarlet.

The Walk » On the opposite side of Cañon Perdido St, Handlebar Coffee Roasters is a

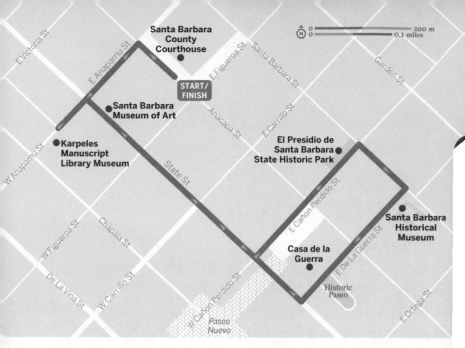

refueling stop. Otherwise, walk one block southeast along Santa Barbara St, turning right onto De La Guerra St.

Santa Barbara Historical Museum

Embracing a cloistered Spanish-style adobe courtyard, this peaceful little **museum** (☑805-966-1601; www.santabarbara museum.com; 136 E De La Guerra St; ⏱10am-5pm Tue-Sat, from noon Sun) has an interesting collection of local memorabilia, ranging from the simply beautiful, such as Chumash woven baskets and Spanish colonial-era textiles, to the simply odd, like an intricately carved coffer that belonged to missionary Junipero Serra.

The Walk » Keep walking southwest on De La Guerra St, crossing Anacapa St. Casa de la Guerra stands on the north side of the street.

Casa de la Guerra

Your admission ticket to El Presidio de Santa Barbara State Historic Park also includes entry to **Casa de la Guerra** (☑805-965-0093; www.sbthp.org; 15 E De La Guerra St; adult/child under 17yr $5/free; ⏱noon-4pm Fri-Sun), a grand 19th-century colonial home with Spanish, Mexican and American heritage exhibits. Authentically restored, this whitewashed adobe with red-tiled roof was an architectural model for rebuilding all of downtown Santa Barbara after a devastating 1925 earthquake.

The Walk » Continue walking southwest, crossing State St over to the Paseo Nuevo shopping mall. Head northwest four blocks to Anapamu St and turn left.

Karpeles Manuscript Library Museum

Stuffed with a hodgepodge of historical written artifacts, this **museum** (☑805-962-5322; www.rain.org/~karpeles; 21 W Anapamu St; ⏱noon-4pm Wed-Sun) is an embarrassment of riches for history nerds, science geeks, and literature and music lovers. One of a dozen Karpeles manuscript museums nationwide, the rotating exhibits at this museum often spotlight literary masterworks, from Shakespeare to Sherlock Holmes.

The Walk » Head northeast on Anapamu St. Turn right onto Anacapa St to return to the county courthouse.

287

Southern California Trips

Surf, sand and sex will always sell SoCal, especially in Hollywood's star-studded dreamscapes. The reality won't disappoint either: the swimsuits are smaller, the water warmer and summers less foggy here than in NorCal. Los Angeles, the 'City of Angels,' is the place for celebrity spotting. Surf culture rules San Diego and Orange County, where Disneyland proves an irresistible attraction for kids.

You'll find even more road-tripping adventures inland. Turn up the heat in SoCal's deserts, starting with the chic resorts of Palm Springs. Then dig deep into the backcountry beauty of Death Valley and Joshua Tree, where dusty 4WD roads lead to remote ghost towns and hidden springs. Finally, leave all of the crowds behind on SoCal's most iconic road trip: Route 66, the USA's legendary 'Mother Road'.

Joshua Tree National Park Exploring the park's boulders
STEPHEN SIMPSON / GETY IMAGES ©

Southern California Trips

Los Banos

Madera

Fresno

Orange Cove

Kings Canyon National Park

Three Rivers

Lone Pine

Sequoia National Park

Visalia

King City

Coalinga

Porterville

Cholame

Woody

Ridgecrest

Paso Robles

Lake Isabella

Bakersfield

Red Mountain

San Luis Obispo

Taft

Mojave

Santa Maria

Ventucopa

Palmdale

Los Alamos

Los Olivos

Lompoc

PACIFIC OCEAN

Angeles National Forest

Santa Barbara

Ventura

Pasadena

Oxnard

29

Santa Monica

Anaheim

Los Angeles

Long Beach

27

Channel Islands

Laguna Beach

Santa Catalina Island

Capistrano Beach

San Nicolas Island

San Clemente Island

---

27 **Disneyland & Orange County Beaches 2–4 Days**
Meet Mickey Mouse, then surf the sun-bronzed 'OC' coast. (p293)

28 **Fun on the San Diego Coast 2–4 Days**
Surf's up and the sun almost always shines, from Coronado to Carlsbad. (p303)

29 **SoCal Pop Culture 3 Days**
Where film and TV stars, new-age hippies and surfer punks collide. (p313)

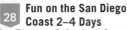
30 **Route 66 3–4 Days**
Dilly-dally through the desert, then zoom past retro icons into LA. (p321)

31 **Life in Death Valley 3 Days**
Old West mining ghost towns, strange geology and inspiring panoramic views. (p331)

Seal Beach

Slow way down for this old-fashioned beach town, just south of LA, where you can learn to surf by a weather-beaten pier on Trip 27

Sunny Jim Cave

In coastal La Jolla, walk down spooky steps through a tunnel into California's only sea cave accessible to landlubbers on Trip 28

Burbank

Take a behind-the-scenes movie studio tour, attend a live TV show taping or buy fashions worn by real-life stars on Trip 29

Amboy

Watch desert tumbleweeds blow by on Route 66 outside landmark Roy's Motel & Cafe, with its giant-sized neon sign, on Trip 30

Tecopa

Soak in hot-springs pools where Native Americans traditionally camped, then grab a snack at China Ranch Date Farm on Trip 31

32 Palm Springs & Joshua Tree Oases 2–3 Days
Where palm trees shade hot springs and date gardens in the desert. (p341)

33 Temecula, Julian & Anza-Borrego 3 Days
Vineyards and apple farms, plus off-roading in California's biggest state park. (p349)

Classic Trip
Disneyland & Orange County Beaches

27

On this fun coastal getaway, let the kids loose at the 'Happiest Place on Earth,' then strike out for sunny SoCal beaches – as seen on TV and the silver screen.

TRIP HIGHLIGHTS

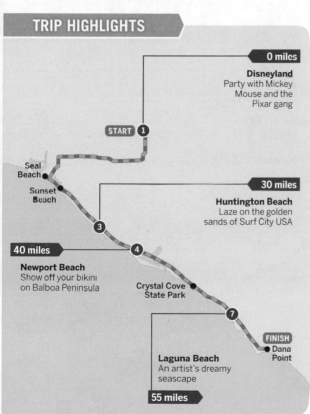

0 miles

Disneyland
Party with Mickey Mouse and the Pixar gang

START ①

Seal Beach

Sunset Beach

30 miles

Huntington Beach
Laze on the golden sands of Surf City USA

③

40 miles

Newport Beach
Show off your bikini on Balboa Peninsula

④

Crystal Cove State Park

⑦

FINISH
Dana Point

Laguna Beach
An artist's dreamy seascape

55 miles

2–4 DAYS
65 MILES / 105KM

GREAT FOR...

BEST TIME TO GO
June to September for summer beach season.

ESSENTIAL PHOTO
Surfers at Huntington Beach Pier.

BEST FOR VIEWS
Corona del Mar's Lookout Point.

Laguna Beach View of the beach from Heisler Park

Disneyland & Orange County Beaches

27

It's true you'll find gorgeous sunsets, prime surfing breaks and just-off-the-boat seafood when road tripping down the OC's sun-kissed coastal Hwy 1. Yet it's the unexpected and serendipitous discoveries you'll remember long after you've left this blissful 42 miles of surf and sand behind. Start it all off with a day or two at Disneyland's theme parks and let's call it a wrap for the perfect SoCal family vacation.

❶ Disneyland

No SoCal theme park welcomes more millions of visitors every year than **Disneyland** (☎714-781-4565; https://disneyland. disney.go.com; 1313 Disneyland Dr, Anaheim; 1-day pass adult/child from $95/89, both parks $155/149; ⏱ open daily, seasonal hours vary; 🅿 ♿). From the ghostly skeletons of Pirates of the Caribbean to the screeching monkeys of the Indiana Jones Adventure, there's magical detail everywhere. Retro-futuristic Tomorrowland is where the Finding Nemo Submarine Voyage and *Star Wars*–themed Star Tours and Jedi Training: Trials

LINK YOUR TRIP

2 Pacific Coast Highways

Orange County is California's official section of the Pacific Coast Hwy (PCH), running along Hwy 1 between Seal Beach and Dana Point.

28 Fun on the San Diego Coast

It's just a 30-mile drive from Dana Point along I-5 south to Carlsbad in San Diego's family-friendly North County.

of the Temple await. Use the Fastpass system and you'll be hurtling through Space Mountain – still the park's best adrenaline pumper – in no time. After dark, watch fireworks explode over Sleeping Beauty's Castle.

Any fear of heights? Then ditch the Twilight Zone Tower of Terror at **Disney California Adventure** (DCA; ☎714-781-4565; https://disneyland.disney. go.com; 1313 Harbor Blvd, Anaheim; 1-day pass adult/child from $95/89, both parks $155/149; 🅿 ♿), Disneyland's younger neighbor. DCA's lightheartedly themed areas highlight the best of the Golden State, while plenty of adventures like Route 66–themed Cars Land don't involve losing your lunch. An exception is rockin' California Screamin' at Paradise Pier: this whip-fast coaster looks like an old-school carnival ride, but from the moment it blasts forward with a cannon-shot whoosh, this monster never lets go. Catch the enthusiasm of the Pixar Play Parade by day and World of Color special-effects show at night.

Just outside the parks, **Downtown Disney** pedestrian mall is packed with souvenir shops, family restaurants, after-dark bars and entertainment venues.

🛏 p301

The Drive » Follow I-5 south, then take Hwy 22 west through inland Orange County, merging onto the I-405 north. After another mile or so, exit onto Seal Beach Blvd, which crawls 3 miles toward the coast. Turn right onto Hwy 1, also known as the Pacific Coast Hwy (PCH) throughout Orange County, then take a left onto Main St in Seal Beach.

❷ Seal Beach

In the SoCal beauty pageant for pint-sized beach towns, Seal Beach is the winner of the crown. It's a refreshingly unhurried alternative to the more crowded Orange County coast further south. Its three-block **Main St** is a stoplight-free zone that bustles with mom-and-pop restaurants and indie shops that are low on 'tude and high on nostalgia. Follow barefoot surfers trotting toward the beach where Main St ends, then walk out onto **Seal Beach Pier**. The 1906 original first fell victim to winter storms in the 1930s, and since then it has been rebuilt three times with a splintery, wooden boardwalk. Down on the **beach**, you'll find families spread out on blankets, building sandcastles and playing in the water – all of them ignoring that hideous oil derrick offshore. The gentle waves make Seal Beach a great place to learn to surf. **M&M Surfing School** (☎714-846-7873; www.surfingschool.

Classic Trip

com; 802 Ocean Ave; 1hr/3hr group lesson $72/82, wetsuit/ surfboard rental $15/25; 🚻) parks its van in the lot just north of the pier, off Ocean Ave at 8th St.

The Drive » Past a short bridge south along Hwy 1, drivers drop onto a mile-long spit of land known as Sunset Beach, with its biker bars and harborside kayak and stand-up paddle boarding (SUP) rental shops. Keep cruising Hwy 1 south another 6 miles past Bolsa Chica State Beach and Ecological Reserve to Huntington Beach Pier.

- - - - - - - - - - - -

TRIP HIGHLIGHT

❸ Huntington Beach

In 'Surf City USA,' SoCal's obsessions with wave riding hits its frenzied peak. There's a statue of Hawaiian surfer Duke Kahanamoku at the intersection of Main St and PCH, and if you look down, you'll see names of legendary surfers in the sidewalk **Surfers' Hall of Fame** (www.hssurf.com/ shof/; 300 Pacific Coast Highway). A few blocks east, the **International Surfing Museum** (☎714-960-3483; www.surfingmuseum. org; 411 Olive Ave; donations welcome; ⊗noon-5pm Wed & Fri-Sun, to 9pm Tue, to 4pm Thu) honors those same legends. Join the crowds on the **Huntington Beach Pier**, where you

can catch up-close views of daredevils barreling through tubes. The surf here may not be the ideal place to test your newbie skills, however – locals can be territorial. In summer, the US Open of Surfing draws more than 600 world-class surfers and 500,000 spectators with a minivillage of concerts and more. As for **Huntington City Beach** (www.huntingtonbeachca.gov; ⊗5am-10pm; **P** 🚻) itself, it's wide and flat – a perfect place to snooze on the sand on a giant beach towel. Snag a fire pit just south of the pier to build an evening bonfire with friends.

⚔ 🛏 p301

**DETOUR:
KNOTT'S BERRY FARM**

Start: ❶ Disneyland (p295)

Hear the screams? Got teens? Hello, **Knott's Berry Farm** (☎714-220-5200; www.knotts.com; 8039 Beach Blvd, Buena Park; adult/child 3-11yr $72/42; ⊗from 10am, closing time varies 5-11pm; **P**🚻), America's first theme park, which opened in 1940. Today, high-scream coasters lure fast-track fanatics. Look up as you enter to see the bare feet of riders who've removed their flip-flops for the Silver Bullet, the suspended coaster careening past overhead, famed for its corkscrew, double spiral and outside loop. In October, Knott's hosts SoCal's scariest after-dark Halloween party. Year-round, the *Peanuts* gang keeps moppets happy in Camp Snoopy, while the next-door water park **Knott's Soak City Orange County** (☎714-220-5200; www.soakcityoc.com; 8039 Beach Blvd, Buena Park; adult/ child 3-11yr $43/38; ⊗10am-5pm, 6pm or 7pm mid-May– mid-Sep; 🚻) keeps you cool on blazing-hot summer days. Knott's is a 20-minute drive from Disneyland via I-5 north to Hwy 91 west to Beach Blvd south.

The Drive » From the Huntington Beach Pier at the intersection of Main St, drive south on Hwy 1 alongside the ocean for another 4 miles to Newport Beach. Turn right onto W Balboa Blvd, leading onto the Balboa Peninsula, squeezed between the ocean and Balboa Island, off Newport Harbor.

- - - - - - - - - - - -

TRIP HIGHLIGHT

❹ Newport Beach

As seen on Bravo's *Real Housewives of Orange County* and Fox's *The OC* and *Arrested Development,* in glitzy Newport Beach wealthy socialites, glamorous teens and gorgeous beaches all share the spotlight. Bikini vixens strut down the sandy beach stretching between the peninsula's twin piers, while boogie boarders brave human-eating waves at the **Wedge** and the ballet of yachts in the harbor makes you dream of being rich and famous. From the harbor, hop aboard a ferry over to old-fashioned **Balboa Island** (http://explore balboaisland.com; P) or climb aboard the Ferris wheel at the pint-sized **Balboa Fun Zone** (www.thebalboa funzone.com; 600 E Bay Ave; ⊘Ferris wheel 11am-7pm Sun-Thu, to 9pm Fri, to 10pm Sat; ∰), near the landmark 1906 **Balboa Pavilion** (www.balboapavilion. com; 400 Main St). Just inland, visit the cutting-edge contemporary **Orange County Museum of Art** (☏949-759-1122; www. ocma.net; 850 San Clemente Dr; adult/students & seniors/ child under 12yr $10/7.50/ free; ⊘11am-5pm Wed-Sun, to 8pm Fri; P ∰) to escape SoCal's vainglorious pop culture.

 p301, p319

The Drive » South of Newport Beach, prime-time ocean views are just a short detour off Hwy 1. First drive south across the bridge over Newport Channel, then after 3 miles turn right onto Marguerite Ave in Corona del Mar. Once you reach the coast, take another right onto Ocean Blvd.

Corona del Mar Houses on cliffs above the main beach

⑤ Corona del Mar

Savor some of SoCal's most celebrated ocean views from the bluffs of Corona del Mar, a chichi commuter town south of Newport Channel. Several postcard beaches, rocky coves and child-friendly tidepools beckon along this idyllic stretch of coast. One of the best viewpoints is at breezy **Lookout Point** on Ocean Blvd near Heliotrope Ave. Below the rocky cliffs to the east is half-mile-long **Main Beach** (Corona del Mar State Beach; ☏949-644-3151; www.newportbeachca.gov; off E Shore Ave; ⊘6am-10pm; P ∰), with fire rings and volleyball courts (arrive early on weekends to get a parking spot). Stairs lead down to **Pirates Cove** which has a great, waveless pocket beach for families – scenes from the classic TV show *Gilligan's*

Island were shot here. Head east on Ocean Blvd to **Inspiration Point**, near the corner of Orchid Ave, for more vistas of surf, sand and sea.

The Drive » Follow Orchid Ave back north to Hwy 1, then turn right and drive southbound. Traffic thins out as ocean views become more wild and uncluttered by housing developments that head up into the hills on your left. It's just a couple of miles to the entrance of Crystal Cove State Park.

⑥ Crystal Cove State Park

With more than 3 miles of open beach and 2400 acres of undeveloped woodland, **Crystal Cove State Park** (☏949-494-3539; www.parks.ca.gov; 8471 N Coast Hwy; per car $15; ⊘6am-sunset; P ∰) lets you almost forget that you're in a crowded metro area. That is, once

Classic Trip

ROBERT POSTMA / GETTY IMAGES ©

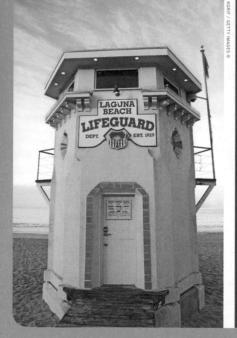

KGRIF / GETTY IMAGES ©

WHY THIS IS A CLASSIC TRIP
SARA BENSON, WRITER

Orange County's beach towns are so beautiful that they're almost a Southern California cliché. Surf rolling beside sunset piers, sparkling white sands, tanned surfers riding bicycles with surfboards attached – this is real life, not a fantasy. But it's the wilder, more natural stretches of coast that are most memorable for me, like at postcard-perfect Crystal Cove State Park, north of Laguna Beach along Hwy 1.

Top: Rock formations at Crystal Cove State Park
Left: Lifeguard station at Laguna Beach
Right: The Silver Bullet ride at Knott's Berry Farm

you get past the parking lot and stake out a place on the sand. Many visitors don't know it, but it's also an underwater park where scuba enthusiasts can check out the wreck of a Navy Corsair fighter plane that went down in 1949. Or just go tidepooling, fishing, kayaking and surfing along Crystal Cove's exhilaratingly wild, windy shoreline. On the inland side of Hwy 1, miles of hiking and mountain-biking trails wait for landlubbers.

✕ ⊨ p301

The Drive » Drive south on Hwy 1 for another 4 miles or so. As shops, restaurants, art galleries, motels and hotels start to crowd the highway once again, you've arrived in Laguna Beach. Downtown is a maze of one-way streets just east of the Laguna Canyon Rd (Hwy 133) intersection.

- - - - - - - - - - - -

TRIP HIGHLIGHT

❼ Laguna Beach

This early 20th-century artists colony's secluded coves, romantic-looking cliffs and Arts and Crafts bungalows come as a relief after miles of suburban beige-box architecture. With joie de vivre, Laguna celebrates its bohemian roots with summer arts festivals, dozens of galleries and the acclaimed **Laguna Art Museum** (☎949-494-8971; www.lagunaart museum.org; 307 Cliff Dr; adult/student & senior/child under 13yr $7/5/free, 5-9pm

Classic Trip

1st Thu of month free; ☺11am-5pm Fri-Tue, to 9pm Thu). In downtown's village, it's easy to while away an afternoon browsing the chic boutiques. Down on the shore, **Main Beach** is crowded with volleyball players and sunbathers. Just north atop the bluffs, **Heisler Park** winds past public art, palm trees, picnic tables and grand views of rocky shores and tidepools. Drop down to **Divers Cove**, a deep, protected inlet. Heading south, dozens of public beaches sprawl along just a few miles of coastline. Keep a sharp eye out for 'beach access' signs off Hwy 1, or pull into locals' favorite **Aliso Beach County Park** (☎949-923-2280; http://ocparks.com/beaches/aliso; 31131 S Pacific Coast Hwy; parking per hr $1; ☺6am-10pm; P 🚻).

✖ 🛏 p301

The Drive » Keep driving south of downtown Laguna Beach on Hwy 1 (PCH) for about 3 miles to Aliso Beach County

↱ DETOUR: PACIFIC MARINE MAMMAL CENTER

Start: ❼ Laguna Beach (p299)

About 3 miles inland from Laguna Beach is the heartwarming **Pacific Marine Mammal Center** (☎949-494-3050; www.pacificmmc.org; 20612 Laguna Canyon Rd; admission by donation; ☺10am-4pm; P 🚻), dedicated to rescuing and rehabilitating injured or ill marine mammals. This nonprofit center has a small staff and many volunteers who help nurse rescued pinnipeds (mostly sea lions and seals) back to health before releasing them into the wild. Stop by and take a self-guided facility tour to learn more about these marine mammals and to visit the 'patients' out back.

Park, then another 4 miles into the town of Dana Point. Turn right onto Green Lantern St, then left onto Cove Rd, which winds past the state beach and Ocean Institute onto Dana Point Harbor Dr.

- - - - - - - - - - - - - -

❽ Dana Point

Marina-flanked Dana Point is the namesake of 19th-century adventurer Richard Dana, who famously thought it was the only romantic place on the coast. These days it's more about family fun and sportfishing boats at **Dana Point Harbor**. Designed for kids, the **Ocean Institute** (☎949-496-2274; www.ocean-

institute.org; 24200 Dana Pt Harbor Dr; adult/child 2-12yr $10/7.50; ☺10am-3pm Sat & Sun, last entry 2:15pm; P 🚻) owns replicas of historic tall ships, maritime-related exhibits and a floating research lab. East of the harbor, **Doheny State Beach** (☎949-496-6172; www.dohenystate beach.org; 25300 Dana Point Harbor Dr; per car $15; ☺park 6am-10pm, visitor center 10am-4pm Wed-Sun; P 🚻) is where you'll find picnic tables, volleyball courts, an oceanfront bike path and a sandy beach for swimming, surfing and tidepooling.

Eating & Sleeping

Disneyland ❶

🛏 Disney's Grand Californian Hotel & Spa
Luxury Hotel $$$

(📞info 714-635-2300, reservations 714-956-6425; https://disneyland.disney.go.com/grand-californian-hotel; 1600 S Disneyland Dr; d from $360; P ❄ @ 🛜 ☟) Soaring timber beams rise above the cathedral-like lobby of the six-story Grand Californian, Disney's homage to the Arts and Crafts architectural movement.

Huntington Beach ❸

✖ Sugar Shack
Cafe $

(📞714-536-0355; www.hbsugarshack.com; 213½ Main St; mains $4-10; ⏰6am-2pm Mon-Tue & Thu-Fri, to 8pm Wed, to 3pm Sat & Sun; 🚹) Expect a wait at this HB institution, or get here early to see surfer dudes don their wet suits. Breakfast is served all day on the bustling Main St patio and inside, where you can grab a spot at the counter or a table for two.

🛏 Shorebreak Hotel
Boutique Hotel $$$

(📞714-861-4470; www.shorebreakhotel.com; 500 Pacific Coast Hwy; r from $269; P ❄ @ 🛜 ☟) Stow your surfboard (lockers provided) as you head inside HB's hippest hotel, a stone's throw from the pier. The Shorebreak has a surf concierge, a fitness center and yoga studio, bean-bag chairs in the lobby and rattan and hardwood furniture in geometric-patterned rooms.

Newport Beach ❹

✖ Bear Flag Fish Company
Seafood $

(📞949-673-3434; www.bearflagfishco.com; 3421 Via Lido; mains $10-16; ⏰11am-9pm Tue-Sat, to 8pm Sun & Mon; 🚹) This is *the* place for generously sized, grilled and panko-breaded fish tacos, ahi burritos, spankin' fresh ceviche and oysters. Pick out what you want from the ice-cold display cases, then grab a picnic-table seat.

🛏 Bay Shores Peninsula Hotel
Hotel $$$

(📞949-675-3463, 800-222-6675; www.thebestinn.com; 1800 W Balboa Blvd; r incl breakfast $190-300; P ❄ @ 🛜) This three-story, reimagined motel is ready to flex some surf-themed muscle. From *Endless Summer* surfing murals and complimentary fresh-baked cookies, free rental movies and a 360-degree-view sun deck, Bay Shores is beachy, casual and customer-focused.

Crystal Cove State Park ❻

✖ Ruby's Crystal Cove Shake Shack
American $

(📞949-464-0100; www.rubys.com; 7703 E Coast Hwy; items $3-11; ⏰7am-8pm Sun-Thu, to 9pm Fri & Sat; 🚹) Although this been-here-forever wooden shake stand is now owned by the Ruby's Diner chain, the ocean views are as good as ever.

🛏 Crystal Cove Beach Cottages
Cabin $$

(📞reservations 800-444-7275; www.crystalcovealliance.org; 35 Crystal Cove, Newport Beach; r with shared bath $36-140, cottages $171-249; ⏰check-in 4-9pm; P) To snag one of these little oceanfront cottages in the park's historic district, book on the first day of the month seven months before your intended stay – or pray for last-minute cancellations.

Laguna Beach ❼

✖ Stand
Vegetarian, Vegan $

(📞949-494-8101; www.thestandnaturalfoods.com; 238 Thalia St; mains $6-11; ⏰7am-8pm; 🍴 🚹) With its friendly, indie-spirited vibe comes this tiny tribute to healthy cuisine. From hummus and guac sandwiches to sunflower sprout salads and black-beans-and-rice burritos, the menu is varied and all of it soul-satisfying.

🛏 Laguna Beach House
Hotel $$$

(📞949-497-6645, 800-297-0007; www.thelagunabeachhouse.com; 475 N Coast Hwy; r $205-419; P ❄ @ 🛜 ☟ ☟) Be it good feng shui, friendly staff or proximity to the beach, something just feels right at this renovated 36-room courtyard inn. From the colorful pillows and hardwood floors to air-con and flat-screen TVs, the decor is contemporary, comfy and clean.

Fun on the San Diego Coast

28

With 70 miles of coastline and a near-perfect climate, it's tough to know where to start. So just do as the locals do: grab a fish taco and a surfboard and head for the beaches.

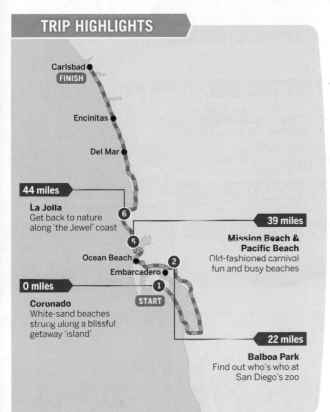

Carlsbad
FINISH

Encinitas

Del Mar

44 miles

La Jolla
Get back to nature along 'the Jewel' coast

6

39 miles

Mission Beach & Pacific Beach
Old-fashioned carnival fun and busy beaches

5

Ocean Beach

2

Embarcadero

0 miles

1

START

Coronado
White-sand beaches strung along a blissful getaway 'island'

22 miles

Balboa Park
Find out who's who at San Diego's zoo

2–4 DAYS
80 MILES / 130KM

GREAT FOR...

BEST TIME TO GO

June to September for prime-time beach weather.

ESSENTIAL PHOTO

The red-turreted Hotel del Coronado.

BEST FOR OUTDOORS

La Jolla's coves, beaches and nature preserves.

Coronado Hotel del Coronado

Fun on the San Diego Coast

Most Americans work all year for a two-week vacation. San Diegans work all week for a two-day vacation at the beach. Family-fun attractions found just off the county's gorgeous coastal highways include the USS Midway Museum, Balboa Park's zoo and the Legoland theme park, along with dozens of beaches from ritzy to raucous. With SoCal's most idyllic weather, it's time to roll down the windows and chillax, dudes.

25 miles to

27

78

Carlsbad 9 *San Elijo Lagoon*
FINISH

Batiqui Lagoo

5

Leucadia

Encinitas 8

Cardiff-by-the-Sea

Solana Beach

Del Mar

La Jolla

PACIFIC OCEAN

TRIP HIGHLIGHT

1 Coronado

With the landmark 1888 Hotel del Coronado (p310) and one of America's top-rated beaches, the city of Coronado sits across San Diego Bay from downtown. It's miles away from the concrete jumble of the city and the chaos of more crowded beaches further north. After crossing the bay via the curved Coronado Bay Bridge, follow the tree-lined, manicured median strip of Orange Ave a mile toward Ocean Blvd, then park your car and walk around. Sprawling in front of the 'Hotel Del' is postcard-perfect **Coronado Municipal**

Beach (www.coronado.ca.us; P 🚻). Less than 5 miles further south, **Silver Strand State Beach** (☎619-435-5184; www.parks.ca.gov; 5000 Hwy 75, Coronado; per car $10; ◷7am-sunset; P 🚻) also offers calm waters for family-friendly swimming. The strand's long, narrow sand spit connects back to the mainland, though people still call this 'Coronado Island.'

🛏 p310

The Drive » Follow Hwy 75 south of Silver Strand past San Diego Bay National Wildlife Refuge, curving inland by Imperial Beach. Merge onto the I-5 northbound, then exit onto Hwy 163 northbound toward Balboa Park. Take exit 1C and follow the signs for the park and zoo.

TRIP HIGHLIGHT

❷ Balboa Park

Spanish Revival–style pavilions from the 1915–16 Panama-California Exposition add a dash of the exotic to a day spent in Balboa Park. This 1200-acre urban retreat is home to gardens, theaters, 15 museums and one giant outdoor organ pavilion, all of which you can see on foot (p358). Without a doubt, the highlight is the **San Diego Zoo** (619-231-1515; http://zoo.sandiego.org; 2920 Zoo Dr; 1-day admission adult/child from $50/40, 2-visit pass to zoo and/or safari park adult/child $90/70; ⊙9am-9pm mid-Jun–early Sep, to 5pm or 6pm early Sep–mid-Jun; [P] [♿]). If it slithers, crawls, stomps, swims, leaps or flies, chances

🔗 LINK YOUR TRIP

27 Disneyland & Orange County Beaches

Cruise 30 miles north on I-5 to Dana Point for another kid-friendly trip, combining knockout beaches with Disneyland's magic.

33 Temecula, Julian & Anza-Borrego

Escape to wine country, apple farms and desert resorts, starting 35 miles inland from Carlsbad via Hwy 76 east to I-15 north.

are you'll find it living inside this world-famous zoo. Arrive early, when the animal denizens are most active – though many perk up again in the afternoon. Nearby at the **Spanish Village Art Center** (☎619-233-9050; http://spanishvillageart.com; 1770 Village Place; ☺11am-4pm), an enclave of small tiled cottages that are rented out as artists' studios, you can watch potters, jewelry makers, glass blowers, sculptors and painters at work.

✕ p310

The Drive ›› Exit Balboa Park to the east via Zoo Pl, turning right onto Florida Dr and right again onto Pershing Dr. Merge onto I-5 north for over a mile, then take exit 17A. Drive almost another mile west on Hawthorn St toward the waterfront, then turn left onto Harbor Dr.

---

❸ Embarcadero

The Coronado ferry and cruise ships moor along downtown San Diego's waterfront Embarcadero. Well-manicured ocean-front promenades stretch along Harbor Dr, where a line-up of historical sailing ships points the way to the **Maritime Museum** (☎619-234-9153; www.sdmaritime.org; 1492 N Harbor Dr; adult/child $16/8; ☺9am-9pm late May-early Sep, to 8pm early Sep-late May; ⊕). Climb aboard the 1863 *Star of India* and don't miss seeing the B-39 Soviet attack sub-marine. More massive is the **USS Midway Museum** (☎619-544-9600; www.midway.org; 910 N Harbor Dr; adult/child $20/10; ☺10am-5pm, last entry 4pm; ⓟ ⊕).

┌─────────────────────────────
│ ↱ **DETOUR:**
│ **SAN DIEGO ZOO**
│ **SAFARI PARK**

Start: ❷ Balboa Park (p305)

Take a walk on the 'wild' side at **San Diego Zoo Safari Park** (☎760-747-8702; www.sdzsafaripark.org; 15500 San Pasqual Valley Rd, Escondido; 1-day admission adult/child $50/40, 2-visit pass to zoo and/or safari park adult/child $90/70; ☺9am-5pm, to 7pm late Jun–mid-Aug; ⓟ⊕), where giraffes graze, lions lounge and rhinos romp more or less freely across 1800 acres of open range. For that instant safari feel, board the Africa Tram, which tours you around some of the field exhibits in just 25 minutes. Elsewhere, animals are in giant outdoor enclosures so naturalistic it's as if the humans are guests. There's a petting kraal, zookeeper talks and animal encounters too. The park is in Escondido, 30 miles northeast of Balboa Park via Hwy 163 and I-15 northbound; alternatively, it's 25 miles east of coastal Carlsbad via Hwy 78. Parking costs $12.

The Navy's longest-serving aircraft carrier (1945–92), it saw action in WWII, Vietnam and the Gulf War. *Top Gun's* Goose and Maverick may spring to mind at the sight of this floating city. A self-guided tour is the best way to experience history: crawl into berth-ing spaces, the galley and sick bay and, of course, peer over the flight deck with its restored aircraft, including an F-14 Tomcat.

The Drive ›› Follow Harbor Dr northwest for 3 miles as it curves along the waterfront past the airport. Turn right onto Nimitz Blvd for another mile, then left onto Chatsworth Blvd and right on Narragansett Ave. After a mile, you'll intersect Sunset Cliffs Blvd in Ocean Beach.

---

❹ Ocean Beach

San Diego's most bohe-mian seaside community, OB is a place of seriously scruffy haircuts and tattooed and pierced body art. **Newport Ave**, the main drag, runs per-pendicular to the beach through a downtown district of bars, street-food eateries, surf and music shops, and vintage-clothing and antique boutiques. Half-mile-long **Ocean Beach Pier** has all the architectural allure of a freeway ramp, but at its end you'll get a great perspective on the coast. A bait-and-tackle shop rents fishing poles if you want to try your luck. Fur-ther north on **Dog Beach**, pups chase birds around the marshy area where the river meets the sea, or you could walk a few blocks south of the pier to **Sunset Cliffs Park** for surfing and yes, brilliant sunsets.

 p310

The Drive » Follow stop-and-go Sunset Cliffs Blvd north. Merge onto W Mission Bay Dr, which crosses over the water twice and curves past SeaWorld San Diego. Less than 4 miles from Ocean Beach, you'll intersect Mission Blvd; turn left to reach the main beach and Belmont Park.

Mission Beach

TRIP HIGHLIGHT

❺ Mission Beach & Pacific Beach

This is the SoCal of the movies: buffed surfers and bronzed sun worshippers pack the 3-mile-long stretch of beach from South Mission Jetty north to Pacific Beach Point. San Diego's best people-watching is along **Ocean Front Walk**, the boardwalk that connects the two beaches. For old-fashioned carnival fun in Mission Beach, **Belmont Park** (☏858-458-1549; www.belmontpark.com; 3146 Mission Blvd; per ride $3-6, all-day pass adult/child $29/18; ⊘from 11am daily, closing time varies; P) has been giving kids a thrill with its Giant Dipper wooden roller coaster since 1925. There's also a large indoor pool and wave machines for faux-surfing, plus bumper cars,

a tilt-a-whirl, carousel and other classic rides. At the ocean end of Garnet Ave in Pacific Beach, **Crystal Pier** is a mellow place to gaze out to sea or fish. Just inland at **Mission Bay** (www.sandiego.gov/park-and-recreation; P 🚻), you can play beach volleyball and zip around **Fiesta Island** on water skis or fly a kite at **Mission Bay Park**. Sailing, windsurfing and kayaking dominate northwest Mission Bay, and there's delightful cycling and inline skating on miles of paved recreational paths.

 p310

The Drive » Heading north of Pacific Beach on Mission Blvd, turn left onto Loring St, which curves right onto La Jolla Blvd. Winding through several traffic circles, the boulevard streams along the coast for 3 miles to downtown La Jolla, stretched along Pearl St east of the beach.

TRIP HIGHLIGHT

❻ La Jolla

Sitting pretty on one of SoCal's loveliest sweeps of coast, La Jolla (Spanish for 'the jewel'; say la-*hoy*-ah, if you please) is a ritzy town of shimmering beaches, downtown fashionista boutiques and clifftop mansions. Take advantage of the sunshine by kayaking and snorkeling at **La Jolla Cove**, or go scuba diving and snorkeling in **San Diego-La Jolla Underwater Park**, a protected ecological zone harboring a variety of marine life, kelp forests, reefs and canyons. Waves have carved a series of caves into the sandstone cliffs east of La Jolla Cove. You can walk down 145 spooky steps to the largest, **Sunny Jim Cave**, accessed via the **Cave Store** (☏858-459-0746;

TIJUANA, MEXICO

Just beyond the most crossed border in the world, Tijuana, Mexico (population 1.8 million) was for decades a cheap, convivial escape for hard-partying San Diegans, sailors and college kids. Around 2008 a double-whammy of drug-related violence and global recession turned once-bustling tourist areas into ghost towns, but Tijuanenses (as the locals call themselves) have been slowly but surely reclaiming their city. The difference from squeaky-clean San Diego is palpable from the moment you cross the border, but so are signs of new life for those who knew TJ in the bad old days.

The main tourist drag is **Avenida Revolución** ('La Revo'), though its charm is marred by cheap clothing and souvenir stores, strip joints, pharmacies selling bargain-priced medications to Americans, and touts best rebuffed with a firm 'no.' It's a lot more appealing just beyond La Revo, toward and around **Avenida Constitución**, where sightseeing highlights include **Catedral de Tijuana**, the city's oldest church; **Mercado El Popo**, an atmospheric market hall selling everything from tamarind pods to religious iconography; and **Pasaje Rodríguez**, an arcade filled with youthful art galleries, bars and trendsetters. A short taxi ride away, **Museo de las Californias**, inside the architecturally daring **Centro Cultural Tijuana**, aka El Cubo (the Cube), offers an excellent history of the border region from prehistory to the present; there's signage in English.

A passport is required for the border crossing (p363). Driving into Mexico is not recommended. By public transportation, the San Diego Trolley Blue Line runs from downtown San Diego to **San Ysidro**, at the border. Cross the border on foot, and pick up a map at the border station for the approximately 20-minute walk to La Revo; follow signs reading 'Centro Downtown.' If traveling by taxi on the Mexican side of the border, be sure to take a taxi with a meter.

www.cavestore.com; 1325 Coast Blvd; adult/child $5/3; ☺10am-4:30pm Mon-Fri, to 5pm Sat & Sun; ⟨⟩).

Heading north along La Jolla Shores Dr, the oceanfront **Birch Aquarium at Scripps** (✆858-534-3474; www.aquarium.ucsd.edu; 2300 Expedition Way; adult/child $17/12.50; ☺9am-5pm; P ⟨⟩) has kid-friendly tidepool displays. Another 5 miles further north, **Torrey Pines State Natural Reserve** (✆858-755-2063; www.torreypine.org; 12600 N Torrey Pines Rd; per car $12-15; ☺7:15am-sunset, visitor center 10am-4pm Oct-Apr, 9am-6pm May-Sep; P ⟨⟩) protects the endangered Torrey pine

tree and offers nature walks above a state beach.

🍴 p311

The Drive » Driving below the natural preserve next to Torrey Pines State Beach, panoramic ocean views open up as the coastal highway narrows and crosses over a lagoon, then climbs the sandstone cliffs toward Del Mar, just over 2 miles away.

- - - - - - - - - - - -

❼ Del Mar

The ritziest of North County's seaside suburbs is home to the pink, Mediterranean-style **Del Mar Racetrack & Fairgrounds** (✆858-792-4242; www.dmtc.com;

2260 Jimmy Durante Blvd; admission from $6; ☺race season mid-Jul–early Sep), cofounded in 1937 by celebrities including Bing Crosby and Oliver Hardy. It's worth braving the crowds on opening day, if nothing else to see the amazing spectacle of the ladies' over-the-top hats. Brightly colored hot-air balloons are another trademark sight in Del Mar – book ahead for a sunset flight with **California Dreamin'** (✆800-373-3359; www.california dreamin.com; per person $298). Downtown Del Mar (sometimes called 'the village') extends for about a mile along Camino del Mar. At its hub, **Del Mar Plaza** (☎858-847-2284; http://delmarplaza.com; 1555 Camino Del Mar) shopping center has restaurants, boutiques and upper-level terraces that look out to sea. At the west end of 15th St, beach-front **Seagrove Park** has grassy lawns, perfect for picnicking.

🛏 p311

The Drive » Continue up the coast on Camino del Mar, leading onto S Coast Hwy 101 into Solana Beach, where the arts, fashion and antiques shops of Cedros Ave Design District are just one block inland. Continue north on S Coast Hwy 101 into Encinitas, about 6 miles north of Del Mar.

❽ Encinitas

Technically part of Encinitas, the southern satellite of **Cardiff-by-the-Sea** has groovy restaurants, surf shops and new-agey businesses lined up along the coast. Known for its surfing breaks and laid-back crowds, Cardiff sits by the coastal **San Elijo Lagoon** (☎760-623-3026; www.sanelijo.org; 2710 Manchester Ave; ☻nature center 9am-5pm; P 🚻), a 979-acre ecological preserve that is popular with bird watchers and hikers. Stop by the nature center for kid-friendly educational exhibits and wide-angle views from the 2nd-floor observation deck.

Since Paramahansa Yogananda built his **Self-Realization Fellowship Retreat** (☎760-436-7220; http://encinitastemple.org; 215 K St; ☻meditation garden 9am-5pm Tue-Sat, from 11am Sun, hermitage 2-4pm Sun) by the sea here in 1937, Encinitas has been a magnet for healers and spiritual seekers. The fellowship's compact but lovely meditation garden has wonderful ocean vistas, a stream and koi pond. The gold lotus domes of the hermitage mark the turn-out for **Swami's**, a powerful reef break surfed by territorial locals. Apart from outdoor cafes, bars, restaurants and surf shops, downtown's main attraction is the 1928 **La Paloma Theatre** (☎760-436-7469; www.lapalomatheatre.com; 471 S Coast Hwy 101), an arthouse cinema screening indie, international and cult films nightly.

✗ p311

The Drive » About 4 miles north of Encinitas, S Coast Hwy 101 becomes Carlsbad Blvd, slowly rolling north along the ocean cliffs for just over 5 miles into Carlsbad Village. If you go too far, you'll hit Oceanside, largely a commuter town for Marine Corps Base Camp Pendleton.

❾ Carlsbad

One of California's last remaining tidal wetlands, **Batiquitos Lagoon** (☎760-931-0800; www.batiquitosfoundation.org; 7380 Gab-

biano Lane; ☻nature center 9am-12:30pm Mon-Fri, to 3pm Sat & Sun; P 🚻) separates Carlsbad from Encinitas. Go hiking here to see prickly pear cactus, coastal sage scrub and eucalyptus trees, as well as great heron and snowy egrets. Then detour inland past the springtime blooms of **Carlsbad Ranch Flower Fields** (☎760-431-0352; www.theflowerfields.com; 5704 Paseo del Norte; adult/child 3-10yr $14/7; ☻usually 9am-6pm Mar–mid-May; P 🚻) to **Legoland California Resort** (☎760-918-5346; www.legoland.com/california; 1 Legoland Dr; adult/child 3-12yr from $93/87; ☻open almost daily year-round, hours vary; P 🚻), a fun fantasy park of rides, shows and attractions for the elementary-school set. Tots can dig for dinosaur bones, pilot helicopters and earn their driver's license, while mom and dad will probably get a kick out of Miniland USA, recreating such national landmarks as the White House, the Golden Gate Bridge and Las Vegas, all made entirely of Lego blocks. Back at the coast, you can go beachcombing for seashells on the long, sandy beaches, off Carlsbad Blvd. The beaches run south of Carlsbad Village Dr, where a free beach boardwalk beckons for sunset strolls.

✗ 🛏 p311

Eating & Sleeping

Coronado ❶

🛏 Hotel del Coronado
Luxury Hotel $$$

(☎619-435-6611, 800-468-3533; www.
hoteldel.com; 1500 Orange Ave, Coronado; r
from $289; P 🐾 ❄ @ 🛜 🏊 🐾) San Diego's
iconic hotel provides the essential Coronado
experience: over a century of history, a pool,
full-service spa, shops, restaurants, manicured
grounds, a white-sand beach and an ice-skating
rink in winter. Even the basic rooms have
luxurious marbled bathrooms. Note: half the
accommodations are not in the main Victorian-
era hotel (368 rooms) but in an adjacent seven-
story building constructed in the 1970s. For a
sense of place, book a room in the original hotel.
Parking is $37.

Balboa Park ❷

🍴 Prado
Californian $$$

(☎619-557-9441; www.pradobalboa.com;
House of Hospitality, 1549 El Prado; mains lunch
$14-19, dinner $22-37; ⏰11:30am-3pm Mon-Fri,
from 11am Sat & Sun, 5-9pm Sun & Tue-Thu, to
10pm Fri & Sat; 🐾) In one of San Diego's most
beautiful dining rooms, feast on Cal-eclectic
cooking by one of San Diego's most renowned
chefs: bakery sandwiches, lobster bucatini,
and jidori chicken. Go for a civilized lunch on
the verandah or for afternoon cocktails and
appetizers in the bar.

Ocean Beach ❹

🍴 South Beach Bar & Grille
Seafood, Mexican $

(☎619-226-4577; www.southbeachob.com;
5059 Newport Ave, Ocean Beach; most dishes
$3-12; ⏰11am-2am) Maybe it's the lightly fried
mahi and wahoo fish. Or the zippy white sauce.
Or layered fresh cabbage and peppery tomato
salsa. Whatever the secret, the fish tacos at this
raucous beachside bar and grill are stand-outs.
All ages welcome before 6pm.

🛏 Inn at Sunset Cliffs
Inn $$

(☎866-786-2453, 619-222-7901; http://
innatsunsetcliffs.com; 1370 Sunset Cliffs
Blvd, Ocean Beach; r/ste from $175/289;
P 🐾 ❄ @ 🛜 🏊) At the south end of Ocean
Beach, wake up to the sound of surf crashing
onto the rocky shore. This low-key 1950s
charmer wraps around a flower-bedecked
courtyard with a small heated pool. Its 24
breezy rooms are compact, but most have
attractive stone and tile bathrooms, and some
suites have full kitchens. Even if the ocean air
occasionally takes its toll on exterior surfaces,
it's hard not to love this place. Free parking.

Mission Beach & Pacific Beach ❺

🍴 Kono's Surf Club
Cafe $

(☎858-483-1669; www.konoscafe.com; 704
Garnet Ave, Pacific Beach; mains $5-10; ⏰7am-
3pm Mon-Fri, to 4pm Sat & Sun; 🐾) This place
makes four kinds of breakfast burritos that you
eat out of a basket in view of Crystal Pier (patio
seating available) alongside pancakes, eggs
and Kono potatoes. It's always crowded but well
worth the wait.

🛏 Crystal Pier Hotel & Cottages
Cottage $$$

(☎800-748-5894; www.crystalpier.com;
4500 Ocean Blvd, Pacific Beach; d $185-525;
P 🐾 🛜) Charming, wonderful and unlike
anyplace else in San Diego, Crystal Pier has
cottages built right on the pier above the water.
Almost all 29 cottages have full ocean views
and kitchens; most date from the 1930s. Newer,
larger cottages sleep up to six. Book eight to 11
months in advance for summer reservations.
Minimum-stay requirements vary by season. No
air-con. Rates include parking.

La Jolla ❻

✗ George's at the Cove
Californian $$$

(☎858-454-4244; www.georgesatthecove.com; 1250 Prospect St; mains $13-50; ⊗11am-10pm Sun-Thu, to 11pm Fri & Sat) The Euro-Cal cooking is as dramatic as the oceanfront location thanks to the bottomless imagination of chef Trey Foshee. George's has graced just about every list of top restaurants in California, and indeed the USA. Four venues allow you to enjoy it at different price points: Ocean Terrace, George's California Modern and the no-reservations Level 2 and Modern Bar.

Del Mar ❼

🛏 Hotel Indigo San Diego Del Mar
Boutique Hotel $$

(☎877-846-3446, 858-755-1501; www. hotelindigosddelmar.com; 710 Camino Del Mar; r from $165; P ⊖ ❀ @ 🎧 🐾 🏊) This collection of white-washed buildings with gray clay-tiled roofs, two pools, a spa and new fitness and business centers recently received a tip-to-toe renovation. Rooms boast hardwood floors, mosaic tile accents and beach-inspired motifs. Some units have kitchenettes and distant ocean views. The hotel's Ocean View Bar & Grill serves breakfast, lunch and dinner.

Encinitas ❽

✗ Swami's Café
Cafe $

(☎760-944-0612; http://swamiscafe.com; 1163 S Coast Hwy 101; mains $5-11; ⊗7am-5pm; 🥦 ❹) This local institution can't be beat for breakfast burritos, multigrain pancakes, stir-fries, salads, smoothies and three-egg *ohm*-lettes (sorry, we couldn't resist). Vegetarians will be satisfied too. Most of the seating is out on an umbrella-covered patio. It's across from the Self-Realization Fellowship Retreat. There's another location in Carlsbad.

Carlsbad ❾

✗ Pizza Port
Pizza $$

(☎760-720-7007; www.pizzaport.com; 571 Carlsbad Village Dr; pizzas $9-24; ⊗11am-10pm Sun-Thu, to midnight Fri & Sat; ❹) Rockin' and raucous local brewpub chain with surf art, rock music and 'anti-wimpy' pizzas to go with the signature Sharkbite Red ale. Multiple locations.

🛏 Legoland Hotel
Hotel $$$

(☎760-918-5346, 877-534-6526; www.legoland. com/california; 5885 The Crossings Dr; r from $369, P ⊖ ❀ @ 🎧 🏊) Lego designers were let loose on this hotel, just outside Legoland's main gate, and boy is it fun: 3500 Lego models (dragons to surfers) populate the property, and the elevator turns into a disco between floors. Each floor has its own theme (pirate, adventure, kingdom), down to the rooms' wallpaper, props (Lego cannonballs – cool!), even the shower curtains.

SoCal Pop Culture

29

Pretend to be the star of your own reality-TV travel show on this whirlwind tour of SoCal, which samples eye-popping film sets, superstar hangouts and Hollywood's cult of celebrity.

TRIP HIGHLIGHTS

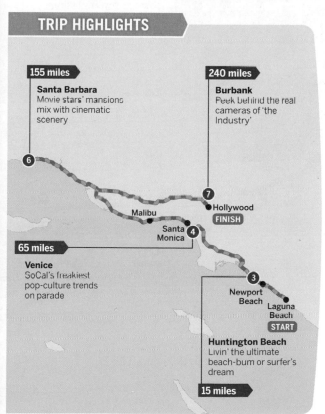

155 miles

Santa Barbara
Movie stars' mansions mix with cinematic scenery

240 miles

Burbank
Peek behind the real cameras of 'the Industry'

Hollywood **FINISH**

Malibu

Santa Monica **4**

65 miles

Venice
SoCal's freakiest pop-culture trends on parade

3

Newport Beach

Laguna Beach **START**

Huntington Beach
Livin' the ultimate beach-bum or surfer's dream

15 miles

3 DAYS
245 MILES / 395KM

GREAT FOR...

BEST TIME TO GO
Year-round, although winter can be rainy.

ESSENTIAL PHOTO
Your favorite star on the Hollywood Walk of Fame.

BEST FOR MOVIE FANS
Burbank's behind-the-scenes studio tours.

Malibu Pier

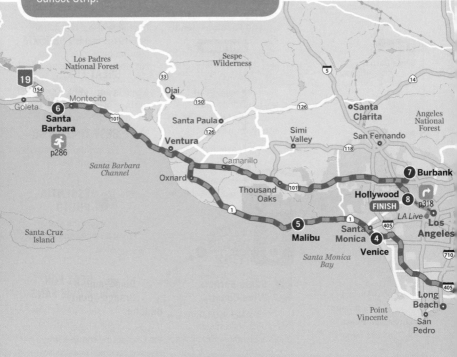

29 | SoCal Pop Culture

This trip starts in SoCal's epicenter of pop culture, Orange County, with its cinematic beaches. Zoom north along the Pacific Ocean past the skater punks of Venice Beach, Hollywood moguls' mansions in Malibu and famous TV and movie film locations in Santa Barbara. Swing back to LA's San Fernando Valley for a TV and movie studio tour, then wind up in Hollywood with a cruise down the rockin' Sunset Strip.

❶ Laguna Beach

When it comes to SoCal pop culture, you can't just ignore the reality-TV phenomenon, including MTV's *Laguna Beach*. Lauren Conrad and the show's other beauties are focused on scoring magazine covers, but the city's most wealthy residents are more about bohemian bonhomie than Hollywood elitism, so don't be shy. Shop the chic boutiques in downtown's **village**, then strike a pose on **Main Beach** in your teeny-weeny bikini.

Jealously guarded by locals, **Thousand Steps Beach** (off 9th Ave) is hidden off Hwy 1 just south of Mission Hospital, where a stairway leads down to a rocky beach, postcard-perfect for sunbathing.

 p301

The Drive » Join Hwy 1, aka Pacific Coast Hwy (PCH), for the quick 10-mile trip north to Newport Beach, passing oceanfront Crystal Cove State Park. Exit onto Newport Blvd, following it down onto the Balboa Peninsula.

❷ Newport Beach

Welcome to the superficial charms of glitzy Newport Beach. Primetime soap *The OC* may be long over, but the angst-ridden adventures of its glamorous teens have given a hipper, youthful sheen to the city's longstanding image as a paradise for yachtsmen and their trophy wives, as parodied by *Arrested Development*. On the **Balboa Peninsula**, the two-mile oceanfront strip between **Balboa Pier** and **Newport Pier** teems with young glamazons. Inland, more lifestyles of the rich and famous revolve around **Fashion Island** (☎855-658-8527, 949 721-2000; www.shopfashionisland. com; 401 Newport Center Dr; ⏱10am-9pm Mon-Fri, to 7pm Sat, 11am-6pm Sun; 🚗), a posh outdoor mall that's one of the OC's biggest shopping meccas.

 p319, p301

The Drive » Keep going north up Hwy 1, often crawling with bumper-to-bumper traffic

on summer weekends when everyone's heading to the beach. Relax, it's only 4 miles to Huntington Beach, at the intersection of Main St and PCH.

TRIP HIGHLIGHT

❸ Huntington Beach

Time to make the pop-cultural switch from the boob tube to surfing. Huntington Beach has been *the* SoCal surf hot-spot since George Freeth first demonstrated the Hawaiian sport of wave-riding here a century ago. The city recently trademarked its nick-name 'Surf City USA' (the moniker from Jan and Dean's 1963 pop-music hit). Surfing is seriously big business in HB, with buyers for major retailers coming here to see what surfers are wearing and then marketing the look, while beautiful blondes blithely play volleyball on the golden sand and skaters whiz past the oceanfront pier.

✕ 🛏 p301

The Drive » Keep going north for 12 miles on Hwy 1

🔗 LINK YOUR TRIP

19 **Santa Barbara Wine Country**

Follow Hwy 154 up into the mountains of the Santa Ynez Valley, where *Sideways* wine country is ready for its close-up.

27 **Disneyland & Orange County Beaches**

If you can't get enough of the OC's sunny sands, keep cruising south on coastal Hwy 1, then hit Disneyland.

passing Sunset Beach. Then join the I-405 north, driving past industrial areas of Los Angeles. Take the Hwy 90 westbound exit toward Marina del Rey, slingshot around the marina to Pacific Ave by the beach, turn right and roll north to Venice.

TRIP HIGHLIGHT

❹ Venice

Created in 1905 by eccentric tobacco heir Abbot Kinney as an amusement park, the 'Venice of America' became complete with Italian *gondolieri* poling the canals. Now new-age hippies, muscled bodybuilders à la Arnold Schwarzenegger, goth punks, tribal drummers and freaks have taken over the **Venice Boardwalk** (Ocean Front Walk; Venice Pier to Rose Ave) – you may recognize it from the opening scenes of *Three's Company* – where the crazy side of SoCal really lets it all hang out. Imagine an experimental human zoo, and strap on those rollerblades, hop on a fluorescent-painted beach cruiser or just shake what yo' mama gave you. Venice is also the birthplace of SoCal skater-punk culture, as chronicled in the movie *Lords of Dogtown*.

✕ ⊨ p319

The Drive » Drive north on Ocean Ave and rejoin PCH past the I-10 Fwy. Cruise past Santa Monica's carnival pier with its solar-powered Ferris wheel. Keep following PCH north as it curves alongside the ocean to Malibu, just over a dozen miles away.

- - - - - - - - - -

❺ Malibu

Measured mile for fabulous oceanfront mile, Malibu may have the densest collection of celebrities anywhere in SoCal. Keep your eye peeled for the paparazzi, especially at the **Malibu Country Mart** (☎310-456-7300; www.malibucountry mart.com; 3835 Cross Creek Rd; ☺8am-9pm; 🚻) mini-mall, where the A-list crowd sips iced lattes as they shop. About 15 miles further west, pull into **Leo Carrillo State Park** (☎310-457-8143; www.parks. ca.gov; 35000 W Pacific Coast Hwy; per car $12; ☺8am-10pm; P 🚻). This beach's hidden coves made a romantic backdrop in *Pirates of the Caribbean*, *The Karate Kid* and *50 First Dates*. Beware of rough surf: John Travolta and Olivia Newton-John almost got swept out to sea here in the opening scene of *Grease*.

✕ p60

The Drive » Hug the coast by following Hwy 1 north, which turns inland to intersect Hwy 101, a multilane freeway that swings back to the coast at Ventura, then flows past ocean cliffs and beaches northwest to Santa Barbara, about a 90-minute trip from Malibu without traffic jams.

- - - - - - - - - -

TRIP HIGHLIGHT

❻ Santa Barbara

A Mediterranean vibe and red-roofed, white-stucco buildings give credence to Santa Barbara's claim of being the 'American Riviera.' Spanish Colonial Revival buildings clustered along downtown's **State St** have made cameos in countless movies, including *It's Complicated*. A 45-minute drive up into the mountains via scenic Hwy 154, Santa Barbara's **wine country** sets the hilarious scene for the

Venice Homes line the canal

Oscar-winning 2004 hit film *Sideways*. Just east of Santa Barbara off Hwy 101, celeb-heavy **Montecito** is a leafy suburb tucked between the mountains and the Pacific. Heavy hitters like Oprah Winfrey, Steven Spielberg and Ellen DeGeneres have homes here and occasionally venture out along downtown's boutique-and-patio-lined main drag, **Coast Village Rd**.

✗ ▭ p60, p70, p217, p319

The Drive » Take Hwy 101 south back to Ventura, then head up into the mountains via the steep Conjeo (Camarillo) Grade. Leveling off, Hwy 101 zooms east through the San Fernando Valley. Veer left onto Hwy 134 toward Burbank, almost 90 miles after leaving Santa Barbara.

— — — — — — — —

TRIP HIGHLIGHT

7 Burbank

Long ago, the TV and movie biz (locals just call it 'the Industry') decamped from Hollywood into the San Fernando Valley. Scores of Hollywood blockbusters, from *The Terminator* to *Chinatown,* have been shot on location here. (Infamously, 'the Valley' is also ground zero for SoCal's XXX porn-movie industry.) It also birthed 1980s 'Valley Girl' speak (gag me with a spoon!) and popularized SoCal's ubiquitous mall-rat culture.

Take a look behind the scenes on the **Warner Bros Studio Tour** (☏818-972-8687, 877-492-8687; www.wbstudiotour.com; 3400 W Riverside Dr, Burbank; tours adult/child 8-12yr from $62/52; ⊙9am-3:15pm Mon-Sat, extended hours Jun-Aug), or take your screaming tweens and teens to **Universal Studios Hollywood** (☏800-864-8377; www.universalstudios hollywood.com; 100 Universal

DETOUR: LA LIVE

Start: ❽ Hollywood

Next to downtown's **Staples Center** (📞213-742-7340; www.staplescenter.com; 1111 S Figueroa St; 🚇), a saucer-shaped sports and entertainment arena, **LA Live** (📞866-548-3452, 213-763-5483; www.lalive.com; 800 W Olympic Blvd; 🅿🚇) is a shiny corporate entertainment hub. Glimpse larger-than-life statues of Magic Johnson and Wayne Gretzky, and party at the **Conga Room** co-owned by J Lo and will.i.am. But only after you pay homage to the **Grammy Museum** (📞213-765-6800; www.grammymuseum.org; 800 W Olympic Blvd; adult/child $13/11; ⏰11:30am-6:30pm Mon-Fri, from 10am Sat & Sun; 🅿🚇). Music lovers will get lost in interactive exhibits, where sound chambers let you try mixing and remixing, singing and rapping. Glimpse such things as GnR's bass drum, Yo-Yo Ma's cello and MJ's glove enshrined like holy relics (though exhibitions and collections do rotate). It's about 8 miles southeast of Hollywood via Hwy 101 and the I-110 Fwy south (exit at 8th St).

City Plaza, Universal City; admission from $99, child under 3yr free; ⏰daily, hours vary; 🅿🚇) theme park, where you can escape into the Wizarding World of Harry Potter, ride a tram tour past working sound stages and pick up free tickets for a live TV show taping from **Audiences Unlimited** (📞818-260-0041; www.tvtickets.com). To buy cast-off TV and movie star fashions, stop off at **It's a Wrap!** (📞818-567-7366; www.itsawraphollywood.com; 3315 W Magnolia

Blvd, Burbank; ⏰11am-7pm Mon-Fri, 11am-6pm Sat, noon-6pm Sun).

The Drive » It's a quick 3-mile trip south on Hwy 101 from Universal Studios to Hollywood. Take the Highland Ave exit and drive south on Highland Ave, which intersects Hollywood Blvd.

- - - - - - - - - - - - - -

❽ Hollywood

Like an aging starlet making a comeback, this once-gritty Los Angeles neighborhood is undergoing a rebirth of cool with hip hotels, restored movie

palaces and glitzy, velvet-roped bars and nightclubs. Even though you aren't likely to see any real celebrities, the pink-starred **Hollywood Walk of Fame** (www.walkoffame.com; Hollywood Blvd) still attracts millions of wide-eyed visitors every year. Snap a souvenir photo outside the **TCL Chinese Theatre** (📞323-461-3331; www.tclchinesetheatres.com; 6925 Hollywood Blvd; tours & movie tickets adult/senior/child from $15/12.50/7.50; 🚇) – go ahead, we know you can't resist. Step inside the slightly musty **Hollywood Museum** (📞323-464-7776; www.thehollywoodmuseum.com; 1660 N Highland Ave; adult/child $15/5; ⏰10am-5pm Wed-Sun; 🚇), crammed with costumes, memorabilia and props from Charlie Chaplin to *Glee*.

Cruise west along the **Sunset Strip**, packed with celeb-slumming bars and dog-eared rock venues where the Rolling Stones and the Doors once tore up the stages. For late-night star-peeping, sneak into the lobby lounge at the **Chateau Marmont**, cosseting A-listers like Bono, Brad Pitt and Angelina Jolie.

🍴 🛏 p319, p329

Eating & Sleeping

Newport Beach ②

✖ Crab Cooker   Seafood $$

(☎949-673-0100; www.crabcooker.com; 2200
Newport Blvd; mains $12-24, lobster $32-40;
⊙11am-9pm Sun-Thu, to 10pm Fri & Sat; 🚻)
Expect a wait at this always-busy joint, a
landmark since 1951. It serves great seafood and
fresh crab on paper plates to an appreciative
crowd wearing flip-flops and jeans. Don't miss
the delish chowder – it's loaded with clams.

Venice ④

✖ Abbot's Pizza Company   Pizza $

(☎310-396-7334; www.abbotspizzaco.com;
1407 Abbot Kinney Blvd; slices $3-5, pizzas
$14-26; ⊙11am-11pm Sun-Thu, to midnight Fri
& Sat; 🅿 🚻) Join the flip-flop crowd at this
shoebox-sized pizza kitchen for habit-forming
bagel crust pies tastily decorated with tequila-
lime chicken, portobello mushrooms, goat
cheese and other gourmet morsels.

🛏 Hotel Erwin   Boutique Hotel $$$

(☎310 452 1111, 800 786 7789; www.
hotelerwin.com; 1697 Pacific Ave; r from $280;
🅿 ❄ @ 🛜) This old motor inn has been
dressed up, colored and otherwise funkified in
retro style. Think: eye-popping oranges, yellows
and greens, framed photos of graffiti art,
flat-screen TVs, and ergo sofas in the spacious
rooms. Book online for the best deals.

Santa Barbara ⑥

✖ Jeannine's   Cafe, Bakery $

(☎805-969-0088; http://jeannines.com; 1253
Coast Village Rd; mains $8-16; ⊙7am-3pm;
🅿 🚻) Nab a table on the outdoor patio and
watch socialites stroll past. At breakfast or
brunch, the from-scratch kitchen goodness
includes challah French toast with bananas
caramelized in Kahlua.

🛏 Four Seasons Biltmore   Resort $$$

(☎info 805-969-2261, reservations
805-565-8299; www.fourseasons.com/
santabarbara; 1260 Channel Dr; r from $425;
🅿 ❄ ❄ @ 🛜 🏊 🐾) Wear white linen and

live like Jay Gatsby at the oh-so-cushy 1927
Biltmore hotel on Butterfly Beach. Every detail
is perfect, from bathrooms with Spanish tiles,
French-milled soaps, deep soaking tubs and
waterfall showers to bedrooms decked out with
ultra-high-thread-count sheets.

Hollywood ⑧

✖ Pikey   Pub Food $$

(☎323-850-5400; www.thepikeyla.com; 7617
W Sunset Blvd; dinner mains $15-32; ⊙11:45am-
1:30am Mon-Fri, from 10:30am Sat & Sun) A
tasteful kitchen that began life as Coach &
Horses, one of Hollywood's favorite dives before
it was reimagined into a place where you can
get roasted broccolini with buffalo burrata, fish
crudo with pickled rhubarb and fennel or seared
squid with curried chickpeas. The cocktails rock.

✖ Pink's   Fast Food $

(☎323-931-4223; www.pinkshollywood.com; 709
N La Brea Ave; items $4-8; ⊙9:30am-2am Sun-
Thu, to 3am Fri & Sat; 🚻) Landmark doggeria
with glacially moving lines thanks to the droves
who descend for garlicky, all-beef frankfurters,
painted with mustard or drenched in chili.

🛏 Magic Castle Hotel   Hotel $$

(☎323-851-0800; http://magiccastlehotel.com;
7025 Franklin Ave; r from $189; 🅿 ❄ @ 🛜 🏊)
Walls at this perennial pleaser are a bit thin,
but otherwise it's a charming base of operation
with large, modern rooms, exceptional staff and
a petite courtyard pool where days start with
fresh pastries and gourmet coffee.

🛏 Hollywood
Roosevelt Hotel   Historic Hotel $$$

(☎323-856-1970; www.thehollywoodroosevelt.
com; 7000 Hollywood Blvd; ⊙24hr; 🅿 🛜)
Great architecture, rich history and gossip
rendezvous at this venerable hotel, where the
first Academy Awards ceremony was held in
1929. After a renovation, it briefly became the
new millennium's poolside hot spot as tabloid
regulars were frequently spotted misbehaving
at the pool bar. Back in her day, glamazon
Marilyn Monroe shot her first print ad (for suntan
lotion) posing on the diving board of said pool,
the bottom of which was later decorated with
squiggles by artist David Hockney.

Classic Trip

Route 66 **30**

Search for the American dream along Route 66, America's 'Mother Road.' This is a trip of retro roadside relics, vintage motor lodges and milkshakes from mom-and-pop diners.

TRIP HIGHLIGHTS

335 miles

Hollywood
Get your kicks in
Tinseltown

95 miles

Amboy
The big sky and empty
byways are starkly
photogenic

START
Needles

Victorville

3

San
Bernardino

10
Los Angeles

11
FINISH

Santa Monica
End this epic trip on
the Pacific shore

350 miles

3–4 DAYS
350 MILES / 565KM

GREAT FOR...

BEST TIME TO GO
Spring, for cruising
with the windows
down before the heat
of summer.

 ESSENTIAL PHOTO

Laying down on the
faded blacktop next to
a Route 66 sign.

✓ **BEST ROAD**
National Trails
Hwy between Goffs
and Amboy is the
quintessential middle-
of-nowhere stretch.

Classic Trip

30 Route 66

For generations of Americans, California, with its sparkling waters and sunny skies, was the promised land for road-trippers on Route 66. Follow their tracks through the gauntlet of Mojave Desert ghost towns, railway whistle-stops like Barstow and Victorville, and across the Cajon Summit. Finally, wind through the LA Basin and put it in park near the crashing ocean waves at the end of Santa Monica Pier.

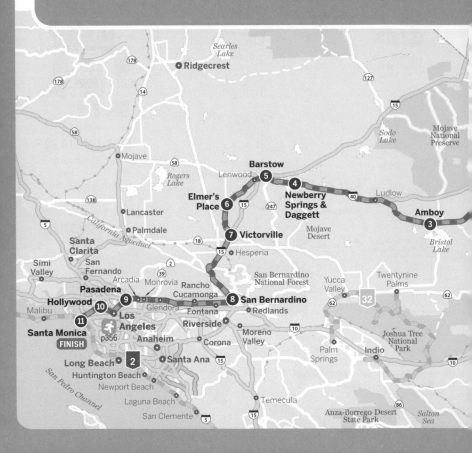

❶ Needles

At the Arizona border south of I-40 the arched **Old Trails Bridge** (🕓no public access) welcomes the Mother Road to California under endless blue skies. You might recognize the bridge: the Depression-era Joad family used it to cross the Colorado River in the movie version of John Steinbeck's novel *Grapes of Wrath*. Drive west past Needles, a dusty throwback railroad town with a historic depot down by the river.

Frozen in a half-restored state, the **El Garces Depot** is one of only a few frontier-era Harvey Houses left standing in the American West. The Harvey Houses were a chain of railway hotels and restaurants popular in the late 19th and early 20th centuries that were famed for traveling waitresses – portrayed by Judy Garland in the 1946 MGM musical *The Harvey Girls*. Head a bit south on Broadway and you'll pass a freshly restored **66 Motel Sign** at the corner of Desnok Street – a great photo.

The Drive » About 15 miles west of Needles, follow Hwy 95 north of I-40 for 6 miles, then turn left onto Goffs Rd. You'll inevitably be running alongside a long locomotive – this is a primary rail shipping route to the West Coast.

❷ Goffs

The shade of cotton-wood trees make the 1914 Mission-style **Goffs**

Schoolhouse (📞760-733-4482; www.mdhca.org; 37198 Lanfair Rd, Essex; donations welcome; 🕓 usually 9am-4pm Sat-Mon Oct-Jun; 🅿) a soothing stop along this sun-drenched stretch of highway. It stands as part of the best-preserved pioneer settlement in the Mojave Desert (although to be quite honest it looks a bit like an empty Taco Bell). Browsing the black-and-white photographs of hardscrabble Dust Bowl migrants gives an evocative glimpse into tough life on the edge of the Mojave.

The Drive » If the bridge beyond Goffs has been restored, keep going on Goffs Rd through Fenner, crossing under I-40; otherwise, backtrack to I-40 via Hwy 95. Turn right onto National Old Trails Hwy (known as National Trails Hwy on some maps and signs) and drive for about an hour, passing abandoned graffiti covered service stations and vintage signs rusting in the sun.

LINK YOUR TRIP

32 Palm Springs & Joshua Tree Oases

Cut south on I-10 out of San Bernardino and head for the breezy palms of Palm Springs.

2 Pacific Coast Highways

This equally classic route lets you cruise along an equally iconic numbered route: Highway 1. When you finish Route 66, follow Hwy 1 north.

Classic Trip

SOUTHERN CALIFORNIA **30** ROUTE 66

TRIP HIGHLIGHT

❸ Amboy

Potholed and crumbling in a romantic way, the USA's original transnational highway was established in 1912, more than a decade before Route 66 first ran through here. The rutted highway races through tiny towns, sparsely scattered across the Mojave. Only a few landmarks interrupt the horizon, including **Roy's Motel & Cafe** (www.rt66roys.com; National Old Trails Hwy, Amboy; ⊙vary; P), a landmark watering hole for decades of Route 66 travelers. If you believe the lore, Roy once cooked his famous Route 66 double cheeseburger on the hood of a '63 Mercury. Although the motel is abandoned, the gas station and cafe are occasionally open. It's east of **Amboy Crater** (📞760-326-7000; www.blm. gov/ca; ⊙sunrise-sunset; P), an almost perfectly symmetrical volcanic cinder cone. You can hike to the top, but not in summer and it's best to avoid the midday sun – the 3-mile round-trip hike doesn't have a stitch of shade.

The Drive ≫ From Amboy travel almost 30 miles along National Old Trails Highway to Ludlow. Turn right onto Crucero Rd and pass under I-40, then take the north frontage road west and turn left at Lavic Rd. Back on the south side of I-40, keep heading west on National Old Trails Hwy. The entire trip takes about one hour and 45 minutes.

❹ Newberry Springs & Daggett

The highway passes under I-40 on its way through **Daggett**, site of the harsh California inspection station faced by Dust Bowl refugees in *Grapes of Wrath*. Today, there ain't much action, but it's a windswept, picturesque place. Pay your respects to early desert adventurers at the old **Stone Hotel** (National Old Trails Hwy, Daggett; ⊙no public entry). This late-19th-century hotel once housed miners, desert explorers and wanderers, including Sierra Nevada naturalist John Muir and Death Valley Scotty. Then make your way out of town to visit **Calico Ghost Town** (📞800-862-2542; www.calicotown.com; 36600 Ghost Town Rd, Yermo; adult/child $8/5; ⊙9am-5pm; P 🚻). This endearingly hokey Old West attraction sets a cluster of reconstructed pioneer-era buildings amid ruins of a late-19th-century silver mining town. You'll pay extra to go gold panning,

take a mine tour or ride a narrow-gauge railway. Old-timey heritage celebrations include Civil War reenactments and a bluegrass 'hootenanny.'

The Drive ≫ From Daggett, drive west to Nebo Rd, turning left to rejoin I-40. You'll drive about 4 miles before taking the exit for E Main St.

❺ Barstow

Exit the interstate onto Main St, which runs through Barstow, a railroad settlement and historic crossroads, where murals adorn empty buildings downtown. Follow 1st St north across the Mojave River over a trestle bridge to the 1911 Harvey House, nicknamed **Casa del Desierto**, designed by Western architect Mary Colter. Inside is the **Route 66 'Mother Road' Museum** (📞760-255-1890; www.route66museum.org; 681 N 1st St; ⊙10am-4pm Fri & Sat, 11am-4pm Sun, or by appointment; P 🚻) **FREE**, displaying black-and-white historical photographs and odds and ends of everyday life in the early 20th century. Next door is the small **Western America Railroad Museum** (WARM; 📞760-256-9276; www.barstowrailmuseum.org; 685 N 1st St; ⊙11am-4pm Fri-Sun; P) **FREE**.

✕ 🍴 p329

The Drive ≫ Leaving Barstow via Main St, rejoin the National Old Trails Hwy west. It curves

TOP TIP: NAVIGATING THE MOTHER ROAD

Nostalgia for the Mother Road draws its share of completists who want to drive every inch. For Route 66 enthusiasts who need to cover every mile, a free turn-by-turn driving guide is available online at www.historic66.com. Also surf to http://route66ca.org for more historical background, photos and info about special events.

alongside the Mojave River through Lenwood. After about 25 miles you'll arrive at Elmer's Place.

---

⑥ Elmer's Place

Loved by Harley bikers, this rural byway is like a scavenger hunt for Mother Road ruins, including antique filling stations and tumbledown motor courts. Colorful as a box of crayons, **Elmer's Place** (Elmer's Place; 24266 National Trails Hwy, Oro Grande; ⊙vary; **P**) is a roadside folk-art collection of 'bottle trees,' made from recycled soda pop and beer containers, telephone poles and railroad signs. Elmer Long, who was a career man at the cement factory you'll pass just out of town, is the proprietor and cracked artistic genius. If you see someone with a long white beard and leathery skin cementing a statue of a bronze deity to some elk antlers, you've found the right guy. Want to leave a little part of yourself along Route 66? Bring a little something for Elmer Long's colorful

forest, constructed lovingly out of little pieces of junk.

The Drive » Cross over the Mojave River on a 1930s steel-truss bridge, then roll into downtown Victorville, a trip of almost 12 miles.

---

⑦ Victorville

Opposite the railroad tracks in quiet little Victorville, visitors poke around a mishmash of historical exhibits and contemporary art inside the **California Route 66 Museum** (📞760-951-0434; www.califrt66museum.org; 16825 D St, Victorville; donations welcome; ⊙10am-4pm Thu-Sat & Mon, 11am-3pm Sun; **P** ♿). The museum building itself was once the Red Rooster Cafe, a famous Route 66 roadhouse. It's a bit of a cluttered nostalgia trip – piled with old signs and roadside memorabilia – but worth a quick look.

The Drive » Get back on I-15 south over the daunting Cajon Summit. If you're hungry, pull off in Hesperia at the Summit Inn, a classic diner. Descending into

San Bernardino, take I-215 and exit at Devore. Follow Cajon Blvd to Mt Vernon Ave, detour east on Base Line St and go left onto 'E' St. This trip takes about 40 minutes.

---

⑧ San Bernardino

Look for the Golden Arches outside the unofficial **First McDonalds Museum** (📞909-885-6324; 1398 N E St, San Bernardino; admission by donation; ⊙10am-5pm; **P** ♿). It was here that salesman Ray Kroc dropped in to sell Richard and Maurice McDonald a mixer. Eventually Kroc bought the rights to the brothers' name and built an empire. Half of the museum is devoted to Route 66, with particularly interesting photographs and maps. Turn west on 5th St, leaving San Bernardino via Foothill Blvd, which continues straight into the urban sprawl of greater Los Angeles. It's a long haul west to Pasadena, with stop-and-go traffic most of the way, but there are more than a handful of gems to uncover. Cruising through Fontana, birthplace of the Hells Angels biker club, pause for a photo by the **Giant Orange** (15395 Foothill Blvd, Fontana; ⊙no public entry; **P**), a 1930s juice stand of the kind that was once a fixture alongside SoCal's citrus groves.

🛏 p329

WHY THIS IS A CLASSIC TRIP

Maybe it goes back to the transient vagabonds who founded this country, but there's a persistent call, deep in the American psyche, that compels us to hit the open road. And no road is quite as satisfying as the endless two-lane blacktop of Route 66. The subject of singalongs and fodder for daydreams, traveling this classic trail to the Pacific shore is an essentially American experience.

Top: Calico Ghost Town, Mojave Desert
Left: Pacific Park's Ferris wheel, Santa Monica Pier
Right: Roy's Motel & Cafe, Amboy

The Drive › Stay on Route 66 as it detours briefly from Foothill Blvd onto Alosta Ave in Glendora, where you can stop for lunch at the Hat. Shortly after 66 rejoins Foothill Blvd in Azusa, continue onto Huntington Dr in Duarte, where a boisterous Route 66 parade happens in September.

❾ Pasadena

Just before you reach Pasadena, you'll pass through **Arcadia**, home to the 1930s **Santa Anita Park** (☏tickets 626-574-6366, tour info 626-574-6677; www.santaanita.com; 285 W Huntington Dr, Arcadia; adult/child from $5/free; ⊗racing season Christmas–mid-Apr, late Sep–early Nov, tram tours 8:30am & 9:45am Sat & Sun during racing season; ☏⏍). This track is where the Marx Brothers' *A Day at the Races* was filmed (and more recently the HBO series *Luck*) and where legendary thoroughbred Seabiscuit once ran. Stepping through the soaring art-deco entrance into the grandstands, you'll feel like a million bucks – even if you don't win any wagers. During race season, free tram tours go behind the scenes into the jockeys' room and training areas; reservations required. Continue along Colorado Blvd into wealthy **Old Pasadena**, a bustling shopping district west of Arroyo Pkwy, where boutiques and cafes are housed in handsomely restored historic Spanish Colonial Revival style buildings.

327

Classic Trip

🍴 🛏 p329

The Drive » Join the jet-set modern world on the Pasadena Fwy (Hwy 110), which streams south into LA. One of the first freeways in the US, it's a truck-free state historic freeway – the whole trip will take less than 20 minutes. Take the Santa Monica Blvd exit, then follow Sunset Blvd northwest to Santa Monica Blvd westbound.

⑩ Hollywood

Like a resurrected diva of the silver screen, Holly-wood is making a come-back. Although it hasn't recaptured the Golden Age glamour that brought would-be starlets cruising here on Route 66, this historic neighborhood is still worth visiting for its restored movie palaces, unique museums and the pink stars on the **Hollywood Walk of Fame**. The exact track that Route 66 ran through the neighborhood isn't pos-sible to follow these days (it changed officially a couple times and has long been paved over). Start exploring at the **Holly-wood & Highland** (www.hollywoodandhighland.com; 6801 Hollywood Blvd; ☺10am-10pm Mon-Sat, to 7pm Sun; 🚇) shopping, dining and entertainment complex, north of Santa Monica Blvd, in the center of the action. The **Los Angeles Visitor Information Center** (☎323-467-6412; www.discoverlosangeles.com; Hollywood & Highland complex, 6801 Hollywood Blvd, Hollywood; ☺10am-10pm Mon-Sat, to 7pm Sun) is upstairs. Travelers looking for a fun, creepy communion with stars of yesteryear should stroll the **Hollywood Forever Cemetery** (☎323-469-1181; www.hollywoodforever.com; 6000 Santa Monica Blvd; ☺usually 8:30am-5pm; 🅿) next to Paramount Pic-tures, which is crowded with famous 'immor-tals,' including Rudolph Valentino, Tyrone Power, Jayne Mansfield and Cecil B DeMille. Buy a map at the flower shop near the entrance.

🍴 🛏 p319, p329

The Drive » Follow Santa Monica Blvd west for 13 miles to reach the end of the road – it meets Ocean Ave at Palisades Park. Hwy 1 is downhill from Ocean Ave heading north. The pier is a few blocks to the south.

⑪ Santa Monica

This is the end of the line: Route 66 reaches its finish, over 2200 miles from its starting point in Chicago, on an ocean bluff in **Palisades Park**, where a Will Rogers Hwy memorial plaque marks the official end of the Mother Road. Celebrate on **Santa Monica Pier** (☎310-458-8901; www.santamonicapier.org; 🚇), where you can ride a 1920s carousel featured in *The Sting*, gently touch tidepool critters at the **Santa Monica Pier Aquarium** (☎310-393-6149; www.healthebay.org; 1600 Ocean Front Walk; adult/child $5/free; ☺2pm-6pm Tue-Fri, 12:30pm-6pm Sat & Sun; 🚇), and soak up a sunset atop the solar-powered Ferris wheel at **Pacific Park** (☎310-260-8744; www.pacpark.com; 380 Santa Monica Pier; per ride $5-8, all-day pass adult/child under 8yr $30/18; ☺daily, seasonal hours vary; 🚇). Year-round carnival rides include the West Coast's only oceanfront steel roller coaster – a thrilling ride to end this classic trip.

🛏 p329

Eating & Sleeping

Barstow ❺

✖ Idle Spurs Steakhouse — Steak $$

(☎760-256-8888; www.thespurs.us; 690 Old Hwy 58; mains lunch $8-16, dinner $18-45; ⊙11am-9pm Tue-Fri, from 4pm Sat & Sun; 🚹) In the saddle since 1950, this Western-themed spot, ringed around an atrium and a full bar, is a fave with locals and RVers. Surrender to your inner carnivore with slow-roasted prime rib, hand-cut steaks and succulent lobster tail.

▦ Oak Tree Inn — Motel $

(☎888-456-8733, 760-254-1148; www.oaktreeinn.com; 35450 Yermo Rd, Yermo; r $55-105; P ☕ ❄ 🛜 ♿ 🐾) For class and comfort, steer towards this three-story, 65-room motel near the freeway, where rooms have black-out draperies and triple-paned windows. It's less than 10 miles east of Barstow (exit Ghost Town Rd off I-15). Breakfast is served at the adjacent 1950s-style Penny's Diner.

San Bernardino ❽

▦ Wigwam Motel — Motel $

(☎909-875-3005; www.wigwammotel.com; 2728 W Foothill Blvd, Rialto; r $75-100; P ☕ ❄ 🛜 ♿ 🐾) Get your kitsch on Rte 66: stay snug in a concrete tipi, with a kidney-shaped pool out the back.

Pasadena ❾

✖ Fair Oaks Pharmacy — Diner, Ice Cream $

(☎626-799-1414; www.fairoakspharmacy.net; 1526 Mission St, South Pasadena; mains $6-11; ⊙9am-9pm Mon-Sat, 10am-7pm Sun; 🚹) Get your kicks at this original 1915 soda fountain right on Route 66. Slurp an old-fashioned 'phosphate' (flavored syrup, soda water and 'secret potion') while waiting for a heaping sandwich or hamburger or stocking up on classic candy in the gift shops. It's touristy, sure, but fun nonetheless.

Saga Motor Hotel — Motel $$

(☎800-793-7242, 626-795-0431; www.thesagamotorhotel.com; 1633 E Colorado Blvd, Pasadena; r from $105; P ❄ @ 🛜 ♿ 🐾) This peach-tinted, palm-shaded motel isn't fancy or as cool as the sign makes it look, but even if some of the beds are saggy and the carpet faded, rooms are clean, have tubs and showers, and some homey touches – such as shutters on the windows and books on the shelves.

Hollywood ❿

✖ Hungry Cat — Seafood $$

(☎323-462-2155; www.thehungrycat.com; 1535 Vine St; mains $13-34; ⊙noon-10pm Mon-Fri, 11am-11pm Sat & 11am-10pm Sun) This kitty is small and sleek and hides out across Sunset Blvd from the ArcLight cinema. It fancies fresh seafood and will have you salivating for a hunky lobster roll, portly crab cakes and savory specials. The Pug Burger – slathered with avocado, bacon and blue cheese – is a meaty alternative.

▦ Farmer's Daughter Hotel — Motel $$$

(☎323-937-3930, 800 334-1658; http://farmersdaughterhotel.com; 115 S Fairfax Ave; r from $240; P ❄ @ 🛜 ♿) Denim bedspreads and rocking chairs lend this flirty motel a farmhouse vibe. Long before the renovation, a young Charlize Theron stayed here with mom when they were hunting for a Hollywood career. Adventurous lovers should ask about the No Tell Room, which has mirrored headboards and another mirror on the ceiling.

Santa Monica ⓫

▦ Sea Shore Motel — Motel $$

(☎310-392-2787; www.seashoremotel.com; 2637 Main St; r $125-240, ste $225-325; P ❄ 🛜) These friendly, family-run lodgings put you just a Frisbee toss from the beach on happening Main St (expect some street noise). The tiled rooms are basic, but families can stretch out comfortably in the modern suites with kitchen and balcony in a nearby building.

Classic Trip

Life in Death Valley

31

Drive where California pioneers and gold miners once rolled their wagons in Death Valley National Park, a place where the magnum forces of natural and human history collide.

TRIP HIGHLIGHTS

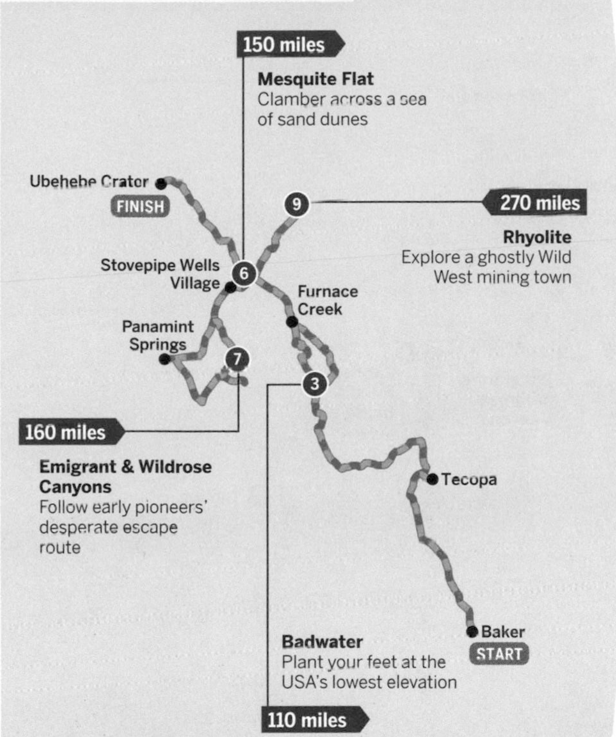

150 miles

Mesquite Flat
Clamber across a sea of sand dunes

Ubehebe Crater
FINISH

9

270 miles

Rhyolite
Explore a ghostly Wild West mining town

Stovepipe Wells Village
6

Furnace Creek

Panamint Springs

7

3

160 miles

Emigrant & Wildrose Canyons
Follow early pioneers' desperate escape route

Tecopa

Badwater
Plant your feet at the USA's lowest elevation

Baker
START

110 miles

**3 DAYS
365 MILES / 585KM**

GREAT FOR...

BEST TIME TO GO
February to April for spring wildflower blooms and cooler temperatures.

 ESSENTIAL PHOTO
Elevation sign at Badwater Basin.

 BEST FOR HISTORY
Abandoned towns and ruins in Emigrant and Wildrose Canyons.

Death Valley National Park Mesquite Flat sand dunes

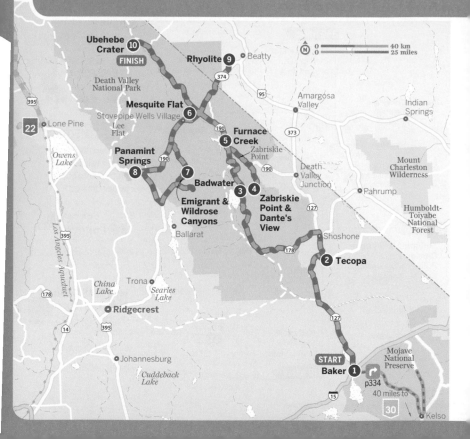

Classic Trip

31 Life in Death Valley

The name itself evokes all that is harsh, hot and hellish — a punishing, barren and lifeless place of Old Testament severity. Ghost towns and abandoned mines are proof of the human struggle to survive here. Yet a scenic drive through the park reveals that in Death Valley, nature is spectacularly alive: 'singing' sand dunes, water-sculpted canyons, boulders mysteriously moving across the desert floor, extinct volcanic craters and palm-shaded oases.

① Baker

Death Valley is a land of extremes – you'll find the lowest elevation in North America here, not far from Mt Whitney, the highest peak in the US outside Alaska. More infamously, Death Valley is the hottest place in the nation. Just take a look at the **World's Largest Thermometer**, right off the I-15 Fwy. It stands 134ft tall to commemorate the record-breaking temperature of 134°F (57°C) measured in Death Valley on July 10, 1913. Recently fixed, the thermometer is an eye-catching tower of roadside kitsch.

The Drive » From Baker, follow Hwy 127 (Death Valley Rd) north for almost 50 miles, crossing railroad tracks and zooming

LINK YOUR TRIP

22 **Eastern Sierra Scenic Byway**

From Panamint Springs, it's 50 miles northwest to Lone Pine, a gateway to lofty Sierra Nevada peaks, via Hwys 190, 136 and 395.

30 **Route 66**
From Baker, drive south through the Mojave National Preserve and across I-40 to meet California's original road trip.

through a sere desert landscape. Turn right onto Old Spanish Trail Hwy and drive 4 miles east toward Tecopa, turning left onto Tecopa Hot Springs Rd for the hot-springs resorts.

② Tecopa

Even when the desert looks bone-dry, you can still find oases in the dusty outpost of Tecopa. In the middle of town at **Tecopa Hot Springs Resort** (📞760-852-4420; www.tecopahotsprings.org; 860 Tecopa Hot Springs Rd; bathing $8, incl towel $10; 🕐 call ahead Jun-Sep), you can soak in the natural mineral springs used by Native Americans for centuries. Sex-segregated bathhouses let tribal elders, snowbird RVers and curious travelers all soak together, or you could rent a private pool. Outside town, **China Ranch Date Farm** (📞760-852-4415; www.chinaranch.com; off Furnace Creek Rd; 🕐9am-5pm; P 👶) is a refreshingly green refuge where you can go hiking or bird-watching, then stock up on fresh dates or try their yummy date shakes. To get to the ranch, follow the Old Spanish Trail Hwy east of Tecopa Hot Springs Rd, turn right onto Furnace Creek Rd, then follow the signs. The last stretch is unpaved, steep and winding, sometimes requiring 4WD.

🛏 p339

The Drive » Continue northwest on Tecopa Hot Springs Rd to rejoin Hwy 127. Turn right and drive north to Shoshone, your last chance for gas, drinks and snacks until Furnace Creek, over 70 miles away. Turn left onto Hwy 178 (Jubilee Pass Rd), which wrenches right at Ashford Junction, becoming Badwater Rd and curving lazily north along the valley floor.

TRIP HIGHLIGHT

③ Badwater

Cresting Jubilee Pass (1290ft), the highway dips down into Death Valley itself. Despite its harsh name, the valley is actually a thriving wildlife habitat and has supported human life for millennia, from Shoshone tribespeople to Old West pioneers, gold seekers and borax miners. It's the silence and solemnity of the vast expanse that inspires today. That cracked, parched-looking salt pan extending across the valley floor, which suddenly sears your retinas with its dazzling white light, is Badwater. At 282ft below sea level, it's the lowest point in North America. A **boardwalk** hovers over the constantly evaporating bed of salty, mineralized water, almost alien in its beauty. Prehistoric **Lake Manly**, which covered the entire valley during the last ice age, reappeared here in 2005 for the first time in recorded human history, then again in 2015.

Classic Trip

Although the lake evaporated within weeks each time, its reemergence just goes to show the tenacity of life in this deceptively barren-looking valley.

The Drive » Eight miles north of Badwater, past the Natural Bridge turnoff on your right and the bizarre salt crystals of Devils Golf Course on your left, detour along Artists Drive, a one-way 9-mile scenic loop (no vehicles with trailers or over 25ft long). Rejoining Badwater Rd, drive 5 miles north, then go right on Hwy 190 for 3.5 miles to Zabriskie Point.

❹ Zabriskie Point & Dante's View

For spectacular valley views across Death Valley's golden badlands eroded into waves, pleats and gullies, head east of the Inn at Furnace Creek on Hwy 190 to **Zabriskie Point** (Hwy 190; **P**). Escape the valley's midday heat or catch a memorable sunset by continuing 20 miles to **Dante's View** (www.nps.gov/deva; **P**), where you can simultaneously view the highest (Mt Whitney) and lowest (Badwater) points in the contiguous USA. From Zabriskie Point, it's about a half-hour drive: follow Hwy 190, then turn right onto Furnace

Creek Rd, which becomes Dante's View Rd.

The Drive » Backtrack along Dante's View and Furnace Creek Rds to Hwy 190. Turn left and drive 12 miles northwest, staying on Hwy 190 past the Inn at Furnace Creek and the Badwater Rd turnoff before rolling to a dusty stop at Furnace Creek Ranch.

❺ Furnace Creek

At Furnace Creek Ranch, Death Valley National Park's busiest tourist hub, the Borax Museum (p339) lets you poke around historical exhibits about mining and the famous 20-mule teams that hauled mineral ore out of Death Valley. Out back are authentic pioneer-era wagons and stagecoaches. A short drive north of the park's **Furnace Creek Visitor Center** (**✆**760-786-3200; www.nps.gov/deva; ☺8am-5pm; **♿**), walk in the footsteps of Chinese laborers as you examine the adobe ruins of the 1880s **Harmony Borax Works** on a scenic side-trip loop through twisting **Mustard Canyon**.

✕ 🛏 p339

The Drive » If you didn't fill up outside the park, Furnace Creek has an expensive gas station with 24-hour, credit-card pumps. Head north from Furnace Creek on Hwy 190. After fewer than 20 miles, turn left to stay on Hwy 190 west toward Stovepipe Wells Village. Just over 5 miles later, pull into the Mesquite Flat parking lot on your right.

DETOUR: MOJAVE NATIONAL PRESERVE

Start: ❶ Baker (p333)

For even more Wild West history than you'll find in Death Valley's abandoned mines and ghost towns, head into the lonely **Mojave National Preserve** (**✆**760-252-6100; www.nps.gov/moja; **P♿**), southeast of Baker off I-15. Start by touring the beautifully restored **Kelso Depot**, with its modern museum of local history and lore. Drive south to scramble around the **Kelso Dunes**, a field of 'singing' sand that makes strange music when the wind blows just so. Further east at **Hole-in-the-Wall**, scale the cliffs Native Americans used to escape Western ranchers, then drive through **Wild Horse Canyon** or follow the old Mojave Rd blazed by Spanish missionaries, fur trappers and traders and, oddly enough, camels on an 1867 military expedition. Northwest of Cima look for the trailhead for **Teutonia Peak**, a 3-mile round-trip hike through the world's largest forest of Joshua trees, ending with panoramic desert views peppered with colorful cinder cones.

Death Valley National Park Zabriskie Point at sunset

TRIP HIGHLIGHT

6 Mesquite Flat

It's time to take up a famous strand of history in Death Valley: the story of the lost '49ers. When the California gold rush took off in 1849, a small group of pioneers chanced what they hoped would be a shortcut to the California goldfields, leaving behind the Old Spanish Trail. Exhausted, dangerously running out of food and water, and struggling with broken wagons and worn-out pack animals, the woeful group arrived near Furnace Creek on Christmas Eve. Failing to get their wagons across the Panamint Mountains, the survivors slaughtered their oxen and burned their wagons near what today is the Mesquite Flat. Get out of the car to hike up and down across the rolling field of sand dunes that look like a mini Sahara.

🛏 p339

The Drive » You can fill up the gas tank and buy food and drinks at Stovepipe Wells Village. 2 miles further west along Hwy 190. Heading west, you'll pass the side road to Mosaic Canyon on your left before reaching Emigrant Canyon Rd after 9 miles. Turn left and start winding uphill toward Emigrant Pass.

TRIP HIGHLIGHT

7 Emigrant & Wildrose Canyons

Faced with no other choice, the '49er pioneers eventually walked out of torturous Death Valley over **Emigrant Pass**. As they left, one woman reputedly looked back and fatalistically uttered the words: good-bye, death valley. Later pioneers flooded back when gold was discovered in Death Valley, including at **Skidoo**, a boomtown that went bust in the early 20th century, and where the influential silent movie *Greed* was filmed in 1923. Nothing remains of the ghost town site today. Further south, the ruined **Eureka Mine** is en route to vertigo-inducing **Aguereberry Point**, where you can see the Funeral Mountains and the parched valley spread out below. Both of these side trips travel on rough, rutted dirt roads (high-clearance 4WD vehicles recommended). Turn left onto Wildrose Canyon Rd to reach the abandoned **Wildrose Charcoal Kilns**. Built in 1876, these beehive-shaped kilns made the fuel miners needed to process Death Valley's silver and lead

Classic Trip

WHY THIS IS A CLASSIC TRIP
SARA BENSON,
WRITER

Most people think of sunny beaches when you mention southern California But some of the most epic scenery I've ever witnessed through my car's windshield has been in the Mojave Desert. In every season, Death Valley's landscape looks startlingly different. You'll never forget your first view of hillsides painted in spring wildflowers or the sight of vanished prehistoric lakes suddenly reappearing in the salt flats after heavy winter rains.

Top: Decorative doorways at Scotty's Castle
Left: Desert iguana in Death Valley
Right: Goldwell Open Air Museum, Rhyolite

ore. The landscape is subalpine, with forests of piñon pine and juniper; it can be covered with snow, even in spring.

The Drive » Backtrack downhill, turning left at the intersection with Emigrant Canyon Rd onto Wildrose Canyon Rd, which snakes through a flash-flood zone (don't attempt this road except during dry weather). At Panamint Valley Rd, turn right and drive north to Hwy 190, then turn left. The longer all-weather route is to backtrack down Emigrant Canyon Rd to Hwy 190, then turn left for the 22-mile drive to Panamint Springs.

⑧ Panamint Springs

At the far western edge of Death Valley National Park, Panamint Springs is a remote base camp. In spring, you can drive the 2.5-mile graded gravel road, followed by a mile-long cross-country hike, to **Darwin Falls**, where a hidden natural-spring cascade plunges into a gorge, embraced by shady willows and migratory birds. Or get more adventurous and follow roughshod Saline Valley Rd out to **Lee Flat**, where Joshua trees thrive. Or play it safe and stay on the paved highway for about 8 miles west of Panamint Springs Resort to **Father Crowley Point**, which peers deep into **Rainbow Canyon**, created by lava flows and scattered with painterly volcanic cinders.

Classic Trip

The Drive » Turn around and drive back downhill east on Hwy 190. About 7 miles east of Stovepipe Wells Village, turn left and then right onto Daylight Pass Rd for 16 miles, exiting the park and following Hwy 374 into Nevada for 9 miles to the signposted turn-off for Rhyolite on your left.

TRIP HIGHLIGHT

9 Rhyolite

Just 4 miles west of Beatty, Nevada (see Sleeping option, p339), **Rhyolite** (www.rhyolitesite.com; off Hwy 374; ☼ sunrise-sunset; P 🚻) was the queen of Death Valley's mines during its heyday. It epitomizes the hurly-burly, boom-and-bust story of Western gold-rush mining towns. Don't miss the 1906 'bottle house' or the skeletal remains of a three-story bank. Also here is the bizarre **Goldwell Open Air Museum** (☎702-870-9946; www.goldwellmuseum.org; off Hwy 374; ☼24hr; P 🚻), a trippy art installation started by Belgian artist Albert Szukalski in 1984. One favorite piece: the giant-sized miner with a pet penguin.

SCOTTY'S CASTLE

Walter E Scott, alias 'Death Valley Scotty,' was the quintessential tall-tale teller who captivated people with his stories of gold. His most lucrative friendship was with Albert and Bessie Johnson, a wealthy insurance magnate and his wife from Chicago. Despite knowing that Scotty was a freeloading liar, the Johnsons bankrolled a whimsical, elaborately constructed desert estate here in Death Valley during the 1920s. Nicknamed Scotty's Castle, the Johnsons' historic home has been restored to its 1939 appearance, featuring sheepskin drapes, carved California redwood, handmade tiles, wrought iron, woven Shoshone baskets and a bellowing pipe organ upstairs.

In 2015, a massive flood in Grapevine Canyon significantly damaged the access road to Scotty's Castle and several historic structures. While repairs are ongoing, the castle remains closed to visitors, probably until 2019. Check the official national park website (www.nps.gov/deva) for updates.

The Drive » Backtrack down Daylight Pass Rd, turning right onto Scotty's Castle Rd, which winds for over 33 miles through the valley, shadowed by the Grapevine Mountains. Turn left near the ranger station at Grapevine Junction onto the side road leading over 5 miles northwest toward Ubehebe Crater.

10 Ubehebe Crater

West of Grapevine Junction, a rough dirt road rumbles out to an overlook of 600ft-deep Ubehebe Crater, formed by the explosive meeting of fiery magma and cool ground-water. Once thought to be an ancient volcano, scientists have come to believe that this volcano exploded possibly as recently as just 300 years ago. Hikers can make a 1.5-mile loop around the rim and over to younger **Little Hebe Crater**, for astounding views into the volcanic depths and over rainbow-colored cinder fields lying scattered over the valley floor.

Eating & Sleeping

Tecopa ❷

🛏 Cynthia's   Hostel, Inn $$

(📞760-852-4580; www.discovercynthias.com; 2001 Old Spanish Trail Hwy, Tecopa; dm $25, r $100-140, tipis from $165; ⊙ check-in 3-8pm; [P] 🛜) Match your budget to a bed at this congenial inn helmed by the friendly Cynthia, about 3 miles from central Tecopa. Your choices: a colorful and eclectically decorated private room in a vintage trailer, a bed in a dorm, or a Native American–style tipi (a short drive away) with thick rugs, fire pits and comfy king-size beds.

Furnace Creek ❺

✖ 19th Hole Bar & Grill   American $

(📞760-786-2345; www.furnacecreekresort. com; Furnace Creek Golf Course, off Hwy 190; mains $8-12; ⊙ seasonal hours vary; [♿]) On the golf course, this place has the juiciest burgers in the park. Sit on the verandah with views of the Panamint Range.

✖ 49'er Cafe   American $$

(📞760-786-2345; www.furnacecreekresort. com; Ranch at Furnace Creek, Hwy 190; mains breakfast $9-16, lunch $13-20, dinner $10-25; ⊙6-10am & 11am-9pm Oct-May, 4-9pm only Jun-Sep; 🛜[♿]) The smallest of the Ranch's main restaurants, this family-friendly stop serves giant omelets, eggs Benedict and pancakes for breakfast, plus fish and chips, sandwiches and burgers for lunch.

🛏 Death Valley National Park Campgrounds   Campground $

(www.nps.gov/deva; campsites free-$30; [P]🐾) Of the park's nine campgrounds, only Furnace Creek accepts **reservations** (📞877-444-6777, international 518-885-3639; www. recreation.gov) between mid-October and mid-April. In summer, Furnace Creek is first-come, first-served, and the only other campgrounds open are Mesquite Spring, near Scotty's Castle,

and those along Emigrant Canyon Rd, west of Stovepipe Wells.

🛏 Ranch at Furnace Creek   Resort $$

(📞760-786-2345; www.furnacecreekresort.com; Hwy 190, Furnace Creek; cabin/r from $149/189; [P]⊖❄🛜💦) Tailor-made for families, this rambling resort with multiple, motel-style buildings has received a vigorous facelift, resulting in spiffy rooms swathed in desert colors, updated bathrooms and French doors leading to porches with comfortable patio furniture. The grounds encompass a playground, spring-fed swimming pool, tennis courts, golf course, restaurants, shops and the **Borax Museum** (⊙9am-9pm Oct-May, variable in summer; [P][♿]).

Mesquite Flat ❻

🛏 Stovepipe Wells Hotel   Motel $$

(📞760-786-2387; www.deathvalleyhotels. com; 51880 Hwy 190, Stovepipe Wells; RV sites $33, r $120-210; [P]⊖❄@🛜💦🐾) The 83 rooms at this sea-level tourist village are newly spruced-up and have quality linens beneath Death Valley–themed artwork, cheerful Native American–patterned bedspreads, coffeemakers and TVs (but no phones). The small pool is cool and the cowboy-style **Toll Road Restaurant** (dinner mains $13-26; ⊙7-10am & 5:30-9pm; 🛜[♿]) serves breakfast and dinner daily, with lunch available in the next-door **Badwater Saloon** (⊙11:30am-9pm or later).

Beatty, Nevada

🛏 Stagecoach Hotel & Casino   Motel $

(📞800-424-4946, 775-553-2419; www. bestdeathvalleyhotels.com; 900 E Hwy 95 N; r $70-100; [P]❄🛜💦🐾) At the edge of town, rooms are pretty bland but large and comfy, while the pool is a nice place to lounge away a dusty day in Death Valley. There's also a small, smoky casino – hello, Nevada! – for slots, blackjack and roulette, and a kids' arcade.

Palm Springs & Joshua Tree Oases

32

Southern California's deserts can be brutally hot, barren places — escape to Palm Springs and Joshua Tree National Park, where shady fan-palm oases and date gardens await.

TRIP HIGHLIGHTS

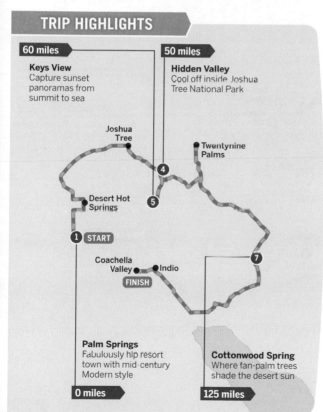

60 miles

Keys View
Capture sunset panoramas from summit to sea

50 miles

Hidden Valley
Cool off inside Joshua Tree National Park

Joshua Tree

Twentynine Palms

4

Desert Hot Springs

5

1 START

Coachella Valley • Indio

FINISH

7

Palm Springs
Fabulously hip resort town with mid-century Modern style

0 miles

Cottonwood Spring
Where fan-palm trees shade the desert sun

125 miles

2–3 DAYS
170 MILES / 275KM

GREAT FOR...

BEST TIME TO GO

February to April for spring wildflower blooms and cooler temperatures.

ESSENTIAL PHOTO

Sunset from Keys View.

BEST FOR SOLITUDE

Hike to the Lost Palms Oasis.

Joshua Tree National Park Standing among larger-than-life boulders

32

Palm Springs & Joshua Tree Oases

Just a short drive from the chic resorts of Palm Springs, the vast Mojave and Sonoran Deserts are serenely spiritual places. You may find that what at first looked like desolate sands transform on foot into perfect beauty: shady palm tree and cactus gardens, tiny wildflowers pushing up from hard-baked soil in spring, natural hot-springs pools for soaking, and uncountable stars overhead in the inky dark.

TRIP HIGHLIGHT

❶ Palm Springs

Hollywood celebs have always counted on Palm Springs as a quick escape from LA. Today, this desert resort town shows off a trove of well-preserved mid-Century Modern buildings. Stop at the **Palm Springs Official Visitors Center** (☎800-347-7746, 760-778-8418; www.visitpalmsprings. com; 2901 N Palm Canyon Dr; ⏰9am-5pm), inside a 1965 gas station by modernist Albert Frey, to pick up a

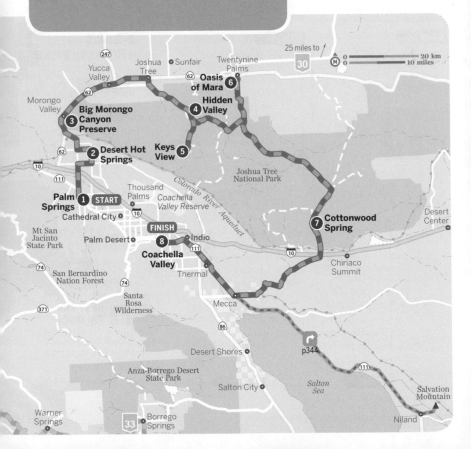

self-guided architectural tour map. Then drive uphill to clamber aboard the **Palm Springs Aerial Tramway** (📞760-325-1449, 888-515-8726; www.pstramway.com; 1 Tram Way; adult/child $25/17; ⏰1st tram up 10am Mon-Fri, 8am Sat & Sun, last tram down 8pm daily; 🅿🚻), which climbs nearly 6000 vertical feet from the hot Sonoran Desert floor to the cool, even snowy, San Jacinto Mountains in less than 15 minutes. Back down on the ground, drive south on Palm Canyon Dr, where you can hop between art galleries, cafes, cocktail bars and chic boutiques such as fashionistas' find **Trina Turk** (📞760-416-2856; www.trinaturk.com; 891 N Palm Canyon Dr; ⏰10am-6pm Mon-Sat, 11am-5pm Sun).

LINK YOUR TRIP

30 **Route 66**
Follow Hwy 62 east of Twentynine Palms, turn left onto Godwin Rd, then right onto Amboy Rd for a 50-mile journey to join America's 'Mother Road.'

33 **Temecula, Julian & Anza-Borrego**
From Mecca, drive along the Salton Sea's western shore, then head inland to Borrego Springs, a 50-mile trip.

🍴 🛏 p47, p346

The Drive » Drive north out of downtown Palm Springs along Indian Canyon Dr for 7 miles, passing over the I-10. Turn right onto Dillon Rd, then after 2.5 miles turn left onto Palm Dr, which heads north into central Desert Hot Springs.

② Desert Hot Springs

In 1774 Spanish explorer Juan Bautista de Anza was the first European to encounter the desert Cahuilla tribe. Afterward, the Spanish name Agua Caliente came to refer to both the indigenous people and the natural hot springs, which still flow restoratively today through the town of **Desert Hot Springs** (www.visitdeserthotsprings.com), where newly hip boutique hotels have appeared atop healing waters bubbling up from deep below. Imitate Tim Robbins in Robert Altman's film *The Player* and have a mud bath at **Two Bunch Palms Spa Resort** (📞760-329-8791; www.twobunchpalms.com; 67425 Two Bunch Palms Trail; day-spa package from $195; ⏰by reservation only), which sits atop an actual oasis. Bounce between a variety of pools and sunbathing areas, but maintain the code of silence (actually, whispers only).

🍴 🛏 p346

The Drive » Head west on Pierson Blvd back to Indian Canyon Dr. Turn right and drive northwest through the dusty outskirts of Desert Hot Springs. Turn right onto Hwy 62 eastbound toward Yucca Valley; after about 4 miles, turn right onto East Dr and look for signs for Big Morongo Canyon Preserve.

③ Big Morongo Canyon Preserve

An oasis hidden in the high desert, **Big Morongo Canyon Preserve** (📞760-363-7190; www.bigmorongo.org; 11055 East Dr, Yucca Valley; donations accepted; ⏰7:30am-sunset; 🅿🚻) is a bird-watching hotspot. Tucked into the Little San Bernardino Mountains, this stream-fed riparian habitat is flush with cottonwood and willow trees. Start from the educational kiosk by the parking lot, then tramp along wooden boardwalks through marshy woodlands as hummingbirds flutter atop flowers and woodpeckers hammer away.

The Drive » Rejoin Hwy 62 eastbound past Yucca Valley, with its roadside antiques and vintage shops, art galleries and cafes, to the town of Joshua Tree (see Sleeping & Eating options, p346 and p347) about 16 miles away, where you'll find places to sleep and eat. At the intersection with Park Blvd, turn right and drive 5 miles to Joshua Tree National Park's west entrance. Make sure you've got a full tank of gas first.

❹ Hidden Valley

It's time to jump into **Joshua Tree National Park** (📞760-367-5500; www.nps.gov/jotr; 7-day entry per car $20; 🕐24hr; [P] [♿]), a wonderland of jumbo rocks interspersed with sandy forests of Joshua trees. Related to agave plants, Joshua trees were named by Mormon settlers who thought the twisted, spiky arms resembled a prophet's arms stretching toward God. Revel in the scenery as you drive along the winding park road for about 8 miles to Hidden Valley picnic area. Turn left and drive past the campground to the trailhead for **Barker Dam**. Here a kid-friendly nature trail loops for just over a mile past a pretty

little artificial lake and a rock incised with Native American petroglyphs. If you enjoy history and Western lore, reserve ahead for a 90-minute guided walking tour of nearby **Keys Ranch** (📞reservations 760-367-5522; www.nps.gov/jotr/; tour adult/child $10/5; 🕐 tour schedules vary, reservations required; [P] [♿]), where 19th-century pioneer homesteaders tried their hand at cattle ranching, mining and desert farming.

🛏 p347

The Drive » Backtrack to Park Blvd, turn left and head south again past jumbled rock formations and fields of spiky Joshua trees. Take the well-signed right turn toward Keys View. You'll pass several trailheads and roadside interpretive exhibits over the next 5.5 miles leading up to the viewpoint.

DETOUR: SALTON SEA & SALVATION MOUNTAIN

Start: ❼ Cottonwood Spring (p345)

Driving along Hwy 111 southeast of Mecca, it's a most unexpected sight: California's largest lake in the middle of its largest desert. In 1905 the Colorado River breached, giving birth to the Salton Sea. Marketed to mid-20th-century tourists as the 'California Riviera' with beachfront vacation homes, the Salton Sea has been mostly abandoned because of the stinky annual fish die-offs caused by chemical runoff from surrounding farmland. An even stranger sight is folk-art **Salvation Mountain** (www.salvationmountaininc.org; 601 E Beal Rd, Niland; donations accepted; [P]), an artificial hill covered in acrylic paint and found objects and inscribed with Christian religious messages. It's outside Niland, about 3 miles east of Hwy 111 en route to Slab City.

❺ Keys View

Make sure you embark at least an hour before sunset for the drive up to Keys View (5185ft), where panoramic views look into the **Coachella Valley** and reach as far south as the shimmering Salton Sea or, on an unusually clear day, Mexico's **Signal Mountain**. Looming in front of you are **Mt San Jacinto** (10,800ft) and **Mt San Gorgonio** (11,500ft), two of Southern California's highest peaks, often snow-dusted even in spring. Down below snakes the shaky **San Andreas Fault**.

The Drive » Head back downhill to Park Blvd. Turn right and wind through the park's Wonderland of Rocks, where boulders call out to scampering kids and serious rock jocks alike, passing more campgrounds. After 10 miles, veer left to stay on Park Blvd and drive north for 8 miles toward the town of Twentynine Palms onto Utah Trail.

❻ Oasis of Mara

Drop by Joshua Tree National Park's **Oasis Park Visitor Center** (www.nps.gov/jotr; 74485 National Park Dr, Twentynine Palms; 🕐8:30am-5pm; [♿]) for its educational exhibits about Southern California's desert fan palms. These palms are often found growing along fault lines, where cracks in the earth's crust allow subterranean water to surface. Outside the visitors center, a gentle half-mile nature trail leads around the Oasis of Mara, where Serrano peoples once camped. Ask for directions to the trailhead off Hwy 62 for the 3-mile, round-trip hike to **49 Palms Oasis**, where a sun-exposed dirt trail marches you over a ridge, then drops you into a rocky gorge, doggedly heading down toward a distant speck of green.

🛏 p347

The Drive » Drive back south on Utah Trail and re-enter the park. Follow Park Blvd south, turning left at the first major junction onto Pinto Basin Rd for a winding 30-mile drive southeast to Cottonwood Spring.

Joshua Tree National Park Cholla Cactus Garden

TRIP HIGHLIGHT

7 Cottonwood Spring

On your drive to Cottonwood Spring, you'll pass from the high Mojave Desert into the lower Sonoran Desert. At the **Cholla Cactus Garden**, handily labeled specimens burst into bloom in spring, including unmistakable ocotillo plants, which look like green octopus tentacles adorned with flaming scarlet flowers. Turn left at the **Cottonwood Visitor Center** (www. nps.gov/jotr; Cottonwood Springs, 8 miles north of I-10 Fwy; ◷8:30am-4pm; 🚻) for

a short drive east past the campground to Cottonwood Spring. Once used by the Cahuilla, who left behind archaeological evidence such as mortars and clay pots, the springs became a hotbed for gold mining in the late 19th century. The now-dry springs are the start of the moderately strenuous 7.2-mile round-trip trek out to **Lost Palms Oasis**, a fan-palm oasis blessed with solitude and scenery.

🛏 p347

The Drive » Head south from Cottonwood Springs and drive across the I-10 to pick up scenic Box Canyon Rd, which twists its way toward the Salton Sea. Take 66th Ave west to Mecca, then turn right onto Hwy 111 and drive northwest (up valley) toward Indio.

8 Coachella Valley

The hot but fertile Coachella Valley is the ideal place to find the date of your dreams – the kind that grows on trees, that is. Date farms let you sample exotic-sounding varieties like halawy, deglet noor and zahidi for free, but the signature taste of the valley is a rich date shake from certified-organic **Oasis Date Gardens** (📞760-399-5665; www.oasisdate.com; 59-111 Grapefruit Blvd, Thermal; ◷9am-4pm; P 🚻) or the 1920s pioneer **Shields Date Garden** (📞760-347-7768; www.shieldsdategarden. com; 80-225 Hwy 111, Indio; ◷9am-5pm; P 🚻).

Eating & Sleeping

Palm Springs ❶

✖ Cheeky's   Californian $

(☎760-327-7595; www.cheekysps.com; 622
N Palm Canyon Dr; mains $9-14; ⊙8am-2pm
Thu-Mon, last seating 1:30pm) Waits can be long
and service only so-so, but the farm-to-table
menu dazzles with witty inventiveness. Dishes
change weekly, but custardy scrambled eggs,
chilaquiles and bacon bar 'flights' keep making
appearances.

✖ Sherman's   Deli, Bakery $$

(☎760-325-1199; www.shermansdeli.com; 401 E
Tahquitz Canyon Way; mains $9-19; ⊙7am-9pm;
⊕ 🏵) Every community with a sizeable retired
contingent needs a good Jewish deli. Sherman's
is it. With a breezy sidewalk patio, it pulls in an
all-ages crowd with its 40 sandwich varieties
(great hot pastrami!), finger-lickin' rotisserie
chicken, lox and bagels, and to-die-for pies.
Walls are festooned with head shots of celebrity
regulars, including Don Rickles.

🛏 Orbit In   Boutique Hotel $$

(☎877-966-7248, 760-323-3585; www.
orbitin.com; 562 W Arenas Rd; r $139-269;
P ⊖ ❄ 🛜 🏊) Swing back to the '50s – pinkie
raised and all – during the 'Orbitini' happy hour
at this fabulously retro property, with high-end
mid-Century Modern furniture (Eames, Noguchi
et al) in rooms set around a quiet saline pool
with a spa bath and fire pit. The long list of
freebies includes bike rentals and poolside
refreshments.

🛏 Parker Palm Springs   Resort $$$

(☎760-770-5000; www.theparkerpalmsprings.
com; 4200 E Palm Canyon Dr; r from $280;
P ⊖ ❄ @ 🛜 🏊 🏵) Featured in the Bravo
TV series *Welcome to the Parker*, this posh
resort highlights whimsical decor by Jonathan
Adler. Drop by for a cocktail at Mister Parker's
or a posh brunch at Norma's five-star coffee
shop. The grounds boast hammocks, croquet,
petanque and a fabulous spa. The $30 resort
charge covers parking, wi-fi, and access to the

Palm Springs Yacht Club spa (☎760-
321-4606; www.theparkerpalmsprings.com/spa;
⊙by appointment only).

Desert Hot Springs ❷

🛏 El Morocco
Inn & Spa   Boutique Hotel $$

(☎760-288-2527, 888-288-9905; http://
elmoroccoinn.com; 66810 4th St, Desert Hot
Springs; r $179-219; P ⊖ ❄ 🛜 🏊) Heed the
call of the casbah at this drop-dead gorgeous
hideaway where the scene is set for romance.
Twelve exotically furnished rooms wrap around
a pool deck where your enthusiastic host
serves free 'Morocco-tinis' during happy hour.
Other perks: on-site spa, huge DVD library and
delicious homemade mint iced tea.

🛏 Spring   Boutique Hotel $$

(☎760-251-6700; www.the-spring.com; 12699
Reposo Way; r $159-299; P ⊖ ❄ 🛜 🏊)
Splash out in this humble 1950s motel that's
morphed into a chic, whisper-quiet spa retreat
where natural hot mineral water feeds three
pools. The dozen rooms are minimalist in design
but not in amenities (rich linens, fluffy robes,
small kitchens). Achieve a state of bliss while
enjoying a treatment or simply calming valley
and mountain views.

Joshua Tree

✖ Pie for the People   Pizza $$

(☎760-366-0400; www.pieforthepeople.
com; 61740 Hwy 62, Joshua Tree; pizzas $11-25;
⊙11am-9pm Mon-Thu, to 10pm Fri & Sat, to
8pm Sun; ⊕) Thin-crust pizzas for takeout and
delivery. Flavors span standards to the David
Bowie: white pizza with mozzarella, Guinness
caramelized onions, jalapenos, pineapple,
bacon, and sweet plum sauce. Enjoy yours
under the exposed rafters in the wood and
corrugated-metal dining room, or under the
tree on the back patio.

🛏 Hicksville Trailer Palace   Motel $$

(📞310-584-1086; www.hicksville.com; d $100-250; P ❄ 📶 🖥 🐾) Fancy sleeping among glowing wigs, in a haunted house, or in a horse stall? Check in at Hicksville, where 'rooms' are eight outlandishly decorated vintage trailers set around a kidney-shaped, saltwater swimming pool. The vision of LA writer and director Morgan Higby Night, each offers a journey into a unique, surreal and slightly wicked world. All but two share facilities.

🛏 Spin & Margie's Desert Hide-a-Way   Inn $$

(📞760-774-0850, 760-366-9124; www.deserthideaway.com; 64491 Hwy 62; d $145-185; P 🚭 ❄ 📶) This handsome hacienda-style inn is perfect for restoring calm after a long day on the road. The five boldly colored suites are an eccentric symphony of corrugated tin, old license plates and cartoon art. Each has its own kitchen and flat-screen TV with DVD and CD player. Knowledgeable, gregarious owners ensure a relaxed visit.

It's down the dirt Sunkist Rd, off Hwy 62, about 3 miles east of downtown Joshua Tree.

Joshua Tree National Park ❹❻❼

🛏 Joshua Tree National Park Campgrounds   Campground $

(📞reservations 877-444-6777; www.recreation.gov; tent & RV sites $15-20; P 🐾) Of the park's eight campgrounds, only Cottonwood and Black Rock have potable water, flush toilets and dump stations. Indian Cove and Black Rock accept reservations between October and May; the others are first-come, first-served. None have showers. Backcountry camping (no campfires) is allowed 1 mile from any road and 500ft from any trail or water source; free self-registration required.

Temecula, Julian & Anza-Borrego

33

Make a weekend getaway from San Diego to Temecula's Wild West wine country; Julian, a gold-mining town surrounded by hills and fruit orchards; and the desert resort of Borrego Springs.

TRIP HIGHLIGHTS

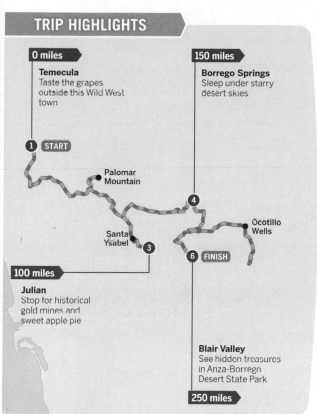

0 miles

Temecula
Taste the grapes outside this Wild West town

1 START

Palomar Mountain

Santa Ysabel

3

100 miles

Julian
Stop for historical gold mines and sweet apple pie

150 miles

Borrego Springs
Sleep under starry desert skies

4

Ocotillo Wells

6 FINISH

Blair Valley
See hidden treasures in Anza-Borrego Desert State Park

250 miles

**3 DAYS
250 MILES / 402KM**

GREAT FOR...

BEST TIME TO GO

February to April for wildflowers and moderate temperatures.

ESSENTIAL PHOTO

Font's Point in Anza-Borrego Desert State Park.

BEST FOR FAMILIES

Julian's apple pie and gold mine tours.

33 Temecula, Julian & Anza-Borrego

In just about any season, incredible scenery will roll past your windshield on this SoCal sojourn. In spring, the desert comes alive with a riot of wildflowers and ocotillo plants with scarlet blooms. In autumn, you can pick apples in Julian's pastoral orchards and celebrate the grape harvest in Temecula's vineyards. For a winter warm-up, escape to Borrego Springs' desert resorts. In summer, cool off in the mountains outside Julian.

TRIP HIGHLIGHT

❶ Temecula

Luiseño peoples, who were present when the first Spanish missionary visited in 1797, called this desert place *temecunga* (place of the sun). It became a ranching outpost for Mission San Luis Rey in the 1820s, and later a stop along the Butterfield stagecoach line and California Southern Railroad. Hiding behind the Old West facades lining Front St in **Old Town** today are antique shops

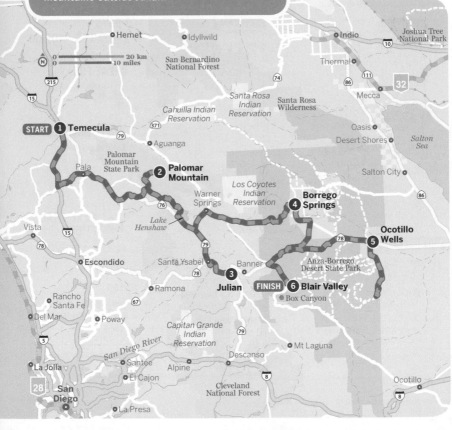

and wine-tasting bars. **Temecula Olive Oil Company** (951-693-4029; www.temeculaoliveoil.com; 28653 Old Town Front St; ⏱9:30am-6pm Sun-Thu, to 7pm Fri & Sat) offers free samples of its herb- and citrus-infused oils, some pressed from the same types of olives that Spanish priests cultivated at 18th-century California missions.

Although you may imagine there's nothing but desert down here, Temecula is only 20 miles inland from the Pacific. Every night, coastal fog and ocean breezes blow inland to cool down the valley's citrus groves and vineyards. Wine grapes flourish, especially sun-seeking Mediterranean varietals. A 10-minute drive east of Old Town

LINK YOUR TRIP

28 Fun on the San Diego Coast

San Diego's sunny and bodacious beach towns are only an hour's drive southwest of Temecula's vineyards.

32 Palm Springs & Joshua Tree Oases

From Borrego Springs, drive east toward the Salton Sea, then north to the Coachella Valley's date farms, a 50-mile trip.

along Rancho California Rd, you'll find the most popular **wineries** (www.temeculawines.org) with patio views of vine-planted hillsides. If you don't like crowds, start your wine tasting fairly early in the day, especially on weekends. Visit family-owned wineries with less crowded tasting rooms by following the **De Portola Wine Trail** (www.deportolawinetrail.com).

 p355

The Drive » From Temecula, take the I-15 south 11 miles to the Pala exit. Turn left onto Hwy 76 eastbound, which winds through wide green valleys bordered by citrus groves, protea farms and mountains. After about 20 miles, take the signposted left turn onto County Rd (CR) S6, aka South Grade Rd, which climbs 11.5 miles up Palomar Mountain.

- - - - - - - - - - - -

❷ Palomar Mountain

Run by Pasadena's prestigious California Institute of Technology (CalTech) university, white-domed **Palomar Observatory** (760-742-2119; www.astro.caltech.edu/palomar/visitor/; 35899 Canfield Rd; tour adult/child $5/3; ⏱ usually 9am-4pm, to 3pm early Nov-mid-Mar; P ⏺) has a lofty perch atop Palomar Mountain (6140ft). On weekends between April and October, guided tours (no reservations) focus on the dome's history and current

scientific research. They'll also let you peek at the 200in Hale Telescope, once the world's largest. Bring a fleece jacket – temperatures inside the observatory hover just above freezing during some months of the year. Call ahead to check road conditions and opening hours before making the long, winding drive here. Even if you're not a science geek, the sprawling views of the San Diego backcountry from the summit are worth the trip. To stretch your legs, nearby **Palomar Mountain State Park** (760-742-3462; www.parks.ca.gov; 19952 State Park Dr, Palomar Mountain; per car $8; ⏱dawn-dusk; P ⏺) has forested hikes along panoramic-view trails where wildflowers bloom in early summer.

 p355

The Drive » Drive 4.5 miles back down CR S6, then turn left onto CR S7, which winds southeast 11 miles down the mountain. Turn left onto Hwy 76 and drive east past Lake Henshaw to Hwy 79. Turn right, heading south toward Santa Ysabel, where you can stop for a bite to eat (see p355), then take a left onto Hwy 78 to Julian.

- - - - - - - - - - - -

TRIP HIGHLIGHT

❸ Julian

Winding through pine-covered mountains and tree-shaded valleys, you'll arrive at Julian. Settled by ex-Confederate soldiers after the Civil War, flecks of gold were found in the creek here in 1869, sparking a short-lived burst of speculation. Be regaled with tales of the hardscrabble life of early pioneers at **Eagle Mining Co** (📞442-777-8646; www.theeaglemining.com; 2320 C St; adult/child $10/5; ⏰10am-4pm Mon-Fri, to 5pm Sat & Sun; 🅿️ ♿), where tour guides lead you through the underground tunnels of the authentic 19th-century hard-rock Eagle and High Peak gold mines.

Although not much mineral ore was ever extracted from Julian's hills, more lasting riches were found in its fertile soil. Today, apple orchards fill the surrounding countryside. The **Apple Days** harvest festival takes place in late September, but crowds descend year-round on Julian's pint-sized **Main Street**, where false-fronted shops along the wooden sidewalks all claim to make the very best apple pie – you'll have to be the judge of that.

 p355

The Drive » Backtrack 7 miles west of Julian on Hwy 78. Turn right onto Hwy 79 northbound through Santa Ysabel toward Warner Springs. Turn right onto CR S2 (San Felipe Rd), then almost 5 miles later take a left onto CR S22 (Montezuma Valley Rd), which twists and turns its way down to Borrego Springs, revealing panoramic desert views.

- - - - - - - - - -

TRIP HIGHLIGHT

❹ Borrego Springs

Lonely, wind-buffeted Borrego Springs is the only settlement to speak of in **Anza-Borrego Desert State Park** (📞760-767-5311; www.parks.ca.gov; per car $5; 🅿️ ♿), the largest US state park outside Alaska, comprising almost a fifth of San Diego County and extending south almost to Mexico. Pick up information on hiking trails and road conditions at the visitor center.

Northeast of Borrego Springs, where CR S22 takes a 90-degree turn to the east, there's a pile of rocks just north of the road. This, the **Peg Leg Smith Monument**, commemorates Thomas

Long Smith: mountain man, fur trapper, horse thief, liar and Wild West legend. Show up on the first Saturday of April for the hilarious **Peg Leg Smith Liars Contest**.

Further east of Borrego, a signed 4-mile dirt road (sometimes passable without a 4WD) heads south of CR S22 to **Font's Point**, where the desert seemingly drops from beneath your feet. Views stretch over the entire Borrego Valley to the west and the park's eroded badlands to the south.

🍴 🛏️ p355

The Drive » From Christmas Tree Circle in Borrego Springs, follow Borrego Springs Rd south onto Yaqui Pass Rd, which dramatically twists down a narrow pass into the desert badlands below, passing hiking trailheads and campgrounds. Turn left onto Hwy 78 and drive 16 miles east to Ocotillo Wells. By the airport, turn right and drive south on Split Mountain Rd.

- - - - - - - - - - - - -

❺ Ocotillo Wells

To escape the roaring off-highway vehicles (OHVs) around Ocotillo Wells, follow Split Mountain Rd onto state park land. About 6 miles south of Hwy 78, you'll pass the **Elephant Trees Discovery Trail**. Related to myrrh, these fragrant trees were thought not to exist in the Colorado Desert until a full-fledged hunt was launched in

WATCHING WILDFLOWERS

Depending on winter rains, wildflowers bloom brilliantly, albeit briefly, in Anza-Borrego Desert State Park starting in late February, making a striking contrast to the desert's usually subtle earth tones. Call the Wildflower Hotline (📞760-767-4684) or check the park website (www.parks.ca.gov) to find out what's blooming right now.

Anza-Borrego Desert State Park Spring wildflowers in bloom

1937. Today, several dozen living trees survive, and you'll encounter plenty of other desert flora along this 1.5-mile loop hike. Another 4 miles south along Split Mountain Rd is the dirt-road turnoff for primitive Fish Creek campground. A 4WD road continues for another 6 miles right through **Split Mountain**, its 600ft-high walls created by earthquakes and erosion. At the gorge's southern end, a steep trail leads up to delicate wind caves carved into the sandstone outcrops.

The Drive » Retrace your drive on Split Mountain Rd to Hwy 78, turning left and heading back west past the Yaqui Pass turnoff for another 7 miles to Scissors Crossing. Turn left

onto CR S2 south, which passes ranchlands for the next 6 miles before reaching the signed Blair Valley turnoff on your left.

- - - - - - - - - - - - - -

TRIP HIGHLIGHT

❻ Blair Valley

This peaceful desert valley abounds with Native American pictographs and *morteros* (hollows in rocks used for grinding seeds), which you can see along hiking trails leading off the dirt road that loops around the valley east of CR S2. A steep scramble of less than a mile leads to **Ghost Mountain** and the remains of a Depression-era homestead occupied by the family of desert recluse Marshal South. On the north side of

the valley at Foot and Walker Pass, a roadside **historical monument** marks a difficult spot on the Butterfield Overland Mail Route. A few miles further south along CR S2 at **Box Canyon**, you can still see the marks where wagons had to hack through the rocks to widen the Mormon pioneers' original trail.

The Drive » Keep following CR S2 south through the park, winding downhill though grassy valleys that look like oases, and county-run campgrounds and parks, including hot-springs pools. About 26 miles after leaving Box Canyon, look for the Carrizo Badlands Overlook pull-off on your left. From there, it's just 13 miles south to the I-8, which heads west to San Diego.

Eating & Sleeping

Temecula ❶

✗ Restaurant at Ponte   Californian **$$$**
(📞951-252-1770; www.pontewinery.com; Ponte Winery, 35053 Rancho California Rd; mains $18-42; ⏱11am-4pm Mon-Thu, to 8pm Fri & Sat, to 5pm Sun) New American cuisine melds with farm-fresh flavors at this busy winery bistro, a favorite for weekend brunch on the airy patio.

✗ Swing Inn Cafe   Diner **$**
(📞951-676-2321; www.swinginncafe.com; 28676 Old Town Front St; mains $7-13; ⏱5am-9pm; 🚹) A proud local institution since 1927, with red leatherette seating and windows to watch the world go by. The Swing Inn serves three square meals, but everyone goes for breakfast – luckily it's served all day.

🛏 South Coast Winery Resort & Spa   Hotel **$$$**
(📞866-994-6379, 951-587-9463; www.southcoastwinery.com; 34843 Rancho California Rd; d from $199; P⊖❄🕸🎱) A very Temecula way to stay – 76 spacious villa rooms dot the edge of the vineyards, around a spa, fitness facility and recently built 50-suite hotel. Your room key comes with a wine glossary, and rates include a bottle of wine, but not the nightly 'resort fee' ($19).

Palomar Mountain ❷

✗ Round Up Grill   American **$**
(📞760-782-2729; www.lakehenshawresort.com; 26439 Hwy 76; mains $7-17; ⏱ usually 11am-7pm Mon-Thu, from 7am Fri-Sun; 🚹) Fuel up after your trip up Palomar Mountain with a burger or a rib-sticking Western barbecue. It's across the road from Lake Henshaw.

Santa Ysabel

✗ Dudley's Famous Bakery   Deli, Bakery **$**
(📞760-765-0488; www.dudleysbakery.com; 30218 Hwy 78; items $3-10; ⏱shop 8am-5pm Thu-Sun, deli 9am-3pm Thu, 8am-4pm Fri-Sun; 🚹) Generations of San Diegans have stopped by Dudley's to pick up picnic lunches and fresh-baked loaves of bread in almost two dozen different flavors.

Julian ❸

✗ Julian Pie Company   Bakery **$**
(📞760-765-2449; www.julianpie.com; 2225 Main St; snacks & pies $3-15; ⏱9am-5pm; 🍴🚹) This popular joint churns out apple cider, cinnamon-dusted cider donuts and classic apple-filled pies and pastries.

🛏 Julian Gold Rush Hotel   B&B **$$**
(📞760-765-0201; www.julianhotel.com; 2032 Main St; d $95-210; P⊖❄🎱) At this 1897 antique-filled B&B, lace curtains, claw-foot tubs and other paraphernalia evoke a bygone era.

Borrego Springs ❹

✗ Carlee's Place   American **$$**
(📞760-767-3262; www.carleesplace.com; 660 Palm Canyon Dr, Borrego Springs; mains lunch $8-14, dinner $12-27; ⏱11am-9pm, bar to 10pm Sun-Thu, midnight Fri & Sat) Even though the decor feels like it hasn't been updated since the 1970s, locals pick Carlee's for its burgers, pastas and steak dinners.

🛏 Borrego Palm Canyon Campground   Campground **$**
(📞800-444-7275; www.reserveamerica.com; off Palm Canyon Dr; tent/RV sites $25/35; P🎱) Near the state-park visitor center, this campground has award-winning toilets, close-together campsites and an amphitheater with ranger programs.

🛏 Borrego Valley Inn   Inn **$$**
(📞760 767 0311; www.highwaywestvacations.com; 405 Palm Canyon Dr, Borrego Springs; r $140-275; P⊖❄🕸🎱) This petite inn, filled with Southwestern knickknacks and Native American weavings, is an intimate spa resort, perfect for adults. There are 15 rooms on almost 10 acres; most rooms have kitchenettes.

STRETCH YOUR LEGS LOS ANGELES

Start/Finish Union Station

Distance 3.5 miles

Duration 4–6 hours

Nobody walks in LA? That's just not true in Downtown's historic core. Sample the jumbled sights, sounds and tastes of the city's Mexican, Asian and European heritage, with iconic architecture and famous TV and film locations, on this half-day ramble.

Take this walk on Trips

Union Station

This majestic 1939 **edifice** (www.amtrak. com; 800 N Alameda St; **P**) was the last of America's grand railway stations to be built. Walk into the waiting room, its glamorous interior glimpsed in dozens of movies and hit TV shows from *Speed* to *24*. Bordered by tall palm trees, the stately exterior is a uniquely Californian fusion of Mission Revival and art-deco streamline moderne styles.

The Walk ≫ Walk a block up N Alameda St, cross over W Cesar E Chavez Ave and walk west a half block. Turn left down the passageway of Olvera St.

El Pueblo de Los Angeles

Compact, colorful and car-free, this **historical monument** (p66) sits near the spot where LA's first Spanish colonists plunked down in 1781. Preserving some of the city's oldest buildings beside tiny museums and churches, El Pueblo is a microcosm of LA's multiethnic immigrant history. Grab a map at the visitor center inside **Avila Adobe** (213-628-1274; www.elpueblo.lacity.org; 10 Olvera St; 9am-4pm), then wander through narrow Olvera St's vibrant Mexican-themed stalls. Free guided tours leave from the **Old Plaza Firehouse** (134 Paseo de la Plaza; 10am-3pm Tue-Sun).

The Walk ≫ Northwest of the open-air bandstand, cross Main St. To your right is 'La Placita,' LA's oldest Catholic church. After peeking inside, walk back down Main St a half block.

La Plaza de Cultura y Artes

This **museum** (p66) tells the whole truth about the Mexican American experience in LA, from Zoot Suit Riots to the Chicana movement. Calle Principal recreates Main Street in the 1920s. Rotating gallery exhibitions showcase Latino art, documentary films and oral history.

The Walk ≫ Continue southwest along Main St, crossing over Hwy 101 toward LA's City Hall (1928). Turn left onto E Temple St, right onto N Los Angeles St and left onto E 1st St, entering Little Tokyo.

Little Tokyo

Walk past ramen shops and *izakaya* (Japanese pubs serving food) to the

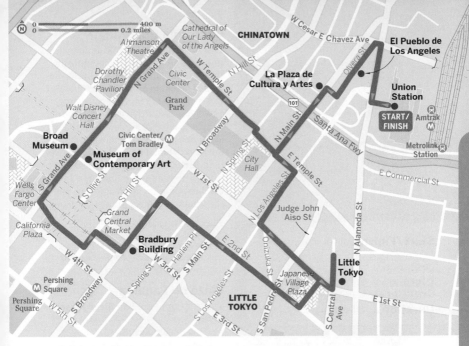

Japanese American National Museum

(📞213-625-0414; www.janm.org; 100 N Central Ave; adult/child $9/5, Thu 5-8pm free, 1st Thu of month free; 🕐11am-5pm Tue, Wed & Fri-Sun, noon-8pm Thu; ♿). Exhibits include those on WWII internment camps and life for immigrant families. Around the corner, the **Geffen Contemporary at MOCA** (📞213-625-4390; www.moca.org; 152 N Central Ave; adult/student/child under 12yr $12/6/free; 🕐11am-6pm Mon, Wed & Fri, to 8pm Thu, to 5pm Sat & Sun) houses cutting-edge art installations.

The Walk » West of Central Ave, turn left to walk through Japanese Village Plaza. Turn right onto E 2nd St, walk five blocks uphill to S Broadway, then turn left and walk a block southwest to W 3rd St.

Bradbury Building

A favorite of movie location scouts since *Blade Runner* was shot here, the 1893 **Bradbury Building** (www.laconservancy.org; 304 S Broadway; 🕐 lobby usually 9am-5pm) is one of LA's architectural treasures. Its red-brick facade conceals a glass-roofed atrium with inky filigree grillwork, a rickety birdcage elevator and brick walls that look golden in the afternoon light.

The Walk » Opposite, walk through LA's Grand Central Market, with its multicultural food stalls. Walk uphill to California Plaza, veering northwest to Grand Ave. Turn right and walk a block northeast.

Museum of Contemporary Art & Broad Museum

With collections from the 1940s to the present day, including works by Mark Rothko and Joseph Cornell, the **Museum of Contemporary Art** (MOCA; 📞213-626-6222; www.moca.org; 250 S Grand Ave; adult/child $12/free, 5-8pm Thu free; 🕐11am-6pm Mon, Wed & Fri, to 8pm Thu, to 5pm Sat & Sun) inhabits a geometrically post-modern building designed by Arata Isozaki. Across the street is the impressive **Broad Museum** (📞213-232-6200; www.thebroad.org; 221 S Grand Ave; 🕐11am-5pm Tue & Wed, to 8pm Thu-Sat, to 6pm Sun; 🅿♿), an even bigger trove of contemporary art that's free to the public (advance ticket reservation required).

The Walk » Continue northeast up Grand Ave, passing Walt Disney Concert Hall. Turn right on Temple St and roll downhill past the Cathedral of Our Lady of the Angels to City Hall, retracing your steps north through El Pueblo to Union Station.

STRETCH YOUR LEGS SAN DIEGO

Start/Finish California Quadrangle

Distance 2.5 miles

Duration 2–6 hours

The zoo, museums and gardens of sun-drenched Balboa Park, originally built for the 1915–16 Panama-California Exposition, make it a highlight of any San Diego stopover. Explore fantastical architecture along its curved walking paths.

Take this walk on Trips

California Quadrangle

East of Cabrillo Bridge, El Prado passes under an archway into the California Quadrangle. Just north, the anthropological **Museum of Man** (☎619-239-2001; www.museumofman.org; Plaza de California, 1350 El Prado; adult/teen/child $12.50/8/6; ⊙10am-5pm, to 8:30pm late May-early Sep; ▮) is one of the park's most ornate Spanish Colonial Revival creations, its landmark **California Tower** richly decorated with blue and yellow tiles. Inside, exhibits span Egypt, the Mayans and the local indigenous Kumeyaay people.

The Walk » Amble east under the white colonnades along the south side of El Prado. Duck into the formally hedged Alcazar Garden on your right, then continue east toward the spritzing fountain in Plaza de Panama.

Plaza de Panama

The exterior of the **San Diego Museum of Art** (SDMA; ☎619-232-7931; www.sdmart. org; 1450 El Prado; adult/child $12/4.50; ⊙10am-5pm Mon, Tue & Thu-Sat, from noon Sun, also 5-8pm Fri mid-May–early Sep) was designed in 16th-century Spanish Renaissance plateresque style. Nearby, the **Timken Museum of Art** (☎619-239-5548; www.timkenmuseum.org; 1500 El Prado; ⊙10am-4:30pm Tue-Sat, from noon Sun) has an impressive collection of artworks by European masters, while the **Mingei International Museum** (☎619-239-0003; www.mingei.org; 1439 El Prado; adult/child $10/7; ⊙10am-5pm Tue-Sun; ▮) exhibits folk art from around the globe.

The Walk » Stroll north alongside the lily pond into the Botanical Building greenhouse. Back outside, cut east to Village Pl, then turn left and walk north past the giant Moreton Bay fig tree and the shops of the Spanish Village Art Center.

San Diego Zoo

Since its grand opening in 1916, San Diego Zoo (p305) has pioneered ways to house animals that mimic their natural habitat, in the process also becoming one of the country's great botanical gardens. A guided double-decker bus tour gives you a good overview of the

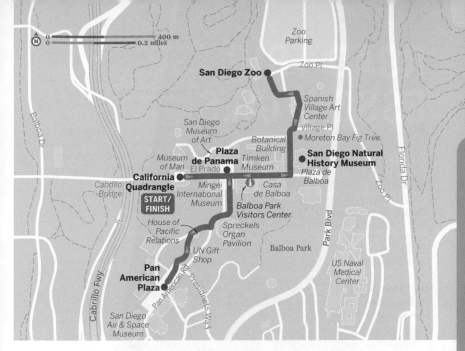

zoo – sitting downstairs puts you even closer to the animals.

The Walk » Retrace your steps south to El Prado, turning left and walking straight ahead to Bea Evenson Fountain. Then backtrack a short distance west to the natural history museum.

San Diego Natural History Museum

With its giant-screen cinema and mega traveling exhibitions, **'the Nat'** (📞877-946-7797, 619-232-3821; www.sdnhm.org; 1788 El Prado; adult/youth 7-17yr/ child 3-6yr $19/14/11; ⊕10am-5pm; 👪) houses 7.5 million specimens, including rocks, fossils, taxidermy animals and skulls, as well as an educational and eco-conscious exhibit on SoCal's water resources.

The Walk » Backtrack west along El Prado, passing the Casa de Balboa, which houses photography, city history and model-railroad museums, on your left. Turn left at Plaza del Panama, heading south past the Japanese Friendship Garden and Spreckels Organ Pavilion.

Pan American Plaza

Fast-food stands and ice-cream vendors set up shop on Balboa Park's central plaza. The **UN Gift Shop** (📞619-233-5044; http://unasd.org/unasd-gift-shop; 2171 Pan American Plaza; ⊕10am-4:30pm; 👪) sells globally minded crafts, jewelry and souvenirs, donating profits to worldwide children's charities. Nearby, the **House of Pacific Relations** (📞619-234-0739; www.sdhpr.org; 2191 W Pan American Rd; ⊕noon-5pm Sun; 👪) actually comprises 15 cottages, inside which you can view furnishings, artworks and museum-like displays from an Olympian mix of countries. Further south is the famous **San Diego Air & Space Museum** (📞619-234-8291; www.sandiegoairandspace.org; 2001 Pan American Plaza; adult/child $19.50/10.50; ⊕10am-4:30pm; 👪).

The Walk » Make a U-turn and walk back up Pan American Rd all the way northeast to Plaza de Panama. Turn left onto El Prado and head west back to California Quadrangle, where your walk began.

ROAD TRIP ESSENTIALS

California Driving Guide

With jaw-dropping scenery and one of the USA's most comprehensive highway networks, California is an all-star destination for a road trip.

DRIVER'S LICENSE & DOCUMENTS

Out-of-state and international visitors may legally drive a car in California with their home driver's license. If you're driving into the USA from Canada or Mexico, bring your vehicle's registration papers, liability insurance and home driver's license; an International Driving Permit (IDP) is a good supplement but isn't currently required.

If you're from overseas, an IDP will have more credibility with traffic police and simplify the car-rental process, especially if your license doesn't have a photo or isn't written in English. International automobile associations can issue IDPs, valid for one year, for a fee. Always carry your home license together with the IDP.

The American Automobile Association (AAA) has reciprocal agreements with some international auto clubs (eg Canada's CAA, AAA in Australia), so bring your membership card from home.

INSURANCE

California law requires liability insurance for all vehicles. When renting a car, check your home auto-insurance policy or your travel-insurance policy to see if rental cars are already covered. If not, expect to pay about $20 per day for liability insurance when renting a car.

Insurance against damage to the car itself, called Collision Damage Waiver (CDW) or Loss Damage Waiver (LDW), costs another $10 to $20 or more per day for rental cars. The deductible may require you to pay up to the first $500 for any repairs. If you decline CDW, you will be held liable for all damages up to the full value of the car.

Some credit cards cover CDW/LDW, provided you charge the entire cost of the car rental to that card. If you have an accident, you may have to pay the rental-car company first, then seek reimbursement. Most credit-card coverage isn't valid for rentals over one month or for 'exotic' models (eg convertibles, RVs).

HIRING A VEHICLE

To rent your own wheels, you'll typically need to be at least 25 years old, hold a valid driver's license and have a major credit card, *not* a check or debit card.

Rates generally include unlimited mileage, but expect surcharges for additional drivers and one-way rentals. Airport locations may have cheaper rates but higher fees; if you get a fly-drive package, local taxes may be extra when you pick up the car. Child or infant safety seats are compulsory; reserve them (from $10 per day) when booking your car.

Major car-rental companies:

Alamo (844-341 8645; www.alamo.com)

Avis (800-633-3469; www.avis.com)

Budget (800 218-7992; www.budget.com)

Dollar (800-800-4000; www.dollar.com)

Enterprise (844-362-0812; www.enterprise.com)

Fox (855-571-8410; www.foxrentacar.com)

Hertz (800-654-3131; www.hertz.com)

Road Distances (miles)

	Anaheim	Arcata	Bakersfield	Death Valley	Las Vegas	Los Angeles	Monterey	Napa	Palm Springs	Redding	Sacramento	San Diego	San Francisco	San Luis Obispo	Santa Barbara	Sth Lake Tahoe
Arcata	680															
Bakersfield	135	555														
Death Valley	285	705	235													
Las Vegas	265	840	285	140												
Los Angeles	25	650	110	290	270											
Monterey	370	395	250	495	535	345										
Napa	425	265	300	545	590	400	150									
Palm Springs	95	760	220	300	280	110	450	505								
Redding	570	140	440	565	725	545	315	190	650							
Sacramento	410	300	280	435	565	385	185	60	490	160						
San Diego	95	770	230	350	330	120	465	520	140	665	505					
San Francisco	405	280	285	530	570	380	120	50	490	215	85	500				
San Luis Obispo	225	505	120	365	405	200	145	265	310	430	290	320	230			
Santa Barbara	120	610	145	350	360	95	250	370	205	535	395	215	335	105		
Sth Lake Tahoe	505	400	375	345	460	480	285	160	485	260	100	600	185	390	495	
Yosemite	335	465	200	300	415	310	200	190	415	325	160	430	190	230	345	190

National (☎877-222-9058; www.nationalcar.com)

Payless (☎800-729-5377; www.paylesscar.com)

Thrifty (☎800-847-4389; www.thrifty.com)

Some major car-rental companies offer 'green' hybrid or biofueled rental cars, but they're in short supply; make reservations far in advance and expect to pay significantly more for these models. Many companies rent hand-controlled vehicles and vans with wheelchair lifts at no extra charge, but you must also reserve these well in advance.

For independent car rentals, check:

Car Rental Express (www.carrental express.com) Search for independent car-rental agencies.

Mobility Works (☎877-275-4915; www.mobilityworks.com) Rents wheelchair-accessible vans in LA, San Diego, the San Francisco Bay Area, Sacramento and a few other locations.

Rent-a-Wreck (☎877-877-0700; www.rentawreck.com) Rents to younger drivers and debit-card users, mainly in the LA and San Francisco Bay areas.

Simply Rent-a-Car (☎888-359-0055; www.simplyrac.com) Hybrid and luxury car rentals in LA.

Sixt (☎888-749-8227; www.sixt.com) Economy and luxury car and SUV rentals around LA and the San Francisco Bay Area.

Super Cheap! Car Rental (www.supercheapcar.com) Rents to younger drivers in LA, Orange County and San Francisco.

Wheelchair Getaways (☎800-638-1912; www.wheelchairgetaways.com) Rents wheelchair-accessible vans in San Francisco and LA.

Motorcycles

Motorcycle rentals and insurance are very expensive.

Bartels' Route 66 (☎310-578-0112, 888-434-4473; www.route66riders.com; 4161 Lincoln Blvd, Marina del Rey; ⏰10am-6pm Tue-Sat, 11am-5pm Sun) Harley-Davidson and Indian motorcycle rentals in LA's South Bay.

Dubbelju (☎866-495-2774, 415-495-2774; www.dubbelju.com; 274 Shotwell St; ⏰9am-6pm Mon-Sat) Harley-Davidson and imported motorcycle rentals in San Francisco.

Eagle Rider (☎888-900-9901, 310-321-3180; www.eaglerider.com) Motorcycle rentals in the LA and San Francisco Bay areas, San Diego, Palm Springs, Fresno and Monterey.

Recreational Vehicles & Campervans

Book recreational vehicle (RV) and campervan rentals as far in advance as possible. Rental costs vary by size and model; rates often don't include mileage, bedding or kitchen kits, vehicle prep or taxes.

Cruise America (☎480-464-7300, 800-671-8042; www.cruiseamerica.com) Twenty RV-rental locations statewide, as well as in Las Vegas, Nevada.

El Monte (☎888-337-2214, 562-483-4985; www.elmonterv.com) Over a dozen RV-rental locations across California and in Las Vegas.

Escape Campervans (☎877-270-8267, 310-672-9909; www.escapecampervans.com) Awesomely painted campervans in San Francisco, LA and Las Vegas.

Jucy Rentals (☎800-650-4180; www.jucyrentals.com) Campervan rentals in San Francisco, LA and Las Vegas.

Road Bear (☎866-491-9853, 818-865-2925; www.roadbearrv.com) RV rentals in San Francisco, LA and Las Vegas.

Vintage Surfari Wagons (☎949-716-3135, 714-585-7565; www.vwsurfari.com) VW campervan rentals in Orange County.

BORDER CROSSING

California is an important agricultural state. To prevent the spread of pests and diseases, certain food items (including meats, fresh fruit and vegetables) may not be brought into the state. Bakery items and hard-cured cheeses are admissible. If you drive across the border from Mexico

Road Trip Websites

AUTOMOBILE CLUBS

American Automobile Association (AAA; ☎emergency roadside assistance 800-222-4357, member services 800-922-8228; www.aaa.com; annual membership from $56) Emergency roadside assistance (24-hour), free maps and travel discounts for members.

Better World Club (☎866-238-1137; www.betterworldclub.com) Ecofriendly autoclub alternative to AAA.

DRIVING CONDITIONS & TRAFFIC

511 SF Bay (www.511.org) San Francisco Bay Area traffic updates.

California Department of Transportation (CalTrans; ☎800-427-7623; www.dot.ca.gov/cgi-bin/roads.cgi) Highway conditions, construction updates and road closures.

Go511 (www.go511.com) LA and Southern California traffic updates.

MAPS

Google Maps (http://maps.google.com) Free online maps and driving directions.

National Park Service (www.nps.gov) Links to individual park sites for road condition updates and free downloadable maps.

ROAD RULES

California Department of Motor Vehicles (www.dmv.ca.gov) Statewide driving laws, driver's licenses and vehicle registration.

or the neighboring states of Oregon, Nevada or Arizona, you may have to stop for a quick agricultural inspection.

If you're driving across the Mexican border, check the ever-changing passport and visa requirements with the **US Department of State** (http://travel.state.gov) beforehand. **US Customs and Border Protection** (http://apps.cbp.gov/bwt) tracks current wait times at every border crossing. Between San Diego and Tijuana, Mexico, San Ysidro is the world's busiest border crossing. US citizens do not require a visa for stays in Mexico of 72 hours or less in a border zone, but they do need a passport.

Unless you're planning an extended stay in Tijuana, taking a car across the Mexican border is more trouble than it's worth. Instead, leave your car on the US side of the border and walk. If you drive across, you must buy Mexican car insurance either beforehand or at the border crossing (see box, p308).

MAPS

Visitor centers and tourist information offices distribute free (but often very basic) maps. GPS navigation cannot be entirely relied upon, especially in remote desert or mountain areas. If you are planning on doing a lot of driving, you'll need a more detailed road map or atlas. DeLorme's comprehensive *California Atlas & Gazetteer* ($25) shows campgrounds, recreational areas and topographical land features, although it's less useful for navigating urban areas. Members of the American Automobile Association (AAA) or its international affiliates (bring your membership card from home) can pick up free driving maps from any of AAA's California offices.

ROAD CONDITIONS

For highway conditions, including road closures and construction updates, dial 📞800-427-7623 or visit www.dot.ca.gov.

In places where winter driving is an issue, snow tires and tire chains may be required, especially on mountain highways. Ideally, carry your own chains and learn how to use them before you hit the road. Otherwise, chains can usually be bought (but not cheaply) on the highway, at gas stations or in nearby towns.

Most car-rental companies don't permit the use of tire chains. Driving off-road, or on unpaved roads, is also prohibited by most car-rental companies.

Driving Problem-Buster

What should I do if my car breaks down? Call the roadside emergency assistance number of your car-rental company or, if you're driving your own car, your automobile association.

What if I have an accident? If it's safe to do so, pull over to the side of the road. For minor fender benders with no injuries or significant property damage, exchange insurance information with the other driver and file a report with your insurance provider as soon as possible. For major accidents, call 📞911 and wait for the police and emergency services to arrive.

What should I do if I am stopped by the police? Be courteous. Don't get out of the car unless asked. Keep your hands where the officer can see them (eg on the steering wheel). For traffic violations, there is usually a 30-day period to pay a fine; most matters can be handled by mail. Police can legally give roadside sobriety checks to assess if you've been drinking or using drugs.

What should I do if my car gets towed? Immediately call the police non-emergency number for the town or city that you're in and ask where to pick up your car. Towing and hourly or daily storage fees can quickly total hundreds of dollars.

What if I can't find anywhere to stay? If you're stuck and it's getting late, it's best not to keep driving on aimlessly – just pull into the next roadside chain motel or hotel with the 'Vacancy' light lit up.

Warning!

As of 2016, the **US State Department** (http://travel.state.gov) has issued a travel warning about drug-trafficking violence and crime along the US–Mexico border. Travelers should exercise caution in the northern state of Baja California, including the city of Tijuana.

ROAD RULES

➡ Drive on the right-hand side of the road.

➡ Talking or texting on a cell (mobile) phone without a hands-free device while driving is illegal.

➡ The use of seat belts is required for drivers, front-seat passengers and children under 16.

➡ Infant and child safety seats are required for children under eight years old unless they are at least 4ft 9in tall.

➡ High-occupancy vehicle (HOV) lanes marked with a diamond symbol are reserved for cars with multiple occupants, sometimes only during rush hours.

➡ Unless otherwise posted, the speed limit is 65mph on freeways, 55mph on two-lane undivided highways, 35mph on major city streets and 25mph in business and residential districts.

➡ At intersections, U-turns are permitted unless otherwise posted.

➡ Except where indicated, turning right at red lights after coming to a full stop is permitted, although intersecting traffic still has the right of way.

➡ At four-way stop signs, cars proceed in the order in which they arrived. If two cars arrive simultaneously, the one on the right has the right of way. When in doubt, wave the other driver ahead.

➡ When emergency vehicles (ie police, fire or ambulance) approach from either direction, carefully pull over to the side of the road.

➡ If a police car is pulled off on the shoulder of the road, drivers in the right-hand lane are legally required to merge left, as long as it's safe to do so.

➡ It's illegal to carry open containers of alcohol inside a vehicle, even empty ones. Unless containers are full and still sealed, store them in the trunk.

PARKING

Parking is plentiful and free in small towns and rural areas, but scarce and/or expensive in cities. You can pay municipal parking meters and centralized pay stations with coins (usually quarters) or sometimes credit or debit cards. When parking on the street, read all posted regulations and restrictions (eg street-cleaning hours, permit-only residential areas) and pay attention to colored curbs, or you may be ticketed and towed. Expect to pay at least $2.50 per hour or $30 overnight at a city parking garage. Flat-fee valet parking at hotels and restaurants is common in cities; tip the valet attendant at least $2 when they hand your keys back.

FUEL

➡ Gas stations in California, nearly all of which are self-service, are everywhere, except in national parks and sparsely populated desert and mountain areas.

➡ Gas is sold in gallons (one US gallon equals 3.78L). In mid-2016, the cost for regular fuel in California averaged $2.80.

SAFETY

In rural areas, livestock sometimes graze next to unfenced roads. These areas are typically signed as 'Open Range,' with the silhouette of a steer. Where deer or other wild animals frequently appear roadside, you'll see signs with the silhouette of a leaping deer. Take these signs seriously, particularly at night or in the fog.

In coastal areas, thick fog may impede driving – slow down and if it's too soupy, get off the road. Along coastal cliffs and on twisting mountain roads, watch out for falling rocks, mudslides and snow avalanches that could damage or disable your car if struck.

California Travel Guide

GETTING THERE & AWAY

AIR

California's major international airports are in Los Angeles (www.lawa.org) and San Francisco (www.flysfo.com). Smaller regional airports are served primarily by domestic US carriers, including low-cost and discount airlines.

Major car-rental agencies operate out of all of California's biggest airports, including international and domestic hubs.

BUS

Greyhound (www.greyhound.com) is the major long-distance bus company, with routes throughout the USA, including to/from California. Greyhound has stopped service to many small towns; routes trace major highways and may only stop at larger population centers.

Car rentals are seldom available at bus terminals, though agency branch offices may be located nearby in some cities.

CAR & MOTORCYCLE

If you're driving into the USA from Canada or Mexico, bring your vehicle's registration papers and proof of liability insurance. If you're renting a car or a motorcycle, ask beforehand if the agency allows its vehicles to be taken across international borders. Expect long border-crossing waits, especially on weekends and holidays and during weekday commuter rush hours.

TRAIN

Amtrak (www.amtrak.com) operates a fairly extensive rail system throughout the USA. Trains are comfortable, if a bit slow, and are equipped with dining and lounge cars on long-distance routes. Fares vary according to the type of train and seating (eg coach or business class, sleeping compartments).

A few agencies make rental cars available at some train stations, usually by advance reservation only.

DIRECTORY A–Z

ACCOMMODATIONS

➜ Budget-conscious accommodations include campgrounds, hostels and motels.

➜ At midrange motels and hotels, expect clean, comfortable and decent-sized rooms with at least a private bathroom, and standard amenities such as cable TV, direct-dial telephone, a coffeemaker, and perhaps a microwave and mini fridge.

Sleeping Price Ranges

The following price ranges refer to a private room with bath during high season, unless otherwise specified. Taxes and breakfast are not normally included in the price.

$ less than $100

$$ $100 to $250

$$$ more than $250

→ At top-end hotels and resorts, swimming pools, fitness rooms, business centers, full-service restaurants and bars are all standard.

→ In Southern California, nearly all lodgings have air-conditioning, but in Northern California, where it rarely gets hot, the opposite is true. In coastal areas as far south as Santa Barbara, only fans may be provided.

→ There may be a fee for wireless internet, especially for in-room access. Look for free wi-fi hot spots in hotel public areas (eg lobby, poolside).

→ Many accommodations in California are exclusively nonsmoking. Where they still exist, smoking rooms are often left unrenovated and in less desirable locations. Expect a hefty 'cleaning fee' ($100 or more) if you light up in designated nonsmoking rooms.

Hotels & Motels

Rooms are often priced by the size and number of beds, rather than the number of occupants. A room with one double or queen-size bed usually costs the same for one or two people, while a room with a king-size bed or two double beds costs more.

There is often a small surcharge for the third and fourth person, but children under a certain age (this varies) may stay free. Cribs or rollaway cots usually incur an additional fee. Beware that suites or 'junior suites' may simply be oversized rooms; ask about the layout when booking.

Recently renovated or larger rooms, or those with a view, are likely to cost more. Descriptors like 'oceanfront' and 'oceanview' are often too liberally used, and you may require a periscope to spot the surf.

You can make reservations at chains by calling their central reservation lines, but to learn about specific amenities and local promotions, call the property directly. If you arrive without reservations, ask to see a room before paying for it, especially at motels.

Rates may include breakfast, which could be just a stale donut and wimpy coffee, an all-you-can-eat hot and cold buffet, or anything in between.

B&Bs

For an atmospheric or even romantic alternative to impersonal motels and hotels, bed-and-breakfasts traditionally inhabit fine Victorian houses or other heritage buildings, bedecked with floral wallpaper and antique furnishings. More modern inns do exist, especially near the coast. Travel-

Practicalities

Electricity 110/120V AC, 50/60Hz

Radio National Public Radio (NPR), lower end of FM dial

Smoking Illegal indoors in all public buildings, including restaurants and bars. Some lodgings offer smoking rooms upon request.

Time California is on Pacific Standard Time (UTC-8). Clocks are set one hour ahead during Daylight Saving Time (DST), from the second Sunday in March until the first Sunday in November.

Weights & Measures Imperial (except 1 US gallon = 0.83 gallons)

ers who prefer privacy may find B&Bs too intimate.

Rates often include breakfast, but occasionally do not (never mind what the name 'B&B' suggests). Amenities vary widely, but rooms with TV and telephone are the exception; the cheapest units share bathrooms. Standards are high at places certified by the **California Association of Boutique & Breakfast Inns** (www.cabbi.com).

Most B&Bs require advance reservations; only a few will accommodate drop-in guests. Smoking is generally prohibited and children are often not welcome. Multiple-night minimum stays may be required, especially on weekends and in high season.

Camping

→ On public lands, primitive campsites usually have fire pits, picnic tables and vault toilets. Developed campgrounds, such as those in state and national parks, usually offer more amenities, including flush toilets, BBQ grills and occasionally hot showers.

→ Private campgrounds often cater to RVs (recreational vehicles) with full electricity and water hookups and dump stations; tent sites may be sparse and uninviting. Hot showers and coin-op laundry are often available, and possibly a pool, wi-fi and camping cabins.

→ Many public campgrounds, especially in the mountains, are closed from late fall through early spring or summer. Opening and closing dates vary each year, depending on weather and snow conditions. Private campgrounds closer to cities, beaches and major highways are often open year-round.

➡ Many public and private campgrounds accept reservations for all or some of their sites, while a few are strictly first-come, first-served. Overnight rates range from free for the most primitive campsites to $60 or more for pull-through RV sites with full hookups.

➡ If you can't get a campsite reservation, plan to show up at the campground between 10am and noon, when last night's campers may be leaving. Otherwise, ask about overflow camping and dispersed camping nearby.

➡ If you didn't bring your own tent, you can buy (and occasionally rent) camping gear at outdoor outfitters and sporting-goods shops in most cities and some towns, especially near national parks.

Rates & Reservations

➡ Generally, midweek rates are lower except at urban hotels geared toward business travelers, which lure leisure travelers with weekend deals.

➡ Discount membership cards (eg AAA, AARP) may get you about 10% off standard rates at participating hotels and motels.

➡ Look for freebie ad magazines packed with hotel and motel discount coupons at gas stations, highway rest areas, tourist offices and online at **HotelCoupons** (www.hotelcoupons. com).

➡ High season is from June to August everywhere, except the deserts and mountain ski areas, where December through April are the busiest months.

➡ Demand and prices spike even higher around major holidays and for festivals, when some properties may impose multiday minimum stays.

Book Your Stay Online

For more accommodations reviews by Lonely Planet authors, check out http://hotels.lonelyplanet.com. You'll find independent reviews, as well as recommendations on the best places to stay. Best of all, you can book online.

➡ Reservations are recommended for weekend and holiday travel year-round, and every day of the week during high season.

➡ Bargaining may be possible for walk-in guests without reservations, especially at off-peak times.

ELECTRICITY

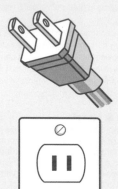

120V/60Hz

FOOD

➡ Lunch is generally served between 11:30am and 2:30pm, and dinner between 5pm and 9pm daily, though some restaurants stay open later, especially on Friday and Saturday nights. A few roadside diners are open 24 hours.

➡ If breakfast is served, it's usually between 7:30am and 10:30am. Some diners and cafes keep serving breakfast into the afternoon, or all day. Weekend brunch is a laid-back affair, usually available from 11am until 3pm on Saturdays and Sundays.

➡ Like all things Californian, restaurant etiquette tends to be informal. Only a handful of restaurants require more than a dressy shirt, slacks and a decent pair of shoes; most places require far less, especially near the beaches.

➡ Tipping 18% to 20% is expected anywhere you receive table service, unless the menu or your bill specifically states that tipping and/or

Eating Price Ranges

The following price ranges refer to an average main course at dinner, unless otherwise stated. These prices don't include taxes or tip. Note the same dishes at lunch will usually be cheaper, even half-price.

$ less than $15

$$ $15 to $25

$$$ more than $25

a service charge is already included (common for groups of six or more).

➡ Smoking is illegal indoors. Some restaurants have patios or sidewalk tables where smoking is tolerated (ask first, or look around for ashtrays), but don't expect your neighbors to be happy about secondhand smoke.

➡ You can bring your own wine to most restaurants; a 'corkage' fee of $15 to $30 usually applies. At lunch, a glass of wine or beer is socially acceptable at most places.

➡ If you ask the kitchen to divide a plate between two (or more) people, there may be a small split-plate surcharge.

➡ Vegetarians, vegans and travelers with food allergies or restrictions are in luck – many restaurants are used to catering to specific dietary needs.

LGBTQ TRAVELERS

California is a magnet for LGBTQ travelers. Hot spots include the Castro in San Francisco, West Hollywood (WeHo), Silver Lake and Long Beach in LA, San Diego's Hillcrest neighborhood, the desert resort of Palm Springs, Guerneville in the Russian River Valley and Calistoga in Napa Valley. Some scenes are predominantly male-oriented, but women usually won't feel too left out.

Same-sex marriage is legal in California. Despite widespread tolerance, homophobic bigotry still exists. In small towns, especially away from the coast, tolerance often comes down to a 'don't ask, don't tell' policy.

Helpful Resources

Advocate (www.advocate.com/travel) Online news, gay travel features and destination guides.

Damron (www.damron.com) Classic, advertiser-driven gay travel guides and 'Gay Scout' mobile app.

Gay & Lesbian National Hotline (☑888-843-4564) For counseling and referrals of any kind.

GayCities (www.gaycities.com) Activities, tours, lodging, shopping, restaurants and nightlife in a dozen California cities.

misterb&b (www.misterb&b.com) Like Airbnb, but for gay (mostly male) travelers.

Out Traveler (www.outtraveler.com) Free online magazine with travel tips, destination guides and hotel reviews.

Purple Roofs (www.purpleroofs.com) Online directory of LGBTQ accommodations.

INTERNET ACCESS

➡ Cybercafes typically charge $6 to $12 per hour for online access.

➡ With branches in most cities and towns, **FedEx Office** (☑800-463-3339; www.fedex. com) offers internet access at self-service computer workstations (around 30¢ per minute) and sometimes free wi-fi, plus digital-photo printing and CD-burning stations.

➡ Free or fee-based wi-fi hot spots can be found at major airports; many hotels, motels and coffee shops (eg Starbucks); and some tourist information centers, campgrounds (eg KOA), stores (eg Apple), bars and restaurants (including fast-food chains like McDonald's).

➡ Public libraries have internet terminals (online time may be limited, advance sign-up required and a nominal fee charged for out-of-network visitors) and, increasingly, free wi-fi.

MONEY

ATMs

➡ ATMs are available 24/7 at most banks, shopping malls, airports, and grocery and convenience stores.

Tipping Guide

Tipping is not optional. Only withhold tips in cases of outrageously bad service.

Airport skycaps & hotel bellhops $2 per bag, minimum $5 per cart.

Bartenders 15% to 20% per round, minimum $1 per drink.

Concierges Nothing for simple information, up to $20 for securing last-minute restaurant reservations, sold-out show tickets etc.

Housekeeping staff $2 to $4 daily, left under the card provided; more if you're messy.

Parking valets At least $2 when handed back your car keys.

Restaurant servers & room service 18% to 20%, unless a gratuity is already charged (common for groups of six or more).

Taxi drivers 10% to 15% of metered fare, rounded up to the next dollar.

➡ Expect a minimum surcharge of around $3 per transaction, in addition to any fees charged by your home bank.

➡ Most ATMs are connected to international networks and offer decent foreign-exchange rates.

➡ Withdrawing cash from an ATM using a credit card usually incurs a hefty fee and high interest rates; contact your credit-card company for details and a PIN number.

Cash

➡ Most people do not carry large amounts of cash for everyday use, relying instead on credit and debit cards. Some businesses refuse to accept bills over $20.

Credit Cards

➡ Major credit cards are almost universally accepted. In fact, it's almost impossible to rent a car, book a hotel room or buy tickets over the phone without one. A credit card may also be vital in emergencies.

➡ Visa, MasterCard and American Express are the most widely accepted.

Money Changers

➡ You can exchange money at major airports, some banks and all currency-exchange offices such as **American Express** (www.american express.com) or **Travelex** (www.travelex.com). Always enquire about rates and fees.

➡ Outside big cities, exchanging money may be a problem, so make sure you have a credit card and sufficient cash on hand.

Taxes

➡ California state sales tax (7.5%) is added to the retail price of most goods and services (gasoline is an exception).

➡ Local and city sales taxes may tack on up to an additional 2.5%.

➡ Tourist lodging taxes vary statewide, but currently average 12% or more.

Traveler's Checks

➡ Traveler's checks have pretty much fallen out of use.

➡ Big-city restaurants, hotels and department stores will often accept traveler's checks (in US dollars only), but small businesses, markets and fast-food chains may refuse them.

➡ Visa and American Express are the most widely accepted issuers of traveler's checks.

OPENING HOURS

Businesses, restaurants and shops may close earlier and on additional days during the off-season (usually winter, except summer in the deserts). Otherwise, standard opening hours are as follows:

Banks 9am to 5pm Monday to Thursday, to 6pm Friday, some 9am to 1:30pm Saturday

Bars 5pm to 2am daily

Business hours (general) 9am to 5pm Monday to Friday

Pharmacies 8am–9pm Monday–Friday, 9am–5pm Saturday and Sunday, some 24 hours

Post offices 8:30am to 4:30pm Monday to Friday, some 9am to noon Saturday

Restaurants 7:30am to 10:30am, 11:30am to 2:30pm and 5pm to 9pm daily, some later Friday and Saturday

Shops 10am to 6pm Monday to Saturday, noon to 5pm Sunday (malls open later)

Supermarkets 8am–9pm or 10pm daily, some 24 hours

PUBLIC HOLIDAYS

On the following national holidays, banks, schools and government offices (including post offices) are closed, and transportation, museums and other services operate on a Sunday schedule. Holidays falling on a weekend are usually observed the following Monday.

New Year's Day January 1

Martin Luther King Jr Day Third Monday in January

Presidents Day Third Monday in February

Good Friday Friday before Easter in March/April

Memorial Day Last Monday in May

Independence Day July 4

Labor Day First Monday in September

Columbus Day Second Monday in October

Veterans Day November 11

Thanksgiving Day Fourth Thursday in November

Christmas Day December 25

School Holidays

➡ Schools take a one or two-week 'spring break' around Easter, sometime in March or April. Some hotels and resorts, especially along the coast, near SoCal's theme parks and in the deserts, raise their rates during this time.

➡ School summer vacations run from mid-June until mid-August, making July and August the busiest travel months almost everywhere except the deserts.

SAFE TRAVEL

Despite its seemingly apocalyptic list of dangers – guns, violent crime, riots, earthquakes – California is a reasonably safe place to visit. The greatest danger is posed by car accidents (buckle up – it's the law),

while the biggest annoyances are metro-area traffic and crowds. Wildlife poses some small threats, and of course there is the dramatic, albeit unlikely, possibility of a natural disaster.

Earthquakes

Earthquakes happen all the time but most are so tiny they are detectable only by sensitive seismological instruments. If you're caught in a serious shaker:

➡ If indoors, get under a desk or table or stand in a doorway.

➡ Protect your head and stay clear of windows, mirrors or anything that might fall.

➡ Don't head for elevators or go running into the street.

➡ If you're in a shopping mall or large public building, expect the alarm and/or sprinkler systems to come on.

➡ If outdoors, get away from buildings, trees and power lines.

➡ If you're driving, pull over to the side of the road away from bridges, overpasses and power lines. Stay inside the car until the shaking stops.

➡ If you're on a sidewalk near buildings, duck into a doorway to protect yourself from falling bricks, glass and debris.

➡ Prepare for aftershocks.

➡ Turn on the radio and listen for bulletins.

➡ Use the telephone only if absolutely necessary.

TELEPHONE

➡ US phone numbers consist of a three-letter area code followed by a seven-digit local number.

➡ When dialing a number within the same area code, use the seven-digit number (if that doesn't work, try all 10 digits).

➡ For long-distance calls, dial 1 plus the area code plus the local number.

➡ Toll-free numbers begin with ☏800, 844, 855, 866, 877 or 888 and must be preceded by 1.

➡ For direct international calls, dial ☏011 plus the country code plus the area code (usually without the initial '0') plus the local phone number.

➡ If you're calling Canada, the country code is ☏1 (the same as for the US, but beware international rates apply between the two countries).

Important Numbers

Country code ☏1

International dialing code ☏011

Operator ☏0

Emergency (ambulance, fire & police) ☏911

Directory assistance (local) ☏411

Cell Phones

➡ You'll need a multiband GSM phone to make calls in the USA. Popping in a US prepaid rechargeable SIM card is usually cheaper than using your network.

➡ SIM cards are sold at telecommunications and electronics stores. These stores also sell inexpensive prepaid phones, including some airtime.

Payphones & Phonecards

➡ Where payphones still exist, they're usually coin-operated, although some may only accept credit cards (eg in national parks). Local calls usually cost 50¢ minimum.

➡ For long-distance calls, you're usually better off buying a prepaid phonecard, sold at supermarkets, pharmacies, newsstands and electronics and convenience stores.

TOURIST INFORMATION

➡ For pretrip planning, peruse the information-packed website of the **California Travel and Tourism Commission** (www.visitcalifornia.com).

➡ The same government agency operates nearly 20 statewide **California Welcome Centers** (www.visitcwc.com), where staff dispense maps and brochures and may be able to help find accommodations.

➡ Almost every city and town has a local visitor center or a chamber of commerce where you can pick up maps, brochures and information.

TRAVELERS WITH DISABILITIES

Much of California is reasonably well-equipped for travelers with disabilities,
especially in metro areas and popular tourist spots.

Lonely Planet's free Accessible Travel guide can be downloaded here: http://lptravel.to/AccessibleTravel.

Accessibility

➡ Most traffic intersections have dropped curbs and sometimes audible crossing signals.

➡ The Americans with Disabilities Act (ADA) requires public buildings built after 1993 to be wheelchair-accessible, including restrooms.

➡ Motels and hotels built after 1993 must have at least one ADA-compliant accessible room; state your specific needs when making reservations.

➡ For nonpublic buildings built prior to 1993, including hotels, restaurants, museums and theaters, there are no accessibility guarantees; call ahead to find out what to expect.

➡ Most national and many state parks and some other outdoor recreation areas offer paved or boardwalk-style nature trails accessible by wheelchairs.

➡ Many theme parks go out of their way to be accessible to wheelchairs and guests with mobility limitations and other disabilities.

Communications

➡ Telephone companies provide relay operators (dial ☏711) for the hearing impaired.

➡ Many banks provide ATM instructions in Braille.

Discount Passes

➡ US citizens and permanent residents with a permanent disability qualify for a free lifetime **'America the Beautiful' Access Pass** (http://store.usgs.gov/pass/access.html), which waives entry fees to all national parks and federal recreational lands and offers 50% discounts on some recreation fees (eg camping).

➡ California State Parks' disabled discount pass ($3.50) entitles those with permanent disabilities to 50% off day-use parking and camping fees; for an application, click to www.parks.ca.gov.

Helpful Resources

A Wheelchair Rider's Guide to the California Coast (www.wheelingcalscoast.org) Free accessibility information covering beaches, parks and trails, plus downloadable PDF guides to the San Francisco Bay Area and Los Angeles and Orange County coasts.

Access Northern California (http://accessnca.org) Links to accessible-travel resources, publications, tours and transportation, including outdoor recreation opportunities.

Accessible San Diego (http://access-sandiego.org) Free online city guide (downloadable/print version $4/5) with listings of lodgings, restaurants, attractions and transportation.

Active Tahoe (http://achievetahoe.org) Organizes summer and winter sports and 4WD adventures around Lake Tahoe in the Sierra Nevada.

Disabled Sports Eastern Sierra (http://disabledsportseasternsierra.org) Offers summer and winter outdoor activity programs around Mammoth Lakes.

Los Angeles for Disabled Visitors (www.discoverlosangeles.com/search/site/disabled) Tips for accessible sightseeing, entertainment and transportation.

Tapooz Travel (www.tapooztravel.com) Travel agency organizes personalized itineraries, including accessible road trips, for travelers with disabilities, mobility issues and other special needs.

Wheelchair Traveling (www.wheelchairtraveling.com) Travel tips, lodging and helpful California destination info.

Yosemite National Park Accessibility (www.nps.gov/yose/planyourvisit/accessibility.htm) Detailed, downloadable accessibility information for Yosemite National Park, including sign-language interpretation services (usually available by advance request).

Transportation

➡ All major airlines, Greyhound buses and Amtrak trains can accommodate people with disabilities, usually with 48 hours of advance notice required.

➡ Major car-rental agencies offer hand-controlled vehicles and vans with wheelchair lifts at no extra charge, but you must reserve these well in advance.

➡ For wheelchair-accessible van rentals, also try **Wheelchair Getaways** (☏800-638-1912; www.wheelchairgetaways.com) in LA and San Francisco or **Mobility Works** (☏877-275-4915; www.mobilityworks.com) in LA, San Diego, San Francisco, Oakland, San Jose, Sacramento, Fresno and Chico.

➡ Local buses, trains and subway lines usually have wheelchair lifts. Service dogs are permitted to accompany passengers on public transportation.

➡ Taxi companies have at least one wheelchair-accessible van, but you'll usually need to call and then wait for one.

VISAS

➡ Visa information is highly likely to change. Depending on your country of origin, the rules for entering the USA keep changing. Double-check current visa requirements *before* coming to the USA.

➡ Currently, under the US Visa Waiver Program (VWP), visas are not required for citizens of 38 countries for stays up to 90 days (no extensions) as long as you have a machine-readable passport (MRP) that meets current US standards and is valid for six months beyond your intended stay.

➡ Citizens of VWP countries must still register with the Electronic System for Travel Authorization (ESTA) online (https://esta.cbp.dhs.gov) at least 72 hours before travel. Once approved, ESTA registration ($14) is valid for up to two years or until your passport expires, whichever comes first.

➡ For most Canadian citizens traveling with Canadian passports that meet current US standards, a visa for short-term visits (usually up to six months) and ESTA registration aren't required.

➡ Citizens from all other countries or whose passports don't meet US standards need to apply for a visa in their home country. The process costs a nonrefundable fee (minimum $160), involves a personal interview and can take several weeks, so apply as early as possible.

➡ For up-to-date information about entry requirements and eligibility, check the visa section of the **US Department of State website** (http://travel.state.gov) or contact the nearest USA embassy or consulate in your home country (for a complete list, visit www.usembassy.gov).

BEHIND THE SCENES

SEND US YOUR FEEDBACK

We love to hear from travelers – your comments help make our books better. We read every word, and we guarantee that your feedback goes straight to the authors. Visit **lonelyplanet. com/contact** to submit your updates and suggestions.

Note: We may edit, reproduce and incorporate your comments in Lonely Planet products such as guidebooks, websites and digital products, so let us know if you don't want your comments reproduced or your name acknowledged. For a copy of our privacy policy visit lonelyplanet.com/privacy.

WRITER'S THANKS

SARA BENSON

Thank you to editors Cliff Wilkinson and Alex Howard for guidance and long-distance support. A big thank you to Jonathan Hayes for driving thousands of miles with me through Gold Country, Wine Country, the Sierra Nevada and all around the Bay Area. PS Hi, Beth!

ACKNOWLEDGMENTS

Climate map data adapted from Peel MC, Finlayson BL & McMahon TA (2007) 'Updated World Map of the Köppen-Geiger Climate Classification', *Hydrology and Earth System Sciences*, 11, 163344.

Front cover photographs (clockwise from top): An evening in Big Sur, Kan Khampanya/500px©; a lifeguard tower on Santa Monica beach, holbox/Shutterstock©; a dog waits for its owner in Santa Barbara, Patricia Marroquin/Getty©

Back cover photograph: La Jolla, San Diego, Dancestrokes/Shutterstock©

THIS BOOK

This 3rd edition of Lonely Planet's *California's Best Trips* guidebook was researched and written by Sara Benson. The previous edition was written by Sara Benson, Nate Cavalieri and Beth Kohn. This guidebook was produced by the following:

Destination Editors Alexander Howard, Clifton Wilkinson

Product Editor Jenna Myers

Senior Cartographers Mark Griffiths, Corey Hutchison, Alison Lyall

Book Designer Virginia Moreno

Assisting Editors Katie Connolly, Monique Perrin, Fionnuala Twomey, Simon Williamson

Cover Researcher Naomi Parker

Thanks to Nate Cavalieri, Kate Chapman, Victoria Harrison, Liz Heynes, Beth Kohn, Andi Jones, Catherine Naghten, Kirsten Rawlings, Angela Tinson, Amanda Williamson

INDEX

– – – – – – – – – – – – –
T